IFIP Advances in Information and Communication Technology 751

IFIP Advances in Information and Communication Technology

The IFIP AICT series publishes state-of-the-art results in the sciences and technologies of information and communication. The scope of the series includes: foundations of computer science; software theory and practice; education; computer applications in technology; communication systems; systems modeling and optimization; information systems; ICT and society; computer systems technology; security and protection in information processing systems; artificial intelligence; and human-computer interaction.

Edited volumes and proceedings of refereed international conferences in computer science and interdisciplinary fields are featured. These results often precede journal publication and represent the most current research.

The principal aim of the IFIP AICT series is to encourage education and the dissemination and exchange of information about all aspects of computing.

More information about this series at https://link.springer.com/bookseries/6102

Barbara Rita Barricelli · Stefano Valtolina ·
Elodie Bouzekri · Angela Locoro · Tilo Mentler
Editors

Human Work Interaction Design

Sustainable Workplaces by Design

IFIP WG 13.6 and WG 13.5 Joint Working Conference, HWID 2024
Milan, Italy, September 5–6, 2024
Revised Selected Papers

Springer

Editors
Barbara Rita Barricelli
Università degli Studi di Brescia
Brescia, Italy

Stefano Valtolina
Università degli Studi di Milano
Milan, Italy

Elodie Bouzekri
University of Western Brittany
Brest, France

Angela Locoro
Università degli Studi di Brescia
Brescia, Italy

Tilo Mentler
Hochschule Trier
Trier, Germany

ISSN 1868-4238 ISSN 1868-422X (electronic)
IFIP Advances in Information and Communication Technology
ISBN 978-3-031-95333-0 ISBN 978-3-031-95334-7 (eBook)
https://doi.org/10.1007/978-3-031-95334-7

This Springer imprint is published by the registered company Springer Nature Switzerland AG
The registered company address is: Gewerbestrasse 11, 6330 Cham, Switzerland

Preface

The Human Work Interaction Design working group (HWID) was created in 2005 by Annelise Mark-Pejtersen, Torkil Clemmensen, and Rikke Orngreen as part of the IFIP Technical Committee 13 (Working Group 13.6) on Human-Computer Interaction. Initially grounded on the Cognitive Work Analysis (CWA) method, today the working group studies the concept of work in HCI. The HWID working group aims to empower workers and enable the design of workplaces through a lightweight version of CWA integrated with interaction design methods. The working group is not limited to a particular work domain. On the contrary, HWID aims to attract researchers studying the notion of work across various sectors and domains through empirical studies, as well as the definition of concepts, techniques, and methods.

This volume includes extended papers presented during the joint conference of IFIP WG 13.6 Human Work Interaction Design and IFIP WG 13.5 on Human Error, Resilience, Reliability, Safety and System Development, held in Milan, Italy, on September 5–6, 2024. This conference was dedicated to "Sustainable Workplaces by Design", continuing the exploration of this theme by the HWID working group, which was initiated in 2023 during a workshop exploring research directions for sustainable HWID.

This working conference attracted 33 participants and 23 full papers were presented after acceptance resulting from a blind peer review process. Participants were invited to submit an extended version of their paper using the EquinOCS system. From the review process in which each extended paper was reviewed (single blind) by three reviewers, 15 papers were accepted for publication in this volume. The pool of reviewers was the same as that of the conference, with the addition of some external reviewers.

HWID 2024 proposed to explore sustainability through a Human Work Interaction Design lens encompassing its environmental, economical, ethical, and social dimensions. This conference proposed to emphasize insights into the relationship between the sustainability of workplaces, the anticipatory potentials of design, and how automation and AI may fit the picture. Because AI systems increasingly handle high-level cognitive tasks, workers' roles change, and known issues must be considered, such as complacency or the deskilling of workers using these systems. It calls for a workplace design oriented towards environmental responsibility, engagement, well-being, and meaningful collaboration with explainable intelligent artificial systems. This focus was driven by the need to anticipate the impact on future generations, social equity, and justice between workers, while also considering performance supported by intelligent interactive system design for the workplace.

The chapters of this book seek to investigate these questions considering different aspects of Human Work Interaction Design. The first section of this book discusses *theories and processes for sustainable HWID*. Chapters of this section compare design theories based on experts' opinions collected during workshops, or propose exploring new design approaches. A human-centered design process to tackle uncertainty of future work contexts and a framework to design and evaluate sustainable interactive systems for workspace are presented. The second section explores *engagement and well-being during work and training*. The chapters in this section present projects and designs proposing gamification or immersive interaction techniques, or the development of digital twins to foster engagement, safety, and well-being at work or during training in various work sectors (i.e., art, sport, health, waste management, education). The third section emphasizes the need to consider *collaboration with intelligent artificial team members at work*. The first chapters of this section question the engagement of workers collaborating with such systems in the information technology sector, the impact on their roles and responsibilities in the aviation sector, and the performance decision-making of different forms of collaboration with intelligent agents. The last two chapters of this section explore opportunities for the design of robots to enhance diagnostic performance and well-being in healthcare or to allow novice workers without programming skills to access robot data using Large Language Models. The last section of this book focuses on *working with complex data and data visualization*. The chapters of this section propose a framework to deal with the complexity of data and their visualization and a tool for archaeological data storage, management, and visualization.

March 2025

Barbara Rita Barricelli
Stefano Valtolina
Elodie Bouzekri
Angela Locoro
Tilo Mentler

Organization

General Chairs

Barbara Rita Barricelli	University of Brescia, Italy
Stefano Valtolina	University of Milan, Italy

Program Committee Chairs

Elodie Bouzekri	McGill University, Canada
Angela Locoro	University of Brescia, Italy
Tilo Mentler	Trier University of Applied Sciences, Germany

Program Committee

Ganesh D. Bhutkar	Vishwakarma Institute of Technology, India
Pedro Campos	University of Madeira, Portugal
Torkil Clemmensen	Copenhagen Business School, Denmark
Daniela Fogli	University of Brescia, Italy
Anant Bhaskar Garg	HaritaDhara Research Development and Education Foundation, India
Luigi Gargioni	University of Brescia, Italy
Frederica Gonçalves	University of Madeira, Portugal
Antony William Joseph	Aalto University, Finland
Dinesh Katre	Centre for Development of Advanced Computing, India
Hanna Koskinen	VTT Technical Research Centre of Finland, Finland
Arminda Guerra Lopes	Polytechnic Institute of Castelo Branco/ITI-LARSys, Portugal
Mashrura Musharraf	Aalto University, Finland
Judith Molka-Danielsen	Molde University College, Norway
Philippe Palanque	Université Toulouse III - Paul Sabatier, France
Xiangang Qin	Beijing University of Posts and Telecommunications, China
Dorina Rajanen	University of Oulu, Finland

Shrikant Salve	Indian Institute of Information Technology Pune, India
Osiris A. Valdez Banda	Aalto University, Finland

Additional Reviewers

Virpi Roto
Åsa Cajander
Marta Larusdottir
Arminda Guerra
Benjamin Berton
Jose Abdelnour-Nocera
Ines Di Loreto
Athina Belsi
Sofia Ouhbi
Aglaia Gantzopoulou
Teresa Macchia

Sponsors

Social Thingum
WhoTeach

Contents

Collaboration with Intelligent Artificial Team Members at Work

Working With Complex Data and Data Visualization

Theories and Processes for Sustainable Human Work Interaction Designs

Design Theory Qualities: Which Socio-Technical Design Theory is Most Sustainable, Responsible, and Explainable?

Torkil Clemmensen(✉)

Copenhagen Business School, 2000 Frederiksberg, Denmark
Tc.digi@cbs.dk

Abstract. This paper is about socio-technical design qualities. Sustainable, responsible, and explainable design qualities are conceptualized by using previous Human Work Interaction Design (HWID) literature. The notion of design theory and four design theories are explained. Comparative 'theorizing workshops' followed by thematic analysis of the design theory qualities illustrate that the design theory shapes the design qualities. The discussion touches on the reciprocity of design theory and design solutions in relation to design qualities. The conclusion promotes HWID Relation Artefact Design as bringing the qualities discussed.

Keywords: Design theory qualities · Socio-technical design · Human Work Interaction Design · Sustainable design · Responsible design · Explainable design

SDGs: 8 · 9 · 12

1 Introduction

What does the very notion of design imply from the point of view of being sustainable, responsible, and explainable, and how can these values be embodied in workplaces? This inspiring question was raised by the conference organizers in the call-for-papers. Given that Human Work Interaction Design (HWID) somewhat relates to Human-Computer Interaction (HCI), Information Systems (IS), and Human Factors (HF) research and practice fields, the question seemed to call for designs to be studied as software or hardware products for workplace use with certain positive qualities. For example, sustainable designs can be studied by connecting designs to the Sustainable Development Goals (Hansson et al., 2021), responsible designs can be studied by social and economic inclusive designs (Monson, 2023), and explainable designs can be studied as users' folk theories of how algorithms work (Ngo & Krämer, 2022). These 'definitions' are of course not the only possible definitions, and they are selected here because they are human (user) centered. These positive values in these definitions can then be embodied in workplaces through design research that builds and evaluates prototypes.

Published by Springer Nature Switzerland AG 2026
B. R. Barricelli et al. (Eds.): HWID 2024, IFIP AICT 751, pp. 3–19, 2026.
https://doi.org/10.1007/978-3-031-95334-7_1

However, an important part of the question raised was what a "…notion of design imply…". This calls for an evaluation of design theories, rather than evaluation of (only) concrete prototypes' qualities such as sustainability, responsibility, and explainability. In contrast, design theories' qualities would in a scientific context be discussed as the validity of both the prototypes and the grounded knowledge connected to those prototypes (Goldkuhl, 2020). On the other hand, it remains a bit unclear if the wanted qualities can be achieved with design theories that do not themselves display such qualities, since the design theory so to speak *is* the design solution (Dorst, 2019). It could be expected that design theories beyond being valid must be sustainable, responsible, and explainable. In a weird way, this raises the question which design theory is most sustainable, responsible, and explainable?

This paper presents previous literature on sustainable, responsible, and explainable design qualities, followed by a theoretical background chapter on the notion of design and a presentation of a small subset of socio-technical, mostly HCI-related, design theories. Then it compares the design theories, using a baseline provided by HWID. By participant observation of a design exercise in design theory groups, followed by thematic analysis, a large data set was created from which this paper analyzes a subset for design theory qualities. The findings suggest that the qualities are shared by each design theory and that they are somewhat specific for each design step. The discussion and conclusion underscore the reciprocity between design theory and design solution for any study of design qualities in HWID.

2 Previous Literature

This section presents the design qualities of sustainable, responsible, and explainable design, with a focus on how they have been discussed in the HWID literature and mostly from a research perspective. The sustainable development goals that have been used as qualities in sustainable design (Hansson et al., 2021) should clearly be relevant to HWID sustainable design, in particular SDG8 'decent work' about sustained, inclusive and sustainable economic growth, full and productive employment and decent work for all. Responsible designs can be studied by social and economic inclusive designs (Monson, 2023), which resonates well with HWID as shown below. The last design quality, explainable design might be studied as users' folk theories of how algorithms work (Ngo & Krämer, 2022); however, very little research on explainable design has found its way into the HWID literature. Not surprisingly, there are some connections and overlaps between the design qualities. For example, sustainability is a multidimensional concept with environmental, economic, and social dimensions of sustainability (Bouzekri et al., 2023). The previous literature is presented below.

2.1 Sustainable Design Qualities

An assumption behind sustainable design is perhaps that it is possible to create an efficient and sustainable workplace in a general sense, regardless of the type of working environment (Hald et al., 2019). Some working environments are perhaps more difficult to make sustainable, such as when environmental sustainability conflict with decent work sustainability in the waste management sector (Barricelli & Reshtehroudi, 2024). Sustainable design is socio-technical design; for example, the design of a sustainable workplace in terms of building design will include the building's energy efficiency and the management of the building from the employee's perspective (Ianeva et al., 2015). Sustainable design is about how both the organizational work procedures and structures and the digital tools and technologies can be designed to provide sustainable work for employees; in this sense usability concerns not only the physical work environment (Johansson & Sandblad, 2006). Evaluating an ethical value attitude as part of usability evaluation help emphasize sustainability design (Kurosu, 2010). Sustainable design is thus about operational efficiency, social equity, and ethical ways of doing things at work (Akram et al., 2024).

Because it helps design ethically solutions that provides relief from physical and mental stress, sustainable design is associated with applying worker-centric-design, (Kaasinen et al., 2019). A skilled worker should have full control when experiencing challenging situations (Cajander et al., 2015). Sustainable design should – as part of corporate social responsibility and social sustainability – support the worker with organizational culture, adaptation of job descriptions, skills training, and in general design the content and format of information shared with employees to create an experience of certainty and trust (Saadati et al., 2022).

Sustainable design qualities are already a part of mainstream *design thinking* methodology. It aims to use empathy to engage in transparent and authentic ways with employees to identify problems to be solved with prototypes that fits into organizational workflows and employer-employee relationships; in short, it aims to achieve flourishing of employees and organizations (Molka-Danielsen et al., 2022), which is a classic socio-technical design goal.

In sustainable design *research* the aim is not only the project results, but also to anchor results and to create sustainable theories and solutions (Ørngreen, 2015). For example, sustainable design research in greenhouse climate management can provide a reference platform for research into environmental sustainability using a series of prototyping studies that explore interaction designs for growers' interaction with the greenhouse climate in view of global climate changes, and thus underscore how sustainable design is also an expression of value-sensitive design (Pedersen & Clemmensen, 2012). The working with alternative designs to avoid confirming existing assumptions, apply rigor in the analysis, and full use of findings, are important part of sustainable design research that aims to identify the rare, crucial incidents that provide new knowledge (Ørngreen, 2015).

2.2 Responsible Design Qualities

For large power distance national or organizational cultures, responsible design can build on the assumption that employees carrying out their ascribed duties responsibly and asymmetrically is responsible design (Camara et al., 2010). Employees responsible for the design work should be told the required knowledge including interaction design knowledge (Johansson & Sandblad, 2006). This view of responsible design focusses on allocating responsibility between the employees and the systems; the operator and the designer of the automated system will, dependent on the design, to different degrees be mutually responsible and liable for what happens with a button is pressed (Bouzekri et al., 2018). Responsible design qualities refer to the explicit description of allocation of responsibility to actors – employee or system – and how these are accountable for the result of an action (Bouzekri et al., 2018). However, responsibility allocation is not always clearly defined in design, which is a classic human factors problem (Quercioli & Amaldi, 2015). A clear identification of responsibilities of different types of users is a quality of responsible design (Kale et al., 2015).

However, what is a clear identification of responsibilities of different types of users is not simple. For example, in a study of procurement in a national defense setting it turned out that the setting consisted of several organizations where two of the most prominent had different goals. One was carrying out international missions, protected the integrity of national orders and supports the society in major crisis, while the other aimed to strengthen the operational capability of the defense system by acquiring materiel in a cost-effective way, by acting as a facilitator between the other organisation forces and external designers. Neither of the two main organizations were allowed to do any kind of development of artifacts supporting actual defense activities (e.g., armed combat). When usability requirements should be designed, it was not clear if one or the other organisation were the users, but everybody agreed that that there was nobody there to take on this responsibility (Eriksson & Swartling, 2013). It is a well-known situation that nobody takes total responsibility for the maintenance, ant that the actual design perspectives fluctuate between different user groups with responsibility for some processes within the larger setting, including the actual end-users of the design (Björndal et al., 2015). As a solution to the problem with the quality in the identification of responsibilities of different types of users, user personas can be applied to describe responsibility, e.g. "X who is responsible for the company's online marketing" (Nielsen, 2010).

Responsible design qualities in the sense of allocating responsibility is not necessarily about equity, as employees may desire from higher levels of the organization to be primarily responsible for the design including the interaction design to be used by the employees in their everyday work (Clemmensen, 2006) and the resulting wellbeing of employees (Gantzopoulou et al., 2024). In addition, the expectation may be that the technical system or systems help allocate responsibility and give feedback on employees' preferences (Campos & Nunes, 2006), and thus take on a dominating responsibility. This situation is also sometimes described as t in design of automation usually a range of alternatives are proposed, leaving operators responsible for making the final choice (Amaldi & Smoker, 2013). Responsible design qualities can be determined by identifying what is the responsibility of the human, over time, and in relation to the allocation of responsibility to artificial agents, and under the consideration of supervision and leadership in the organisation (Amaldi & Smoker, 2013).

In contrast to the above management-led responsible design, a worker-centric responsible design may move somewhat away from the user-centered design (UCD) methodologies of professional designers and move towards variants of participatory design (PD) involvement of laypeople as co-designers (Lopes, 2022). Socially responsible design is a democratic research practice that is value-added (Ørngreen, 2015). For example, employees can be involved in the design of key performance indicators (KPI) – usually a management tool – by allowing employees to co-select KPIs and be responsible for them and the implied goals (Lárusdóttir & Guðmundsdóttir, 2024). A responsible design quality is then that it is clear who is responsible for KPIs and their impact on employees and organizational success (Lárusdóttir & Guðmundsdóttir, 2024). Another example is when employees who participated as decision-makers in design workshops considering the principles and requirements of Industry 4.0 felt responsible for redesigning their organization's business models (Saadati et al., 2022). The examples indicate that responsible design is classic socio-technical design in terms of balancing employee wellbeing and organizational success.

Given the socio-technical approach to responsible design, ethical issues require that these are considered during design and by thinking about the future; they need to be extrapolated into business processes and strategies(Molka-Danielsen et al., 2022). An example is the social competencies, students and staff awareness of, and responsibility for, environmental issues in design of the smart university. How can designers facilitate and encourage sharing of thermal comfort strategies (keeping cool or warm) that do not endanger the environment by waste or CO2-production, while at the same time learning from others? (Abdelnour-Nocera, Oussena, et al., 2015). Responsible design requires that employees perceive themselves as personally accountable and responsible for the work outcomes (Kaasinen et al., 2019). However, researchers may not achieve the trust of the responsible stakeholders in the design context, as employees have concerns and doubts about anonymity of their data (Wurhofer et al., 2015). Despite these concerns, when employees point to events of interest, the design researcher(s) have the responsibility to interpret these events and to relate them to theories relevant to the phenomenon.(Ørngreen, 2015). Sometimes researchers get access to information that would benefit the organisation, but due to research ethics this cannot be shared, which raises the question when and to what extent a researcher should engage in organizational politics? (Eriksson & Swartling, 2013).

2.3 Explainable Design Qualities

Explainable design is perhaps the most recent design quality, as it came around with the newest wave of AI research. It is by now clear that complex AI systems, such as GenAI, can produce outcomes that are non-transparent and unexplainable (Molka-Danielsen et al., 2022). The outcomes may well appear to be unjustifiable to users of the AI (Molka-Danielsen et al., 2022). Explainable design is needed for the design of AI, robotics, and IoT, since these technologies are overwhelming and often directive for employes and can be directive for human action (Clemmensen, 2021). Explainable design guidelines acknowledge that employees have a need for directives from the AI (Liao et al., 2020). Employees adapt their interaction behaviors to better use the AI, e.g., employee chatbot users follow directions towards what kind of things they could ask the AI chatbot (Liao et al., 2020). The perhaps most promising direction for studying explainable design qualities for employees is to study users' folk theories of how algorithms work (Ngo & Krämer, 2022). In addition, explaining algorithmic bias on social media can be seen as a question of communication (Lopes, 2022).

3 Theoretical Background

3.1 The Notion of Design in Design Theory

The background of this paper is a larger project that aims to dig out a notion of design for HWID by internationalize, finalize, and evaluate a specific HWID design theory, called ***Relation Artefact Design*** to distinguish it from other theoretical perspectives on HWID (Clemmensen, 2021). The idea was to do this by comparing and combining the HWID framework presented in (Abdelnour-Nocera, Barricelli, et al., 2015; Campos et al., 2012; Clemmensen et al., 2006; Katre et al., 2010) with related research socio-technical design theories. At the time of the research, the Information Systems (IS) and New Media research group from School of Economic Disciplines at University of Siegen had a strong HCI and CSCW presence, and also published in IS. Furthermore, the Siegen group included several well-known socio-technical design theories that were suitable for comparison, including 'Practice-Based Computing' (Wulf et al., 2015, 2018) and Experience Design (Hassenzahl, 2010). In addition, at a research group at a nearby university had developed another relevant socio-technical design theory, Design Tension (Gross, 2013). The expectation to the comparing and combining of different design theories was that there would be sufficient overlap and similarities of the notion of design in these theories, so that there would be several benefits of a consolidated HWID framework. A consolidated HWID theory could be a development platform for analytical tools for socio-technical interventions in various work domains. This would be relevant for SME's with potentials for human-oriented digitalization, e.g., employee-robot collaboration, in the production of goods and professional services.

3.2 The Socio-Technical Design Theories

In ***Relation Artefact Design*** (RA) theory, it is critical not to reduce the understanding of how work analysis and interaction design are connected to a series of steps, but instead to see HWID as a *holistic design gestalt that includes several relation-theories* (Clemmensen, 2011, 2021). The Relation Artefacts type I-IV includes a total of 12 selected socio-technical designs, which systematically in a lightweight way supports design moves from social to technical perspectives and vice-versa on the design case. The theory presents itself as a platform that supports the development of domain specific theoretical gestalts that is expressed as the Relation Artefacts.

Practice-Based Computing/Design (PBD) theory (Wulf et al., 2015, 2018) argues that even a strong work domain analysis paired with good user centered design with real user participation is not enough to account for the changes in social practices resulting from new technological artifacts. Rather, research should build a repository of design case studies and generalize by doing comparative analysis with concept building. The focus of concept and theory building should be on *features of social practice* (e.g., awareness), *IT design principles* (e.g., tailorability), and social changes stemming directly from *appropriation* of IT artifacts (e.g., over the shoulder learning). Thus, PBD emphasizes the conceptualization of notions of social changes across empirical cases.

Experience Design (ED) theory (Buchenau & Suri, 2000; Hassenzahl, 2010) assumes that experiences are subjective, holistic, situated, dynamic, and (sometimes) positive. Subjective because experiences depend on the individual's psychology, holistic since it takes design for including not only the product but the wider experience, situated in the sense that experiences are both unique and common patterns at the same time, dynamic as IT artefacts often change over time in the distribution of their pragmatic and hedonic qualities and overall experiences, and finally, positive at least by designers' intent. The idea of ED is to put the experience before the design. Designers should aim at designing user experiences which are experiences mediated by technology. Designers work with materials and tools. Hence, in ED the IT artefact (product, system) is seen as having qualities. These qualities are pragmatic (related to DO goals) and hedonic (related to BE goals) qualities. In ED, the value or the why of a design is seen as hedonic (identity and stimulation)-related psychological need fulfilment, while the 'what' and 'how' of design are the pragmatic-related task performance goals. There is a difference between what are qualities of an IT artefact (pragmatic and hedonic) and what are the subjective, holistic, situated, and dynamic character of an experience (Hassenzahl et al., 2015).

Design Tension (DT) theory (Gross, 2013) sees design as designing compromises towards a set of basic tensions: availability, privacy, conventions, and tailoring. First, the design tension of availability stems from conflicting user needs: users want to interact with computers and with other users, but they also want not be disrupted. Second, the design tension of privacy stems from conflicting user needs related to that data must be captured and shared because it is important for productive group work that the group members know about all team members' situations, activities, and results, but from a privacy perspective users have the right to have their data protected. Third, the design tension of conventions originates from a conflict about informal rules in a group on how members should behave and what to expect from others. There is a conflict between having few conventions that allow for great personal freedom and having many conventions that mediates mutual expectations and a common ground to stand on in the group. Fourth, the design tension for tailoring refers to the need to make domain-specific adaptations in the system. While it is desirable to have a preconfigured system with well thought-out defaults for individual functionality and team functionality, individual user needs and the team requirements could be highly domain specific.

4 Method

4.1 Comparing Design Theories

The author collected data from three research groups on their design theory. Applying participant observation techniques, the design theories were compared in three theorizing workshops to explore variations of the HWID framework for socio-technical interventions in various work domains in a German context. Each workshop began with an introduction to HWID Relation Artefact theory and a design exercise with that design theory, which was followed by a presentation of the research group leader of their design theory and a design exercise with that theory. The design exercises were based on based on analysis of design case of the use of a Cobot (small industrial robot) in a Danish SME (Clemmensen & Nørbjerg, 2019). Each of the three workshops used the theorizing workshop format, Fig. 1.

Instructions to participants: Compare and contrast two socio-technical HCI approaches that are both based on design cases, 'Human Work Interaction Design' (HWID) and 'Practice-Based Computing' (PBD), to explore if and in what ways to theorize, that is, to develop a set of ideas, about socio-technical design cases.
Agenda:
10:00-10:15 *Welcome*
10:15-10:45 *Introduction* to the theorizing exercise, the HWID platform, and the design case
10:45-12:00 *Groupwork*, developing analytical tools for socio-technical interventions in work

- HWID theorizing with two design cases
- Cases: 1) design the use of collaborative robots in a glass processing factory, 2) production planning
- Material: LEGO, to 'build' theory, illustrate developed concepts and relations and their links to data material
- Outcome: Documented with group video explaining HWID principles, using theorizing material
- Coffee will be available

12:00-13:00 *Forum,* presentation and discussion of theory building videos
Lunch (provided by workshop)
13:30-13:45 *Introduction* to Practice-Based Computing
13:45-14:45 *Groupwork*, using PBC to combine, contrast and compare to HWID based on the group's case analysis from the morning session.

- Reflective exercise with HWID+PBD.
- Material: Praxlab spaces (user, method, management and creative spaces)
- Outcome: documented with uploaded group video presenting combinations, contrasts and comparisons HWID+PDB

14:45-15:15 *Forum* presentation and discussion of comparison videos
15:15-15:30 Summary and evaluation of the day and next step
Readings <list>

Fig. 1. Workshop 1. HWID compared to Practice-Based Computing

The workshops were facilitated by the author in cooperation with the respective research group leaders. The data collection was done by video and audio recording the workshops by a research assistant, who was the same for all three workshops. In addition, workshop participants upload their design exercise material and videos made during the workshop in a cloud service (Sciebo, shared by German universities). The data analysis proceeded in two steps, one was done during the workshops by the participants as the outcome and upload in the cloud service, and another was done later by the author with the aim of publishing insights from the workshops. In these three workshops the outcome was theory comparison. An overview of the three workshops is in Table 1.

Table 1. Overview of HWID theorizing workshops for comparing and consolidating theory

Workshops	Month 1 Workshop	Month 2 Workshop	Month 3 Workshop
Theory variation	'Practice based' & HWID framework	'Experience Design' & HWID framework	'Design tensions' & HWID framework
Responsible	The author and PBD research leader and group	The author and ED research leader and group	The PI and DT research leader and group
Participants	Researchers, students and practitioners using PBD	Researchers, students and practitioners using ED	Researchers, students and practitioners using DT
Theorizing material for MORNING session	LEGO, wood and other mock-up material, prototype tools	LEGO, wood and other mock-up material, prototype tools	LEGO, wood and other mock-up material, prototype tools
Reflective material for AFTERNOON session	Praxlab spaces (user, method, management and creative spaces) (Wulf et al., 2018)	Experience Design Tools (Need Cards, interaction vocabulary cards) (Hassenzahl, 2010)	Design tension categories (Gross, 2013)

Over three months, six forum discussions and more than 15 interviews were held, and 12 design videos produced by participants were collected. The initial findings indicated that (1) HWID is less contextual and less technical, and more social and theory-oriented compared to PBC, (2) HWID is less theoretical/conceptual, and more contextual and more work and social oriented, compared to ED, and (3) HWID is less philosophically focused and has broader view of the socio-technical relations compared to DT (Clemmensen, 2021). On this basis, it was decided to explore these design theories from the perspective of qualities of sustainability, responsibility, and explainability.

4.2 Coding and Analysis

The collected data were analyzed thematically by first two coders, and when consensus was reached, by one coder using MAXQDA 2020–2022. This resulted in 10 documents groups, 46 text documents, 187 codes, 1652 coded segments, and 212 memos.

5 Analysis

For this paper, the author further analyzed a subset of the coded material, which were four main codes and 18 subcodes related to design theory steps coding 201 text segments. These segments were additionally coded for sustainable design by interpreting their possible relation to the UN Sustainable Development Goals (Hansson et al., 2021), responsible designs for their social and economic inclusiveness (Monson, 2023), and for explainability by their reliance on folk theories of how algorithms work (Ngo & Krämer, 2022). The result of the analysis is shown in Table 2.

Table 2. Analysis of design theory qualities in design steps for socio-technical design theories.

	HWID Human work interaction Design	PBD Practice Based Design	ED Experience Design	DT Design tensions
Problem definition and need finding	Multiple interrelated notions of needs and problems: Organizational problem definitions, Workers' need findings, Persona creations. + **Responsible design:** "a multi-sided platform. So, a platform for a meeting point for different stakeholders. So, in any project that you are dealing with, maybe think about how the different stakeholders are involved (Forum 1, Pos. 48)"	Participatory design approach to requirement specification. + **Explainable design:** "I can talk to like the guy working at this 100-person company around the corner, he's responsible for the machines there, and he will like, yeah, this is main, I do this maintenance of the machine and yesterday I did this and this and this. And he's really, really, really keen on doing his job…you can see that there are more, probably more people in German companies, especially in the Mittelstand sector, that are really keen on doing work they like or which they really do. (WM interview, Pos. 146)"	Basic psychological needs defined a priori; specific needs found from sampling positive experiences. No organizational problem definition but focus on human experience. + **Responsible design**: "[in critique of an interaction design case] they found that some people are dyslexic. So from that they jumped to video, never actually really questioned that mechanism at all, never questioned the robot, but working on minor details, which I find quite typical for interaction design. Don't you think? Because it's like our how-level. (Group 2, Pos. 335)	Considered early in the design process by consulting theory. + **Responsible design:** "xx was more responsible. He was more reflective and could come up with his own ideas. Yes. It's one of the things I'm also working on. (Group1, Pos. 55)"
Ideation	Multiple sketching on different organizational levels: Interaction patterns, Collaborative sketches, Workflows. +**Explainable design:** "like a turning point for a creative trigger, because the worker here just has the basic knowledge and doesn't use the robot at all or just in a certain way. Now he starts learning by sharing the knowledge from someone else. Learns, learns, learns and then falls down, but as the worker here learned that you can explore creative ways, he might be able to use the experience of experiencing new ways to explore his own new ways (Group 1, Pos. 143–144)"	Sketching not important	Experimental and embodied sketching is a central activity; purpose to empathize and speculate. +**Explainable design:** "I give them on the one hand workshops. So, a kind of coaching of the employees or coaching of some people regarding strategy. On the other hand, I also give them prototypes. So, user interface like mock-ups. And sometimes they are also happy with getting bits of like just a theory. So, how I think certain things work and how they should be designed. But it's not very concrete designs, but more a kind of theory. (DL interview, Pos. 11)"	More than visually brainstorm solutions only, due to theory-driven approach. +**Explainable design:** "…she came with a mood board. So here is the mood board. Here is what I want to design for the users. Here is what I want to, the designers basically to feel. And the user who is using my application should be in this motion basically….in order to make it a scientific research question that I personally also find exciting, I would make it into attention [a theoretical concept]. So I drew this literally…. (Forum 2, Pos. 79) "

(*continued*)

Table 2. (*continued*)

	HWID Human work interaction Design	PBD Practice Based Design	ED Experience Design	DT Design tensions
Prototyping	Individual and collective UX prototypes: Organizational action hypotheses, Prototyped worker experiences, Field evaluations and UX tests. +**Sustainable design:** "I think the job design has to be flexible. I mean, the medium has to be flexible. It shouldn't be just one static video. It has to be maybe telling the people how to be creative with the robot, and then they can be creative with the robot and take videos themselves again. (Group 1, Pos. 158)"	Mature, industry-level prototypes, accepted by companies into daily operation. +**Responsible design:** "typically with companies you start with small, for them not very relevant projects and only after they build trust they work with you on more strategic projects. (Research group leader presentation, Pos. 38)"	UX prototypes, focus on the individual experiences. +**Responsible design:** "robot designers are usually fixed or focusing on the human as a design strategy. So how can we overcome it? We are using performative prototyping methods like dressing roboticists as their robots, giving them prosthesis that change their perception, and let them act the robot. And then let them reflect about what are the strengths of robots, what are the strengths of human and how can we make the robot more robotish in its unique, we call it always superpowers, (DL interview, Pos. 81)"	Design concept-driven low, mid, hi fi prototypes. +**Sustainable:** "We try to distill a lot out of these theories. We also work, as the video shows, we also work empirically of course. Sometimes in our movie project that we had for many years, we really looked at movie theaters, that's a movie theater in Bamberg, and look how people are there and how they interact with each other, how they choose movies. And then we develop theoretical models, like here for example, we also work a lot with, as you all know, with Goffman. (Forum 2, Pos. 74)"
Intervention and evaluation	Sociomaterial focus with Interaction interoperability checks, Digital legacy interventions, & Organizational strategy alignment. +**Sustainable design**: "there needs to be a content strategy because there need to be certain lines of content inside to make it work. So there needs to be something like a knowledge share. What we just said. First of all, they share the knowledge, and then they share the fun part, parts, and using. (Group 1, Pos. 159)"	Ethnographic studies of companies and workers appropriation of prototypes. +**Sustainable design:**" I think in a case like that where it is very important how the person facilitate pick the person regarding the practices and commented it for a sustainable, for a long term sustainable practice and learning, and training of workers to consolidate the practices, and I found that very interesting. (Group1, Pos. 25)"	UX evaluation, focus on assessing need fulfilment. +**Sustainable design:** "in the end, I identified four practices that indigenous people actually use to differentiate between subject and object, or between themselves and the other [the technology]. And I'm transferring these practices or methods, one could maybe say, to design, research, or HCI. (J interview, Pos. 20)"	Theory before testing, evaluation with respect to specific design tensions. + **Sustainable design:** "for me, theorizing before at least, was that one really knows a lot about a topic in order to develop a theory. You really have to study and can't just come up with a theory. Like for me, the theories we developed are more assumptions or hypotheses that need to be tested, but it's not, for me, I wouldn't go out and say, well, I have a new theory, so it's more like one might assume, but it's nothing really that one can grasp. (Forum 3, Pos. 73)"

6 Discussion and Conclusion

This section discusses if the answer to the research question is that HWID Relation Artefact Design is the most sustainable, responsible, and explainable socio-technical design theory. The analysis in Table 2 indicates that Relation Artefact Design to a large degree offers a holistic approach to dealing with sustainability, responsibility, and explainability at work, compared to the others. Relation Artefact Design is sustainable by meeting SDG 8 on decent work by prototyping for worker experiences of creativity with technology. It is responsible by being socially inclusive with a wide range of stakeholders, including management, and economic inclusive by considering both worker and business goals. Finally, Table 2 indicates that HWID is explainable by workers' sharing their cultural models of use of a technology.

However, despite the answer given above, obviously it cannot really be said which design theory is most sustainable, responsible, and explainable, since the design theory qualities discussed here cannot or should not be quantified. First, what is at stake here is perhaps not (only) what does the very notion of design imply from the point of view of being sustainable, responsible, and explainable; rather the notion of design, the design theory, shapes what is sustainable, responsible, and explainable design, Table 3.

Table 3. Design theory qualities.

Qualities	HWID Relation Artefact Design	PBD Practice Based Design	ED Experience Design	DT Design tensions
Sustainable	Provide content for workers creativity with technology	Facilitate workers long-term appropriation of technology	Built on known ways of positive need fulfilment	Based on repeated studies of work
Responsible	Involve all stakeholders in work, including management	Design for organizational strategy	Experience and empathize user categories	Include reflective others
Explainable	By sharing cultural models of use	By referring to worker qualities	Giving prototypes with bits of theory	In terms of theory

This reciprocity between design theory and design solution is perhaps not so different from the insight that design should move beyond problem solving toward being the solution in itself (Dorst, 2019). However, to discuss the subcategories of sustainable, responsible, and explainable design for different design theories require more in-depth analysis of each design theory and the large body of knowledge created by each of those theories; e.g., HWID Relation Artefact Design (Clemmensen, 2021); PBD (Wulf et al., 2018); ED (Hassenzahl, 2010); DT (Gross, 2013). Arguably, sustainable design requires anchoring design outcomes in sustainable theories (Ørngreen, 2015), which happens for all the compared theories, albeit most stable for ED Experience Design and DT Design Tensions, Table 3. In contrast, responsible design requires worker-centric design with clear and full involvement of a widest possible set of stakeholders in the design (Lárusdóttir & Guðmundsdóttir, 2024), which PBD Practice Based Design and in particular HWID Relation Artefact Design provide. Explainable design can be studied by digging out employees' folk theories of how algorithms work (Ngo & Krämer, 2022) and seeing explains as communications (Lopes, 2022), which is something ED Experience Design and in particular HWID Relation Artefact Design does, Table 3.

Second, it is interesting to consider if design theory qualities are different for each design theory step. There does indeed seem to be a sequence in design theory qualities: 1) problem identification and need finding has to be responsible and explainable, 2) ideation has to be explainable, 3) prototyping has to be sustainable and responsible, and 4) intervention and evaluation has to be sustainable, Table 4.

Table 4. Sequence of design qualities.

Design phase/Design theory	1. Problem definition and need finding	2. Ideation	3. Prototyping	4. Intervention and evaluation
HWID Relation Artefact Design	Responsible design	Explainable design	Sustainable design	Sustainable design
PBD Practice Based Design	Explainable design	n/a	Responsible design	Sustainable design
ED Experience Design	Responsible design	Explainable design	Responsible design	Sustainable design
DT Design tensions	Responsible design	Explainable design	Sustainable	Sustainable design

The sequential variation in design qualities illustrated in Table 4 aligns somewhat with previous literature statements that design research has different steps/phases/moves/mechanisms, which each should have design qualities in order not to omit rare, interesting, and crucial incidents of knowledge creation (Ørngreen, 2015). Furthermore, it calls for research into the concrete content of for example responsible design in need finding versus responsible design in prototyping, that is, what is in each of the cells in Table 4. For example, does it make a difference if different design qualities or different version of same design qualities guide the design activities? Future research could analyze design cases, such as the case of defining software company's KPIs from customers' and employees' perspectives (Lárusdóttir & Guðmundsdóttir, 2024). If problem definition and needs finding are done as "…key performance indicators were selected in collaboration with the employees" (Lárusdóttir & Guðmundsdóttir, 2024), is that to considered responsible or explainable design? And which version of responsible design?

Disclosure of Interests. Torkil Clemmensen is a vice-chair of HWID TC WG 13.6.

References

Abdelnour-Nocera, J., Barricelli, B.R., Lopes, A., Campos, P., Clemmensen, T.: Human work interaction design : work analysis and interaction design methods for pervasive and smart workplaces. In: Abdelnour Nocera, J., Barricelli, B.R., Lopes, A., Campos, P., Clemmensen, T. (eds.) 4th IFIP 13.6 Working Conference, HWID 2015, London, UK, June 25–26, 2015, Revised selected papers, vol. 468. Springer (2015). https://doi.org/10.1007/978-3-319-27048-7

Abdelnour-Nocera, J., Oussena, S., Burns, C.: Human Work Interaction Design of the Smart University. In: Abdelnour Nocera, J., Barricelli, B., Lopes, A., Campos, P., Clemmensen, T. (eds.) Human Work Interaction Design. Work Analysis and Interaction Design Methods for Pervasive and Smart Workplaces. HWID 2015. IFIP Advances in Information and Communication Technology, vol 468. Springer, Cham (2015). https://doi.org/10.1007/978-3-319-27048-7_9

Akram, S., Buono, P., Lanzilotti, R.: Rethinking Recruitment Processes through Human-centric Chatbot Design for Sustainable Workplaces. HWID2024-This Volume (2025)

Amaldi, P., Smoker, A.: An organizational study into the concept of automation in a safety critical socio-technical system. In: Campos, P., Clemmensen, T., Nocera, J.A., Katre, D., Lopes, A., Ørngreen, R. (eds.) Human Work Interaction Design. Work Analysis and HCI. HWID 2012. IFIP Advances in Information and Communication Technology, vol 407. Springer, Berlin, Heidelberg (2013). https://doi.org/10.1007/978-3-642-41145-8_16

Barricelli, B.R., Reshtehroudi, R.B.: Interaction Design for Gamified Training in Waste Management Plants: The SOHS Project. HWID2024-This Volume (2025)

Björndal, P., Eriksson, E., Artman, H.: From transactions to relationships: making sense of user-centered perspectives in large technology-intensive companies. In: Abdelnour Nocera, J., Barricelli, B., Lopes, A., Campos, P., Clemmensen, T. (eds.) Human Work Interaction Design. Work Analysis and Interaction Design Methods for Pervasive and Smart Workplaces. HWID 2015. IFIP Advances in Information and Communication Technology, vol 468. Springer, Cham (2015). https://doi.org/10.1007/978-3-319-27048-7_8

Bouzekri, E., Barricelli, B.R., Clemmensen, T., Hertzum, M., Masoodian, M.: Sustainable human-work interaction designs. In: Abdelnour Nocera, J., Kristín Lárusdóttir, M., Petrie, H., Piccinno, A., Winckler, M. (eds.) Human-Computer Interaction – INTERACT 2023. INTERACT 2023. Lecture Notes in Computer Science, vol 14145. Springer, Cham (2023). https://doi.org/10.1007/978-3-031-42293-5_92

Bouzekri, E., Canny, A., Martinie, C., Palanque, P., Gris, C.: Using task descriptions with explicit representation of allocation of functions, authority and responsibility to design and assess automation. In: Barricelli, B., et al. Human Work Interaction Design. Designing Engaging Automation. HWID 2018. IFIP Advances in Information and Communication Technology, vol 544. Springer, Cham (2019). https://doi.org/10.1007/978-3-030-05297-3_3

Buchenau, M., Suri, J.F.: Experience prototyping. In: Proceedings of the Conference on Designing Interactive Systems Processes, Practices, Methods, and Techniques - DIS 2000, pp. 424–433 (2000). https://doi.org/10.1145/347642.347802

Cajander, Å., Larusdottir, M., Eriksson, E., Nauwerck, G. (2015). Contextual personas as a method for understanding digital work environments. In: Abdelnour Nocera, J., Barricelli, B., Lopes, A., Campos, P., Clemmensen, T. (eds.) Human Work Interaction Design. Work Analysis and Interaction Design Methods for Pervasive and Smart Workplaces. HWID 2015. IFIP Advances in Information and Communication Technology, vol 468. Springer, Cham. https://doi.org/10.1007/978-3-319-27048-7_10

Camara, S.B., Oyugi, C., Abdelnour-Nocera, J., Smith, A.: Augmenting usability: cultural elicitation in HCI. In: Katre, D., Orngreen, R., Yammiyavar, P., Clemmensen, T. (eds.) Human Work Interaction Design: Usability in Social, Cultural and Organizational Contexts. HWID 2009. IFIP Advances in Information and Communication Technology, vol 316. Springer, Berlin, Heidelberg (2010). https://doi.org/10.1007/978-3-642-11762-6_4

Campos, P., Clemmensen, T., Nocera, J.A., Katre, D., Lopes, A., Ørngreen, R. (eds.): Human work interaction design. Work Analysis and HCI. HWID 2012. IFIP Advances in Information and Communication Technology, vol 407. Springer, Berlin, Heidelberg (2012). https://doi.org/10.1007/978-3-642-41145-8_10

Campos, P., Nunes, N.J.: Principles and practice of work style modeling: sketching design tools. In: Clemmensen, T., Campos, P., Orngreen, R., Pejtersen, A.M., Wong, W. (eds.) Human Work Interaction Design: Designing for Human Work. HWID 2006. IFIP International Federation for Information Processing, vol 221. Springer, Boston, MA (2006). https://doi.org/10.1007/978-0-387-36792-7_12

Clemmensen, T.: A simple design for a complex work domain - the role of sketches in the design of a Bachelor study's new folder structure for use by teachers, students and administrators. In: Clemmensen, T., Campos, P., Orngreen, R., Pejtersen, A.M., Wong, W. (eds.) Human Work Interaction Design: Designing for Human Work. HWID 2006. IFIP International Federation for Information Processing, vol 221. Springer, Boston, MA (2006). https://doi.org/10.1007/978-0-387-36792-7_13

Clemmensen, T.: A human work interaction design (HWID) case study in e-government and public information systems. Int. J. Public Inf. Syst. **7**(3) (2011)

Clemmensen, T.: Human work interaction design: a platform for theory and action. Springer (2021)

Clemmensen, T., Campos, P., Orngreen, R., Pejtersen, A.M., Wong, W. (eds.): Human work interaction design: designing for human work. HWID 2006. IFIP International Federation for Information Processing, vol 221. Springer, Boston, MA. https://doi.org/10.1007/978-0-387-36792-7

Clemmensen, T., Nørbjerg, J.: (not) Working (with) Collaborative Robots in a Glass Processing Factory. Paper presented at ECSCW workshop: Worst Case Practices Teaching us the Bright Side, Salzburg, Austria (2019)

Dorst, K.: Design beyond design. She Ji J. Des. Econ. Innov. **5**(2), 117–127 (2019)

Eriksson, E., Swartling, A.: UCD Guerrilla Tactics. In: Campos, P., Clemmensen, T., Nocera, J.A., Katre, D., Lopes, A., Ørngreen, R. (eds.) Human Work Interaction Design. Work Analysis and HCI. HWID 2012. IFIP Advances in Information and Communication Technology, vol 407. Springer, Berlin, Heidelberg (2013). https://doi.org/10.1007/978-3-642-41145-8_10

Gantzopoulou, A., et al.: Virtual reality headsets for work-related stress among midwives. HWID2024-This Volume (2025)

Goldkuhl, G.: Design science epistemology. A pragmatist inquiry. Scand. J. Inf. Syst. **32**(1), 2 (2020)

Gross, T.: Supporting effortless coordination: 25 years of awareness research. Comput. Supported Coop. Work (CSCW) **22**(4), 425–474 (2013). https://doi.org/10.1007/s10606-013-9190-x

Hald, K., Rehm, M., Moeslund, T.B.: Testing Augmented Reality Systems for Spotting Sub-Surface Impurities. In: Barricelli, B., et al. Human Work Interaction Design. Designing Engaging Automation. HWID 2018. IFIP Advances in Information and Communication Technology, vol 544. Springer, Cham (2019). https://doi.org/10.1007/978-3-030-05297-3_7

Hansson, L.Å.E.J., Cerratto Pargman, T., Pargman, D.S.: A decade of sustainable HCI: connecting SHCI to the sustainable development goals. In: Proceedings of the 2021 CHI Conference on Human Factors in Computing Systems, pp. 1–19 (2021)

Hassenzahl, M.: Experience design: technology for all the right reasons. Synth. Lect. Hum.-Centered Inform. **3**(1), 1–95 (2010). https://doi.org/10.2200/s00261ed1v01y201003hci008

Hassenzahl, M., Wiklund-Engblom, A., Bengs, A., Hägglund, S., Diefenbach, S.: Experience-oriented and product-oriented evaluation: psychological need fulfillment, positive affect, and product perception. Int. J. Hum.-Comput. Interact. **31**(8), 530–544 (2015)

Ianeva, M., et al.: Pervasive technologies for smart workplaces: a workplace efficiency solution for office design and building management from an occupier's perspective. In: Abdelnour Nocera,

J., Barricelli, B., Lopes, A., Campos, P., Clemmensen, T. (eds.) Human Work Interaction Design. Work Analysis and Interaction Design Methods for Pervasive and Smart Workplaces. HWID 2015. IFIP Advances in Information and Communication Technology, vol 468. Springer, Cham (2015). https://doi.org/10.1007/978-3-319-27048-7_5

Johansson, N., Sandblad, B.: VIHO - Efficient IT Support in Home Care Services. In: Clemmensen, T., Campos, P., Orngreen, R., Pejtersen, A.M., Wong, W. (eds) Human Work Interaction Design: Designing for Human Work. HWID 2006. IFIP International Federation for Information Processing, vol 221. Springer, Boston, MA (2006). https://doi.org/10.1007/978-0-387-36792-7_3

Kaasinen, E., et al.: A worker-centric design and evaluation framework for operator 4.0 solutions that support work well-being. In: Barricelli, B., et al. Human Work Interaction Design. Designing Engaging Automation. HWID 2018. IFIP Advances in Information and Communication Technology, vol 544. Springer, Cham (2019). https://doi.org/10.1007/978-3-030-05297-3_18

Kale, P., Bhutkar, G., Pawar, V., Jathar, N.: Contextual design of intelligent food carrier in refrigerator: an indian perspective. In: Abdelnour Nocera, J., Barricelli, B., Lopes, A., Campos, P., Clemmensen, T. (eds.) Human Work Interaction Design. Work Analysis and Interaction Design Methods for Pervasive and Smart Workplaces. HWID 2015. IFIP Advances in Information and Communication Technology, vol 468. Springer, Cham (2015). https://doi.org/10.1007/978-3-319-27048-7_15

Katre, D., Orngreen, R., Yammiyavar, P., Clemmensen, T. (eds.): Human work interaction design: usability in social, cultural and organizational contexts. HWID 2009. IFIP Advances in Information and Communication Technology, vol 316. Springer, Berlin, Heidelberg. https://doi.org/10.1007/978-3-642-11762-6

Kurosu, M.: Usability and culture as two of the value criteria for evaluating the artifact. In: Katre, D., Orngreen, R., Yammiyavar, P., Clemmensen, T. (eds.) Human Work Interaction Design: Usability in Social, Cultural and Organizational Contexts. HWID 2009. IFIP Advances in Information and Communication Technology, vol 316. Springer, Berlin, Heidelberg (2010). https://doi.org/10.1007/978-3-642-11762-6_6

Lárusdóttir, M., Guðmundsdóttir, G.L.: Defining software company's KPIs from customers' and employees' perspectives. In: Lárusdóttir, M.K., Naqvi, B., Bernhaupt, R., Ardito, C., Sauer, S. (eds.) Human-Centered Software Engineering. HCSE 2024. Lecture Notes in Computer Science, vol 14793. Springer, Cham (2024). https://doi.org/10.1007/978-3-031-64576-1_8

Liao, Q.V., Gruen, D., Miller, S.: Questioning the AI: informing design practices for explainable AI user experiences. In: Proceedings of the 2020 CHI Conference on Human Factors in Computing Systems, pp. 1–15 (2020). https://doi.org/10.1145/3313831.3376590

Lopes, A.G. (2022). HCI four waves within different interaction design examples. In: Bhutkar, G., et al. Human Work Interaction Design. Artificial Intelligence and Designing for a Positive Work Experience in a Low Desire Society. HWID 2021. IFIP Advances in Information and Communication Technology, vol 609. Springer, Cham. https://doi.org/10.1007/978-3-031-029 04-2_4

Molka-Danielsen, J., Rasool, J., Smith, C.H.: Design and deployment considerations for ethically advanced technologies for human flourishing in the workplace. In: Bhutkar, G., et al. Human Work Interaction Design. Artificial Intelligence and Designing for a Positive Work Experience in a Low Desire Society. HWID 2021. IFIP Advances in Information and Communication Technology, vol 609. Springer, Cham (2022). https://doi.org/10.1007/978-3-031-02904-2_5

Monson, M.: Socially responsible design science in information systems for sustainable development: a critical research methodology. Eur. J. Inf. Syst. **32**(2), 207–237 (2023)

Ngo, T., Krämer, N.: Exploring folk theories of algorithmic news curation for explainable design. Behav. Inf. Technol. **41**(15), 3346–3359 (2022)

Nielsen, L.: Personas in cross-cultural projects. In: Katre, D., Orngreen, R., Yammiyavar, P., Clemmensen, T. (eds.) Human Work Interaction Design: Usability in Social, Cultural and Organizational Contexts. HWID 2009. IFIP Advances in Information and Communication Technology, vol. 316. Springer, Berlin, Heidelberg (2010). https://doi.org/10.1007/978-3-642-11762-6_7

Ørngreen, R.: Reflections on design-based research. In: Abdelnour Nocera, J., Barricelli, B., Lopes, A., Campos, P., Clemmensen, T. (eds.) Human Work Interaction Design. Work Analysis and Interaction Design Methods for Pervasive and Smart Workplaces. HWID 2015. IFIP Advances in Information and Communication Technology, vol. 468. Springer, Cham (2015). https://doi.org/10.1007/978-3-319-27048-7_2

Pedersen, R.U., Clemmensen, T.: A design science approach to interactive greenhouse climate control using lego mindstorms for sensor-intensive prototyping. In: Campos, P., Clemmensen, T., Nocera, J.A., Katre, D., Lopes, A., Ørngreen, R. (eds.) Human Work Interaction Design. Work Analysis and HCI. HWID 2012. IFIP Advances in Information and Communication Technology, vol. 407. Springer, Berlin, Heidelberg (2013). https://doi.org/10.1007/978-3-642-41145-8_7

Quercioli, M.S., Amaldi, P.: A multi-perspective view on human-automation interactions in aviation. In: Abdelnour Nocera, J., Barricelli, B., Lopes, A., Campos, P., Clemmensen, T. (eds) Human Work Interaction Design. Work Analysis and Interaction Design Methods for Pervasive and Smart Workplaces. HWID 2015. IFIP Advances in Information and Communication Technology, vol. 468. Springer, Cham (2015). https://doi.org/10.1007/978-3-319-27048-7_12

Saadati, P., Abdelnour-Nocera, J., Clemmensen, T.: Co-designing prototypes for user experience and engagement in automation. In: Bhutkar, G., et al. Human Work Interaction Design. Artificial Intelligence and Designing for a Positive Work Experience in a Low Desire Society. HWID 2021. IFIP Advances in Information and Communication Technology, vol. 609. Springer, Cham (2022). https://doi.org/10.1007/978-3-031-02904-2_8

Wulf, V., Müller, C., Volkmar, P., Randall, D., Rohde, M., Stevens, G.: Practice-based computing: empirically grounded conceptualizations derived from design case studies. In: Wulf, V., Schmidt, K., Randall, D. (eds.) Designing Socially Embedded Technologies in the Real-World, pp. 111–150. Springer, London (2015). https://doi.org/10.1007/978-1-4471-6720-4_7

Wulf, V., Pipek, V., Randall, D., Rohde, M., Schmidt, K., Stevens, G.: Socio-informatics. In: Wulf, V., Pipek, V., Randall, D., Rohde, M., Schmidt, K., Stevens, G. (eds.) Vol. 1. Oxford University Press (2018). https://doi.org/10.1093/oso/9780198733249.001.0001

Wurhofer, D., Fuchsberger, V., Meneweger, T., Moser, C., Tscheligi, M.: Insights from user experience research in the factory: What to consider in interaction design. In: Nocera, J.A., Barricelli, B., Lopes, A., Campos, P., Clemmensen, T. (eds.) HWID2015 -Human Work Interaction Design. Work Analysis and Interaction Design Methods for Pervasive and Smart Workplaces. IFIP Advances in Information and Communication Technology, vol. 468, pp. 39–56. Springer, Heidelberg (2015). https://doi.org/10.1007/978-3-319-27048-7_3

Futures HCD - Human-Centred Design for Uncertain Future

Antony William Joseph(✉), Virpi Roto, and Vivian Stolt

School of Art, Design and Architecture, Department of Design, Aalto University, Helsinki, Finland
antony.joseph@aalto.fi

Abstract. Four industrial revolutions have not only affected how products are manufactured, but they have also transformed the ways of working in industry. Human-Work Interaction Design (HWID) research could play an important role in the fifth industrial revolution, since Industry 5.0 is visioned to be human-centred and placing worker's well-being at the centre of the production process. At this point, HWID can steer this next industrial revolution by developing Human-Centred Design (HCD) methods for Industry 5.0 designers. A natural role for HWID researchers is to influence the work tool design process, which normally starts by studying the present work, and making incremental changes. However, it is difficult to turn the findings from the present to a future that is revolutionarily different, such as Industry 5.0. In this paper, we introduce a Futures HCD methodology that starts by predicting the future work context with a Futures Wheel method. This means modifying the standard Human-Centred Design cycle to start from collective understanding of the possible futures instead of studying the present context. This paper introduces the Futures HCD methodology and evaluates it in a maritime project targeting human-centred Industry 5.0.

Keywords: Human-Centred Design · Future of work · Uncertain Future · Futures HCD · User experience design · UX@Work · Industrial revolution

1 Introduction

The industrial revolutions have led to significant transformations, rendering current problems obsolete and giving rise to new challenges. Technological advancements have significantly impacted the design of work within organizations [3] and have reshaped the way employees work under different conditions [42]. The effects of macro trends, such as digitalisation, automation, and sustainability, are being felt at work across all sectors.

The ongoing fourth industrial revolution (Industry 4.0 or I4.0) with Cyber-Physical Systems introduces significant changes in many industries. These new digital technologies are opening up new forms of human-machine interaction which have a direct impact on the employees and the nature of work [30]. The revolution requires rethinking the work structure, roles, and tools. In this context, uncertainty of the future work presents

Published by Springer Nature Switzerland AG 2026
B. R. Barricelli et al. (Eds.): HWID 2024, IFIP AICT 751, pp. 20–38, 2026.
https://doi.org/10.1007/978-3-031-95334-7_2

itself as a challenge and requires attention. Design has been always involved in envisioning and shaping the future, and it is increasingly important for designers to engage with stakeholders and users to understand their perspectives and actively involve them in decision making through scenarios and stories to envision future contexts [12].

Despite the fact that I4.0 has not yet been completely deployed and integrated internationally, several industries are already anticipating the effect of Industry 5.0 (I5.0) [60]. The European Commission conceived the term Industry 5.0 to tackle the social and environmental challenges introduced by I4.0 and to encourage companies and industries to adapt and become more sustainable, resilient, and human-centric [8]. While automation is the major emphasis of I4.0, I5.0 emphasizes collaboration between humans and autonomous machines [40].

The emerging paradigm of I5.0 aims to bring greater attention to worker well-being, placing "the well-being of the worker at the centre of the production process"[1]. Coronado et al. [11] describe I5.0 as a radical shift that promotes human-centered intelligent systems and human-robot interaction in order to address societal and environmental issues brought on by earlier industrial revolutions. This suggests that I5.0 is value-driven rather than technology-driven [60]. Nahavandi [40] expects that in I5.0, the human worker will have a distinct sense of fulfillment and can work stress-free and with a human touch. Addressing these goals requires a human-centred design (HCD) methodology, which enables designing work tools and conditions fulfilling the needs of human employees.

One of the industries under a significant transformation towards I5.0 is the waterborne transport industry. As the maritime industry is advancing towards autonomous ships and remote operations, it is important to design for the well-being of workers [14]. Since the user experience of digital tools in future work have an important role in worker well-being, early involvement of Human-Work Interaction Design experts in this transformation is required.

Our research question is *How to design human-centred work tools for an uncertain industrial future?* We approach this question by developing a Human-Centred Design methodology that pays more attention than the standard version of HCD [27] to understanding the revolutionary changes that the future with I5.0 may bring. The proposed methodology focuses on the first phase of the iterative HCD process, *Understanding and specifying the context of use* [27]. Therefore, our goal is to provide an additional tool to understand the potential future contexts. We adopted a participatory tool for this purpose, Futures Wheel [6, 10, 20]. In this paper, we report a case study where the Futures Wheel was integrated to the HCD process to gain understanding of the potential futures of remote operation work in the maritime industry. **The case study tested the Futures HCD methodology in the case of maritime mission planning**. This study contributes to human work interaction design research by suggesting and testing a methodology for human-centred design of future work in I5.0.

[1] https://research-and-innovation.ec.europa.eu/research-area/industrial-research-and-innovation/industry-50_en.

2 Related Research

Recognizing the need for improved collaboration between humans and intelligent systems, recent technological advancements paved the way for human-centred design approach for AI systems. It is challenging to design usable and explainable AI systems, and even more challenging to address the psychological needs of the users. Still, Human-Centred Industry 5.0 needs to address user experiences at work, including the users' emotional needs.

Good HCD approach leads to good user experience (UX) by placing the users at the center of the design process, ensuring their needs and preferences are carefully addressed. In the context of creating human-centred future work tools for autonomous maritime operations, this section aims to understand specific challenges and requirements of the maritime sector. The related research of this paper reviews user experience at work and human-centred methods for uncertain future.

2.1 User Experience at Work

The advancement of AI is accelerating automation in the design of technology, and workers may be more concerned that AI in the workplace may remove human autonomy and jobs [38]. This is one of the reasons why several policy making organizations call for a human-centred future of work. The International Labour Organization (ILO) has selected the human-centred future of work as a priority theme in its centennial declaration [50]. Similarly, the EU High-Level Expert Group on Artificial Intelligence emphasizes human-centred AI in the workplace [17]. Human well-being is given top priority in the design of autonomous and intelligent systems by the IEEE Ethically aligned design [26] and Global Initiatives on Ethics of Autonomous and Intelligent Systems.

The majority of goods and services targeted at the consumer market aim to provide good UX. UX design of tools used at workplaces has focused on improving work efficiency and safety, e.g., through improving usability and avoiding errors. Employees' psychological well-being has gained little attention, since UX research is largely focused on the pragmatic rather than psychological needs of employees, as shown by Simsek et al. [52]. According to Kaasinen et al. [29], UX at work refers to 'The way a person feels about using a product, service, or system in a work context, and how this shapes the image of oneself as a professional'. The goal of Experience Design is to explain how technology might be designed to promote positive experiences [24, 25], which goes beyond removing usability problems or safety hazards towards providing meaningful experiences at work context [35] and making employees proud of their work [35]. Based on these developments in UX at work research, this paper focuses on the positive UX design of digital work tools.

2.2 From I4.0 to I5.0 in Maritime Industry

Looking back in history the industry revolution has gone through four technological and social revolutions that have transformed industrial concepts and operating methods [58]. Currently, industries are experiencing an evolutionary migration from I3.0 to I4.0 through digitalisation of manufacturing processes [15, 19]. I4.0 has created a massive influence on the digital system, promoting high levels of manufacturing efficiency and quality through novel technologies [39]. The advancement of I4.0 has also given a new perspective on humans' role and their tasks in the industrial context [23]. I4.0 requires skilled employees to handle several responsibilities related to communication with machines through human-machine interfaces and offers methods to interface with digital systems [55].

The effects of I4.0 are becoming noticeable in the key areas of the maritime sector, such as shipping, shipbuilding, seaports, terminals and their operations and services [45, 54]. Digitalisation is expected to result in better connectivity between sea and land as well as land-based operations more frequently [2]. Better connectivity is an opportunity that brings all key areas of the maritime sector, from sea to port, to connect and grow simultaneously and modernize the process through digitalization [43]. Innovative technologies used in the maritime sector include Artificial Intelligence, automation, remote monitoring, IoT, and innovative propulsion system [16].

In the maritime sector, though several attempts are made to embrace new technologies or I4.0, the pace and implementation process is slow [1, 47, 56]. The shortcoming of I4.0 is already being felt by the industries and at the same time, they are also able to perceive the effects of I5.0 [31]. The future of the shipping sector is largely dependent on autonomous shipping [28], which has immense potential if the shortcomings are effectively addressed [49].

The digital transformation (I4.0) primarily focused on automating processes and emphasized technology-centred approach rather than human-centred approach (I5.0) [13, 36, 40, 49, 60]. The future of the maritime sector is progressively moving towards automation and remote monitoring and it is important to study the uncertain future through human-centred design approach. Our research study focuses on human-centred design of future work in I5.0.

2.3 Human-Centred Methods for Uncertain Future

Human-centred design (HCD) is a widely recognized participatory approach to the design and development of interactive systems that places emphasis on the users, their needs and requirements [27]. The HCD activities in the development process of the project consists of four phases: Understanding and specifying the context of use, Specifying the user requirements, Producing design solutions, and Evaluating the design.

The field of futures research gained recognition as a research paradigm in the early 1970s [5, 20]. According to Ramos [44, P. 825], there are "five major stages of futures research: Predictive, Systemic, Critical, Participatory, and Action oriented". This study aligns with the participatory and action-oriented approaches that involve qualitative data gathering through workshops, allowing individuals to explore future scenarios and actively prioritize actions, determining potential consequences.

The Futures Wheel, originally developed by Glenn [22], is interesting due to its alignment with participatory approach, which is a prominent human-centred design approach [27]. Futures researchers employ qualitative methods, primarily scenario-based, to identify and analyze potential futures [48] and those methods are more valuable in cases of high level uncertainty of the future [9].

Previous studies have demonstrated the use of futures methods in various design contexts across different industries. Behboudi and Javidani [4] employed the Futures Wheel as a tool to identify potential opportunities in the initial stages of the design process and examined the outcomes of design choices in later stages. Later, Wright [59] investigated the implications of design decisions through consequence mapping. Kouri et al. [32] focused on predicting the future of healthcare and e-health. Their findings suggest that the Futures Wheel method effectively enables envisioning and understanding the possible consequences and cascading effects of future changes.

Farrow [18] explored the potential implications of varying ratios of human and artificial intelligence within future operating models using the Futures Wheel method and emphasize the necessity for organizations to carefully consider the prioritization of AI investments. Similarly, Simões et al. [51] employed Futures Wheel to examine the future of digital transformation and AI in the context of I4.0 and presented probable future events that may occur in the 2020s and 2030s.

Nielsen et al. [41] conducted a Futures Wheel workshop with transport experts to assess the impact of open science in the transport section. This study identified specific impacts of open science on the transport sector, such as reduced emissions, shorter travel times, improved traffic safety, increased awareness of transport policies and the utilization of AI to enhance mobility services.

Futures methods have the flexibility to be integrated into any phase of the HCD process [37, 46, 53]. For instance, Wright [59] employed a consequence mapping tool to assess future implications of their design while Behboudi and Javidani [4] incorporated a Futures Wheel activity to evaluate future implications. Their primary motivation behind combining HCD and Futures design is to instill long-term design implications within the HCD process [57]. However, it can be challenging to identify specific instances where design methods are used within the Futures Design process [57]. A larger number of research literature predominantly focuses on using design methods to generate design futures rather than addressing the Futures Design [10] that envision futures and explore alternatives [33].

In conclusion, the futures studies in various sectors inadequately address the design of human-centred work tools for an uncertain future. When designing for human-centred Industry 5.0, there is a need to consider potential futures and the positive user experience in the design of work tools. The present study aims to address this gap by applying a participatory futures research method, Futures Wheel, in the beginning of a human-centred design process.

3 Methodology

This case study developed and tested Futures HCD, a human-centred design approach [27] for an uncertain future. The key phase to gain clarity of the possible futures is the "Understanding and specifying the context of use" phase of the HCD process. The other phases include semi-structured interviews to identify user needs, designing use scenarios, and evaluating the scenarios with stakeholders (see Fig. 1).

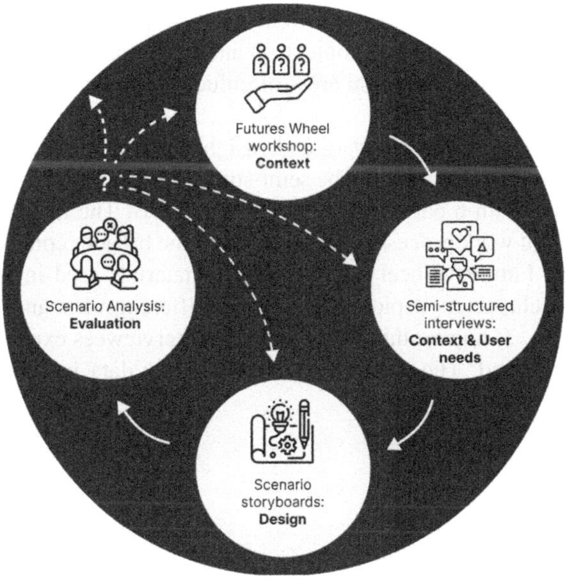

Fig. 1. Futures HCD - a human-centred design methodology proposed for uncertain future.

The method we propose for phase "Understanding and specifying the future context of use" is a workshop utilizing the Futures Wheel [18, 21, 22]. The purpose of this workshop is to gain a collective understanding of the possible futures by addressing not only the technology to be designed but also the themes affecting the future more broadly.

This study employed the Futures Wheel method, originally proposed by Glenn [22] to anticipate and prepare for potential future consequences in the context of remote operation of autonomous ships. The Futures Wheel is a graphical visualization method that facilitates the identification and evaluation of the potential future consequences of various forms of change, encompassing technical, sociological, ethical, environmental, political, and jurisdictional aspects [6]. The visualization process of the Futures Wheel enables participants to uncover multiple layers of consequences, including first-order, second-order, and third-order ramifications, thereby creating a comprehensive map of direct and indirect impacts [6].

In this study, the Futures Wheel [22] workshop was conducted remotely with 10 participants from Company A (developers of the new work tool) and Company B (potential users of the tool). All participants were employees in the client company who were directly involved or had a relevant skill in envisioning the future Mission Planning tool. The reason to organize the workshop internally was inspired by the objective of building a shared knowledge of the Mission planning system, the employee experience, and the company's future direction. Microsoft Teams was used as the online meeting call solution between participants. Additionally, Miro, an online whiteboard tool enabled sharing the Futures Wheel and allowing all participants to add their input to the whiteboard. The goal of the workshop was to build a shared knowledge of the future context in which the new tool would be used, addressing the employee experience. The 2.5-h workshop consisted of three phases: 1) scanning the environment for significant forces in important areas affecting the future work context, 2) analyzing the impacts of the discovered forces, and 3) determining the critical areas of influence to evaluate for a probable event based on the prior consequences.

The Futures Wheel workshop data and insights served as a foundation for planning the semi-structured interviews. The semi-structured interviews [7] were conducted individually on-site with 6 participants from Company B. The interviews investigated details of the present work processes to complement the broader contextual information gathered from the Futures Wheel workshop. The materials used included a map (see Fig. 2) with chess characters depicting workers in different roles, and 3D-printed ships and cargos (see Fig. 3) hoping this would help the interviewees explain their work and the procedures involved. The semi-structured interview data was analyzed using the Affinity Diagram method [34].

Fig. 2. A map illustrating the voyage between two harbors was one of the physical materials aimed at concretizing discussion during semi-structured interviews.

Fig. 3. A participant interacting with chess characters, 3D-printed ships, and cargos during the interview.

The outcomes of the interviews and the scenarios generated through the Futures Wheel workshop contributed to the creation of several storyboards. The storyboards aimed to capture the essence of the envisioned tool and explore workflows. While the interface design and workflow-related features were not the primary focus at this stage, attention was given to incorporating small details that would make the interface more insightful and contribute to a positive user experience.

Storyboard evaluation was conducted with 6 participants from Company A and Company B. The evaluation was conducted online using Microsoft Teams and the Miro Board platform. The scenarios were visualized as storyboards and evaluated through both individual and group sessions. The individual sessions were conducted to gather detailed feedback and explore personal perspective and opinions on storyboards. The group sessions were aimed to obtain broader perspectives from professionals across different disciplines. The facilitator played an important role in creating an atmosphere where participants feel confident in expressing their opinions.

4 Case Study of Futures HCD

The future-oriented human-centred design methodology of work tools for I5.0 was evaluated in a case project that aimed to develop a new way of mission planning for autonomous ships. The practical aim of the case project was to provide ideas for a human-centred mission planning user interface defined as "Mission Planner 2028". The interface would be used by employees in a remote operation centre, and the planning is aided by an intelligent system. Since the focus of this paper is on the Futures HCD method, we introduce the four phases of the Futures HCD methodology (see Fig. 1) with examples.

4.1 Understanding and Specifying the Context of Use with Futures Wheel

Organizing a Futures Wheel workshop was the duty of the research team, and it consisted of three steps: Preparing the Futures Wheel and the workshop arrangements, Running the Workshop, and Analyzing the workshop. First, the macro theme of the Futures Wheel was defined as "Mission Planner 2028" which aimed to foster a human-centred approach. Then, the research team defined six Macro Themes relevant to this context, namely Technology, Organizations, Sustainability, Social connection, Decision making, and Regulations (see Fig. 4). When running the workshop, the participants were asked to identify the second-level consequences relating to mission planning based on the first-level Macro Themes as either "improvements that could happen" or "risks that could realize". The next phase of the workshop was taking the participants from identifying the context aspects to human-centred thinking of third-level consequences through the question "What does the employee want?". Examples of the employee's wants under Sustainability theme included *Easy visual indication of sustainability parameters for the mission*, and in Decision Making theme *[Human operator] always knows who is in charge of all systems.* As the last activity of the session, participants presented their group work to the whole group, describing the key features that emerged within various categories.

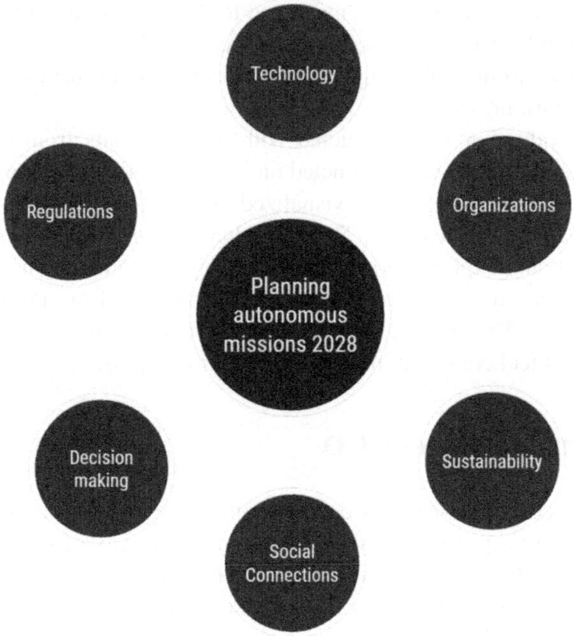

Fig. 4. Futures Wheel including the six themes to be discussed in the workshop.

During the Futures Wheel workshop, data was generated and stored on the Miro board facilitating convenient analysis within the same environment. The Futures Wheel workshop provided a total of 106 notes, including 47 notes on future improvements, 37 notes on future risks, and 22 notes on desired employee experiences. Analyzing the workshop activity started by grouping similar notes together, forming themes such as "Planning the Mission", "Ongoing Mission", and "Need for Change or Help". Second, the notes related to the employee experience were extracted and analyzed through thematic analysis to extract the experiences important in this context. The resulting employee experience themes included themes related to efficiency, feeling important and confident with the decisions, and the need for help. The themes represent the relevant factors affecting human-centred design of mission planning tool. They form the basis for further consideration in the subsequent phases of design from the perspective of the employee.

4.2 Semi-structured Interviews

A significant outcome of the Futures Wheel workshop was the identification of recurrent scenarios such as communication, variable parameters, connection loss, and shift change. These scenarios were considered important and thus required further exploration to understand how the new mission planning tool would fit the work of the early adopters of the remote ship operation tools in Company B. The interviews aimed to gather an understanding of the current practices and experiences of these employees and to find the employees' perspectives on the future direction of the company.

The interview questions focused on understanding participants' perspectives on mission planning, communication problems, shift change, unexpected challenges, connection loss, and finally understanding their perspective on future mission planning. The recurring scenarios identified during the Futures Wheel workshop served as a framework for further exploration and discussion during the interviews.

The analysis of the data collected from the interviews using an Affinity Diagram yielded valuable insights into the characteristics of potential users and their relationship to the employee experience in mission planning. The responses from each interviewee were grouped based on the scenario-based questions posed during the interviews. The interviews revealed important aspects of the employees' relationship with the company's ship automation initiatives. The outcomes of the interviews complemented the scenarios generated through the Futures Wheel workshop, providing valuable perspectives from potential users.

4.3 Design

The goal of the design phase in the HCD process is to produce design solutions that align with user needs and requirements. This phase involves creating scenarios of use through storyboards. In our study, the storyboarding process commenced with a careful evaluation and synthesis of the outcomes derived from the Futures Wheel workshops and interview data. The workshop yielded valuable insights and ideas pertaining to future scenarios and challenges within the realm of mission planning and autonomous shipping. The subsequent interviews provided additional perspectives and experiences from professionals actively engaged in the field. The objective was to provide insights and services for potential employees who would be utilizing the entire Mission Planning system. The storyboards aimed to depict how the system could facilitate transparent and efficient communication between employees and the Mission Planning system. Although interface design and flow-related features were not the primary emphasis during this stage, particular attention was given to incorporating relevant details that would enhance the interface's insightfulness and contribute to a positive user experience.

The first scenario is Starting a Mission Plan (see Fig. 5) which addresses the communication between the user and the system. In this scenario, the mission planner downloads mission details and creates a dashboard. If the AI system was unable to choose the appropriate vessel to achieve balanced container loading onto the ship, the employee would have the capability to make the final selection.

Fig. 5. Scenario 1: Starting a mission plan which shows the colour coding of vessels and mission planning progress.

The second scenario is Assigning Captains (see Fig. 6) depicts how the mission planner assigns captains and shows the progress to the Remote Operating Centre (ROC) members. The AI system informs the mission planner if any information is missing.

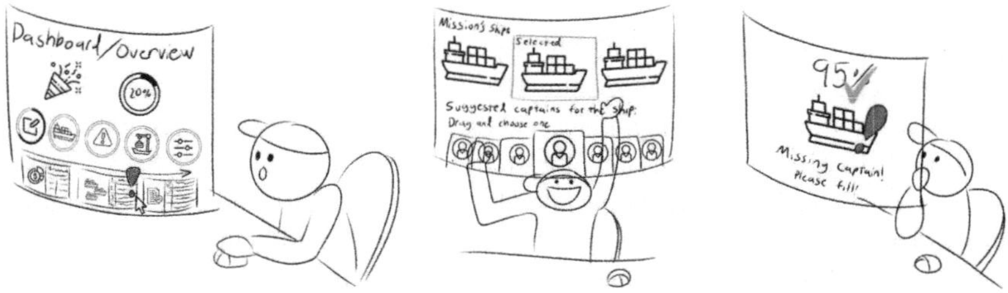

Fig. 6. Scenario 2: Swiping as a playful interaction while assigning captains to the ships.

The third scenario (see Fig. 7) is the Voyage Plan focuses on the details of waypoint, general information about the trip, ship capabilities, reported previous history, weather conditions, regions with low connectivity and other probable causes that might affect the mission. The AI system congratulates the mission planner when the mission planning is completed.

Fig. 7. Scenario 3: AI assisted voyage plan and the AI system congratulate the mission planner on the successful completion of the mission planning.

4.4 Evaluation

The last phase of the Futures HCD methodology is "Evaluating the design". The scenarios produced in the design phase were evaluated with different stakeholders, including potential users of those designs. The evaluation sessions can be individual or group sessions. In our case, individual evaluation sessions of early storyboards were effective in gaining a comprehensive understanding and creating detailed UI outcomes. The individual sessions enable thorough examination of participants' personal opinions of early design ideas without external influences. Once detailed storyboards are created based on the results of individual sessions, a group analysis session with the design team is conducted. During individual sessions, it is easier to keep the discussion organized and gather more detailed feedback on specific details. In group discussion, the focus remains on observing the broader picture and how storyboards bring perspectives from different professionals. The results of the scenario evaluation workshop show that early mission planning, clarity of voyage progress, playful interaction, symbiosis, and social connection can contribute to positive user experience and worker well-being in future work.

Based on the evaluation outcome, the Futures HCD process continues with refining the storyboards to the preferred direction, and by running additional evaluation rounds as needed. Once the evaluation results show positive feedback, the actual development of the work tool can begin, e.g., by following the Agile Software Development process. Our recommendation is to continue rapid iteration of design and evaluation by developing more or less detailed user interface designs and testing them with target user group representatives.

5 Discussion

To address our research question 'How to design human-centred work tools for uncertain industry future', we have developed and tested a four-phase design methodology (see Fig. 1), Futures HCD. This methodology focuses on the early and the most crucial phase of the design process, which develops a work tool concept before the actual system development starts. The methodological basis for the new methodology is the Human-Centred Design process [27], which starts by understanding the work context. This phase of Understanding and Specifying the Context of Use typically uses interview and observation methods in the present contexts of use. It works well for incremental design cases, but in the case of industrial revolution, the present context understanding is not enough. Designers who want to design for I5.0 need to have a method to help them estimate the future contexts, i.e., the potential futures. We see this phase as the most important and also the most demanding one in the Futures HCD methodology, therefore, it is the one that we focus on and provide most guidance for through the case project in the previous chapter and below. Shorter guidance on the three other phases of the HCD cycle is naturally provided also in the coming subchapters, although they are closer to the typical HCD methods.

5.1 Futures Wheel Workshop

The method we propose for understanding and specifying the future context of use is a workshop utilizing the Futures Wheel [18, 21, 22]. This workshop involves both users and other relevant stakeholders representing diverse perspectives as participants. The purpose of this workshop is to gain a collective understanding of the possible futures by addressing not only the technology to be designed, but also the macro themes affecting the future more broadly. The macro themes to be discussed can be adjusted based on the context of the design task.

The process of the Futures Wheel workshop consists of three steps: Preparing the Futures Wheel and the workshop arrangements, Running the Workshop, and Analyzing the workshop. When preparing the Futures Wheel, it is important to verify that the center of the Wheel is a macro theme that should direct the subsequent discussion towards a human-centred one. In our case, the original macro theme suggestion of "Mission Planner 2028" was modified to less human-centred "Planning Autonomous Missions 2028", but it still worked well to keep the focus on the work of mission planners. We identified relevant Macro Themes through a workshop among researchers with experience in this domain area, and adjusted the results based on industry expert comments. When deciding the themes in advance, it is then possible to ensure that people with expertise in the Macro Themes will join the workshop. Another option is to define the Macro Themes as the first step of the workshop, if there is enough time in the workshop for this rather demanding activity, and if the themes are not easy to define beforehand.

The Futures Wheel Workshop should invite participants from many backgrounds. This means that some participants may not agree that the employee should be in the center of operations, therefore it may be useful to provide a short introduction of I5.0 vision at the start or even in the invitation. In our case, the focus change from "Mission Planner" to "Planning Autonomous Missions" targeted at being intriguing to a broader set of participants. It is good to avoid participants with the same background forming a group, so that every group would have some people who can bring the human-centred perspective to discussion. If not others, then make sure the facilitator in each group will take care of this.

As our case shows, it is possible to run the workshop online, which makes it easier also for busy people to join. The online environment for working on the Futures Wheel makes the data collection and analysis easier, compared to the physical workshop with physical equipment and hand-written sticky notes that need to be digitized. Not all participants may be fluent with the online tools, however, so pointing them to a tutorial or sandbox of the online collaboration whiteboard before the workshop might lower the threshold for active use of the tool.

In the analysis phase of the workshop data, we produced several results. First, all notes from the different groups were categorized using a thematic analysis. A similar analysis was then conducted from the employee experience perspective. Finally, the data was scanned to identify scenarios that required deeper understanding and were thus taken as the basis for the semi-structured interviews. These steps help the designer to take best out of Futures Wheel workshop and help designing the futuristic concept that is in line with the participants future vision.

5.2 Semi-structured Interviews

Human-centred automation design involves understanding which parts of the work employees desire to automate and identifying the most promising opportunities for automation. Therefore, the second phase of the proposed process is semi-structured interviews, which build on the findings of the Futures Wheel Workshop and aim to clarify the present context of use and user needs. We propose this semi-structured one-to-one interview method as part of our methodology as it allows the user researchers to delve into the specific work processes of individual employees. The interview results help the design team to get clarity on the present work process, employees' opinions of what works well and what should be improved, stakeholder roles and duties, and the communication channels between them. The data collected from the interviews is analyzed through a thematic analysis, such as an affinity diagram [34].

Semi-structured interviews are frequently used to combine data collection on both the context of use and the user requirements, i.e., the two first phases of the standard HCD cycle. Also in our case, the researcher conducted the interviews at the participants' workplace to better understand the context, but as many times in industry contexts, running the interviews in the interviewee's actual work context turned out to be challenging. Instead, we used tangible 3D printed objects, such as chess characters and ships, and a map of the workplaces to spark contextual discussions in the meeting room interviews but we cannot report success with this tangible technique. Possibly they were not familiar with the nature of chess characters, or they did not see the benefit of using the 3D printed objects when they could simply explain the activities verbally. The verbal interview data provided in-depth understanding of the most important work processes relating to mission planning, which formed a valuable basis for the design phase.

5.3 Design

In the third phase of HCD, a designer uses the findings from the two studies to generate storyboards to propose new solutions where human-centred work tools can best improve the user experience. It is important to lean on the findings from the studies and include both broad and small ideas into the storyboards. In our case, an example of a broad idea is the building of a dashboard (see Fig. 5) and an example of a small idea is the swiping action to complete the mission planning (see Fig. 6 and Fig. 7).

The design phase reported in this article was the first iteration of the HCD process, which would continue over several rounds until the design fulfills the user requirements.

5.4 Evaluation

Once a designer has produced a manageable set of storyboards of the key ideas for the tool UX design, they are evaluated with different stakeholders, including potential users of those designs. The evaluation sessions can be individual or group sessions. In our case, individual evaluation sessions of early storyboards were effective in gaining a comprehensive understanding and creating detailed UI outcomes. The individual sessions enable thorough examination of early design ideas without external influences. Once detailed storyboards are created based on the results of individual sessions, a group analysis session with the design team is conducted. Exploring small details prove significantly more challenging in group discussions. The easiest part of group discussions is brainstorming different problems or situations that UI solutions might encounter, such as evaluating whether the roles were sufficient or needed additional refinement. During individual sessions, it is easier to keep the discussion organized and gather more detailed feedback on specific details. In group discussion, the focus remains on observing the broader picture and how storyboards bring perspectives from different professionals. It's also important to note in individual sessions, as in group situations, that the discussion does not overly focus on a specific theme, potentially overlooking other important aspects. In practice, both sessions are useful depending on whether one seeks a precise assessment of the experience or a more comprehensive perspective from the evaluation of different experts on situations and challenges that UI might encounter. User experience design plays an important role in enhancing worker well-being in the context of an autonomous ship monitoring system.

Based on the evaluation outcome, the design process continues with refining the storyboards to the preferred direction, and by running additional evaluation rounds as needed. Sometimes, it may be required to revisit earlier phases, and gain more clarity on the future context and needs by running more interviews or even going through the whole cycle again, starting from another Futures Wheel workshop. Once positive evaluation results are obtained, the development of the work tool can begin, using the Agile Software Development process. We recommend ongoing rapid iteration of designs and testing user interface designs with target user group representatives.

6 Conclusion

This paper contributes to HWID research by proposing a participatory methodology, Futures HCD, for human-centred design of future work in Industry 5.0. Futures HCD (see Fig. 1) consists of the four phases of the standard HCD cycle, but proposes a specific method for the first phase, the Futures Wheel Workshop. This method aims to bring clarity to the future context, which has a considerable impact on future work. We have reported an application of the Futures HCD methodology in a case project, mission planning of autonomous ships, targeting the human-centred Industry 5.0.

Despite the case being conducted in the maritime context, we expect this methodology to be valuable in other domains as well, when there is a need to develop digital tools for an uncertain and considerably different future. The Futures Wheel Workshop aims to get clarity on the potential futures and prepares organizations to plan and design for them.

The limitations of this study include the single case context for testing the proposed methodology. While the Futures HCD results from this case project are promising, more case studies need to be conducted to learn more about the applicability and effectiveness of Futures HCD in other contexts. Another limitation is, it would be beneficial to use the Futures HCD methodology with a larger groups of participants in testing the design concepts. Despite these limitations, we believe that Futures HCD methodology will help steer the industry towards the utopia of a human-centred future of work with intelligent systems.

Acknowledgments. We are indebted to all the stakeholders, participants, and individuals who generously shared their time and knowledge in shaping the outcome of this research.

Disclosure of Interests. This research was funded through contract research by Kongsberg Maritime Finland Oy. The authors declare that the research was conducted in the absence of any commercial or financial relationships that could be construed as a potential conflict of interest. The methodology that we have developed and reported here is not part of the client's commercial offering.

References

1. Babica, V., Sceulovs, D., Rustenova, E.: Digitalization in maritime industry: prospects and pitfalls. In: ICTE in Transportation and Logistics 2019, pp. 20–27. Springer (2020). https://doi.org/10.1007/978-3-030-39688-6_4
2. Baldauf, M., Fischer, S., Kitada, M., Mehdi, R., Al-Quhali, M.A., Fiorini, M.: Merging conventionally navigating ships and MASS-merging VTS, FOC and SCC? TransNav Int. J. Marine Navig. Saf. Sea Transp. **13**, 495–501 (2019). https://doi.org/10.12716/1001.13.03.02
3. Barley, S.R.: Why the internet makes buying a car less loathsome: how technologies change role relations. Acad. Manag. Discov. **1**, 5–35 (2015). https://doi.org/10.5465/amd.2013.0016
4. Behboudi, M., Javidani, M.: Futures Wheel: Practical Frameworks for Ethical Design (2019). https://medium.com/klickux/futures-wheel-practical-frameworks-for-ethical-design-e40e323b838a. Accessed 03 Feb 2022
5. Bell, W.: Reflections in the mirrors of time. Futures **28**, 527–530 (1996). https://doi.org/10.1016/0016-3287(96)84434-X
6. Bengston, D.N.: The futures wheel: a method for exploring the implications of social–ecological change. Soc. Nat. Resour. **29**, 374–379 (2016). https://doi.org/10.1080/08941920.2015.1054980
7. Blandford, A. E.: Semi-structured qualitative studies. Interaction Design Foundation (2013)
8. Breque, M., De Nul, L., Petridis, A.: Industry 5.0: towards a sustainable, human-centric and resilient European industry. European Commission, Directorate-General for Research and Innovation, Luxembourg, LU, 46 (2021)
9. Bussey, M., et al.: Framing adaptive capacity through a history–futures lens: lessons from the south east Queensland climate adaptation research initiative. Futures **44**, 385–397 (2012). https://doi.org/10.1016/j.futures.2011.12.002
10. Candy, S., Potter, C.: Design and futures. Tamkang University Press Taipei (2019)
11. Coronado, E., Kiyokawa, T., Ricardez, G.A.G., Ramirez-Alpizar, I.G., Venture, G., Yamanobe, N.: Evaluating quality in human-robot interaction: a systematic search and classification of performance and human-centered factors, measures and metrics towards an industry 5.0. J. Manufact. Syst. **63**, 392–410 (2022). https://doi.org/10.1016/j.jmsy.2022.04.007
12. Dash, D.: An overview of futures research for designers. In: Research into Design for a Connected World: Proceedings of ICoRD 2019 Volume 1, pp. 111–121 (2019). https://doi.org/10.1007/978-981-13-5974-3_10
13. Demir, K.A., Döven, G., Sezen, B.: Industry 5.0 and human-robot co-working. Procedia Comput. Sci. **158**, 688–695 (2019). https://doi.org/10.1016/j.procs.2019.09.104
14. Dhiman, H., Nemoto, Y., Fellmann, M., Röcker, C.: Beyond productivity and efficiency: design tools, methods and frameworks for psychological well-being, and (un) exploited potentials to assist employees at work. Front. Comput. Sci. **5**, 1129087 (2023). https://doi.org/10.3389/fcomp.2023.1129087

15. Ehrlich, M., Wisniewski, L., Jasperneite, J.: Usage of retrofitting for migration of industrial production lines to industry 4.0. Jahreskolloquium Kommunikation in der Automation (KommA) (2015)
16. Emad, G.R.: Shipping 4.0 disruption and its impending impact on maritime education. In: 31st Annual Conference of the Australasian Association for Engineering Education (AAEE 2020): Disrupting Business as Usual in Engineering Education: Disrupting Business as Usual in Engineering Education, pp. 202–207. Engineers Australia Barton, ACT (2020). https://search.informit.org/doi/https://doi.org/10.3316/informit.724915764961062
17. EU: High-level expert group on artificial intelligence. Ethics guidelines for trustworthy AI, 6 (2019)
18. Farrow, E.: Determining the human to AI workforce ratio–exploring future organisational scenarios and the implications for anticipatory workforce planning. Technol. Soc. **68**, 101879 (2022). https://doi.org/10.1016/j.techsoc.2022.101879
19. Ghobakhloo, M.: The future of manufacturing industry: a strategic roadmap toward Industry 4.0. J. Manufact. Technol. Manag. **29**, 910–936 (2018). https://doi.org/10.1108/jmtm-02-2018-0057
20. Gidley, J.M.: Globally scanning for "Megatrends of the Mind": potential futures of futures thinking. Futures **42**, 1040–1048 (2010). https://doi.org/10.1016/j.futures.2010.08.002
21. Glenn, J.: Futurizing teaching vs. futures courses. Social Science Record (1972)
22. Glenn, J.C., Gordon, T.J.: Futures research methodology: version 3.0. Millennium Project Washington, DC (2009)
23. Gorecky, D., Schmitt, M., Loskyll, M., Zühlke, D.: Human-machine-interaction in the industry 4.0 era. In: 2014 12th IEEE international conference on industrial informatics (INDIN), pp. 289–294. IEEE (2014). https://doi.org/10.1109/INDIN.2014.6945523
24. Hassenzahl, M., Diefenbach, S., Göritz, A.: Needs, affect, and interactive products–facets of user experience. Interact. Comput. **22**, 353–362 (2010). https://doi.org/10.1016/j.intcom.2010.04.002
25. Hassenzahl, M., Eckoldt, K., Diefenbach, S., Laschke, M., Lenz, E., Kim, J.: Designing moments of meaning and pleasure. Experience design and happiness. Int. J. Des. **7**, 21–31 (2013)
26. IEEE: Ethically Aligned Design: A Vision for Prioritizing Human Well-being with Autonomous and Intelligent Systems, First Edition (2019). https://ethicsinaction.ieee.org
27. ISO 9241-210:2019: Ergonomics of human-system interaction. Part 210: Human-Centred Design for Interactive Systems (2019)
28. Jo, S., D'agostini, E.: Disrupting technologies in the shipping industry: how will MASS development affect the maritime workforce in Korea. Mar. Policy **120**, 104139 (2020). https://doi.org/10.1016/j.marpol.2020.104139
29. Kaasinen, E., et al.: Defining user experience goals to guide the design of industrial systems. Behav. Inf. Technol. **34**, 976–991 (2015). https://doi.org/10.1080/0144929X.2015.1035335
30. Kadir, B.A., Broberg, O.: Human-centered design of work systems in the transition to industry 4.0. Appl. Ergon. **92**, 103334 (2021). https://doi.org/10.1016/j.apergo.2020.103334
31. Kalateh, S., Estrada-Jimenez, L.A., Pulikottil, T., Hojjati, S.N., Barata, J.: The human role in human-centric industry. In: IECON 2022–48th Annual Conference of the IEEE Industrial Electronics Society, pp. 1–6. IEEE (2022). https://doi.org/10.1109/IECON49645.2022.9968440
32. Kouri, P., Hopia, H., Hakala, A.: Predicting the future of healthcare and eHealth with the futures wheel method. J. Int. Soc. Telemed. eHealth **8**, e22–1 (2020). https://doi.org/10.29086/JISfTeH.8.e22
33. Kozubaev, S., et al.: Expanding modes of reflection in design futuring. In: Proceedings of the 2020 CHI Conference on Human Factors in Computing Systems, Honolulu, HI, USA, pp. 1–15. ACM (2020). https://doi.org/10.1145/3313831.3376526

34. Liu, J., Eagan, J.: ADQDA: a cross-device affinity diagramming tool for fluid and holistic qualitative data analysis. Proc. ACM Hum.-Comput. Interact. **5**, 1–19 (2021). https://doi.org/10.1145/3488534
35. Lu, Y., Roto, V.: Design for pride in the workplace. Psych Well-Being **6**, 6 (2016). https://doi.org/10.1186/s13612-016-0041-7
36. Maddikunta, P.K.R., Pham, Q.-V., Deepa, N., Dev, K., Gadekallu, T.R., Ruby, R., Liyanage, M.: Industry 5.0: a survey on enabling technologies and potential applications. J. Ind. Inf. Integr. **26**, 100257 (2022). https://doi.org/10.1016/j.jii.2021.100257
37. Miemis, V.: How can futures thinking amplify design thinking? Core77 (2010)
38. Molka-Danielsen, J., Rasool, J., Smith, C.H.: Design and deployment considerations for ethically advanced technologies for human flourishing in the workplace. In: Bhutkar, G., et al. (eds.) Human Work Interaction Design. Artificial Intelligence and Designing for a Positive Work Experience in a Low Desire Society, pp. 101–122. Springer, Cham (2022). https://doi.org/10.1007/978-3-031-02904-2_5
39. Moller, D.P.F., Vakilzadian, H., Haas, R.E.: From industry 4.0 towards industry 5.0. In: 2022 IEEE International Conference on Electro Information Technology (eIT), Mankato, MN, USA, pp. 61–68. IEEE (2022). https://doi.org/10.1109/eIT53891.2022.9813831
40. Nahavandi, S.: Industry 5.0—a human-centric solution. Sustainability **11**, 4371 (2019). https://doi.org/10.3390/su11164371
41. Nielsen, A.F., et al.: Using the future wheel methodology to assess the impact of open science in the transport sector. Sci. Rep. **13**, 6000 (2023). https://doi.org/10.1038/s41598-023-33102-5
42. Parker, S.K., Wall, T.D., Cordery, J.L.: Future work design research and practice: towards an elaborated model of work design. J Occupat & Organ Psyc. **74**, 413–440 (2001). https://doi.org/10.1348/096317901167460
43. Quitzau, J., Tontara, N., Vöpel, H., Jahn, M., Otto, A. H., Wolf, A.: Shipping in an era of digital transformation (No. 25e). Strategy 2030-Capital and Life in the Next Generation (2018). https://hdl.handle.net/10419/177894
44. Ramos, J.: Linking foresight and action: toward a futures action research. In: Rowell, L.L., Bruce, C.D., Shosh, J.M., Riel, M.M. (eds.) The Palgrave International Handbook of Action Research, pp. 823–842. Palgrave Macmillan US, New York (2017). https://doi.org/10.1057/978-1-137-40523-4_48
45. Razmjooei, D., Alimohammadlou, M., Ranaei Kordshouli, H.-A., Askarifar, K.: Industry 4.0 research in the maritime industry: a bibliometric analysis. WMU J Marit Affairs **22**, 385–416 (2023). https://doi.org/10.1007/s13437-022-00298-8
46. Roumiantseva, A.: The fourth way: Design thinking meets futures thinking (2021)
47. Schröder-Hinrichs, J.U., Song, D.W., Fonseca, T., Lagdami, K., Shi, X., Loer, K.: Transport 2040: Automation, technology, employment-The future of work. World Maritime University (2019). https://doi.org/10.21677/itf.20190104
48. Schwartz, P.: The art of the long view: Planning for the future in an uncertain world. Crown Currency (2012)
49. Shahbakhsh, M., Emad, G.R., Cahoon, S.: Industrial revolutions and transition of the maritime industry: the case of Seafarer's role in autonomous shipping. Asian J. Shipp. Logist. **38**, 10–18 (2022). https://doi.org/10.1016/j.ajsl.2021.11.004
50. Silva, V.: The ILO and the future of work: the politics of global labour policy. Glob. Soc. Policy **22**, 341–358 (2022). https://doi.org/10.1177/14680181211004853
51. Simoes, R.V., Parreiras, M.V.C., Silva, A.C.C.D., Barbosa, C.E., Lima, Y.O.D., Souza, J.M.D.: Artificial intelligence and digital transformation: analyzing future trends. In: 2022 IEEE International Conference on Systems, Man, and Cybernetics (SMC), Prague, Czech Republic, pp. 1462–1467. IEEE (2022). https://doi.org/10.1109/SMC53654.2022.9945429

52. Simsek Caglar, P., Roto, V., Vainio, T.: User experience research in the work context: maps, gaps and agenda. Proc. ACM Hum.-Comput. Interact. **6**, 1–28 (2022). https://doi.org/10.1145/3512979
53. Spencer, F.: Design thinking must be futures empowered. Kedge Futures (2016)
54. Sullivan, B.P., Desai, S., Sole, J., Rossi, M., Ramundo, L., Terzi, S.: Maritime 4.0 – opportunities in digitalization and advanced manufacturing for vessel development. Procedia Manuf. **42**, 246–253 (2020). https://doi.org/10.1016/j.promfg.2020.02.078
55. Taylor, N.C., Bekker, A., Kruger, K.: Mariner 4.0: integrating seafarers into a maritime 4.0 environment. IJME **164**, 373–384 (2023). https://doi.org/10.5750/ijme.v164iA4.773
56. Tijan, E., Jović, M., Aksentijević, S., Pucihar, A.: Digital transformation in the maritime transport sector. Technol. Forecast. Soc. Chang. **170**, 120879 (2021). https://doi.org/10.1016/j.techfore.2021.120879
57. Udoewa, V.: Five modes and nine variations of integration between HCD and futures design. JDT **3** (2022). https://doi.org/10.22059/jdt.2022.349164.1084
58. Vinitha, K., Ambrose Prabhu, R., Bhaskar, R., Hariharan, R.: Review on industrial mathematics and materials at Industry 1.0 to Industry 4.0. Mater. Today Proc. **33**, 3956–3960 (2020). https://doi.org/10.1016/j.matpr.2020.06.331
59. Wright, M.: Consequence scanning - an exercise you can use when designing new services. Online Conference lecture, Service Design in Gov Conference (2021). https://drive.google.com/file/d/1isgp-Qd7a9PQqx2TPbwmDpNOfmIZ_yxH/view?usp=sharing
60. Xu, X., Lu, Y., Vogel-Heuser, B., Wang, L.: Industry 4.0 and industry 5.0—inception, conception and perception. J. Manufact. Syst. **61**, 530–535 (2021). https://doi.org/10.1016/j.jmsy.2021.10.006

Permaengineering: A Framework to Think Interactive Tools in Engineering Sustainable Workspaces

Lou Grimal[1,2](✉), Inès di Loreto[3], and Nadège Troussier[4]

[1] Univ. Bordeaux, CNRS, Bordeaux INP, I2M, UMR 5295, 33400 Talence, France
lou.grimal@ensam.eu

[2] Arts et Metiers Institute of Technology, CNRS, Bordeaux INP, I2M, UMR 5295, 73375 Le Bourget-du-Lac, France

[3] LIST3N, Tech-CICO, Troyes University of Technology, 12 rue Marie Curie, 42060, 10004 Troyes, CS, France

[4] Arts et Metiers Institute of Technology, Paris, France

Abstract. This paper focuses on the interaction and influence between digital tools, engineering methods and paradigms of sustainability. The goal of our work is to better understand how to design digital tools for strong sustainability contexts of engineering work. Using a framework for engineering strong sustainability, we have defined variables to assess whether digital tools align with these principles. Those variables have been gathered to form an assessment grid which can be used to evaluate tools and methods, with life cycle assessment (LCA) serving as a test case. The results show that the grid is functional, but further work is needed to integrate elements related to care ethics. This paper is an extended version of the paper presented at the HWID conference in September 2024.

Keywords: Sustainability · Permaengineering · Design Method · Evaluation

1 Introduction

As the urgency of addressing sustainability intensifies, digital tools are playing an increasingly vital role in transforming organizational processes aimed at achieving sustainability, especially within workplace environments [1]. The design of these tools plays a critical role in empowering users to make informed decisions that align with both environmental goals and the practical realities of their work [2]. However, the sustainability paradigms in which these tools are developed and deployed significantly influence their role and effectiveness. Indeed, the first decades of sustainable Human-Computer Interaction (HCI) efforts has shown that persuasive techniques - which can lead to local optimizations - do not enable stakeholders to fundamentally change their practices [3, 4]. The reason behind this lack of profound transformation is that these persuasive technologies emphasize individual changes, which are necessary but insufficient to meet

Published by Springer Nature Switzerland AG 2026
B. R. Barricelli et al. (Eds.): HWID 2024, IFIP AICT 751, pp. 39–55, 2026.
https://doi.org/10.1007/978-3-031-95334-7_3

the objectives of the Paris Agreement. For this reason, some researchers have claimed that sustainable HCI (SHCI) should move its focus towards more collective actions and participatory approaches [5, 6]. We interpret this shift as a call to explore sustainable HCI from a broader perspective that takes into account not only individual users but the collective workplace environment and the sustainability paradigm within which work takes place. We believe indeed that the challenge of designing tools that meet the needs of both sustainable practices and workplace empowerment becomes more interesting once the type of sustainability paradigm into which the workplace bathes is identified.

Sustainability Paradigms
In the literature, we can find an interesting distinction between weak and strong sustainability, which could be used as a basis for differentiating digital tools.

But what are the characteristics of the weak and strong sustainability paradigms? The two paradigms have been distinguished by economists [7] according to capitals: physical, natural and human. In a weak sustainability perspective, those capitals can be substitutable: as long as the total amount of capital (physical, natural and human) does not decrease. So, it is acceptable to destroy the biosphere to replace it with the anthroposphere (human efforts or technical systems). On the contrary, strong sustainability does not permit this substitution.

Organizations that operate under the principles of weak sustainability often prioritize short-term gains and rely on the substitution of natural resources with technological solutions. These organisations focus heavily on efficiency and optimization with the capitalist economy framework. The limitation of this paradigm is that it does not question the fundamental values and goals of society. This practice can lead to rebound effects i.e., the decrease of environmental impact per unit of production but the increase of absolute environmental impact because of the rise of productions. In contrast, strong sustainability emphasizes the irreplaceability of natural capital, advocating for practices that operate within the Earth's ecological limits [8].

In this paper, we will provide examples of digital tools for both contexts. We believe that the paradigm within which digital tools are designed, developed and deployed impact their purpose and how they are used.

Before addressing our research question, it is important to note that digital tools are often inextricably linked to the methods they support. For instance, applications that calculate CO_2 emissions are inherently tied to the CO_2 calculation methodology itself. Accordingly, we will examine Life Cycle Assessment (LCA) both as a method and as a tool, emphasizing that digital tools should be analysed in conjunction with the methods they derive from. For this reason, in this article, we will analyse both the digital tools and the methods (and thus the paradigm) they are used to support.

Our research effort is driven by the question (RQ): *What digital tools and methods best support strong sustainability practices in professional environments?* As this research question is too wide to be answered in this paper, we decided to focus on a sub-question, focused on evaluation. This sub-research question (RQ1) is the following: *can an engineering framework for strong sustainability be transformed into an evaluation grid to help identify engineering methods and tools that support strong sustainability practice?* The engineering for sustainability framework will be detailed in Sect. 2.3.

Paper Positioning

This paper directly contributes to the Human-Work Interaction Design (HWID) field by proposing a framework to assess digital tools in engineering contexts for strong sustainability where user interaction, context-sensitive design, and work-based empowerment are essential. HWID bridges empirical work-domain studies with interaction design [9, p. 133-172], and this work extends that scope by examining how interactive tools can be tailored to support sustainable practices in complex engineering workspaces. Specifically, by focusing on engineering practices grounded in strong sustainability rather than traditional "business-as-usual" paradigms, this paper explores how sustainability-oriented interaction design can better empower users within their work environments to achieve long-term ecological resilience.

In the following section, we discuss the importance of defining sustainability paradigms in workspaces and the activities carried out within them - activities typically performed by stakeholders and often supported by digital tools. This second section will highlight the need to develop interactive technologies tailored to strong sustainability practices. We will then introduce a theoretical framework for engineering for strong sustainability - permaengineering -, which will serve as the basis for defining an evaluation grid in Sect. 3. In Sect. 2.2, we will detail the method used to define measurable evaluation variables derived from the permaengineering framework, applicable to both engineering methods and digital tools. The proposed grid will first be tested on a sustainability-focused engineering method: life cycle assessment (LCA). This first application of the grid allows us to offer recommendations for designing digital tools that support strong sustainability practices in workspaces.

2 State of the Art: Relations Between Context, Workspaces, Engineers, and Their Tools

Digital tools play a central role in organizational processes, especially in sustainability-focused workplaces. These tools are shaped by the sustainability paradigms - whether weak or strong - under which they are developed, and have distinct implications for workplace empowerment. This section explores the difference between the weak and strong paradigms and their effect on the design and use of digital tools. Although work has been done on the role of IT tools on the work of professional operators and institutions, to our knowledge, none of these studies has focused on the case of sustainable engineering. Indeed, there is a lack of research linking engineering activities and digital tools in contexts of sustainable engineering.

Specifically, we propose to address three levels of interactions: (1) the interaction between sustainability paradigms (weak and strong) and the digital technologies used (Sect. 2.1), (2) the interaction between engineering activities and digital technology in professional tasks (Sect. 2.2), and (2) the interaction between strong sustainability paradigm and engineering activities (Sect. 2.3). To help illustrate these interactions, we have included a visual representation in Fig. 1. The goal of this section is to show how the strong sustainability paradigm can influence the workspace activities (engineering method, goals), and the digital tools at use.

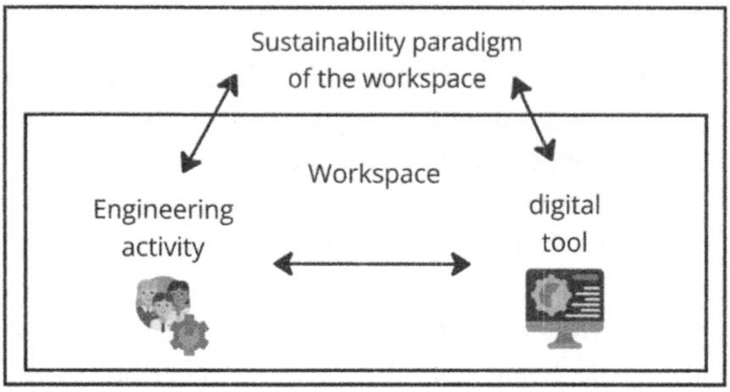

Fig. 1. Representation of 3 interactions: (1) between the digital tool and the sustainability paradigm, (2) between the engineers involved in the professional context and the digital tool, and (3) between the engineering activity (people and engineering method) and the paradigm of sustainability. Made by authors.

2.1 Paradigms of Sustainability and Its Impact on Digital Technologies

Weak and strong sustainability paradigms offer contrasting views on how organizations should balance resource use and environmental responsibility. In weak sustainability, natural capital is seen as replaceable by human-made capital, allowing for technological substitution and prioritizing short-term efficiency. In certain circumstances, weak sustainability can even be understood as a business-as-usual proposal. Indeed "*by assuming a high degree of substitutability between natural and man-made capital, and applying it to the analysis of sustainability, we are in fact diminishing the concern by which it was originally created - namely, the potential conflicts between viable economic development and preservation of the environment.*" [10, p. 151]. As a result, digital tools designed within this paradigm often focus on metrics that optimize immediate productivity and cost-effectiveness, potentially neglecting broader ecological and social impacts. A clear example is in precision agriculture, where sensors are used to optimize chemical usage. While these sensors promote more responsible chemical application, they do not address the fundamental issue of intensive agriculture's role in disrupting biogeochemical cycles [11]. Therefore, when the system's objectives are not aligned with strong sustainability principles, it becomes challenging for the supporting digital tools (sensors, applications, etc.) to meaningfully engage with sustainability concerns. In our examples, the sensors don't enable farmers to change their perspective on the agricultural system.

In contrast, strong sustainability views natural capital as not substitutable and emphasizes the importance of operating within planetary boundaries. Planetary boundaries "introduced in 2009, aimed to define the environmental limits within which humanity can safely operate" [12, p. 1]. Tools developed from the perspective of strong sustainability must empower users to make decisions that address both the immediate needs of their work and the long-term sustainability of the environment. This requires digital tools to be adaptable and context-sensitive, enabling users to balance workplace processes with environmental goals. Using agriculture as an example, the work of [13] shows that a deeper understanding of alternative agricultural systems (for example through ethnography) could enable the development of technologies that do not further widen the divide between nature and culture in food production, and have a very low environmental impact while enabling the living of farmers. Indeed, agroecosystems emphasize the role of polyculture which foster the interaction between plants. Thus, the use of sensors for precision agriculture is less relevant as it is substituted by the symbiosis between plants and the community effort to maintain the agrofood system. Different digital systems have been designed and tested to enable farmers engaged in radical ecological perspectives to practice agriculture with some digital tools supporting their specific practice [14–16]. The paper of Norton et al. [14] documents how a team of researchers in HCI have designed a digital information system supporting a polyculture effort.

Some HCI grassroots initiatives have already shown that sustainable communities (which we consider close to a strong sustainability focus) have specific characteristics in how they approach their relationship with interactive technologies, for example: little trust in technology, a desire to maintain control over their infrastructure, and a determination not to replace human relationships with virtual interactions [15, 17, 18].

2.2 The Link Between Digital Tools and Users

In the previous subsection, we have shown how different paradigms of sustainability impact the final goal and performance of interactive technologies. As a complement, in this section we will show how interactive technologies constrain the action of engineering activities.

Digital tools are far from neutral artifacts; they inherently carry the values, priorities, and assumptions of the environments in which they are created [19]. In workplace settings, these values significantly shape how tools are used and how they empower - or constrain - users. In sustainability contexts, this is particularly important, as the values embedded in tools can either align with or conflict with the broader sustainability goals of the organization [20]. The distinction between weak and strong sustainability paradigms directly impacts the design and functionality of these tools, and by extension, their role in empowering users in their work [21]. Tools designed for weak sustainability tend to emphasize efficiency and cost-reduction, aligning with short-term organizational goals. We have seen in the previous section the example of sensors in monoculture agriculture, which push the user (here the farmer) to optimize the use of pesticides to improve their production. But if the user (farmer) wants to be more in-line with radical sustainability and promote biosphere diversity, the digital tools are not helpful anymore.

Another element can be found in the literature: how digital tools can put at risk the goals of communities. Indeed, intentional communities aiming at creating a significantly different living environment than the normative one, the use of "business-as-usual" digital tools could lead to misalignments between users' decision-making and adaptability in the workplace. This is what is shown by Ghoshal et al. [22] in their example of intentional community focused on creating an equal space for their members (by opposition to our society in which discrimination is present). The introduction of digital tools into the community has disrupted the balance of power by giving more power to those with digital skills. Thus, the fundamental goal of the community was put at risk by the digital infrastructure installed.

Research from Human-Computer Interaction (HCI) and Computer-Supported Cooperative Work (CSCW) has shown that tools are imbued with the values of their creators, and these values affect workplace dynamics [19]. In strong sustainability contexts, where collaboration and long-term thinking are essential, tools designed for efficiency-driven, weak sustainability frameworks, may restrict users' ability to respond to evolving challenges or engage in participatory decision-making. The example we gave earlier about sensors used in intensive agriculture shows well this restriction since sensors are used, in this case, to support the increase of productivity of monocultures. We have chosen to focus on examples related to farming work situations as those examples are very well documented in the SHCI literature. But other examples, more specific to non-farming workspaces do exist. For instance, we can observe (especially in France) the development of low-tech workspaces (Low tech Lab community) who tend to design technologies which are (1) useful, (2) accessible (meaning understandable) by everyone, and (3) sustainable (meaning with a low-environmental impact, long-lasting). Low-technologies are not about having fewer technologies but about having a better understanding of them to design and use technical systems that are non-harmful for the biosphere and human systems. These technologies, when introduced in a workspace, transform the way users interact with them, as they challenge the "notions of need, comfort, and autonomy" [23].

Misaligned digital tools can thus hinder workplace processes in strong sustainability contexts, where flexibility and user empowerment are critical. In particular, tools that prioritize standardized metrics and predefined processes may disempower users, limiting their ability to adapt to context-specific conditions and reducing the effectiveness of sustainability efforts.

To empower users effectively, digital tools must be designed with adaptability and flexibility in mind. This includes supporting collaborative decision-making and allowing users to adjust tools to their specific work contexts. Such tools will enable workers to align their immediate tasks with long-term sustainability goals, enhancing both workplace efficiency and environmental responsibility.

2.3 The Permaengineering Framework

We have shown that sustainability paradigms influence the performance of interactive technologies, and that these technologies, in turn, shape the range of actions available to practitioners. This subsection focuses on the last interaction introduced at the start of the section (Fig. 1), the interaction between engineering practitioners and the strong sustainability paradigm. We introduce the theoretical framework of permaengineering, which has been thoroughly detailed in [24]. Why we choose this framework? We believe this framework can serve as a foundation for identifying key elements that should be considered when discussing strong sustainability engineering practices.

Permaengineering is defined as an activity "*centred on the principle of collaboration between the stakeholders in an engineering process with the aim of moving towards the sustainability of socio-technical systems. This goal is achieved through four main elements: (1) an ethic of care, (2) a goal of strong sustainability, (3) a socio-technical approach to sustainable problems, (4) an interactional expertise and engineering competencies for sustainability.*" [24].

Permaengineering shows 4 facets: ethics, goal, approach, and expertise.

1. Ethics of care: this ethics emphasizes the importance of relationships. Consequently, a permaengineer must prioritize the interconnectedness of the biosphere, Earth's resources, and technologies that are designed for long-term sustainability.
2. The goal of permaengineering activities is to achieve sustainability by respecting planetary boundaries and promoting the well-being of both humans and non-humans. Therefore, permaengineering is founded on a strong sustainability perspective."
3. The approach to solving permaengineering problems differs from traditional engineering methods. Sustainability is considered a wicked problem. Consequently, permaengineers must address engineering challenges not as isolated disciplinary issues but as complex, interconnected problems.
4. The expertise and competencies of permaengineers must focus on managing uncertainty and interacting with various specialists and stakeholders. Interactional expertise, the ability to understand different fields without being a technical expert, is crucial. This competence enables permaengineers to engage with multiple specialized domains, design sustainable scenarios, and test strategies for sustainable transitions, requiring strong collaborative abilities with diverse groups.

Thanks to this state of the art, we have seen that professionals are influenced by the digital tools they use but also by the sustainability paradigm they are anchored in. Thus, our aim is to understand if the conceptual framework of permaengineering can serve as an evaluation grid to assess if certain engineering methods, supported by digital tools, align with permaengineering principles. In other words, we aim to address the following question (RQ1 adapted in this paper): *can the permaengineering framework be applied as an evaluation grid to help identify engineering methods and tools that support strong sustainability practices?* In its current state, the permaengineering framework remains too abstract to be applied to the design of digital tools for engineering workspaces anchored in strong sustainability context. To establish measurable variables, each of the four facets must be defined more precisely, as outlined in the next section.

3 Method

The overall research method used to define the variables is outlined in Fig. 2 and consists of 4 steps. Step 1 consisted of a state-of-the-art review, focusing on the interactions discussed in Sect. 2 of the paper. Step 2 was divided into two parts: the first part involved a review of the art on the four key facets of permaengineering, and the second part focused on defining subcriteria for each of these facets. This second step followed an iterative process, with the results presented in Sect. 3.1. Then, step 3 involved testing these subcriteria on sustainability-focused engineering methods supported by a digital tool, as described in Sect. 3.2. For this step, 30 to 40 papers from the International Journal of Life Cycle Assessment were selected and analysed. Finally, we drafted a final version of the grid, which was step 4 of the research process (formalization and critical perspective on the grid obtained).

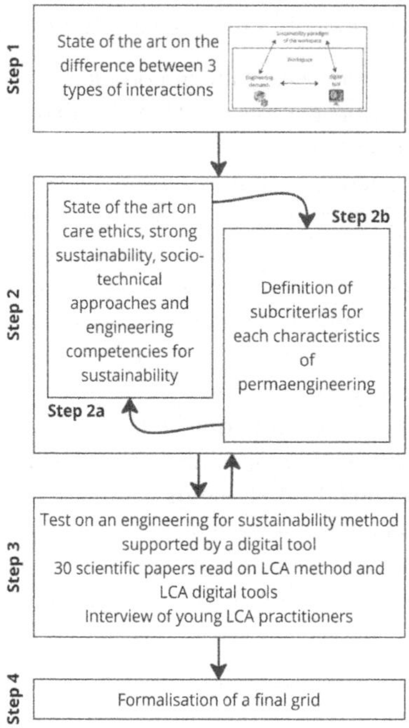

Fig. 2. Scheme representing the method followed to conduct this research. The figure should be read from top to bottom.

The following subsections will focus on steps 2 and 3 of the research method. Section 3.1 will provide a justification for the selection of the variables, clarifying the general facets of permaengineering. Section 3.2 will then focus on applying the evaluation grid to a case study to assess the relevance and effectiveness of the developed grid.

3.1 Definition of the Variables to Evaluate Interactive Tools for Permaengineering

In this section, the facets of permaengineering will be detailed and variables will be attributed to each of them. However, due to the notable lack of research on care ethics in engineering, our focus is limited to the three facets discussed in Sect. 2.3.

3.1.1 Goal of Strong Sustainability (Facet 2)

The ambition of permaengineering is to conduct engineering activities within the planetary boundaries, on the short and long term. Thus, two variables have been defined:

N°	Label	Variable to evaluate	Evaluation of the variable in this paper	Methods for data collection
V1	Planetary boundaries	Presence of planetary limits in the engineering method	Ability of the LCA method to link global limits to impact categories	Analysis of the scientific literature linking LCA impact categories to global limits
V2	Long-term impacts	Presence of long-term effects (>100 years) of impacts in the engineering method	Ability to launch LCA calculations covering long periods (>100 years)	Identifying, in LCA calculation methods, whether long-term phenomena are taken into account and highlighted in the results

3.1.2 Socio-technical Approach (Facet 3)

Permaengineering aims to maintain a socio-technical approach to addressing engineering problems. Thus, permaengineering activities should link technical and social (or organisational) aspects. Form this statement, we can derive two variables:

N°	Label	Variable to evaluate	Evaluation of the variable in this paper	Methods for data collection
V3	Technical aspects	Level of technical knowledge necessary to conduct the engineering method	Level of knowledge required about the technical systems assessed which is necessary to conduct the life cycle assessment	Feedback from LCA experts about the LCA they already conducted, and the difficulties they faced when they didn't know a lot about the technical system analysed
V4	Non-technical aspects	Level of non-technical knowledge related to the production system studied	Level of non-technical knowledge required about production systems in relation to the LCA carried out	Feedback from LCA experts about the LCA they already conducted, and the difficulties they faced when they didn't know a lot about the organisation in which the LCA is conducted
V5	Decisions taking	Level of support provided to the engineer for making informed decisions during a study	During the LCA process, who takes decisions, and what decision-making method is used (possibility of taking a parameter into consideration or not, discussion, etc.)?	Feedback from LCA experts about the LCA they already conducted and how they took decisions during the LCA process

3.1.3 Competence of Interactional Expertise (Facet 4)

Interactional expertise is characterized by the acculturation to the tacit knowledge of a domain, but not the practice of the domain itself. This type of expertise enables interactional experts to discuss with experts of a specific subject in order to work with them on a common goal. Interactional experts are thus very confident in interdisciplinary teams, as they are able to integrate different kinds of knowledge and create links between experts.

Therefore, this facet is more related to the competence of the engineering practicing permaengineering than the approach itself. The variables that can be deduced from this description are the following:

N°	Label	Variable to evaluate	Evaluation of the variable	Methods for data collection
V6	Common goals	Level of integration of different stakeholders	Presence of various stakeholders	Literature review and interviews with LCA experts
V7	Bridge between stakeholders	Links between stakeholders during engineering activities	Ability to create links between stakeholders during engineering activities	Literature review and interviews with LCA experts

3.2 Case Study: Life Cycle Assessment

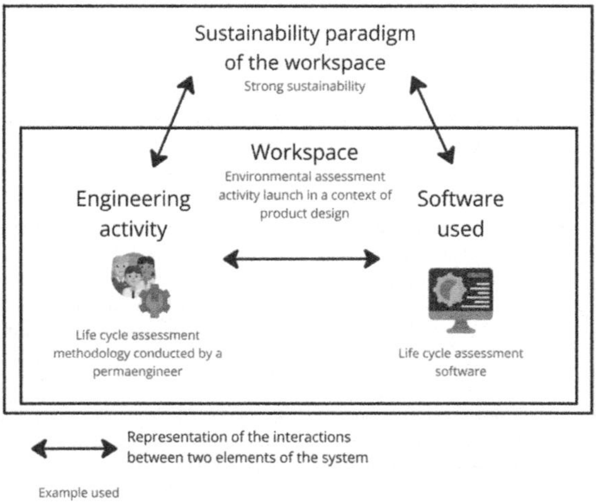

Fig. 3. Representation of the case study analyzed in this paper, regarding the 3 interactions presented in the state of the art: between the digital tool (LCA software), the user (LCA practitioner), and the sustainability context of the workspace (environmental assessment).

As we are interested in engineering activities for sustainability related to digital tools, we decided to analyse life cycle assessment (LCA). Figure 3 represents the different elements from the state of the art applied to this case study.

LCA is a method defined by 2 norms (ISO 14040 and ISO 14044). It was developed in the 70s, initially in the United States. Since the end of the 90s, the development of this method has significantly increased, especially thanks to the integration of policy standards on environmental issues [25]. Indeed, the need for companies to assess their environmental impacts have increased the interest of those companies for environmental assessment and ecodesign. LCA is supported by strong scientific dynamics which work on the transformation of substances emissions (CO2, Lead, Antimony, Phosphorus, etc.) in environmental impacts (climate change, water pollution, acidification of air, eutrophication, etc.). While being based on scientific knowledge (chemical science, environmental science, mathematical sciences), the process of LCA is also related to political aspects, as the choice of the goal of the LCA process, the choice of the technical system to analyse, the choice of the system frontiers, is highly normative [26, 27]. Thus, LCA process is interesting for us as it requires engineering knowledge (to understand production systems which are analysed), environmental knowledge (to understand the results, and to know which impact category to choose), and social competencies (to facilitate the LCA process with the involved stakeholders).

LCA is an environmental assessment method which is supported by software that is used to model the technical system to assess and run the methods to calculate the environmental impacts. Software is also used to visualize the LCA results [28]. LCA software are widely used for measuring environmental impacts but are often rigid, designed for specific datasets and processes. This rigidity can limit users' ability to tailor the tool to local environmental contexts, thereby hindering their ability to fully engage with sustainability goals in workplace environments [28].

The LCA method and software have been evaluated thanks to the grid presented in the previous section. The data used to construct the analysis come from a) literature about LCA practice (the International Journal of Life Cycle Assessment), b) 2 interviews made with young LCA practitioners. The industrial contexts at stakes are various: design of furniture, perfumery, packaging. The practitioners were junior LCA consultants, in contact with one person from a company willing to engage in a LCA for ecodesign.

4 Results

This section describes the results obtained by applying the analysis grid to the LCA approach and to one software (openLCA) supporting the LCA process. We have formalized the results in the form of a table with three columns: (1) the name of the variable, (2) the variable applied to the LCA method, and (3) the variable applied to the digital LCA tool (here openLCA). The results are shown in Table 1.

Through this grid, we can see that the scope of the LCA methodology does not really fit with the scope of the LCA software. Thus, not all the LCA methods are mediatised in the software. Moreover, in variable 8, we see that the use of an LCA software could disrupt the permaengineer in its creation of links between the stakeholders involved in the LCA process. Thus, on this specific variable, the software reduces the ability of the permaengineer to conduct their work properly, following the 4 characteristics of permaengineering. On the other hand, on variable 3, we can see that mathematical models enable LCA practitioners to link the emission of substances to impact categories, to make them understandable to the large public.

Table 1. Representation of the results obtained following application of the method on a life cycle analysis method and software. Each column corresponds to one variable defined in the previous section. Each element regarding LCA method and LCA tool is described in the corresponding cells. Each element is introduced by (+) when elements are corresponding to permaengineering facets, (/) when elements are missing, and (-) when elements are misaligned with permaengineering facets.

Variable	Variable applied to the LCA Method	Variable applied to 1 LCA software (openLCA)
V1. Planetary boundaries	(−) The current LCA method does not integrate the planetary boundaries as thresholds to enable practitioners to stay within the planetary boundaries (+) Nonetheless, some developments are currently going on to relate LCA with the framework of the planetary boundaries [29–32]. The integration of thresholds for certain impacts is possible and is currently being studied in various research projects (working on ethical principles as in [33, p. 1688 (table 1)] on page 1689)	(−) As the planetary boundaries model is not currently integrated in the LCA method, it is not integrated in the software
V2. Long-term impacts	(+) Some impact categories do integrate long-term impacts on human societies. For instance, the characterisation method IPCC (2007) at 500 years takes into account the long-term damage to human health caused by climate change [34, 35] Also, dynamic LCA is a form of LCA integrating long-term changes in the results [36]	(+) The software integrates the different characterisation methods to calculate the environmental impact potentials due to the emission and exposure to some substances
V3. Technical aspects	(+) LCA methodology requires a good understanding of the technical system which is analysed. Indeed, the bill of material has to be defined (phase 2 of the norm). It requires knowledge about the materials used to design the system but also the production steps all along the life cycle of the analysed system (different production processes)	(+) LCA software requires technical competencies to choose the appropriate data, to check if the scope of the generic data corresponds to the corresponding modelling choices
V4. Organisational aspects	(+) LCA methodology requires a good understanding of the organisation of a value chain and the identification of the good stakeholders willing to participate (to access the data, to know about the production processes) [37]	(−) The software does not integrate organisational aspects

(continued)

Table 1. *(continued)*

Variable	Variable applied to the LCA Method	Variable applied to 1 LCA software (openLCA)
V5. Taking decisions	(+) Some decisions on the inventory (phase 2 of LCA) are done in collaboration with different stakeholders and decisions to take into account different parts can be done collectively (-) LCA results are difficult to understand by non-experts and thus, decisions at the end of the LCA process are difficult to take without LCA experts [38]	(−) The LCA experts are taking decisions for what is done on the software
V6. Common goals	(+) The LCA method allows stakeholders to define a common goal, at the very beginning of the methodology. This common goal can be revisited during the process and should be explicitly mentioned	(−) The software does not integrate the definition of the goals of the LCA methodology
V7. Bridge between stakeholders	(/) The LCA method does not impeach the practitioner to facilitate meetings gathering different stakeholders. The LCA method does not force the creation of links between the involved stakeholders all along the process [39]	(−) The software does not enable non-experts stakeholders to participate in the modelling of the technical system on the interface. Also, the use of the software is complex and is not used between the LCA expert and non-experts

This result is not surprising, as LCA emerged and was developed through collaboration between industries and academia to address specific industrial challenges in the US. The challenges included reducing solid waste generation - particularly since landfilling was the dominant waste management practice in the US at that time - and addressing concerns about oil dependency and material efficiency, which were influenced by the energy crisis. Furthermore, the first companies to adopt LCA, such as Coca-Cola, were already well-established within the capitalist economy. t is therefore not surprising to see that there are some mismatches between LCA and the permaengineering framework, due to their different context of development. Nonetheless, the recent development of LCA (integration of planetary boundaries, development of new calculation methods, development of more collaborative and user-friendly software) brings the LCA approach in line with the permaengineering framework.

5 Discussion

For organisations committed to strong sustainability, empowerment in the workplace is a critical factor in achieving both environmental and organisational goals. To support these goals, digital tools must be designed with adaptability, flexibility, and collaboration in mind. Tools should not only provide users with access to data but also empower them to make decisions that are responsive to local conditions, incorporate diverse forms of knowledge, and contribute to long-term ecological resilience. This requires a shift in tool design—from rigid, standardised frameworks to more inclusive, context-sensitive systems that support user empowerment across a range of work domains. This shift can be observed in the LCA ecosystem, as more and more digital tools are being developed to support an LCA-methodology with a more collaborative perspective, such as EcoDesign Studio or ArtoACV [40].

In this paper we wanted to answer the question: *"Can the permaengineering framework be applied as an evaluation grid to help identify engineering methods and tools that support strong sustainability practices?"* Through our paper, we successfully derived variables from three characteristics of permaengineering. We then applied these variables to an engineering method—life cycle analysis (LCA). We found that the selected variables made it possible to identify the limitations of LCA in relation to an engineering practice anchored in a strong sustainability paradigm. We also observed that LCA is an engineering process supported by digital tools and that both the methodological approach and the tools have evolved over time.

The evaluation grid, far from rigidly assigning a compatibility score between the LCA approach and the permaengineering framework, instead highlights the evolutions and potentialities of the LCA method. By distinguishing between the LCA methodology and the digital tools that support it, it was shown that the LCA approach is potentially close to the goals of permaengineering. However, the mediation of this approach through software tools tends to reduce this compatibility.

As a final comment on the results, while in this paper we have decided to focus on LCA, other methods could obviously be tested, such as low-tech design engineering methods and tools.

On a matter of accessibility of the proposed grid, we are aware that in order to fill the grid, a practitioner would need to read a lot of documentation on the engineering method studied, and to have practised it, or to gather testimonials (via interviews) from people who have practised it. For this reason, we believe that the evaluation grid is fairly easier to fill in and can be completed by a group of people rather than an individual. As a summarizing remark, based on our findings, we highly recommend using this framework for qualitatively "measuring" the gap between the engineering method employed, its tools, and the criteria for engineering practices aligned with strong sustainability. We also strongly recommend distinguishing the engineering method itself from the digital tools that mediate its application. Indeed, an engineering method can be supported by different digital tools, empowering or constraining its alignment with strong sustainability principles depending on how these tools are designed, implemented, and utilized.

6 Conclusion

In this paper, we have proposed a first operational grid to better understand if engineering methods and their digital tools used in professional activities are in line with strong sustainability approaches.

Future research and development should focus on creating digital tools that are consistent with the principles of strong sustainability while also supporting empowering workplaces. The grid we have defined could be used as an evaluation method for engineering methods mediating within a digital tool. We believe that this grid should only be used for engineering practices in strong sustainability contexts, as it does not fit weak sustainability contexts (gap in terms of ethics, goals, practices and competences).

Disclosure of Interests. The authors have no competing interests to declare that are relevant to the content of this article.

References

1. Rosário, A.T., Dias, J.C.: Sustainability and the digital transition: a literature review. Sustainability **14**(7), Art. no 7 (2022). https://doi.org/10.3390/su14074072
2. Sparviero, S., Ragnedda, M.: Towards digital sustainability: the long journey to the sustainable development goals 2030. Digit. Policy Regul. Gov. **23**(3), 216–228 (2021). https://doi.org/10.1108/DPRG-01-2021-0015
3. Brynjarsdottir, H., Håkansson, M., Pierce, J., Baumer, E., DiSalvo, C., Sengers, P.: Sustainably unpersuaded: how persuasion narrows our vision of sustainability. In: Proceedings of the SIGCHI Conference on Human Factors in Computing Systems, in CHI 2012, pp. 947–956. Association for Computing Machinery, New York (2012). https://doi.org/10.1145/2207676.2208539
4. DiSalvo, C., Sengers, P., Brynjarsdóttir, H.: Mapping the landscape of sustainable HCI. In: Proceedings of the SIGCHI Conference on Human Factors in Computing Systems, CHI 2010, pp. 1975–1984. Association for Computing Machinery, New York (2010). https://doi.org/10.1145/1753326.1753625
5. Heitlinger, S., Bryan-Kinns, N., Jefferies, J.: UbiComp for grassroots urban food-growing communities. In: Proceedings of the 2013 ACM Conference on Pervasive and Ubiquitous Computing Adjunct Publication, in UbiComp 2013 Adjunct, pp. 589–594. Association for Computing Machinery, New York (2013). https://doi.org/10.1145/2494091.2497617
6. Dourish, P.: HCI and environmental sustainability: the politics of design and the design of politics. In: Proceedings of the 8th ACM Conference on Designing Interactive Systems, DIS 2010, pp. 1–10. Association for Computing Machinery, New York (2010). https://doi.org/10.1145/1858171.1858173
7. Stern, D.I.: The capital theory approach to sustainability: a critical appraisal. J. Econ. Issues (1997). https://www.tandfonline.com/doi/abs/10.1080/00213624.1997.11505895. Accessed 29 Dec 2024
8. Dietz, S., Neumayer, E.: Weak and strong sustainability in the SEEA: concepts and measurement. Ecol. Econ. **61**(4), 617–626 (2007). https://doi.org/10.1016/j.ecolecon.2006.09.007
9. Clemmensen, T.: Human work interaction design: a platform for theory and action. Springer (2021)
10. Cabeza Gutés, M.: The concept of weak sustainability. Ecol. Econ. **17**(3), 147–156 (1996). https://doi.org/10.1016/S0921-8009(96)80003-6
11. Streed, A., Kantar, M., Tomlinson, B., Raghavan, B.: How sustainable is the smart farm?. In: Computing within Limits, LIMITS (2021). https://doi.org/10.21428/bf6fb269.f2d0adaf
12. Steffen, W., et al.: Planetary boundaries: guiding human development on a changing planet. Science **347**(6223), 1259855 (2015). https://doi.org/10.1126/science.1259855
13. Biggs, H., Joshi, T., Murphy, R., Bardzell, J., Bardzell, S.: Alternatives to agrilogistics: designing for ecological thinking. Proc. ACM Hum.-Comput. Interact. **5**(CSCW2), 413:1–413:31 (2021). https://doi.org/10.1145/3479557
14. Norton, J., et al.: The SAGE community coordinator: a demonstration. In: Proceedings of the Fifth Workshop on Computing within Limits, LIMITS 2019, pp. 1–10. Association for Computing Machinery, New York (2019). https://doi.org/10.1145/3338103.3338108

15. Norton, J., Penzenstadler, B., Tomlinson, B.: Implications of grassroots sustainable agriculture community values on the design of information systems. Proc. ACM Hum.-Comput. Interact. **3**(CSCW), 34:1–34:22 (2019). https://doi.org/10.1145/3359136
16. Raghavan, B., Nardi, B., Lovell, S.T., Norton, J., Tomlinson, B., Patterson, D.J.: Computational agroecology: sustainable food ecosystem design. In: Proceedings of the 2016 CHI Conference Extended Abstracts on Human Factors in Computing Systems, CHI EA 2016, pp. 423–435. Association for Computing Machinery, New York (2016). https://doi.org/10.1145/2851581.2892577
17. Heitlinger, S., Bryan-Kinns, N., Jefferies, J.: Sustainable HCI for grassroots urban food-growing communities. In: Proceedings of the 25th Australian Computer-Human Interaction Conference: Augmentation, Application, Innovation, Collaboration, OzCHI 2013, pp. 255–264. Association for Computing Machinery, New York (2013). https://doi.org/10.1145/2541016.2541023
18. Hansen, A.-M.S.: The app is not where the action is: discussing features of an internal communication system for a permaculture village. In: Proceedings of the 7th International Conference on ICT for Sustainability, ICT4S2020, pp. 275–284. Association for Computing Machinery, New York (2020). https://doi.org/10.1145/3401335.3401824
19. van de Poel, I., Kroes, P.: Can technology embody values? In: Kroes, P., Verbeek, P.-P. (eds.) The Moral Status of Technical Artefacts, pp. 103–124. Springer, Dordrecht (2014). https://doi.org/10.1007/978-94-007-7914-3_7
20. Grimal, L., di Loreto, I., Troussier, N.: Le désalignement de valeurs dans les interactions : une opportunité pour l'IHM soutenable: Value misalignments in interactions: an opportunity for sustainable HCI. In: Proceedings of the 34th Conference on l'Interaction Humain-Machine, in IHM 2023, pp. 1–10. Association for Computing Machinery, New York (2023). https://doi.org/10.1145/3583961.3583964
21. Biemans, W.: The impact of digital tools on sales-marketing interactions and perceptions. Ind. Mark. Manag. **115**, 395–407 (2023). https://doi.org/10.1016/j.indmarman.2023.10.015
22. Ghoshal, S., Mendhekar, R., Bruckman, A.: Toward a grassroots culture of technology practice. Proc. ACM Hum.-Comput. Interact. **4**(CSCW1), 54:1–54:28 (2020). https://doi.org/10.1145/3392862
23. Duhamel, R., Lallemand, C., Legardeur, J.: The impact of low-tech systems on user experience: first methodological reflections around the urban biosphere experiment. In: Proceedings of the European Conference on Cognitive Ergonomics 2024, ECCE 2024, pp. 1–5. Association for Computing Machinery, New York (2024). https://doi.org/10.1145/3673805.3673851
24. Grimal, L.: Permaingénierie : un cadre théorique de transition vers un paradigme de soutenabilité forte. Etude par les IHM, thesis, Troyes (2023). https://theses.fr/2023TROY0010. Accessed 29 Dec 2024
25. Jolliet, O., Saadé, M., Crettaz, P.: Analyse du cycle de vie: comprendre et réaliser un écobilan. EPFL Press (2010)
26. Freidberg, S.: From behind the curtain: talking about values in LCA. Int. J. Life Cycle Assess. **23**(7), 1410–1414 (2018). https://doi.org/10.1007/s11367-015-0879-6
27. Sakellariou, N.: A historical perspective on the engineering ideologies of sustainability: the case of SLCA. Int. J. Life Cycle Assess. **23**(3), 445–455 (2018). https://doi.org/10.1007/s11367-016-1167-9
28. Rio, M., Blondin, F., Zwolinski, P.: Investigating product designer LCA preferred logics and visualisations. Procedia CIRP **84**, 191–196 (2019). https://doi.org/10.1016/j.procir.2019.04.293
29. Paulillo, A., Sanyé-Mengual, E.: Approaches to incorporate planetary boundaries in life cycle assessment: a critical review. Resour. Environ. Sustain. **17**, 100169 (2024). https://doi.org/10.1016/j.resenv.2024.100169

30. Bjørn, A., Margni, M., Roy, P.-O., Bulle, C., Hauschild, M.Z.: A proposal to measure absolute environmental sustainability in life cycle assessment. Ecol. Indic. **63**, 1–13 (2016). https://doi.org/10.1016/j.ecolind.2015.11.046
31. Bjørn, A., et al.: Challenges and opportunities towards improved application of the planetary boundary for land-system change in life cycle assessment of products. Sci. Total Environ. **696**, 133964 (2019). https://doi.org/10.1016/j.scitotenv.2019.133964
32. Ryberg, M.W., Owsianiak, M., Richardson, K., Hauschild, M.Z.: Challenges in implementing a planetary boundaries based life-cycle impact assessment methodology. J. Clean. Prod. **139**, 450–459 (2016). https://doi.org/10.1016/j.jclepro.2016.08.074
33. Sandin, G., Peters, G.M., Svanström, M.: Using the planetary boundaries framework for setting impact-reduction targets in LCA contexts. Int. J. Life Cycle Assess. **20**(12), 1684–1700 (2015). https://doi.org/10.1007/s11367-015-0984-6
34. Levasseur, A., Lesage, P., Margni, M., Deschênes, L., Samson, R.: Considering time in LCA: dynamic LCA and its application to global warming impact assessments. Environ. Sci. Technol. **44**(8), 3169–3174 (2010). https://doi.org/10.1021/es9030003
35. Hellweg, S., Frischknecht, R.: Evaluation of long-term impacts in LCA. Int. J. Life Cycle Assess. **9**(5), 339–341 (2004). https://doi.org/10.1007/BF02979427
36. Shimako, A.H., Tiruta-Barna, L., de Faria, A.B.B., Ahmadi, A., Spérandio, M.: Sensitivity analysis of temporal parameters in a dynamic LCA framework. Sci. Total Environ. **624**, 1250–1262 (2018). https://doi.org/10.1016/j.scitotenv.2017.12.220
37. Nilsson-Lindén, H., Baumann, H., Rosén, M., Diedrich, A.: Organizing life cycle management in practice: challenges of a multinational manufacturing corporation. Int. J. Life Cycle Assess. **23**(7), 1368–1382 (2018). https://doi.org/10.1007/s11367-014-0818-y
38. Vizzoto, F., Testa, F., Iraldo, F.: Towards a sustainability facts panel? Life cycle assessment data outperforms simplified communication styles in terms of consumer comprehension. J. Clean. Prod. **323**, 129124 (2021). https://doi.org/10.1016/j.jclepro.2021.129124
39. ISO 14040:2006, ISO. https://www.iso.org/standard/37456.html. Accessed 29 Dec 2024
40. Pongérard, M., San Augustin, F., Paredes, M.: Comparison of tools for simplified life cycle assessment in mechanical engineering. In: Cavas Martínez, F., Peris-Fajarnes, G., Morer Camo, P., Lengua Lengua, I., Defez García, B. (eds.) Advances in Design Engineering II, pp. 71–80. Springer, Cham (2022). https://doi.org/10.1007/978-3-030-92426-3_9

Engagement and Well-being during Work and Training

Human Work Interaction Design in Sustainable Interactive Art

Arminda Guerra(✉)

ITI/LARSyS and Polytechnic University of Castelo Branco, Castelo Branco, Portugal
aglopes@ipcb.pt

Abstract. This article outlines a research study that investigates identity practices related to the environment, specifically focusing on marine debris. Although not the original focus, this subject inspired an artistic endeavor that led to the creation of the AquaPlay installation. AquaPlay, an ongoing collaborative project, seeks to promote awareness about the increasing plastic pollution found on beaches and in waters in Portugal. Through fieldwork, various identity dynamics were observed in different contexts, such as immigrant integration in Portugal and Portuguese migration, covering emotional, ecological, political, and institutional aspects. AquaPlay points to an experimental collaborative installation that uses interactive play to underscore the importance of marine litter, surpassing boundaries and bringing attention to contemporary issues like plastic pollution in the oceans. User participation in multiple exhibitions has impacted the project's development, underscoring the significance of incorporating user experiences in the design process to achieve effective results.

Keywords: Design · Sustainability · Interactive Game · Digital Art

1 Introduction

Identity practices intersect with environmental concerns in various ways, and one significant aspect of this intersection is the problem of marine litter [1, 2]. This research investigates the entanglement of identity practices with ecological consciousness, focusing on the pervasive issue of marine litter. Although marine litter was not the primary focus initially, it emerged as a central theme that sparked an innovative artistic endeavor. The genesis of this project originated from the urgent problem of marine litter, which served as the driving force behind the creation of the AquaPlay installation. AquaPlay is a collaborative artistic initiative about the intensifying pollution caused by plastic materials on Portuguese beaches and waters that aims to raise awareness in society.

The AquaPlay installation draws inspiration from the *Plasticus Maritimus* project, initiated by a marine biologist [3, 5], and [6] to amplify the message of environmental preservation and raise awareness about the detrimental effects of marine litter [7, 8]. *Plasticus Maritimus*, conceived by [4], represents a fusion of educational ecological awareness, creative expression, and activist action.

Published by Springer Nature Switzerland AG 2026
B. R. Barricelli et al. (Eds.): HWID 2024, IFIP AICT 751, pp. 59–76, 2026.
https://doi.org/10.1007/978-3-031-95334-7_4

Initially shared on social media platforms, the project gained well-known attention and engagement from activists, independent ecological groups, and communities, leading to discussions and actions that extended beyond the digital realm [9, 10]. AquaPlay combines the nostalgia of analog toys with digital art techniques, providing a unique platform to explore ideas and efficiently execute tasks while evoking sensory experiences that engage personal emotions, memories, and identity practices.

This research examines semiotic perspectives on marine litter, and presents the interaction design of the artistic installation, emphasizing the crucial role of the user in the design process. Moreover, this study emphasizes the sustainability aspect of such projects, underscoring the importance of integrating ecological considerations into artistic endeavors to foster environmental well-being [10–12]. (Fig. 1).

Fig. 1. Marine Litter

2 AquaPlay

In developing the installation, we drew inspiration from the Tomy toy - Waterful Ringtoss, which debuted in 1976 and gained widespread popularity in Brazil during the 1980s [13]. This iconic toy served as our foundational model, characterized by a compact transparent container filled with water and sealed with a cap at the top. A button at the container's base (some models feature two buttons) triggers a hydraulic mechanism essential for the game's functionality. The specific tasks vary across different models, offering diverse interactive experiences to users (Fig. 2).

Fig. 2. AquaPlay Models: 1. Produced in Brazil 1980; 2. Model of Chinese production, 2017.

The installation features a sizable water container, measuring A0 (84 × 119 cm), positioned at a 45-degree angle atop a plinth. This arrangement offered users a comprehensive view of the container's contents and enabled them to interact with the buttons that surround the installation. Within the container, marine debris floats, encapsulated within small plastic bubbles equipped with embedded RFID markers. These bubbles navigated through a series of targets inside the tank, representing various ecological niches where marine debris accumulated. Each target housed a miniature RFID detector, facilitating the identification of the types of debris present in different natural zones.

The interaction was facilitated through buttons placed around the tank, each connected to a motor that activates a hydraulic plunger, simulating the manual mechanism reminiscent of the original game. To enhance the immersive experience, a rear projection film lined the tank's bottom, allowing a built-in short throw projector within the plinth to project game animations and feedback directly onto the tank's surface. This multi-sensory approach engaged participants in a dynamic exploration of the complex interplay between human actions, marine ecosystems, and environmental sustainability.

2.1 A Semiotic View of Marine Litter

This work holds relevance in its approach to the creative process and methodology, emphasizing collaborative and multidisciplinary efforts. It sheds light on a pertinent issue that warrants discussion across various levels of understanding.

AquaPlay encourages individual interpretations, allowing each participant to contribute to the hybrid composition of the experience. Drawn based on the idea of narrative construction and (re)construction within the game's timeframe, AquaPlay empowers participants to shape their narratives and perspectives, contributing to a rich and dynamic discourse surrounding the environment [5, 14].

Viewing marine litter [15] through a semiotic lens [16] involves examining the signs, symbols, and meanings associated with it within the context of the aquatic environment. The approach taken in this case was the identification of:

- *Symbols of Consumption:*
  Plastic water bottles: Symbolizing convenience and single-use culture.
  Disposable food packaging: Representing fast food and on-the-go eating habits.
  Shopping bags: Reflecting consumerism and the disposable nature of goods.

- *Signs of Pollution:*
  Plastic debris floating in the ocean: Indicating human impact on marine ecosystems.
  Oil slicks and tar balls: Signify pollution from industrial activities and maritime transportation.
  Entangled marine animals: Illustrate the harmful effects of litter on wildlife.
- *Cultural Significance:*
  Discarded fishing nets and gear: Symbolizing the fishing industry and traditional fishing practices in coastal communities.
- *Perception and Meaning:*
  Some people may perceive marine litter as an eyesore and a threat to marine life, while others may view it as a byproduct of economic development.
  Recyclers may see certain types of litter as valuable resources, while conservationists may prioritize its removal to protect marine ecosystems.
- *Communication and Awareness:*
  This project can be considered an alert to different people through their participation in this artistic installation by observing images of marine animals entangled in plastic waste to evoke emotional responses and raise awareness about the consequences of littering.
  Symbols like a crossed-out plastic bottle or a clean ocean wave were used in our pictures to communicate the importance of reducing plastic pollution.
- *Remediation and Mitigation:*
  One objective of this installation was to engage communities in implementing policies to regulate single-use plastics and promote recycling.

These examples demonstrate how different types of marine litter can be interpreted through a semiotic lens, revealing their underlying meanings and implications for environmental stewardship and conservation efforts.

2.2 Interaction Design – Design Process

The development of AquaPlay underwent a co-design process [17, 18], organized into four phases (Fig. 3):

Contextualization and Exploration - This phase involves presenting the theme and examining the initial context, motivations, objectives, and problems to be solved. During this immersive phase, the work team engaged in dialogue and debate to better understand the proposed theme and analyze possible solutions. Additionally, marine litter was collected from the beach and classified, and proposals for AquaPlay models were developed.

Development (idea classification and prototyping) - This phase was more exhaustive, as it required more elaborate research and experimentation on technical procedures (physical structures, mechanical instruments, analog, and digital devices) that could be essential for a feasible model of the production of aimed at the desired space, aggregated relationships, desired experiments, and future developments.

Conceptualization - This phase permeated all the production moments, defining the conceptual approaches involved in the present installation, considering its dimensions: playful, didactic, social, and environmental.

Implementation - This phase sought to effectively integrate functional and conceptual components according to the theme, resulting in a prototype of AquaPlay on a larger scale than the initial reference. The design still resembled the base model but with targets for change.

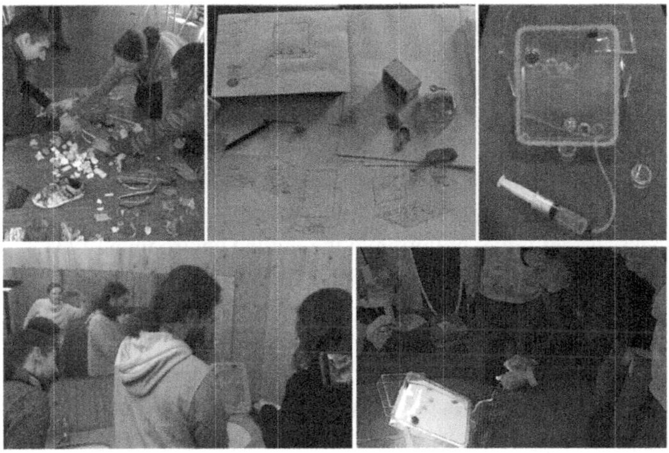

Fig. 3. AquaPlay – Co-design process

2.3 Human Work Interaction Design

Human Work Interaction Design (HWID) is a subfield within Human-Computer Interaction (HCI) that focuses on the interaction between human work practices and the design of computer systems [19, 20]. It emphasizes understanding how technology fits into and supports work environments, recognizing that work contexts are complex, dynamic, and deeply influenced by social, organizational, and cultural factors. HWID aims to design systems that enhance user performance while ensuring they align with the real-world work settings in which they are deployed.

One key aspect of HWID is its interdisciplinary approach, drawing on cognitive psychology, ergonomics, and organizational studies to comprehend the nuanced nature of human work. For instance, it considers how users' cognitive load or workplace stress may influence their interaction with technology [21]. Moreover, HWID is also concerned with how digital tools can transform work practices, often leading to new working methods, rather than merely supporting existing tasks [22].

A guarantee of HWID is its focus on empirical methods, meaning researchers often engage directly with workers through field studies, observations, and interviews to gather insights about their needs and challenges. This bottom-up approach allows designers to create systems that are not only technically robust but also contextually relevant [20]. Additionally, HWID highlights the importance of iterative design, where systems are continuously tested and refined in collaboration with users to ensure long-term efficacy in real-world settings.

Human Work Interaction Design bridges the gap between work practice and system design by focusing on user needs within specific work environments to promote a user-centered, context-aware design philosophy. This approach's application to the development of sustainable designs is explained in Sect. 3.1.

3 Results and Discussion

From this ecological explanation, it was understood that the sea concerning identity and memory encompassed many possibilities for personal and social engagement. The artistic installation took on the responsibility of acting in an activist dimension by developing the sea subject from the perspective of man - nature - technology - society. The installation game recreates a chaotic scenario where plastic consumption is the trigger for discussing a current issue: pollution in the marine environment [23].

AquaPlay is an experimental collaborative installation that, presents marine litter as a semantic object capable of transcending boundaries and revealing contemporary situations worthy of discussion, through playful interaction, such as plastic pollution in the oceans [24–26]. The focus of this interactive installation was to present the significance of marine litter because of practice—a society of social and economic extremes that, to maintain its production, will have to assess the harmful effects caused by this production, not only on nature but also on itself, which indirectly already harbors a legacy of uncertainties.

AquaPlay is based on memory related to mechanically analog toys combined with techniques and concepts in digital art, which when articulated have shown potential to enhance ideas and provide quicker responses in task execution, as well as to observe multiple sensory experiences involving personal feelings, memories, and identity practices.

During the testing of the prototype in a mini artistic residency, participants were prompted to think about the theme through the simulation of the environment proposed by the game, to perceive their emotional relationships, especially those involving memories of childhood games, and their individual and social responsibility towards the environment.

As the interaction process with the game [27, 28] progressed, the narrative paths taken during the experience depended on the interpretations made by each interactant various narrative forms [29] have always allowed for some interaction of the individual through imagination, generating a diversified range of interpretations about a particular story. The interactants gained a deeper understanding of human influence on the dynamics of marine litter through playful experience, being confronted with the results of their actions. AquaPlay's gameplay, featuring "air bubbles" containing plastic waste in a water-filled tank, combines playfulness with urgent narratives, prompting reflection on contemporary issues requiring collective action (Fig. 4).

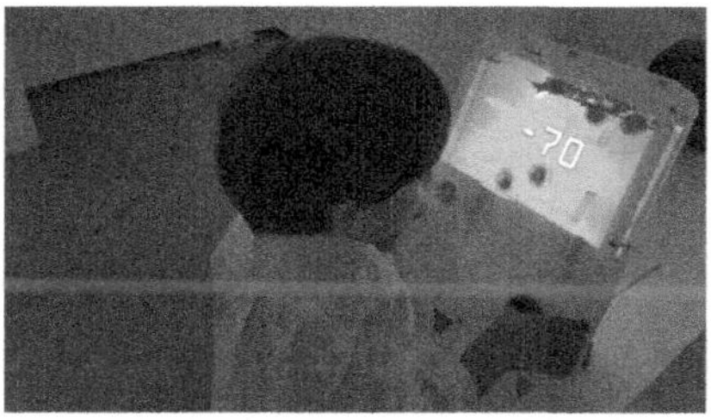

Fig. 4. A moment of interaction with one prototype

Time is important in addressing environmental challenges [30], as players must navigate complex currents to free marine life from pollution (Fig. 5).

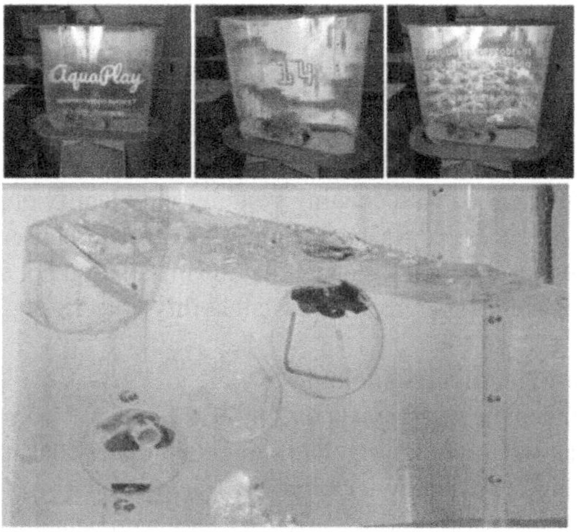

Fig. 5. Final installation

The main strengths of this installation are:

Environmental Awareness: The activity prompts participants to reflect on plastic waste and its environmental impact, fostering a deeper understanding of environmental issues.
Hands-On Learning: Through a beach reconnaissance activity to collect waste, participants engage directly with the issue, enhancing experiential learning.
Artistic Expression: Using an interactive art installation game like AquaPlay allows for creative exploration and engagement with environmental themes in an innovative way.
Interactive Learning: AquaPlay utilizes elements like symbolic bubbles, infographics, and point scores to educate players on the real impact of plastic waste, promoting interactive and engaging learning experiences.
Critical Thinking: The game challenges players to consider their actions and consequences on the ecosystem and biodiversity, fostering critical thinking skills.

Artistic Language: Utilizing artistic language and interactive installations like AquaPlay can engage participants creatively, making environmental education more engaging and memorable.

3.1 Applying Human Work Interactions Design to the Development of Sustainable Designs

During the development of the interactive installation, the application of Human Work Interaction Design (HWID) was crucial in ensuring that the sustainability principles were effectively intertwined with the design process. This approach focuses on aligning HWID principles with sustainability objectives to create systems that meet both human needs and environmental goals. Below are the key steps we took to effectively implement HWID in our sustainable design process:

Contextual Analysis of Work Practices
At the outset, we conducted a detailed contextual analysis to understand the specific work practices of our users within their operational environments. This involved assessing how current workflows might impact resource utilization, energy consumption, and waste generation. We engaged in field studies, interviews, and observations to gain insights into user interactions with existing systems and identify opportunities for integrating sustainable practices. For instance, notes, incorporating user feedback throughout the design process is essential to ensure that the installation not only meets practical operational demands but also aligns with sustainability objectives [20].

Incorporating Eco-Friendly Technologies
Once we comprehended the work practices, our next focus was on integrating materials and technologies that would minimize environmental impacts. The principles of HWID guided us in selecting eco-friendly technologies, such as energy-efficient systems and materials with lower carbon footprints, ensuring they were suitable for the users' real-world contexts.

Iterative and Participatory Design
We adopted an iterative design methodology that involved continuous testing and refinement in partnership with users. This participatory approach was instrumental not only in assessing usability but also in evaluating the environmental implications of our solutions [31]. We conducted user-centered workshops and participatory design sessions to gather feedback and insights on how our sustainable solutions could better integrate into their work processes. This method ensured that our sustainability initiatives did not compromise user productivity or satisfaction [20].

Promoting Sustainable Behaviors through Interaction
Our design aimed to encourage users to adopt more eco-friendly behaviors. By leveraging HWID, we incorporated features that made environmental impacts more transparent and manageable for users. For example, our interactive system provided real-time feedback on energy consumption and material waste, empowering users to make environmentally

conscious decisions during their activities [20]. This enhanced the usability of the installation but also reinforced its sustainability objectives, creating a holistic user experience [32, 33].

Evaluation and Long-Term Adaptability

Recognizing that sustainable design must consider both immediate and long-term impacts, we emphasized ongoing evaluation of the installation in real work settings. HWID principles enabled us to gather continual feedback, ensuring our design evolves to meet users' needs and sustainability goals over time. This iterative and improved process allowed the installation to remain relevant and efficient as work practices and environmental conditions evolved [19].

In summary, applying HWID to our sustainable interactive installation development involved a unified approach that considers human work practices alongside environmental sustainability. By analyzing the context of use, selecting eco-friendly technologies, engaging in participatory design, encouraging sustainable behaviors, and focusing on long-term adaptability, we created a system that effectively supports user productivity while promoting environmental stewardship.

3.1.1 Interaction Between Humans and the Environment

The developed artistic installation explores the interaction between humans and the environment [34, 35] through the concept of Human Work Interaction Design (HWID). The piece reflects on human impact on the marine ecosystem, using the following core elements:

1. **Marine Litter**: The presence of marine litter because of human activity.
2. **Artistic Endeavour**: Artistic expression as a means of raising awareness.
3. **Students**: Involvement of students as future agents of change.
4. **Environment Preservation**: The urgent need for environmental preservation.
5. **Awareness about Detrimental Effects of Marine Litter**: Raising awareness of the harmful effects of marine litter.
6. **Pervasive Issues**: Environmental issues that are ever-present in daily life.
7. **Creative Expression**: The use of art to provoke reflection and foster change.
8. **Activist Action**: The installation is a call for activist involvement.
9. **Social Media Platforms**: The role of social media in spreading the environmental message.
10. **Artistic Installation**: The piece is an immersive artistic installation.
11. **Memories**: The relationship between sensory memories and the natural environment.
12. **Sensory Experiences**: Sensory experiences are provided by the artwork to engage the audience.
13. **Personal Emotions**: The emotional connection participants form with the cause.

Applying the principles of HWID emphasized how **human work** (in this case, creative and activist action) interacts with and is shaped by the social, technological, and environmental context. The artwork seeks to provoke deep reflection on the impact of marine litter, using the emotions and sensory experiences of the audience to create a meaningful connection with the issue. Figure 6 presents the adaptation of the HWID Framework [20].

The framework integrates multiple interconnected dimensions focusing on environmental and social dynamics through a comprehensive methodological approach. At its core, the framework employs collaboration, observation, interviews, and fieldwork to understand the complex relationships between human practices and ecological consciousness, particularly regarding pollution. Through a dialogic process between human work findings and interaction design principles, it explores how these elements intersect and influence each other.

The framework addresses crucial contemporary issues including plastic pollution, migration patterns, and immigration challenges, while also considering broader ecological, political, and institutional aspects. Furthermore, it examines the cultural manifestations of pollution and consumption patterns, analyzing how these factors contribute to and reflect societal attitudes and behaviors. This multi-layered approach enables a deeper understanding of the interconnections between human activities, environmental impact, and social dynamics, providing insights into how these elements shape and influence each other within modern societal contexts.

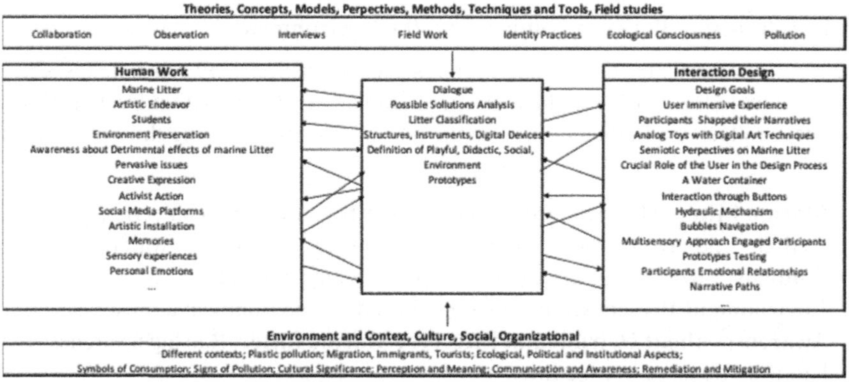

Fig. 6. HWID Framework [20]

3.1.2 Theories, Concepts, Models, Perspectives, Methods, Techniques, and Tools

In this study, several theoretical and practical frameworks were considered to guide the development of the installation [36, 37]:

- **Theories, Concepts, Models, Perspectives**: Foundational theories of human-environment interaction, concepts of sustainability, models of user engagement, and perspectives on ecological design informed the creative process.
- **Methods, Techniques, and Tools**: Various methods, techniques, and tools were used, including digital art, interactive mechanics, and multisensory engagement tools to deepen participant involvement.
- **Field Studies**: Practical field studies were conducted to gain insights into how people perceive and interact with environmental issues.

- **Collaboration**: Collaboration with students, activists, and environmental experts to ensure a comprehensive approach to the subject matter.
- **Observation and Interviews**: Observational studies and interviews were held to gather first-hand experiences regarding marine pollution and human behaviors.
- **Field Work and Identity Practices**: Fieldwork revealed how identity practices and personal attitudes influence ecological consciousness.
- **Ecological Consciousness and Pollution**: The installation highlights the growing ecological consciousness around the pollution of marine ecosystems, engaging users in reflecting on their environmental impact.

3.1.3 Interaction Design and Its Relation to Human Work Interaction Design

The artistic installation was also strongly influenced by the principles of **Interaction Design**, aimed at creating an immersive and meaningful experience for participants. In this context, **Interaction Design** [38] was applied through the following aspects:

1. **Design Goals**: The central goal of designing an interactive experience is to engage participants in raising awareness about marine litter.
2. **User Immersive Experience**: Creating an immersive experience where users shape their narratives, building emotional connections with the subject.
3. **Participants Shaped Their Narratives**: Participants constructed personal stories through their interaction with the installation elements, reinforcing engagement.
4. **Analogue Toys with Digital Art Techniques**: The combination of analog toys and digital art techniques bridged the traditional and modern, enhancing immersion.
5. **Semiotic Perspectives on Marine Litter**: Exploration of cultural and social meanings associated with marine litter, expanding participants' understanding.
6. **Crucial Role of the User in the Design Process**: The central role of the user in the design, directly influences the outcome of the experience.
7. **A Water Container**: A water container as part of the installation symbolizes the marine environment, encouraging hands-on interaction.
8. **Interaction through Buttons**: Buttons allow users to physically interact with the artwork, creating tangible and direct actions.
9. **Hydraulic Mechanism**: A hydraulic mechanism represents the movement of water and ocean currents, intensifying the connection to the subject.
10. **Bubbles Navigation**: Navigation through bubbles provided a playful and multisensory approach to engage participants.
11. **Multisensory Approach Engaged Participants**: A multisensory approach engaged participants through sight, touch, and sound.
12. **Prototypes Testing**: Prototypes were tested during development to ensure smooth and effective user interactions.
13. **Participants' Emotional Relationships**: Exploring participants' emotional relationships with the installation elements deepened the connection to the issue.
14. **Narrative Paths**: Multiple narrative paths were created, allowing participants to follow personalized, engaging experiences.

3.1.4 Methodology and Data Analysis Process

In this research, a comprehensive mixed-methods approach was employed to understand the effectiveness of the artistic installation on marine litter. The primary data collection methods involved systematic observation and designed questionnaires. During the installation, the research team conducted structured observations, documenting how participants interacted with the various interactive elements. Detailed notes on participant behaviors, engagement levels, and the ways they navigated through the installation's different components were taken.

Complementing the observational data, questionnaires were distributed to participants. Participants were asked about their experiences, emotional responses, and understanding of the environmental message we were trying to convey. The questionnaires were structured to encourage deep reflection on their interactions with the installation.

The analysis process was equally demanding. We began with a qualitative content analysis, systematically examining our observational notes and questionnaire responses. The goal was to identify recurring themes and meaningful patterns that emerged from the participants' experiences. We used a thematic coding approach, which allowed us to group similar insights and extract key concepts related to dialogue, environmental awareness, and interactive design.

The thematic analysis revealed several critical connections between Human Work Interaction Design (HWID) and Interaction Design. We found that the installation successfully created a dialogic space where participants could engage critically with the issue of marine litter. The interactive elements encouraged collective reflection and invited participants to explore potential solutions to environmental challenges. We were particularly interested in how the design elements – including physical structures, digital devices, and interactive prototypes – contributed to this engagement.

Prototype testing was crucial to our research approach. We viewed prototyping as an iterative process, continuously refining the installation based on participant feedback and observations. Each iteration allowed us to improve the persuasiveness and impact of the interactive experiences. We paid special attention to how we balanced playful, didactic, social, and environmental elements to ensure that our message remained clear and compelling.

By cross-referencing our observational data with questionnaire responses, we developed a holistic understanding of how interactive design can facilitate environmental awareness. Our theoretical framework, grounded in HWID and Interaction Design principles, guided our interpretation of participant experiences. Finally, we were able to demonstrate how carefully designed interactive experiences can transform complex environmental issues into engaging, reflective encounters that encourage deeper understanding and potential action.

3.1.5 Connecting Human Work Interaction Design and Interaction Design

During the development of the artistic installation, key connections between **Human Work Interaction Design (HWID)** and **Interaction Design** were identified. These elements were essential in shaping the installation, linking human work to interactive design. Some of the key connections observed include:

- **Dialogue**: The installation fostered a continuous dialogue between participants and the interactive elements, encouraging collective reflection on marine litter.
- **Possible Solutions Analysis**: Through interaction, participants were invited to explore and suggest solutions to the environmental problems presented.
- **Litter Classification**: The classification of marine litter was integrated into the narrative, allowing participants to identify and understand different environmental impacts.
- **Structures, Instruments, Digital Devices**: Physical structures, instruments, and digital devices were essential to creating a rich and engaging experience.
- **Definition of Playful, Didactic, Social, and Environmental Elements**: The installation balanced playful, didactic, social, and environmental elements to deliver a clear environmental message while encouraging participant engagement.
- **Prototypes**: Prototyping was crucial in refining the interactive experience, ensuring that the interactions were smooth and impactful.

3.1.6 Environment, Context, Culture, Social and Organizational Aspects

In developing the installation, the **environment**, **context**, **culture**, and **social and organizational aspects** surrounding marine pollution and human interaction with the environment were considered [39]. The following themes were explored:

- **Different Contexts**: The installation acknowledged different contexts where marine pollution occurs, from urban areas to coastal regions.
- **Plastic Pollution**: A core focus was placed on plastic pollution, one of the most pervasive issues affecting marine ecosystems.
- **Migration, Immigrants, Tourists**: The roles of migration, immigrants, and tourists were considered in how they contribute to or are affected by marine pollution.
- **Ecological, Political, and Institutional Aspects**: The ecological implications of pollution alongside political and institutional responses to environmental degradation were examined.
- **Symbols of Consumption**: The installation examined how consumption patterns contribute to marine litter, using symbolic elements to provoke thought.
- **Signs of Pollution**: Various signs and representations of pollution were integrated to make the impact of human behavior visible to participants.
- **Cultural Significance**: The cultural significance of marine ecosystems was explored, highlighting how different cultures perceive and value the marine environment.
- **Perception and Meaning**: The installation aimed to shift participants' perception of marine litter, encouraging them to assign new meanings to their interaction with the environment.
- **Communication and Awareness**: Effective communication strategies were employed to raise awareness about pollution and its consequences.
- **Remediation and Mitigation**: The artwork encouraged participants to consider remediation and mitigation strategies for reducing human activity's environmental impact.

3.1.7 Study Results

The artistic installation on marine litter revealed reflective insights into participant engagement with environmental issues through interactive design. The research demonstrated that carefully crafted interactive experiences can transform complex environmental topics into meaningful, reflective encounters. Participants consistently reported a deep connection with the marine litter theme, moving beyond passive observation to active reflection and potential problem-solving.

The dialogue-driven approach emerged as a particular aspect of the installation. Participants engaged in continuous, meaningful interactions with the interactive elements, encouraging collective reflection on marine environmental challenges. This dialogic process was informative and transformative, allowing participants to explore environmental issues from multiple perspectives and develop a better understanding of marine litter's complex impacts.

One of the most significant findings was the participants' ability to analyze potential solutions actively. The installation's design prompted users to move beyond passive awareness to constructive thinking about environmental challenges. Participants were not just receiving information but were actively invited to explore, suggest, and conceptualize potential approaches to addressing marine litter. This approach demonstrated the potential of interactive design to transform environmental education from a unidirectional information transfer to a collaborative problem-solving experience.

The classification of marine litter within the installation's narrative proved to be a critical component of participant learning. By integrating a systematic approach to understanding different types of marine waste, the installation helped participants develop a more sophisticated comprehension of environmental impacts. Participants could identify, categorize, and understand the nuanced effects of different types of marine litter, transforming abstract environmental concepts into tangible, understandable information.

Physical and digital elements played an important role in creating an engaging and immersive experience. The strategic use of structures, instruments, and digital devices created a rich, multisensory environment that encouraged deeper exploration and understanding. These elements were not mere technological additions but integral components that facilitated meaningful interaction and reflection on environmental themes.

The installation balanced multiple design elements, creating a holistic experience that was simultaneously playful, didactic, social, and environmentally focused. This multifaceted approach ensured that the environmental message was clear and emotionally resonant. By combining educational content with interactive, engaging design, the installation demonstrated an innovative approach to environmental communication that could potentially inspire real-world action.

Prototyping emerged as a critical methodology for refining the interactive experience. Through iterative design and continuous improvement, we were able to create interactions that were not just persuasive but deeply impactful. Each prototype iteration allowed us to fine-tune the installation's ability to engage participants, ensuring that the interactive elements effectively communicated the environmental message while maintaining a high level of user engagement.

Finally, our research highlighted the transformative potential of Human Work Interaction Design (HWID) and Interaction Design in addressing complex environmental challenges. By creating immersive, interactive experiences inviting participation, reflection, and collaborative problem-solving, we demonstrated a powerful approach to ecological education beyond traditional informational methods.

4 Conclusions

This work holds relevance in its approach to the creative process and methodology, emphasizing collaborative and multidisciplinary efforts. It sheds light on a pertinent issue that warrants discussion across various levels of understanding. AquaPlay encourages individual interpretations, allowing each participant to contribute to the hybrid composition of the experience. The notion of narrative construction and (re)construction within the game's timeframe, AquaPlay empowers participants to shape their narratives and perspectives, contributing to a rich and dynamic discourse surrounding environmental stewardship.

This integration of Interaction Design and Human Work Interaction Design, combined with the broader environmental, cultural, and social aspects, underscores the importance of users, their context, and the social environment in creating an artistic experience that not only informs but also inspires action and reflection on urgent environmental issues.

The future work on AquaPlay aims to enhance the digital art experience and explore new dimensions of interaction and engagement. Potential possibilities for development include expanding narrative and gameplay by introducing new storylines, challenges, and interactive elements to provide users with a more immersive experience. Additionally, there is a focus on enhancing the tangible interface for interaction by introducing new input methods like gesture-based controls or haptic feedback.

Furthermore, multiplayer capabilities could be integrated to foster social interaction and collaboration among users. The exploration of augmented reality (AR) or virtual reality (VR) technologies is also on the agenda to increase the digital art experience by overlaying virtual elements onto the physical installation or creating fully immersive virtual environments [40].

Data collection and analysis were planned to be implemented to gather insights into user behavior, preferences, and engagement patterns, allowing for iterative improvements based on user feedback. Ensuring accessibility and inclusivity was a priority, with features and design elements incorporated to meet diverse user needs.

Overall, AquaPlay's future work is driven by a desire to push the boundaries of digital art and interactive experiences, engaging and inspiring users through innovative storytelling. Collaboration with artists, technologists, and audiences is anticipated to shape the future of digital art.

Other future challenges are: Preparing Educational Workshops and Lectures: Conducting educational workshops, lectures, and environmental actions in school environments, cultural spaces (including family, children, and elderly attendees), and community groups can create diverse learning opportunities and promote dialogue on plastic usage. Long-Term Impact: Encouraging participants to confront the contradictions in their daily actions towards the environment can lead to long-term awareness and commitment to sustainable living practices.

Acknowledgments. We want to thank all the participants who engaged with the various prototypes during this study. Their involvement and collaboration were essential to this project's success. Thank you to Adriana Moreno. This research was funded by Funded by FCT projects: https://doi.org/10.54499/LA/P/0083/2020; https://doi.org/10.54499/UIDP/50009/2020 & https://doi.org/10.54499/UIDB/50009/2020.

References

1. Akindele, E.O., Alimba, C.G.: Plastic pollution threat in Africa: current Status and implications for aquatic ecosystem health. Environ. Sci. Pollut. Res. **28**, 7636–7651 (2021). https://doi.org/10.1007/s11356-020-11736-6
2. Chitaka, T.Y., Onianwa, P.C., Nel, H.A.: Marine litter sources and distribution pathways. In: Maes, T., Preston-Whyte, F. (eds.) The African Marine Litter Outlook. Springer, Cham (2023). https://doi.org/10.1007/978-3-031-08626-7_2
3. Pêgo, A.: Plasticus Maritimus: an art intervention to alert society to marine litter. In: Proceedings of the International Conference on Marine Debris (2015)
4. Pêgo, A.: Plasticus Maritimus: shedding light on plastic waste and its consequences for marine ecosystems. Mar. Pollut. Bull. **123**(1–2), 13–19 (2017)
5. Ellen MacArthur Foundation. The Global Commitment 2022 Progress Report: Breaking the Plastic Wave (2022). https://www.ellenmacarthurfoundation.org/global-commitment-2022/resources
6. Verlis, K., Wilson, S.: Paradise trashed: Sources and solutions to marine litter in a small island developing state. Waste Manag. **103**, 128–136 (2019). https://doi.org/10.1016/j.wasman.2019.12.020
7. Smith, J.: Understanding environmental issues (2nd Ed.). SAGE Publications (2014)
8. Jordan, C.: Midway Journey [Documentary] (2013)
9. Lee Coles, L., Pasquier, P.: Digital eco-art: Transformative possibilities. Digit. Creativity **26**(1), 3–15 (2015)
10. Turnbull, J., et al.: Digital Ecologies: Mediating More-Than-Human Worlds. Manchester University Press (2024)
11. Shin, H.D., Bull, R.: Three dimensions of design for sustainable behaviour. Sustainability **11**(17), 4610 (2019). https://doi.org/10.3390/su11174610
12. Digital Ecologies: Materialities, Encounters, Governance: Progress in Environmental Geography **2**(1–2), 3–32 (2022)
13. Water Games. (n.d.). https://toytales.ca/water-games-tomy-1976-2/
14. Robin, B.R.: Digital storytelling: a powerful technology tool for the 21st century classroom. Theory Pract. **47**(3), 220–228 (2009)
15. Râpă, M., et al.: An overview of the current trends in marine plastic litter management for a sustainable development. Recycling **9**(2), 30 (2024). https://doi.org/10.3390/recycling9020030
16. Sathvika, R., Venkatraman, R.: A semiotic analysis of Saussure and Barthes's theories under the purview of print advertisements. J. Lang. Linguist. Stud. **18**, 386–396 (2022). https://doi.org/10.52462/jlls.189
17. Lam, B., Pitsaki, I.: Co-design for the development of new knowledge and practices in not-for-profit organizations. Des. Manag. J. **13**, 70–82 (2018). https://doi.org/10.1111/dmj.12044

18. Thorburn, K., Waks, S., Aadam, B., Fisher, K.R., Spooner, C., Harris, M.F.: Creating the conditions for collaborative decision-making in co-design. CoDesign **20**(4), 567–584 (2024). https://doi.org/10.1080/15710882.2024.2349578
19. Clemmensen, T.: The design and usability of human work interaction design frameworks. Int. J. Hum.-Comput. Interact. **27**(10), 941–962 (2011)
20. Lopes, A.G.: Human work interaction design: designing for human work. In: Clemmensen, T., et al. (eds.) Human Work Interaction Design: Usability in Social, Cultural, and Organizational Contexts, pp. 1–18. Springer, Cham (2011)
21. Kaptelinin, V., Nardi, B.: Acting with Technology: Activity Theory and Interaction Design. MIT Press (2006)
22. Bannon, L.J., Bødker, S.: Beyond the interface: encountering artifacts in use. In: Designing Interaction, pp. 227–253. Cambridge University Press (1991)
23. Jones, L.: Playful reflections: using games to spark environmental awareness. Environ. Educ. Res. **24**(4), 547–561 (2018)
24. Bellou, N., Gambardella, C., Karantzalos, K., et al.: Global assessment of innovative solutions to tackle marine litter. Nat. Sustain. **4**, 516–524 (2021). https://doi.org/10.1038/s41893-021-00726-2
25. Lincoln, S., et al.: Marine litter and climate change: inextricably connected threats to the world's oceans. Sci. Total. Environ. **837**, 155709 (2022). https://doi.org/10.1016/j.scitotenv.2022.155709
26. Löhr, A., Savelli, H., Beunen, R., Kalz, M., Ragas, A., Van Belleghem, F.: Solutions for global marine litter pollution. Curr. Opin. Environ. Sustain. **28**, 90–99 (2017). https://doi.org/10.1016/j.cosust.2017.08.009
27. Miller, S.: Activating society: engaging individuals in environmental action through gameplay. Environ. Commun. **36**(3), 221–234 (2020)
28. Teague, A., Sermet, Y., Demir, I., Muste, M.: Serious gaming for water resources planning and hazard mitigation (2020). https://doi.org/10.31223/osf.io/vcy5e
29. Medema, W., Mayer, I., Adamowski, J., Wals, A.E.J., Chew, C.: The potential of serious games to solve water problems: editorial to the special issue on game-based approaches to sustainable water governance. Water **11**(12), 2562 (2019). https://doi.org/10.3390/w11122562
30. Brown, R.: Time as a narrative device in environmental games. Games Cult. **14**(5), 548–566 (2019)
31. Bratteteig, T., Wagner, I.: Unpacking the notion of participation in participatory design. Comput. Support. Coop. Work (CSCW) **25**, 425–475 (2016). https://doi.org/10.1007/s10606-016-9259-4
32. Pallot, M., Pawar, K.: A holistic model of user experience for living lab experiential design. In: 2012 18th International Conference on Engineering, Technology and Innovation, ICE 2012 - Conference Proceedings, pp. 1–15 (2012). https://doi.org/10.1109/ICE.2012.6297648
33. Pallot, M., et al.: An experiential design process and holistic model of user experience for supporting user co-creation (2015). https://doi.org/10.13140/RG.2.1.4429.8406
34. Dearing, J., Battarbee, R., Dikau, R., Larocque, I., Oldfield, F.: Human-environment interactions: learning from the past. Reg. Environ. Change **6**, 1–16 (2006). https://doi.org/10.1007/s10113-005-0011-8
35. Proskuryakova, L.: The interaction of environmental systems and human development in a time of wild cards: a big data enhanced foresight study. J. Environ. Manage. **316**, 115169 (2022). https://doi.org/10.1016/j.jenvman.2022.115169
36. Lopes, A.G.: Research methods–what is best for developing and evaluating human-computer interaction and interactive artistic installations? In: Human Work Interaction Design. Designing Engaging Automation: 5th IFIP WG 13.6 Working Conference, HWID 2018, pp. 229–241. Springer, Cham (2019)

37. Lopes, A.G.: Using research methods in human-computer interaction to design technology for resilience. JISTEM-J. Inf. Syst. Technol. Manage. **13**, 363–388 (2016)
38. Lopes, A.: Interaction design as a multimodal conversation. In: Katre, D., Orngreen, R., Yammiyavar, P., Clemmensen, T. (eds.), Human Work Interaction Design: Usability in Social, Cultural and Organizational Contexts. HWID 2009. IFIP Advances in Information and Communication Technology, vol. 316. Springer, Cham (2010). https://doi.org/10.1007/978-3-642-11762-6_19
39. Schweitzer, L., Lyons, S., Smith, C.J.: Career sustainability: framing the past to adapt in the present for a sustainable future. Sustainability **15**(15), 11800 (2023). https://doi.org/10.3390/su151511800
40. Wang, F., Zhang, Z., Li, L., Long, S.: Virtual reality and augmented reality in artistic expression: a comprehensive study of innovative technologies. Int. J. Adv. Comput. Sci. Appl. **15**(3) (2024). https://doi.org/10.14569/IJACSA.2024.0150365

Design of Gamified Training in Waste Management Plants: The SOHS Project

Barbara Rita Barricelli[1], Roya Biabani Reshtehroudi[1], Federica Caffaro[2], Giuseppe Carrus[2], Raffaele Cioffi[3], Giuseppe De Palma[1], Daniela Fogli[1](✉), Matteo Gremo[2], Niccolò Leonardi[4], Margherita Micheletti Cremasco[3], Niccolò Pampuro[4], Emma Sala[1], and Mentore Vaccari[1]

[1] Università degli Studi di Brescia, Brescia, Italy
{barbara.barricelli,roya.reshtehroudi,giuseppe.depalma, daniela.fogli,emma.sala,mentore.vaccari}@unibs.it
[2] Università degli Studi Roma Tre, Rome, Italy
{federica.caffaro,giuseppe.carrus,matteo.gremo}@uniroma3.it
[3] Università degli Studi di Torino, Turin, Italy
{r.cioffi,margherita.micheletti}@unito.it
[4] Consiglio Nazionale delle Ricerche, Turin, Italy
{niccolo.leonardi,niccolo.pampuro}@stems.cnr.it

Abstract. Keeping workers safe and healthy is good not only for them but also for business. Strong occupational safety and health (OSH) programs can boost a company's competitiveness and productivity. However, OSH also plays a big role in environmental and social well-being. This connection between being *green* and keeping workers *safe* is especially tricky when it comes to *green jobs*. The number of workers in the fast-growing waste management sector is skyrocketing, so new safety considerations must be addressed. Waste treatment workers are exposed to a combination of risks (chemical, biological, biomechanical, and psychosocial), and very little is known about the possible interactions that may increase or decrease the overall workers' health. Innovative and highly engaging methods are needed to effectively train employees on the risks. In this paper, we present the preliminary results of the SOHS Project that aims to perform a multidimensional occupational risk assessment, define the corresponding risk scenarios, and design and develop a prototype of a gamified tool to offer an engaging training experience. The project applies Human Work Interaction Design (HWID) principles and techniques to ensure that the design aligns with the workers' context, supporting effective interaction between employees and the training system. By embedding HWID principles, the training system balances technology-driven risk insights with the workers' expertise and experience, fostering meaningful engagement while enhancing safety outcomes.

Published by Springer Nature Switzerland AG 2026
B. R. Barricelli et al. (Eds.): HWID 2024, IFIP AICT 751, pp. 77–92, 2026.
https://doi.org/10.1007/978-3-031-95334-7_5

Keywords: Occupational safety and health · Human work interaction design · Sustainability · Gamification

1 Introduction

Municipal solid waste management (MSWM) plays a critical role in achieving the United Nations Sustainable Development Goals (SDGs)[1] and fostering a green economy [16]. However, prioritizing environmental sustainability can sometimes conflict with ensuring workers' occupational safety and health (OSH) in the waste management sector. It is now time to explore this "green paradox" within the context of MSWM, focusing on emerging challenges and potential solutions.

European MSWM strategies have significantly shifted, transitioning towards integrated approaches emphasizing recycling and resource recovery [4]. This has resulted in a rise in waste sorting and recovery facilities, increasing the workforce dedicated to waste-handling activities [20,22]. The growing complexity of integrated MSWM systems presents workers with new OSH risks that require careful consideration.

Data provided by INAIL, the Italian public body that manages the compulsory insurance against accidents at work and occupational diseases on behalf of the State, reveals that between 2018 and 2022, a concerning trend, with over 10,000 work accidents and 1,000 work-related illnesses reported annually in the waste management sector [10]. This high incidence rate can be attributed to several factors: a) workers are exposed to various hazards, including chemical, biological, biomechanical, and psychosocial stressors [13,18]; b) a significant proportion of the waste management workforce may include foreign workers with potentially lower educational levels and with a diverse range of languages and cultures, thus increasing their vulnerability to these hazards [9]; c) the inherent variability of waste materials can pose unforeseen dangers that traditional risk assessments may not adequately capture [18]; and d) beyond physical dangers, individual and psychosocial factors also contribute to adverse OSH outcomes. Unsafe behaviors, low-risk perception, and a lack of adherence to safety protocols can significantly increase the likelihood of accidents and illnesses [2,7].

Effective training is a cornerstone of OSH prevention strategies mandated by Italian legislation [8]. Studies have demonstrated that engaging training methods, such as hands-on demonstrations, can promote safe work practices, reduce stress, and enhance safety commitment [19]. However, these methods can be costly.

The emergence of new technologies presents promising alternatives. Gamification – i.e., using game-like elements in training – offers a cost-effective and flexible approach that can provide realistic simulations and promote learner-centered education [1,15,23]. This approach fosters engagement and knowledge retention, ultimately improving safety outcomes.

[1] https://sdgs.un.org/goals.

To further enhance the effectiveness of these training methods, Human Work Interaction Design (HWID) principles are essential [5,17]. By focusing on the interaction between workers, the technologies they use, and the complex environments in which they operate, HWID ensures that the training tools are aligned with the workers' cognitive and physical needs. This alignment is critical, especially in diverse and multicultural workforces, to ensure that gamified training methods are intuitive, accessible, and adaptive to varying skill levels and safety perceptions. HWID also helps address the psychosocial factors at play, promoting safety protocols in ways that resonate with workers' experiences and perspectives.

The state of the art highlighted a lack of knowledge regarding the OSH risks to which workers employed in the growing waste management sector are exposed and the need for highly engaging safety training methods addressing the specific OSH needs of these operators [12]. Previous studies pointed out the positive impact of game-based safety training activities in many production sectors [23], even though the potential of these training methods has not yet been explored in waste treatment.

2 The SOHS Project

In this paper, we present the preliminary results obtained in the SOHS Project ("Sustainable Occupational Health and Safety in Waste Treatment Plants: A Gamified Training Tool for Workers")[2], a two-year research project funded by the PRIN 2022 Programme (Italian Research and University Ministry and European Union - NextGenerationEU). This project aims to conduct a comprehensive occupational risk assessment in two Italian waste treatment plants, identify the associated risk scenarios, and design and evaluate a prototype of a gamified tool that provides workers with an engaging safety training experience.

2.1 An Interdisciplinary Approach

The researchers involved in the SOHS Project, belonging to four different institutions, have complementary expertise covering all aspects involved in risk assessment, identification of risk scenarios, and design, development, and usability evaluation of a prototype for gamified training.

Università degli Studi Roma Tre, leader of SOHS, participates with the Department of Education, and it holds competencies and expertise in the mixed-methods analysis of the role played by individual and psychosocial variables in affecting OSH and the overall efficiency and sustainability of a working system.

The Italian National Research Council participates in the project with the Institute of Sciences and Technologies for Sustainable Energy and Mobility (STEMS). In detail, the Turin branch research group has developed competencies including the management of waste from the agri-food chain, monitoring of

[2] https://www.sohs.it/.

greenhouse gas emissions generated by the composting process, and the development of innovative processes for the valorization of agro-industrial by-products into organic fertilizers.

Università degli Studi di Torino participates with the group of Physical Anthropology, Anthropometry, and Ergonomics, which operates at the Department of Life Sciences and Systems Biology. The group focuses on anthropometric and biomechanical variability and how they affect human interaction with life and work environment and technological artifacts, ergonomic analysis of work activities, with attention to health, safety, and comfort, to promote wellness at work, healthy lifestyle, and wellbeing.

Università degli Studi di Brescia is involved in this project with 3 different departments and research groups: 1) The Sanitary and Environmental Engineering research group, which operates in the Department of Civil, Architectural, and Environmental Engineering and Mathematics, deals with pollution phenomena and technologies for the protection of the environment and human health. Regarding solid waste, the research group deals with technologies for the management (i.e., collection, treatment, recovery, and final disposal) of municipal and non-municipal solid waste, with attention to treatment plant management; 2) The group of Occupational Health and Industrial Hygiene, which operates in the Department of Medical and Surgical Specialties, Radiological Sciences, and Public Health, is involved in the research activities dealing with occupational health and risk assessment mainly using industrial hygiene resources and methods; 3) The Human-Computer Interaction group, which carries out its research in the Department of Information Engineering, brings to the project its members' expertise in Human Work Interaction Design, usability, and user experience of interactive systems for professionals, typically not experts in IT nor interested in becoming ones, but deeply knowledgeable of their work domain.

2.2 Two Case Studies

Two case studies have been identified as representatives of most of the processes and working procedures related to the MSWM. In this context, recovery and composting facilities are reported as the most hazardous [14].

The first plant is a social cooperative established in Brescia in 1995 to combine social and environmental actions. The activities and services offered by the cooperative in the environmental sector allow the reduction of waste and consumption and support paths of innovation and cooperation for creative recovery and enhancement of human and natural resources.

The second plant is represented by a facility located in Parma managed by a leading company in the recovery of recyclable materials. Since it was founded in 1963, the company has been committed to being a reference point in non-hazardous waste recovery, mainly paper and cardboard. Thanks to the experience acquired in more than 50 years of activity, the company can provide a complete service to find the best solution to the waste management that each company encounters, providing the most suitable equipment for the customers' needs and being technologically advanced.

2.3 Objectives

Based on the abovementioned state of the art, the objectives of the SOHS project are:

1. To perform a multidimensional occupational risk assessment in the two plants selected as case studies. The risk assessment includes biomechanical, chemical, biological, and psychosocial risk factors during on-plant waste processing. This activity is aimed at defining risk scenarios enriched by individual behavioral components.
2. To design and develop a prototype of a gamified tool that allows studying different identified scenarios for workers' training. The scenarios will be replicated as gamified features to support the identification of on-site hazards and learn how to perform correct and safe behaviors.
3. To test the prototype's usability (in terms of effectiveness, efficiency, and satisfaction) with different groups of workers representing the extremes of human variability (in terms of age, gender, cultural differences, and level of work expertise). Evaluating interactive system design with users and improving it based on their feedback effectively minimizes the risk of a system not meeting user or organizational needs [11]. At the end of this activity, a report with suggestions for improvements will be shared with the software development consulting firm that will develop the gamified tool.

Specifically, in what follows we will focus on the second objective, which mostly pertains to the Human Work Interaction Design field.

3 Sustainable Human Work Interaction Design for Waste Sector Workers' Training

To design the gamified tool prototype, we planned the following five activities:

1. **User research:** This activity aims to analyze user profiles, user needs, and requirements through observations, questionnaires, interviews, and focus groups. User needs and requirements specify what users expect to find in a system and how they hope to use it to reach a goal.
2. **Task analysis through Human Work Interaction Design methods**. With this activity, HWID integrates work analysis methods and interaction design to support interactive systems design for domain experts to use in work environments.
3. **User Experience design:** This third activity is aimed to define personas, scenarios, and user journey maps [3,21]. Designing Personas means providing detailed descriptions of the target users of a product under development. They support exploring and discussing contexts, needs, and requirements without describing the software use. Scenarios are meant to provide an informal narrative for describing the interaction between a user and an interactive system that already exists or is under design. User journey maps are graphical representations of the user flow in an application or website.

4. **Scoring system design:** This activity specifies the reward system used in the game designed according to the results of the multidimensional occupational risk assessment carried out in the project's first phase. An appropriate reward system can support the user in being motivated to use the gamified tool and in understanding the risks they are exposed to in the workplace.
5. **Sketches and wireframes:** This activity defines design ideas through sketches, wireframes, and presentations to the users during focus groups. Sketches are hand-drawn and are heavily used in low-fidelity prototyping activities. Wireframes show an interactive system's structure, content, and controls. Active involvement of the users in the discussion about the design ideas is foreseen in this activity.
6. **Design handoff:** Finally, this activity regards debriefing the design team about user research outcomes, user experience design, scoring system design, and sketches and wireframes ideation. The aim is to inform the development phase and discuss and clarify any possible technical challenge or opportunity before implementing the final prototype.

The SOHS Project started in October 2023. The first two activities have been completed at the moment this paper is being written, while the third is currently ongoing, and, specifically, the user journey maps are still being prepared.

4 User Experience Design

The user research and task analysis activities have been completed, and we are now working on the User Experience design activity; in particular, personas and scenarios have been defined, while user journey maps are still under preparation.

Specifically, four sessions of direct observation of the work activity in the plants led us to the identification of key takeaways that can inform the design process of the gamified workers' training prototype:

- *Identification of workers' common behaviors and challenges*: It was possible to analyze how workers perform their tasks and identify several risky situations to which they are exposed.
- *Analysis of work environment and context*: It allowed us to identify physical and social factors that might affect the work practice and represent potential safety issues.
- *Feedback gathering from domain experts*: We collected important knowledge about training procedures, needs, and preferences, which will be useful in the design of engaging, motivating, and effective interaction strategies.

4.1 The Workplace and the Tasks

Analyzing the two waste management plants, we have identified the following workplace areas: conveyor belts, loading and unloading stations, and transit areas (for promiscuous use by people and vehicles). A further situation in which safety issues may occur is when people are assigned to machinery and vehicle handling. In what follows, we will describe four task scenarios.

Scenario #1. The worker on the left side of Fig. 1 performs the task of manual belt sorting. He performs his task in standing posture (often with knees flexed) along one of the two sides of the conveyor belt (*motonastro*, in Italian) placed in an oblique position inside a shed. While working, he wears specific clothing and specific Personal Protective Equipment (PPE): safety shoes, a pair of neon orange reflective shorts, a neon yellow reflective vest, non-disposable gloves, and a respiratory protection mask. Operationally, this activity consists of manually sorting extraneous waste (e.g., mixed packaging, plastic, and paper) sorted according to quality characteristics. Once selected, the worker puts the foreign material into the bins near him. Unselected material remains on the conveyor belt and is directed toward pressing or shredding machines. The conveyor belt can be stopped directly by the operators in case of need or emergency, but the belt speed cannot be changed.

Fig. 1. The first and the second scenarios. On the left, a worker performs manual belt sorting in an oblique position. On the right, a worker performs manual belt sorting on a conveyor belt placed horizontally.

Scenario #2. On the right side of Fig. 1, the worker performs the task of manual belt sorting. She performs her task uprightly along one of the two sides of the conveyor belt placed horizontally inside the sorting cabin. While working, the worker wears specific clothing and specific PPE: safety shoes, a disposable plastic apron (some also wear a full jumpsuit), a neon orange reflective vest, disposable plastic arm covers, non-disposable gloves, and a respiratory protection mask. Operationally, this activity consists of manually sorting extraneous waste (mixed packaging, plastic, and paper) sorted according to quality characteristics. Once sorted, the material is introduced by hand into unloading hoppers and collected in boxes located under or at the sides of the conveyor belt or behind the workers, before being sent for pressing or shredding. The conveyor belt is not operated directly by the operators, but by the foreman operating in the cabin: the speed of the belt cannot be changed, but it can be stopped by the foreman and only in cases of extreme necessity or emergency by the operators.

Scenario #3. The worker on the left side of Fig. 2 performs the task of manual sorting on the ground. He performs his task in standing posture, flexed posture on his legs (and often incorrectly on his back) in an open-air asphalt yard and under the partial cover of a canopy. While working, he wears specific clothing and specific PPE: safety shoes, a neon yellow undershirt, a neon yellow reflective vest, non-disposable gloves, and a respiratory protection mask. Operationally, this activity consists of opening the separated garbage bags (plastic), tipping the contents on the ground, and separating and sorting the different types of material (hard plastics, cellophane). The sorted material is placed in separate piles by type and then transported by hand or forklifts. For plastic and wood waste, manual sorting on the ground removes foreign substances and separates the mixed materials into homogeneous fractions. The separated fractions are then subjected to the operations prescribed for each type of waste.

Fig. 2. The third and fourth scenarios. On the left side, a worker performs manual sorting on the ground. On the right side, a worker stands on a conveyor belt performing manual sorting on the ground. (Color figure online)

Scenario #4. The worker on the right side of Fig. 2 performs the task of manual sorting on the ground. He performs his task standing on top of a conveyor belt placed horizontally below the floor level (−63 cm) inside a shed. While working, he wears specific clothing and specific PPE: safety shoes, a full white jumpsuit, a reflective orange and neon yellow vest, non-disposable gloves, and a respiratory protection mask. Material is placed on the sides of the conveyor belt by forklifts (sometimes driven by the workers themselves). Operationally, the workers' activity consists of opening files/envelopes (paper), tipping the contents on the ground, and separating and sorting the different types of material (paper, white/colored cardboard). The material sorted and dropped on the conveyor belt is moved to the next work area (sorting cabin). The material sorted and placed on the edge of the conveyor belt is placed in separate piles by type, which are then moved by a forklift.

4.2 Hazards in the Workplace

The hazards that one may experience in a waste sorting facility fall into 3 groups:

1. *Biological and chemical*: exposure to pathogens and chemicals, harmful gases, vapors, dust, radiation, inhaling toxic substances, contact with poisonous substances.
2. *Physical*: awkward postures, repetitive movements, falls, collisions with machines, crashes with vehicles, slip risk, entrapment, and danger of being struck by falling objects.
3. *Psychosocial*: stress, anxiety, depression, fatigue, monotony, social isolation.

Also, it is important to detect the places where the hazards may occur to make designing the gamified interaction in realistic scenarios easier.

4.3 Workers' Personas

Data gathered through questionnaires and interviews with 31 workers at the two waste management plants allowed us to start the User Experience design phase by defining four personas. Personas are fictional yet data-driven archetypes representing different user types within a specific domain [6]. They are used in interaction design to provide insight into the needs, goals, behaviors, and challenges of distinct end-user groups. By embodying the diverse characteristics of target audiences, personas help researchers and designers ground their decisions in user-centered considerations, ensuring that the systems or tools developed align with real-world expectations.

In this project, the four personas were created based on data collected from interviews and observational studies: Jelani Niakaté (Fig. 3), Mandisa Yatara (Fig. 4), Elena Filippini (Fig. 5), and Giovanni Savoldi (Fig. 6). These personas were developed to reflect the varying experiences, expertise, and roles of individuals interacting in the workplace. Each persona represents a specific user profile, providing a holistic understanding of the users' needs, expectations, and pain points.

Two personas are male, and two are female. The most experienced persona is Elena Filippini, 50 years old, with 12 years in the role of manual waste disposal. Elena is Italian, single, and holds a primary school diploma. Jelani, a 45-year-old man from Senegal, has 7 years of experience in ground waste collection, is married, and has completed middle school. Another male worker is Giovanni, a 43-year-old Italian, who has worked for 6 years in manual waste disposal, holds a high school diploma, and is single. Lastly, the youngest person is Mandisa, 26 years old, with only 1 year of experience in manual waste disposal. She is from Cameroon, has a high school diploma, and is married.

Besides their differences in biographical details and work experience, the four personas are characterized by varying physical attributes, which are important for the design considerations in the project. Shorter workers will need removable devices to elevate themselves to the correct level relative to the workbench, avoiding strain on their joints. In contrast, taller workers will face more challenges in

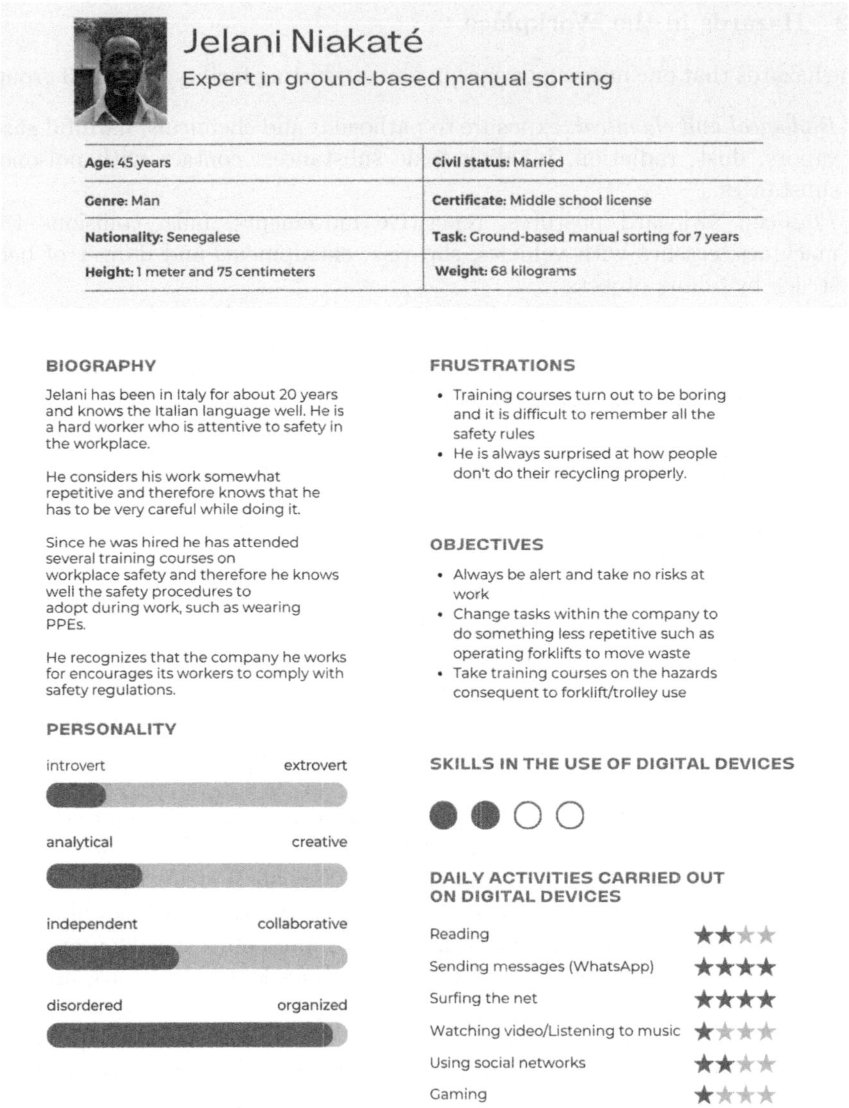

Fig. 3. Persona #1. Jelani Niakaté.

ground-level tasks and will require specific adjustments to protect their health. Naturally, weight also plays an important role in worker well-being, always considered in tandem with height: Jelani is 175 cm tall and weighs 68 kg, Mandisa is 162 cm tall and weighs 54 kg, Elena is 170 cm tall and weighs 77 kg, while Giovanni is 178 cm tall and weighs 101 kg.

As shown in the figures, we have defined various characteristics related to personality, frustrations, and goals for each individual, along with a brief biog-

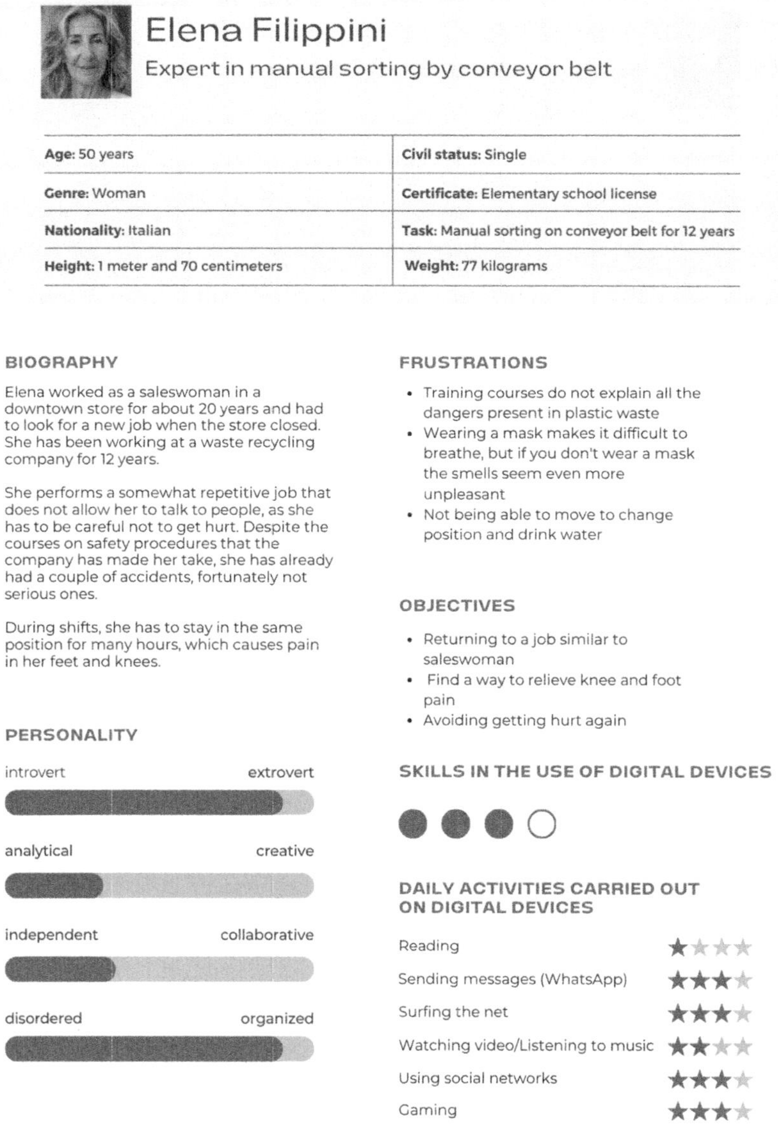

Fig. 4. Persona #2. Elena Filippini.

raphy that outlines their character. A key aspect we focused on is their ability to use digital devices and the type of usage they engage in. Specifically, we defined the types of activities each persona performs to represent individuals with different attitudes toward technology. Jelani considers himself to have average digital skills and primarily uses devices for instant messaging and web browsing. Mandisa is the least familiar with technology, and she mainly uses it to watch videos

Fig. 5. Persona #3. Mandisa Yatara.

and listen to music. Elena believes she has good digital skills and uses devices for various purposes, including instant messaging, web browsing, and social media. Lastly, Giovanni is the most proficient with technology, using it mostly for reading, browsing the web, watching videos, and listening to music.

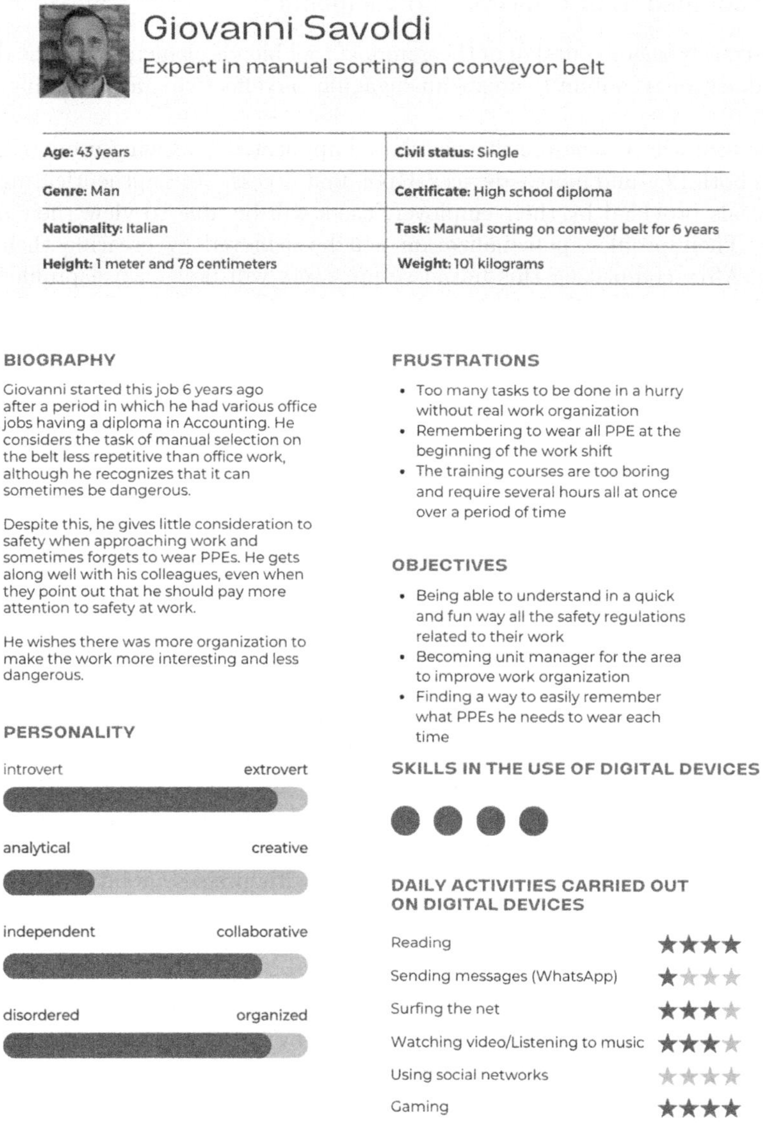

Fig. 6. Persona #4. Giovanni Savoldi.

The final and fundamental aspect of the four personas is their attitude toward gaming. On a scale from 1 to 4, the highest score for the use of electronic games goes to Giovanni (4), followed by Elena (3), Mandisa (2), and lastly Jelani (1).

4.4 Gamified Tool Concept and Elements

The currently ongoing design of the gamified tool blends elements of game design with educational content to create an engaging and effective safety training experience.

The tool will be a responsive web-based application, allowing users to access it from both PCs and mobile devices. Upon first access, after authenticating with credentials provided by their employer, users will be able to view their profile screen. Their profile's personalization will be achieved by creating their own avatar. After completing this initial setup, users will be shown a profile page. On this page, every time they access the tool, their status in terms of safety training and the trophies they have earned will be displayed.

The gamified tool will be organized into levels that include distinct activities corresponding to the various tasks performed within the waste sorting facility. Once a level is completed, users can advance to the next level or replay the completed one (or any of the others they already completed) to improve their score. The proposed levels are five in total, and their order reflects their respective complexities: entrance to the facility, changing room, ground sorting, horizontal conveyor belt sorting, and inclined conveyor belt sorting. This structured approach aims to make the training engaging and relevant to the specific duties of waste management workers.

The challenges in the tool are represented by quizzes and interactive scenarios that simulate real-life safety situations, testing workers' knowledge of safety measures at work and decision-making skills. Correct answers earn points, while incorrect ones provide immediate feedback and learning opportunities.

Implementing successful motivational strategies is pivotal in contributing to solving the psychosocial risks described in Sect. 4.2. To achieve this goal, we plan to include both instant feedback and progress tracking. Instant feedback will provide immediate responses to the workers with praises, points, and virtual rewards to increase engagement with the tool. Also, constructive guidance will be offered in case mistakes are made: hints, explanations, or links to teaching material will be offered. The immediate feedback is aimed at building confidence and trust towards the gamified tool and the training process in general. On the other hand, progress tracking will be achieved by providing users with progress bars and reports to illustrate their advancements.

Last but not least, accessibility strategies will be included in the design to ensure the tool offers mostly visual instructions instead of textual ones to overcome issues related to digital literacy, cognitive abilities, and multiculturalism.

5 Conclusion

In the frame of the SOHS Project, a multidisciplinary team is involved in performing a multidimensional risk assessment at two waste management plants in Italy and designing a gamified solution to foster workers' training in performing correct and safe behaviors. In this paper, we presented the activities that concern the design and development of the training solution, which will be realized as a gamified training system representing a waste management plant endowed with features for virtually and engagingly testing different risk scenarios. For this project, a Human Work Interaction Design approach is adopted. The user research activities allowed the project team to identify key aspects to be considered for the prototype design. These insights will be employed to design gamified scenarios that simulate real-world and realistic challenges, helping the workers practice safe and effective decision-making in a controlled environment. The goal of gamification techniques is to incorporate rewards and recognition systems to motivate the workers to participate in the training activities and make them more engaging. Once the gamified tool is implemented, extensive user tests involving workers in the two waste management plants will be organized. We will not only evaluate system usability and user experience but also game effectiveness in training. Lastly, a longitudinal study will be planned to assess whether the long-term impact of the gamified approach to training is beneficial and if it can be sustained over time.

Acknowledgments. This work has been supported by the Italian MUR PRIN 2022 Project 20227TS4WN, Sustainable Occupational Health and Safety in Waste Treatment Plants: A Gamified Training Tool for Workers, funded by European Union - NextGenerationEU. The authors want to thank the personnel of Cauto c.s.r.l. and Ghirardi s.r.l. for their collaboration in the Project.

References

1. Brahm, F., Singer, M.: Is more engaging safety training always better in reducing accidents? evidence of self-selection from Chilean panel data. J. Safety Res. **47**(1), 85–92 (2013)
2. Caffaro, F., Micheletti Cremasco, M., Roccato, M., Cavallo, E.: It does not occur by chance: a mediation model of the influence of workers' characteristics, work environment factors, and near misses on agricultural machinery-related accidents. Int. J. Occup. Environ. Health **23**(1), 52–59 (2017)
3. Carroll, J.: Making Use: Scenario-Based Design of Human-Computer Interactions. The MIT Press, Cambridge (2003)
4. Chen, X., Geng, Y., Fujita, T.: An overview of municipal solid waste management in china. Waste Manage. **30**(4), 716–724 (2010)
5. Clemmensen, T.: Human Work Interaction Design. A Platform for Theory and Action. Springer, Cham (2021)
6. Cooper, A.: The Inmates are Running the Asylum: Why High-Tech Products Drive Us Crazy and How to Restore the Sanity. Sams Publishing, Indianapolis (1999)
7. Glasscock, D.J., Rasmussen, K., Carstensen, O., Hansen, O.N.: Psychosocial factors and safety behaviour as predictors of accidental work injuries in farming. Work Stress. **20**(2), 173–189 (2006). https://doi.org/10.1080/02678370600879724
8. D.lgs 81/2008. Testo coordinato con il d.lgs. 3 agosto 2009, n. 106. Testo unico sulla salute e sicurezza sul lavoro (2008)
9. Gregson, N., Crang, M., Botticello, J., Calestani, M., Krzywoszynska, A.: Doing the 'dirty work' of the green economy: resource recovery and migrant labour in the EU. Eur. Urban Reg. Stud. **23**, 541–555 (2016)

10. INAIL Istituto Nazionale Assicurazione contro gli Infortuni sul Lavoro. Banca dati statistica (2023). Accessed 07 May 2024
11. ISO 9241-210:2019 Ergonomics of human-system interaction – Part 210: Human-centred design for interactive systems (2019)
12. Jedynska, A., Kuijpers, E., van den Berg, C., Kruizinga, A., Meima, M., Spaan, S.: Biological agents and work-related diseases: results of a literature review, expert survey and analysis of monitoring systems. Technical report, European Agency for Safety and Health at Work (2019)
13. Jilcha, K., Kitaw, D.: Industrial occupational safety and health innovation for sustainable development. Eng. Sci. Technol. Int. J. **20**(1), 372–380 (2017). https://doi.org/10.1016/j.jestch.2016.10.011
14. Kontogianni, S., Moussiopoulos, N.: Investigation of the occupational health and safety conditions in hellenic solid waste management facilities and assessment of the in-situ hazard level. Saf. Sci. **96**, 192–197 (2017). https://doi.org/10.1016/j.ssci.2017.03.025
15. Mohd, N.I., Ali, K.N., Ebrahimi, S.S., Ahmad Fauzi, A.F.A.: Understanding the level of self-directed learning and decision-making style of construction-related workers. Int. J. Interact. Mob. Technol. **13**(07), 44–53 (2019). https://doi.org/10.3991/ijim.v13i07.10749
16. Nandy, S., Fortunato, E., Martins, R.: Green economy and waste management: an inevitable plan for materials science. Progress Nat. Sci. Mater. Int. **32**(1), 1–9 (2022)
17. Abdelnour Nocera, J., Barricelli, B.R., Lopes, A., Campos, P., Clemmensen, T. (eds.): HWID 2015. IAICT, vol. 468. Springer, Cham (2015). https://doi.org/10.1007/978-3-319-27048-7
18. Poole, C.J.M., Basu, S.: Systematic review: occupational illness in the waste and recycling sector. Occup. Med. (Lond.) **67**(8), 626–636 (2017)
19. Ricci, F., Chiesi, A., Bisio, C., Panari, C., Pelosi, A.: Effectiveness of occupational health and safety training: a systematic review with meta-analysis. J. Work. Learn. **28**(6), 355–377 (2016). https://doi.org/10.1108/JWL-11-2015-0087
20. Song, J., et al.: Reinforced urban waste management for resource, energy and environmental benefits: China's regional potentials. Resour. Conserv. Recycl. **178**, 106083 (2022)
21. Stickdorn, M., Schneider, J.: This is Service Design Thinking: Basics, Tools. Wiley, Cases (2012)
22. Szulc, J., et al.: Microbiological and toxicological hazard assessment in a waste sorting plant and proper respiratory protection. J. Environ. Manage. **303**, 114257 (2022). https://doi.org/10.1016/j.jenvman.2021.114257
23. Vigoroso, L., Caffaro, F., Micheletti Cremasco, M., Cavallo, E.: Innovating occupational safety training: a scoping review on digital games and possible applications in agriculture. Int. J. Environ. Res. Public Health **18**(4), 1868 (2021). https://doi.org/10.3390/ijerph18041868

Virtual Reality Headsets for Work-Related Stress Among Midwives

Aglaia Gantzopoulou[1](✉), José Abdelnour-Nocera[2], Athina Belsi[3], Linda McDonald[4], Teresa Macchia[5], Gulsah Cetinkaya[6], Dionysios Kokkoris[1], and Makrina Savvidou[7]

[1] School of Computing and Engineering, University of West London, London, UK
aiglimid@gmail.com
[2] Sociotechnical Group for Innovation and UX, University of West London, London, UK
[3] Clinical Communication, Imperial College, London, London, UK
[4] Mental Health Nursing, University of West London, London, UK
[5] Computer Science, University of West London, London, UK
[6] Research and Development, Chelsea and Westminster Hospital, London, UK
[7] Department of Obstetrics and Gynaecology, Chelsea and Westminster Hospital, London, UK

Abstract. In the healthcare profession, workloads are often demanding, with long working hours and unpredictable schedules. Work-related stress is prevalent in a variety of professions, including the field of midwifery. A combination of their work and the inherent emotional and physical demands may result in anxiety, depression or exhaustion. In recent years, virtual reality (VR) has been explored as a tool for mental health treatments. By wearing VR headsets, individuals can immerse themselves in calming environments or engage in activities that reduce stress and promote positive emotions. However, a new approach to personalisation is needed that provides users with techniques more appropriate to their needs and preferences. Human-Work Interaction Design (HWID) research can steer and play an important role as it influences the human-work interaction design process by understanding user needs and requirements. This research paper summarises a randomised controlled trial to investigate the effectiveness of Virtual Reality (VR) headsets in reducing work-related stress among midwives in maternity services. This novel study will assess the impact of VR-based relaxation devices on midwives' emotional well-being and stress levels, as well as explore the user experience. The results from the study are expected to contribute valuable insights into the potential benefits of implementing Virtual Reality in healthcare settings to improve staff mental wellness and work performance as well as improve VR design for relaxation and interventions from a User Experience (UX) perspective.

Keywords: Work-related stress · Burnout · Midwives · Well-being · Virtual reality · Relaxation · Healthcare

B. R. Barricelli et al. (Eds.): HWID 2024, IFIP AICT 751, pp. 93–109, 2026.
https://doi.org/10.1007/978-3-031-95334-7_6

1 Introduction

A wealth of literature has documented midwives' positive impact on healthcare [13, 22, 54]. Midwives play a vital role in providing quality and safe care to women, newborns, and adolescents in sexual and reproductive health [15], as well as in contributing to research and education [10]. Midwifery care is associated with a reduced need for obstetric interventions, improved birth outcomes, and more efficient use of healthcare resources [54]. However, despite its crucial importance, it is a challenging and ever-evolving profession [52]. It can be critical, as making the appropriate decisions requires constant and careful attention [27]. In addition, traumatic birth events, birth-related trauma and adverse pregnancy outcomes are integral parts of this professional role [60]. As such, midwives are at a greater risk of developing work-related burnout than other fields of medicine [4, 19, 45], leading to up to 30–40% of sickness absence [53]. Workers' health and well-being are critical to Britain's future and worldwide [20]. An individual's mental well-being is defined as the capacity to succeed, cope with, and adapt to change and uncertainty, as well as work and live productively [59].

Wellness in the field of work is one of the most critical elements for contemporary organisations, as global, technological, and social changes in the twenty-first century constantly affect work and workers [20]. Employers should encourage well-being to decrease stress and burnout at work. It is challenging for organisations to ensure long-term success, as they must value employees as workers and individuals. Despite the efforts for interventions to support workers' mental health needs, several reasons, such as miscommunication, regulations and policies, stigma, and others, can pose challenges and barriers to individuals accessing them at the workplace [32]. Thus, there is a need to develop and evaluate new interventions to offer cost-effectiveness and easy access and reduce stigma compared to the traditional ones [7].

Virtual Reality (VR) is a newly developed technology that creates three-dimensional simulated environments. The term comes from two words: 'virtual', which means close by, and 'reality', which refers to human experience [28]. This technology features a head-mounted display and presents a screen the size of a room. With the use of software, it creates an artificial environment that can be accepted as a real one [28]. By wearing the headsets, users are located in different worlds, and through vision, sound and movements, they interact with virtual objects [39]. In that way, users can be transferred to calm and peaceful natural environments that reduce stress [25]. Environmental psychology says natural environments have numerous relaxing and calming benefits. Visiting nature can relieve stress and soothe emotional strain. Nevertheless, access to restorative environments is hampered by various factors, such as specific working environments or medical treatments. It is believed that immersion in natural virtual environments, in such circumstances, can have similar positive effects [37].

Research so far has shown VR's contribution to alleviating symptoms of depression and anxiety disorders. Its therapeutic process is based on interactive scenarios designed to reduce symptoms such as negative thinking and tension [31]. This technology can immerse users in virtual environments such as beaches or forests to reduce stress [50]. Engagement with bright and highly saturated colours can improve their mood and motivation [37]. However, personalising natural VR scenarios can be a critical component in facilitating users' sense of presence and relaxation [22]. Thus, a new approach to this field is needed that provides users with techniques more appropriate to their needs and preferences [46]. This novel study explores the potential of using virtual reality to improve staff well-being and productivity in maternity settings, as well as contributes to HWID by suggesting interfaces through human-centred approach that reduces mental workloads in their daily work in a hospital. Thus, it aims to improve VR design for relaxation and interventions from a User Experience (UX) and adoption perspective.

2 Related Research

The National Health Service (NHS) is the single biggest employer in the UK, with over 1.5 million individuals. Work-related stress is estimated to be responsible for 40% of all NHS employee sickness absences [48], and it is considered the second biggest occupational health problem in England, costing £3.6 billion annually [53]. Chronic occupational stress, defined as burnout [54], may lead to a variety of symptoms such as fatigue, tension headaches, concentrating problems or memory loss, abnormal sleep patterns and sometimes alcohol or drug abuse [27]. There is an estimate that occupational stress is associated with upwards of 120,000 deaths on a yearly basis [23, 30].

A recent National Maternity Review highlighted that midwives are more likely than any other NHS staff group to experience work-related stress [19]. An overstretched maternity service situation can lead to midwives experiencing overwork, frustration, and exhaustion. This results in a rushed, brusque, or chaotic approach to maternal care [62]. Additional studies [26, 45] also highlighted that UK NHS midwives' stress levels were significantly higher than the general population, which has severe implications for delivering high-quality and safe maternity care. Moreover, Hunter *et al.* [26] reported that an online survey among 1,997 midwives showed that 36.7% scored from moderate to severe stress, 38% to anxiety and 33% to depression. Aside from that, Jun *et al.* [30] underlined that burnout and especially emotional exhaustion endanger medical errors and are associated negatively with the safety and quality of care, patients' satisfaction and organisational productivity. According to the Royal College of Midwives (RCM), midwives face colossal pressures due to workplace issues. It is estimated that there is a shortage of over 2000 full-time midwives in England, with June 2022 figures showing a 12-month drop of 677 midwives [53]. According to several publications [3, 10, 19, 21, 27, 44], early-career midwives are the most likely to report burnout and intention to leave the profession despite attempts to resolve the growing midwifery staffing crisis. In addition, 25% of student midwives in the UK leave the course before qualifying [19].

In healthcare, job satisfaction and motivational factors significantly influence employees' well-being [18, 57]. Employers are generally responsible for supporting midwives' emotional well-being and mental health to retain a motivated and healthy workforce [53]. Cull et al. [19] presented a survey of 500 midwives for job satisfaction, where 400 stated that good teamwork is a protective factor against occupational stress. However, it is imperative for employers to develop strategies for preventing and mitigating anxiety, work-related stress, and burnout in maternity services [3, 57].

2.1 Challenges Associated with Current Well-Being Interventions

Despite workplace mental wellness being recognised as a critical policy issue for over two decades, challenges arise with several interventions for managing occupational stress [9]. There are numerous resources available to staff, including helplines, online therapy and group counselling sessions, peer support or 'buddy' programs, as well as online tools designed to help manage anxiety and sleeping difficulties [33]. However, Kinman and Teoh [33] and Keyworth et al. [32] argued that healthcare workers are frequently stigmatised, hindering seeking help. Moreover, all NHS organisations must have policies on managing work-related stress. Nonetheless, challenges arise in implementing, communicating, and understanding those policies [32, 33]. Yet, most workplace wellbeing initiatives, like relaxation or mindfulness meditation, involve skills that are difficult to learn and usually taught by therapists, so they are hard to implement during work [1].

In a randomised controlled trial conducted by Brinkmann et al. [14], the authors compared heart rate variability-biofeedback (HRV-Bfb) with mindfulness-based interventions (MBI) to reduce work-related stress over six weeks. Even though both methods were found to reduce stress, significant challenges have been identified for their application in workplace settings. In midwifery, a Professional Midwifery Advocate (PMA) role was formulated in April 2017 to support midwives in improving their wellbeing [6]. However, barriers such as the availability of advocates and the physical space to have the sessions may hinder the role's success [52]. Last, Jourabchi *et al.* [29] assessed Benson's relaxation techniques to control muscle tension and reduce negative emotions among 65 midwives, concluding that it helps with long-term stress. Despite that, the authors suggested that these techniques would be better practised at home rather than in hospital settings due to the requirement of a silent environment and breathing concentration. Thus, there is a need to identify more effective interventions to reduce cost and stigma [7] and ensure they are flexible enough for medical staff to engage with [45].

2.2 VR for Stress Management

It has emerged recently that Virtual Reality (VR) can be an effective tool to reduce stress based on the principle that interacting with pleasant stimuli in our environment can produce positive emotions [49, 50, 61]. Starting in the 1990s, VR was investigated as a new method of treating various phobias, with reports of a significant reduction in anxiety levels [47]. Through the years, its dynamic growth has made it applicable to the military, psychology, and medicine as a therapy for mental disorders [31]. However, VR mechanisms remain unclear; leading hypotheses suggest that immersive VR contexts and distraction may improve stress control by competing memory or emotion channels that detract from stress-signalling pathways [17].

There has been a recent surge in interest in virtual reality as a method of dealing with workplace stress. With VR's maturation, that field will be a significant focus of study over the next decade [8]. Research so far has demonstrated the potential application of VR headsets for stress management in the workplace, where participants experience a certain degree of ease [2, 8, 40, 47, 56]. As a result of the positive findings, increasing evidence indicates that VR relaxation may be applied in the workplace as a staff support initiative, including healthcare workers [38, 63].

2.3 VR for Stress Relief in Medical Staff

In the early stages of the Covid-19 pandemic, Nijland *et al.* [41] conducted the first study of VR relaxation with medical staff. The authors found 39.9% less perceived stress after using VR. They also interviewed 51 participants, and the qualitative feedback showed increased levels of positive emotions such as calm, relaxation, and happiness among most respondents. However, the absence of a comparison group is a notable limitation of the study. On the other hand, Soh *et al.* [55] compared mindfulness practice with and without VR (only audio) among fifty-one healthcare professionals from several institutions in Singapore. Compared to the audio only, participants reported a reduction in negative mood states with VR intervention. Several attendees found the device too heavy. A similar study took place in the USA among 100 frontline healthcare workers during shift work to test if a Virtual reality plus neurofeedback (VR+NF) meditation experience is more effective than a standard audio-only one [58]. The VR+NF group showed a decrease in fatigue, confusion and vigour, such as an increase in happiness and calmness scales compared to the audio-only group, where no significant changes were noted.

In addition, Adhyaru and Kemp [1] performed research in 2022 to determine if a short VR nature experience could induce a positive mood in NHS clinicians in a fast-paced trauma service during the workday. Thirty-nine participants used the device for 10 min and reported significant increases in happiness and relaxation, while anger and anxiety significantly decreased. Moreover, Beverly *et al.* [11] piloted the VR effectiveness in the USA among 102 COVID-19 frontline healthcare workers. Even though it did not include a comparison group and lacked standardised measures, the conclusions from the study showed that one-third of the attendees met the cut-off for high stress before the session, compared to only 4% after the VR interaction, which makes VR an accessible short-term intervention for stress relief among front-line healthcare professionals. On the other hand, [12] also undertook a crossover study on 88 ICU caregivers for two sessions, one with VR and another without VR, just a usual break. However, this is the only study that evaluated participants before and after sessions and at the end of the work shift. Results showed no difference in fatigue at the end of the work shift, questioning short-lasting VR effects.

So far, all the above studies have included single sessions evaluating the short-term effects of VR interventions in healthcare settings. Alternatively, in a long-term view, Pascual *et al.* [43] compared a VR-based meditation to a standalone mobile meditation application. The trial involved 32 participants in the USA, mainly medical students, for three VR sessions over four weeks. The findings proved VR-based meditation to be a feasible and accessible acute intervention, such as a more effective solution than mobile apps for healthcare clinicians. However, the study did not explore the user experience of the VR device. On the other hand, Williams and Riches [63] conducted the most recent VR study between 14 nurses in a psychiatric inpatient ward of a London hospital in a single session of 30 min. Despite the small number, the authors used qualitative and quantitative data collection methods to explore user experience in this study. They found significant decreases in anxiety, stress, and sadness, as well as a substantial increase in happiness, relaxation, and connectedness to nature. In most of the above studies, minor technical issues were noted with the Oculus Go VR headset, such as out-of-focus visuals, poor general quality, and freezing, which required a restart. Despite these technical difficulties, the positive outcomes support growing evidence that VR well-being interventions can be applied in healthcare workplace settings [1, 38, 51] and support research suggesting that VR can provide medical staff with rapid stress relief [49, 51].

2.4 Personalisation of VR

Last, a key element that can further facilitate users' sense of presence and relaxation is the personalisation of VR-based natural scenarios. Pardini *et al.* [42] conducted a study to understand the user experience between a standard and a personalised VR intervention. Findings showed that personalised VR interactions were preferred by participants who generally experienced a greater sense of immersion, pleasure, engagement, and relaxation compared to the standard one. In addition, Pizzoli *et al.*, [46] argued that despite its major costs, the personalised approach may result in more lasting and sophisticated relaxation in users. This new type of technique opens up a new area of study aimed at improving the experiences of people suffering from mental health problems in general and relaxation therapy in particular [24].

2.5 Human Work Interaction Design

Human Work Interaction Design is a comprehensive approach to Human Computer Interaction. A design artefact may connect work, analysis, and interaction design but may have different relations with these fields [16]. Various contextual factors, such as national, cultural, social, and organisational factors, influence users' interaction with technology. Users' interaction with technology in the workplace and in their daily lives is also influenced by the nature of the application domain, the tasks, and their skills and knowledge. A HWID framework is essential as it offers a structured approach to designing interactive systems that meet human needs and are aligned with work practices. By bridging the gap between human-computer interaction (HCI) and work analysis, it ensures that systems are not only functional, but also efficient [16].

3 Methodology

Midwives working in a busy Antenatal Clinic of a North West London NHS Trust were recruited for this study to create two groups. The Trust's statistician's input was advised for the sample size calculation. A target sample size was estimated based on a prior sample size calculation of similar studies with pwr.t.test in the language R. Three inputs were used: 1) sig. level = 0.05, 2) power = 0.8 and 3) effect size:0.72. The output calculated the sample size of each group of 15, so a total of 30 participants.

One group uses the Virtual Reality (VR) headset while on a break at work, and the other is socialising with colleagues while on a work break. Posters were displayed in the staff room and midwives willing to learn more details about the study and possibly participate were given the Participants Information Sheet (PIS) and time to make an informed decision. Participants who decided to participate were contacted face-to-face to express any questions and complete the screening questionnaire and the consent form. Individuals with a history of epilepsy, vertigo, motion sickness, current facial injuries or regularly used VR were excluded from the study. The randomisation process was performed on the computer (computer-generated random numbers). Midwives who met the criteria and were willing to participate were approached during their breaks. Participants in the Intervention Group interacted with the VR headsets in a calm and quiet environment in the author's presence for three sessions each. Participants in the Control Group approached on their break wherever they wished to socialise for three sessions. Participants were asked not to share any feedback from the sessions until the study finished to avoid influence between them. The Intervention Group received Virtual reality-based relaxation with the Smileyscope VR headset for 3 sessions, once per week for 8 min each. This included relaxation-calming virtual environments based on the water, designed to reduce stress and induce relaxation (see Fig. 1, Fig. 2, Fig. 3).

Fig. 1. Relaxation-calming virtual environment based on beach scenario.

Fig. 2. Relaxation-calming virtual environment based on lake scenario.

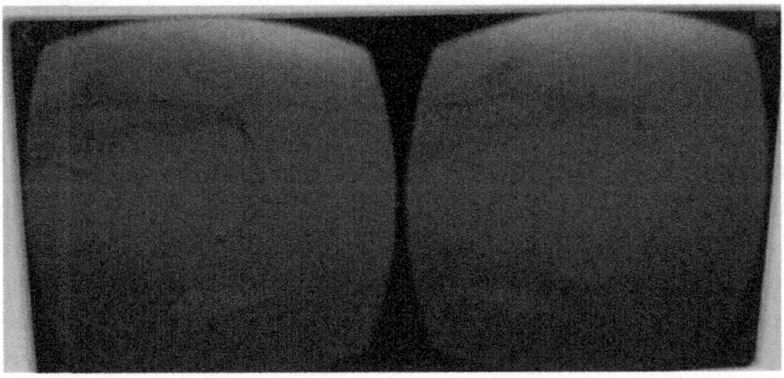

Fig. 3. Relaxation-calming virtual environment based on underwater scenario.

A pilot study was carried out with maternity staff about how they would find the idea of trying the VR headset as a stress relief option on the break, and very positive feedback was gathered. Also, peer support was carried out with the Smileyscope VR headset to get feedback on the time of use and topics to be explored. Seven members of staff tried the device and reported:

- Feeling a bit dizzy in 10 min, but not in 6 min
- Prefer a combination of different topics in water landscapes as it is more exciting
- Members who wear glasses felt a bit uncomfortable at 10 min due to the d vice's pressure on the glasses.

Also, timeframes were discussed and finalised with respect to their break time (to avoid break abuse).

Mixed research methods were used for collecting qualitative and quantitative data. Data was collected by using the Perceived Stress Scale (PSS-10) [36] and Brunel Mood Scale questionnaires [5, 35], by checking the Heart rate levels and by conducting semi-structured interviews online on Microsoft Teams to gather feedback:

- on VR headsets' usability, design, acceptability, adoption, user experience, and effects on stress relief (in the intervention group) and
- to assess stress relief without using VR and socialising with colleagues (in the control group).

Data were analysed using mixed methods in SPSS to assess statistical differences before and after the sessions in both groups. The themes of the interviews emerged based on the interview questions using Nvivo computer software.

4 Results

The active participation of 30 midwives, who eagerly completed the three sessions and pre- and post-questionnaires, significantly contributed to the study. We interviewed 26 of them, and their insights have been instrumental in shaping our research. Four midwives were unable to attend the interviews due to the demanding workload at that time.

Using a Mann-Whitney U test, our SPSS analysis of the Brunes Mood scale revealed a profound difference between the two groups in the variables of tension, calmness, and heart rate levels. In the VR group, tension ($p = 0{,}034$, $U = 63$, $Z = -2{,}11$) and heart rate ($p < 0{,}01$, $U = 8.5$, $Z = -4.3$) were significantly reduced, while calmness ($p = 0{,}021$, $U = 57$, $Z = -2{,}3$) was significantly increased, compared to the control group. No difference was reported in anger, depression, vigour, fatigue and confusion between the two groups. The happiness variable is close to significance, indicating a potential increase in the VR group (see Table 1).

Table 1. Mann-Whitney U test to compare the distributions between VR and control group

Test Statistics[a]

	Anger_Diff	Tension_Diff	Depresssion_Diff	Vigour_Diff	Fatigue_Diff	Confusion_Diff	Happy_Diff	Calmness_Diff	heart_diff
Mann-Whitney U	110.000	63.000	98.000	105.000	111.000	105.000	69.500	57.000	8.500
Wilcoxon W	230.000	183.000	218.000	225.000	231.000	225.000	189.500	177.000	128.500
Z	-.111	-2.115	-.654	-.313	-.063	-.321	-1.804	-2.313	-4.319
Asymp. Sig. (2-tailed)	.911	.034	.513	.754	.950	.748	.071	.021	<.001
Exact Sig. [2*(1-tailed Sig.)]	.935[b]	.041[b]	.567[b]	.775[b]	.967[b]	.775[b]	.074[b]	.021[b]	<.001[b]

a. Grouping Variable: group

b. Not corrected for ties.

The interviews have formed the following themes:

Theme 1 - VR Design. Our research underscores the profound impact of VR applications, particularly their personalisation options, on midwives' stress relief. The sense of realism these applications provide further enhances the experience, making it more engaging and interesting for the users.

Quotes that illustrate the point are:

- 'Feeling at ease, relaxed, and content.'
- 'I felt calm and relaxed'
- 'I found the beach scenario more relaxing than the others.'
- 'I would rather listen to the waves' sound than background music. That would help to relax more.'
- 'The background music is a bit distracting.'

Thirteen of the fifteen midwives who tried the VR technology reported feeling relaxed and reducing their stress levels after the sessions. One reported no difference, and one reported feeling more stressed after, as she didn't enjoy the interaction. The most reported relaxing scenario was the beach and then the underwater one. Moreo-ver, most of the participants asked if we could change the background music. The background music was fixed in the Smileyscope VR device, and no further options were available. By examining the personalised factor, we can see how different types of scenarios affect calmness and stress levels individually.

Theme 2—VR Interaction. This theme examines how interactive features within VR applications can enhance user experience and reduce stress.

Quotes that illustrate the point are:

- 'The moving scenarios were more engaging and interesting.'
- 'Jumping from one scenario to the other is slightly unsettled.'
- 'With the same scenarios, you may actually lose interest in.'
- 'I actually felt in the moment.'
- 'It actually felt like I kind of wanted to get down and walk amongst the beach.'
- 'I think the novelty of it all is wearing off, with the same scenarios you may lose interest in.'

Most of the participants reported being well-engaged with the scenarios. However, in the long term, 2/3 of them reported they would prefer different scenarios in every interaction to keep their interest higher with the element of surprise. It is possible to become bored with constantly predictable experiences. The surprise element breaks this predictability, keeping the experience enjoyable.

Theme 3 – UX (User Experience). This section explores the overall user experience of midwives using VR for stress relief, satisfaction, emotional reactions, and adverse reactions.

Quotes that illustrate the point are:

- 'It didn't fit my face; I was holding it, which was annoying.'
- 'It felt heavier and uncomfortable with glasses in a sitting position'
- 'I felt sad when I had to stop the sessions'
- 'It allowed me to take a proper break and relax'
- 'My head was completely relaxed without stress or anxiety.'
- 'On the day of the scheduled VR session, I was excited all day, waiting for the session.'

The VR experience was positively received, with most midwives reporting significant stress reduction. Two-thirds of them mentioned it didn't affect their motivation to return to work, but half of them highlighted that when they started the afternoon clinic, they felt more proactive due to reduced stress levels. Moreover, two of the participants found the headset heavy and a bit uncomfortable, while the rest thirteen didn't report any discomfort. None of the participants reported adverse reactions in the 8-min interaction, and neither were asked to stop any of the sessions. The constructive feedback highlighted areas for improvement, such as using VR while wearing glasses, better head-mounted headset adjustment, or a solution for lighter devices.

Theme 4 – Use of Interventions in Hospital Settings. This theme explores VR interventions' implementation, practicality, and accessibility in a healthcare environment.

Quotes that illustrate the point are:

- 'You can use the VR on your break quite comfortably.'
- 'The VR is compatible with the work breaks; you still have time to eat.'
- 'We don't have the culture to support relaxation at work breaks.'

The schedule of using the VR for 8 min once per week proved feasible for hospital settings.

Theme 5 – Short and Long-Term Use of VR. This theme presents data obtained from participants on VR's long-term and short-term use.

Quotes that illustrate the point are:

- "I felt relaxed for the whole afternoon.'
- 'The stress relief lasted maybe an hour, then the stress built up again.'
- 'I was relaxed for a couple of hours'

Most of the midwives mentioned that the stress relief from the VR interaction lasted a couple of hours, which concludes with short-term relaxation effects.

Theme 6—Effects of Routine Breaks at Work. This theme shows how routine breaks at work affect midwives.

Quotes that illustrate the point are:

- 'It's not a real break because you just keep thinking about what you need to do after.'
- 'You keep thinking; the brain can't switch off.'
- 'If I don't have a break, I get more stressed.'
- 'I always feel like there is so much to do. It feels wrong taking time out.'
- 'I feel rushed and tired, and I am just thinking about what's happening next.'
- 'We don't have time to change clothes and go out for a walk'

Most of the midwives in the control group reported that the break is needed as it helps them relax and rest for the afternoon clinic. However, 1/3 of the participants mentioned that the high workload generally doesn't allow them to get a proper break, or even if they take one, they cannot switch off as they are overthinking about the rest of the shift. In such situations, relaxing and reaping the benefits of a break may be difficult. Also, due to the nature of the job, it isn't easy to spend a break outside of the hospital setting.

5 Discussion

The main result from the study is that an 8-min VR session for midwives in maternity settings is feasible and beneficial. Overall, the participants were interested in repeating the experience and would use this technology if it was available at work. As a result of our findings, we add weight to the growing body of literature suggesting that virtual reality has the potential to be an effective tool for reducing stress and promoting relaxation [1].

Self-reported measures of effect revealed that the VR interaction was associated with a significant increase in calmness and a significant reduction in participants' heart rate levels and tension. In contrast with other similar studies, VR, in our case, didn't affect fatigue [12]. Qualitative data supported the quantitative results and enhanced the understanding of participants' thoughts and feelings. The VR experience was positively received, with most midwives reporting feeling less stressed and more relaxed, lasting a couple of hours. A significant finding was that in most of the cases, the interaction didn't affect their motivation to go back to work; however, half of the participants reported that when they started the afternoon clinic, they felt more proactive due to reduced stress levels. No significant difference was noted in depression and fatigue; for happiness, a potential effect was indicated, but further investigation with a larger sample size is needed.

To our best knowledge, this is the first paper investigating the effectiveness and feasibility of virtual reality in maternity settings, especially among midwives. The positive outcomes support growing evidence that VR well-being interventions can be applied in healthcare workplace settings [1, 38, 51] and support research suggesting that VR can provide medical staff with rapid stress relief [49, 51]. In addition, it highlights the importance of the personalised factor, which links with a greater sense of immersion, pleasure, engagement, and relaxation [42]. Last, this study points out areas for improvement, such as using VR while wearing glasses, better head-mounted headset adjustment, or a solution for lighter devices, providing insights on how to improve VR design for relaxation and interventions from a User Experience (UX) perspective. Improvements and developments can be considered on several fronts. This study's participants were mostly 30–50-year-old White/English/Welsh/Scottish/Irish females, reflecting the demographics of the staff working in the Trust's antenatal clinic. Future studies should seek a more representative sample of medical staff in maternity settings. Also, a long-term approach would enable us to evaluate the impact of regular VR sessions during work breaks on various factors, including employee retention and job satisfaction.

Human Work Interaction Design is a comprehensive approach to Human Computer Interaction. A design artefact may connect work, analysis, and interaction design but may have different relations with these fields [16].

Looking at the framework in Fig. 4, we can discuss that VR is a mediating work artefact and could be improved for design. In our case, the nature of the midwifery profession often includes long shifts, emotional stress and high-pressure situations. Adopting the VR solution expands the physical and active space where midwives operate and generates an opportunity to decompress and step away from the challenges and risks of their work and profession. The artefact itself becomes a space to act or better in(act) within. The core relation among Human Work (midwives' tasks), Artefact (VR), and Interaction Design (How VR is designed to interact with individuals) becomes the one that is invisible but transformative, which subsequently changes the way to work as discussed above. Midwives are not just using the VR device; the device transforms how they work. VR systems may subtly affect how individuals think, respond to stress, or improve muscle memory without their full awareness at the time. A deeper understanding of this invisible relationship and how technology affects the work environment will allow designers to create more effective and user-centred systems for work. Work environments like hospital settings or medical clinics require design that not only makes tools more straightforward to use but also considers the overall work experience.

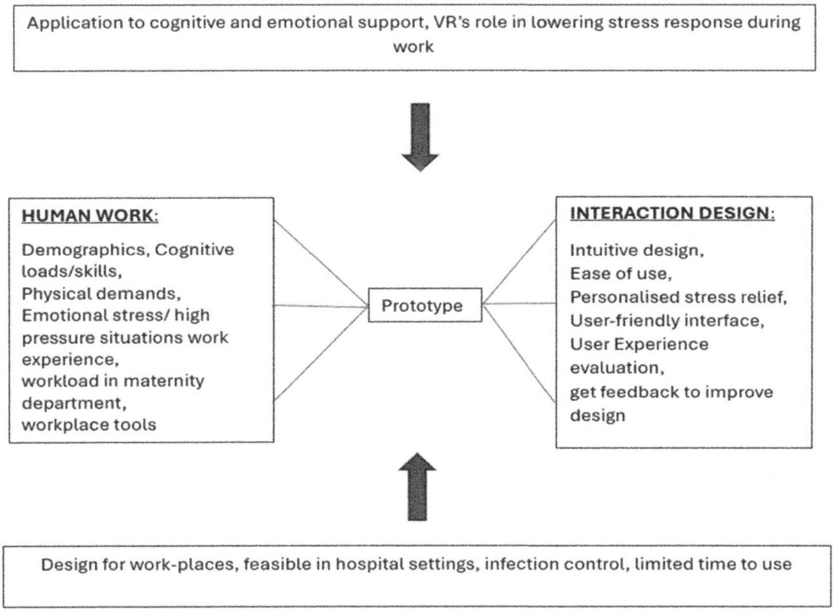

Fig. 4. HWID for VR in work-related stress in midwives.

In our case, VR isn't just about creating a relaxing VR experience for midwives; rather, it is about incorporating it into their emotional rhythms throughout the day. Stress-reduction tools have to be designed with an understanding of how they might affect the mental state of the employee throughout a working shift, and not only during the period when they are interacting directly with the system. The work environment involves more than simply completing tasks. It also serves as a place for managing emotions, cognitive functions, and physical stress.

An effective design should be fluid and supportive, integrating seamlessly into the work process rather than adding a new task to the workflow. The ability to accomplish this requires a deep understanding of how medical staff move through their daily routines, pressures, time, and the mental space they need. Thus, considering the limited time they can spend on a VR during their break and the personalised factor, VR should support options for individuals to select the time of use or the preferred topics for that moment.

6 Conclusion

In summary, Midwifery is a challenging profession, and midwives are at a greater risk of developing work-related psychological distress or burnout, leading to 40% of sickness absence. A central theme revolves around the correlation between job burnout and poor quality of care, lower job satisfaction and increased employee resignations, apart from the financial burden. Despite the efforts to improve staff mental well-being, there are many challenges and barriers for individuals accessing interventions at the workplace. Virtual reality is a newly developed technology that has been proven to reduce symptoms of anxiety and stress, by transferring users to calm and peaceful natural environments. HWID allows designers to identify the complex, yet often unseen dynamics that influence work environments, focus on a work experience that transcends task-based design and provide adaptable and flexible systems that follow the user's needs as they change.

This paper contributes to HWID research by introducing these interfaces for medical staff and proposing ways to reduce their physical and mental workload in hospital settings. This novel study's findings indicated that a short VR relaxation interaction during a workplace break can reduce stress and increase calmness among midwives. Its advantages compared to other methods are its cost-effectiveness, rapid effects, and ease of access and implementation in hospital settings. This is a relatively new field; thus, more evaluations should be conducted in more methodologically robust studies. Also, more qualitative feedback from users and more adaptive technologies will improve the design to reach the very end user and mitigate the challenges around UCD for successful and sustainable VR interactions. Thus, we can further evaluate if VR can affect job satisfaction and staff retention and be the future solution to the prominent staff crisis issue, not only in midwifery but in various healthcare professions in the UK and beyond.

Approvals. Chelsea and Westminster Hospital agreed to Sponsor the study. HRA, HCRW and UWL ethical approvals were received in January 2024.

Acknowledgments. We want to acknowledge the support provided by CW+ by lending us the Smileyscope VR headset device, which made this research possible, as well as thank all the participants for their time and feedback.

Disclosure of Interests. The authors have no competing interests to declare that are relevant to the content of this article.

References

1. Adhyaru, J.S., Kemp, C.: Virtual reality as a tool to promote wellbeing in the workplace. Digit. Health **8**, 205520762210844 (2022)
2. Ahmaniemi, T., Lindholm, H., Muller, K., Taipalus, T.: Virtual reality experience as a stress recovery solution in workplace. In: 2017 IEEE Life Sciences Conference (LSC), Sydney, NSW, pp. 206–209. IEEE (2017)
3. Albendín-García, L., Suleiman-Martos, N., Cañadas-De la Fuente, G.A., Ramírez-Baena, L., Gómez-Urquiza, J.L., De la Fuente-Solana, E.I.: Prevalence, related factors, and levels of burnout among midwives: a systematic review. J. Midwife Womens Health **66**(1), 24–44 (2021)
4. Amir, Z., Reid, A.J.: Impact of traumatic perinatal events on burnout rates among midwives. Occup. Med. **70**(8), 602–605 (2020)
5. Andrade, A., Cruz, W.M.D., Correia, C.K., Santos, A.L.G., Bevilacqua, G.G.: Effect of practice exergames on the mood states and self-esteem of elementary school boys and girls during physical education classes: a cluster-randomized controlled natural experiment. PLoS ONE **15**, e0232392 (2020)
6. Andrews, J., Todd, S., Armato-Harris, P.: The academic PMA....Supporting the future midwifery workforce. TPM **26**(02), 42–46 (2023)

7. Armaou, M., Konstantinidis, S., Blake, H.: The effectiveness of digital interventions for psychological well-being in the workplace: a systematic review protocol. IJERPH **17**(1), 255 (2019)
8. Arora, S., Mahapatra, M.: Virtual reality as a solution for workplace stress. **10**(1) (2022)
9. Bajorek, Z., Holmes, J.: Health and Wellbeing Interventions in Healthcare A rapid evidence review. (2020)
10. Båtsman, A., Fahlbeck, H., Hildingsson, I.: Depression, anxiety and stress in Swedish midwives: a cross-sectional survey. Eur. J. Midwifery **4** (2020)
11. Beverly, E., et al.: A tranquil virtual reality experience to reduce subjective stress among COVID-19 frontline healthcare workers. PLoS One **17**(2), e0262703 (2022)
12. Bodet-Contentin, L., Letourneur, M., Ehrmann, S.: Virtual reality during work breaks to reduce fatigue of intensive unit caregivers: a crossover, pilot, randomised trial. Aust. Crit. Care **36**(3), 345–349 (2023)
13. Bradfield, Z., Officer, K., Barnes, C., Mignacca, E., Butt, J., Hauck, Y.: Sexual and reproductive health education: midwives' confidence and practices. Women Birth **35**(4), 360–366 (2022)
14. Brinkmann, A.E., Press, S.A., Helmert, E., Hautzinger, M., Khazan, I., Vagedes, J.: Comparing effectiveness of HRV-biofeedback and mindfulness for workplace stress reduction: a randomized controlled trial. Appl. Psychophysiol. Biofeedback **45**(4), 307–322 (2020)
15. Carvajal, B., Hancock, A., Lewney, K., Hagan, K., Jamieson, S., Cooke, A.: A global overview of midwives' working conditions: a rapid review of literature on positive practice environment. Women Birth **37**(1), 15–50 (2024)
16. Clemmensen, T.: A human work interaction design (HWID) case study in e-government and public information systems. Int. J. Public Inf. Syst. **3** (2011)
17. Colloca, L., et al.: Virtual reality: physiological and behavioral mechanisms to increase individual pain tolerance limits. Pain **161**(9), 2010–2021 (2020)
18. Cramer, E., Hunter, B.: Relationships between working conditions and emotional wellbeing in midwives. Women Birth **32**(6), 521–532 (2019)
19. Cull, J., Hunter, B., Henley, J., Fenwick, J., Sidebotham, M.: "Overwhelmed and out of my depth": responses from early career midwives in the United Kingdom to the Work, Health and Emotional Lives of Midwives study. Women Birth **33**(6), e549–e557 (2020)
20. Cvenkel, N.: Well-Being in the Workplace: Governance and Sustainability Insights to Promote Workplace Health. Springer Nature (2020)
21. Elliott, R., Fry, M.: Psychological capital, well-being, and patient safety attitudes of nurses and midwives: a cross-sectional survey. Nurs. Health Sci. **23**(1), 237–244 (2021)
22. Gillen, P., et al.: Wellbeing and coping of UK nurses, midwives and allied health professionals during COVID-19-a cross-sectional study. PLOS One **17**(9), e0274036 (2022)
23. Goh, J., Pfeffer, J., Zenios, S.A.: The relationship between workplace stressors and mortality and health costs in the United States. Manage. Sci. **62**(2), 608–628 (2016)
24. Heyse, J., De Jonge, T., Vega, M.T., De Backere, F., De Turck, F.: A personalized virtual reality experience for relaxation therapy. In: 2019 Eleventh International Conference on Quality of Multimedia Experience (QoMEX), Berlin, Germany, pp. 1–3. IEEE (2019)
25. Hsieh, C.H., Yang, J.Y., Huang, C.W., Chin, W.C.B.: The effect of water sound level in virtual reality: a study of restorative benefits in young adults through immersive natural environments. J. Environ. Psychol. **88**, 102012 (2023)
26. Hunter, B., Fenwick, J., Sidebotham, M., Henley, J.: Midwives in the United Kingdom: levels of burnout, depression, anxiety and stress and associated predictors. Midwifery **79**, 102526 (2019)
27. Janighorban, M., Dadkhahtehrani, T., Najimi, A., Hafezi, S.: The correlation between psychological empowerment and job burnout in midwives working in the labor ward of hospitals. Iran. J. Nurs. Midwifery Res. **25**(2), 128–133 (2020)

28. Javaid, M., Haleem, A.: Virtual reality applications toward medical field. Clin. Epidemiol. Glob. Health **8**(2), 600–605 (2020)
29. Jourabchi, Z., Satari, E., Mafi, M., Ranjkesh, F.: Effects of Benson's relaxation technique on occupational stress in midwives. Nursing **50**(9), 64–68 (2020)
30. Jun, J., Ojemeni, M.M., Kalamani, R., Tong, J., Crecelius, M.L.: Relationship between nurse burnout, patient and organizational outcomes: systematic review. Int. J. Nurs. Stud. **119**, 103933 (2021)
31. Kamińska, D., Smółka, K., Zwoliński, G., Wiak, S., Merecz-Kot, D., Anbarjafari, G.: Stress reduction using bilateral stimulation in virtual reality. IEEE Access **8**, 200351–200366 (2020)
32. Keyworth, C., et al.: Barriers and enablers to accessing support services offered by staff wellbeing hubs: a qualitative study. Front. Psychol. **13**, 1008913 (2022)
33. Kinman, G., Teoh, K.: What could make a difference to the mental health of UK doctors? A review of the research evidence. Soc. Occup. Med. (2018)
34. Kinman, G., Teoh, K., Harriss, A.: Supporting the well-being of healthcare workers during and after COVID-19. Occup. Med. **70**(5), 294–296 (2020)
35. Lan, M.F., Lane, A.M., Roy, J., Hanin, N.A.: Validity of the Brunel mood scale for use with Malaysian athletes. J. Sports Sci. Med. **11**, 131–135 (2012)
36. Lee, E.-H.: Review of the psychometric evidence of the perceived stress scale. Asian Nurs. Res. **6**(4), 121–127 (2012)
37. Liszio, S., Graf, L., Masuch, M.: The relaxing effect of virtual nature: immersive technology provides relief in acute stress situations. Annu. Rev. Cyberther. Telemed. **16**, 87–93 (2018)
38. Mistry, D., et al.: Meditating in virtual reality: proof-of-concept intervention for posttraumatic stress. Psychol. Trauma Theory Res. Pract. Policy **12**(8), 847–858 (2020)
39. Mystakidis, S.: Metaverse. Encyclopedia **2**(1), 486–497 (2022)
40. Naylor, M., Ridout, B., Campbell, A.: A scoping review identifying the need for quality research on the use of virtual reality in workplace settings for stress management. Cyberpsychol. Behav. Soc. Netw. **23**(8), 506–518 (2020)
41. Nijland, J.M., Veling, W., Lestestuiver, B.P., Van Driel, C.M.: Virtual reality relaxation for reducing perceived stress of intensive care nurses during the COVID-19 pandemic. Front. Psychol. **12**, 706527 (2021)
42. Pardini, S., et al.: The role of personalization in the user experience, preferences and engagement with virtual reality environments for relaxation. IJERPH **19**(12), 7237 (2022)
43. Pascual, K., Fredman, A., Naum, A., Patil, C., Sikka, N.: Should mindfulness for health care workers go virtual? A mindfulness-based intervention using virtual reality and heart rate variability in the emergency department. Workplace Health Saf. **71**(4), 188–194 (2023)
44. Perry, L., Xu, X., Duffield, C., Gallagher, R., Nicholls, R., Sibbritt, D.: Health, workforce characteristics, quality of life and intention to leave: the 'Fit for the Future' survey of Australian nurses and midwives. J. Adv. Nurs. **73**(11), 2745–2756 (2017)
45. Pezaro, S., Clyne, W., Fulton, E.A.: A systematic mixed-methods review of interventions, outcomes and experiences for midwives and student midwives in work-related psychological distress. Midwifery **50**, 163–173 (2017)
46. Pizzoli, S.F.M., Mazzocco, K., Triberti, S., Monzani, D., Alcañiz Raya, M.L., Pravettoni, G.: User-centered virtual reality for promoting relaxation: an innovative approach. Front. Psychol. **10**, 479 (2019)
47. Pretsch, J., Pretsch, E., Saretzki, J., Kraus, H., Grossmann, G.: Improving employee well-being by means of virtual reality – REALEX: an empirical case study. Eur. J. Econ. Bus. Stud. **6**(1), 95 (2020)
48. Ravalier, J.M., McVicar, A., Boichat, C.: Work stress in NHS employees: a mixed-methods study. IJERPH **17**(18), 6464 (2020)

49. Riches, S., Azevedo, L., Bird, L., Pisani, S., Valmaggia, L.: Virtual reality relaxation for the general population: a systematic review. Soc. Psychiatry Psychiatr. Epidemiol. **56**(10), 1707–1727 (2021)
50. Riches, S., Smith, H.: Editorial: taking a break in the "new normal": virtual reality relaxation for a stressed workforce. MHRJ **27**(2), 133–136 (2022)
51. Riches, S., Taylor, L., Jeyarajaguru, P., Veling, W., Valmaggia, L.: Virtual reality and immersive technologies to promote workplace wellbeing: a systematic review. J. Mental Health 1–21 (2023)
52. Rouse, S.: The role of the PMA and barriers to the successful implementation of restorative clinical supervision. Br. J. Midwifery **27**(6), 381–386 (2019)
53. Royal College of Midwives (online) 'work-related stress'. https://www.rcm.org.uk/media/6370/work-related-stress.pdf. Accessed 20 Apr 2024
54. Sidhu, R., Su, B., Shapiro, K.R., Stoll, K.: Prevalence of and factors associated with burnout in midwifery: a scoping review. Eur. J. Midwifery **4** (2020)
55. Soh, D.J.H., et al.: Exploring the use of virtual reality for the delivery and practice of stress-management exercises. Front. Psychol. **12**, 640341 (2021)
56. Soni, A., Shete, S.: Mixed reality for stress relief. In: Proceedings of the Fourteenth International Conference on Tangible, Embedded, and Embodied Interaction, Sydney, NSW, Australia, pp. 937–942. ACM (2020)
57. Suleiman-Martos, N., et al.: Prevalence and predictors of burnout in midwives: a systematic review and meta-analysis. IJERPH **17**(2), 641 (2020)
58. Tarrant, J., Jackson, R., Viczko, J.: A feasibility test of a brief mobile virtual reality meditation for frontline healthcare workers in a hospital setting. Front. Virtual Real. **3**, 764745 (2022)
59. Teoh, K.R.H., Kinman, G., Harriss, A., Robus, C.: Recommendations to support the mental wellbeing of nurses and midwives in the United Kingdom: a Delphi study. J. Adv. Nurs. **78**(9), 3048–3060 (2022)
60. Toohill, J., Fenwick, J., Sidebotham, M., Gamble, J., Creedy, D.K.: Trauma and fear in Australian midwives. Women Birth **32**(1), 64–71 (2019)
61. Wang, X., Shi, Y., Zhang, B., Chiang, Y.: The influence of forest resting environments on stress using virtual reality. IJERPH **16**(18), 3263 (2019)
62. Warriner, S., Hunter, L., Dymond, M.: Mindfulness in maternity: evaluation of a course for midwives. Br. J. Midwifery **24**(3), 188–195 (2016)
63. Williams, G., Riches, S.: Virtual reality relaxation for staff wellbeing on a psychiatric rehabilitation ward: a feasibility and acceptability study. J. Psych. Intensive Care **19**(1), 51–58 (2023)

Serious Games: Changing the Environments in the Classrooms

Cristiano França[1(✉)], Genesis Betencourt[1], Frederica Gonçalves[1], and Pedro Campos[2]

[1] ITI/LARSyS, University of Madeira, Funchal, Portugal
crisfranca@live.com.pt
[2] ITI/LARSyS, University of Madeira, WowSystems, Funchal, Portugal

Abstract. The classroom environment has a substantial impact on the student's education journey. Not only the physical space where teaching and learning occur, but a dynamic ecosystem that shapes the attitudes, behaviour's, and academic outcomes of students. The objective of this research was to analyse and compare the motivation and engagement of students in two different classroom environments: traditional class and serious game class. The conducted study had 14 participants of which 5 experimented with the serious game while 9 had the conventional class. The results showed that the serious game developed motivated more students than the traditional class, providing positive feedback for future design of educational games, as well as introducing those games in classrooms.

Keywords: Classroom Environment · Serious Games · Motivation

1 Introduction

The classroom environment has a substantial impact on students in their learning process. Various factors such as school infrastructure, the ability of the teacher, and classroom interactions can influence the performance of students [1]. Recent research has shown that using information and communication technologies (ICT), having a competent teacher, and well-equipped school facilities could potentiate students' learning trajectory [4].

Despite the evolution in recent years, students still suffer from a common experience in schools: boredom. Addressing this challenge remains an ongoing struggle, as boredom can arise in multifaceted ways, becoming an obstacle for educators. Boredom can emerge from a lack of student engagement, when the teacher fails to engage the student with the subject, with repetitive or unchallenging content, and if the classroom doesn't have conditions. In this paper, we will focus on how to improve student engagement by changing the class environment.

In today's classes, teachers must create a better and more fun environment for their students to maintain focused learning of the subject. When this task fails, students can become bored and negatively influence their schooling.

Published by Springer Nature Switzerland AG 2026
B. R. Barricelli et al. (Eds.): HWID 2024, IFIP AICT 751, pp. 110–126, 2026.
https://doi.org/10.1007/978-3-031-95334-7_7

The continuous evolution of technology and the interest in putting together digital games to find ways to improve education, occupational choice, training, planning, and problem-solving originated the serious games [5]. Throughout the years many tried to give a true definition for what is a serious game, and taking into this literature review [6] gathered several definitions to try to categorize it. They conclude that a serious game enters two main categories: entertainment education and game-based learning.

In recent years, teachers started changing the traditional environment of the classroom introducing new ways of teaching alongside the evolution of technology. One of the methods was using serious games. Although the interest in serious games in the classroom has increased, there's still a lack of literature to understand if a serious game can have a real impact on students and change the traditional classroom environment [7]. Mostly serious games are designed to look into teaching the subject forgetting many times that students would only want to play if the game was fun in the first place. The application of narratives has been correlated with immersion, engagement, motivation, and learning gains. Using narratives in the design of the serious game can have an impact on creating a more dynamic game for the student [8]. The design of a serious game with the utilization of narratives can stimulate the student to personate as the player and motivate him to continue the story of the game while learning the subject, creating a favourable environment in the classroom [9].

Considering the two papers, [10, 11], where was explored complementary aspects of designing interactive systems to enhance user engagement and productivity in workplace settings. The first paper focuses on design principles that promote work engagement—such as empowerment, feedback, and social interaction—within interactive systems to create an environment where users feel energized, dedicated, and deeply absorbed in their tasks. In contrast, the second paper examine how the concepts of motivation, participation, and engagement are defined and measured in Human Work Interaction Design (HWID) literature, emphasizing the need for clear, standardized definitions and interdisciplinary approaches. Both papers highlight the importance of user-centred design in creating meaningful workplace interactions. Together, these studies underscore the need for thoughtfully designed systems that both address theoretical gaps and apply practical solutions to improve employee experience and well-being. Considering these two previous studies done based on HWID research, our study contributes to HWID research by examining how to redesign the school environment to be more digital, equipping students with tools they are already familiar with in their daily lives. This approach aims to boost student motivation while maintaining the integrity of the learning process. With this study we aim to provide more discussion on the utilization of serious games in schools and give more ideas on how to improve working places on schools.

2 Related Work

2.1 Student's Emotions on School Engagement and Academic Performance

There has been a significant increase in research on student engagement aimed at addressing and attempting to correct persistent educational problems such as low achievement, high dropout rates, and high rates of student boredom [12]. Several studies suggest that when experiencing boredom, individuals perceive their current situation as lacking in meaning, often because of insufficient stimulation. Recognizing boredom as an opportunity for exploration and change has the potential to boost creativity and imagination, as the mind combines various elements from the environment to produce fresh ideas and expressions [13]. For instance, certain researchers have discovered that when student's experiences are connected in a range of positive emotions, this can profoundly impact their engagement in the learning process. If students have a sense of enjoyment from academic tasks, they are more likely to invest greater effort and commitment to completing them. In contrast, students who feel stressed or frustrated tend to withdraw and disengage from learning [14].

While various theoretical approaches aim to boost student's motivation, it's crucial to recognize that school engagement is fundamental to student learning. Research indicates a strong correlation between student's motivation levels and how they navigate academic challenges throughout their educational journey [15].

2.2 Traditional Education Environment vs Modern Education Environment

Nowadays, there are different approaches through which individuals can pursue professional development, such as traditional education (presential classes) and virtual education (online classes) standing out as prominent options. Each of these approaches has its positive and negative aspects. In modern learning, the use of multimedia devices such as television, videos, CD-ROMs, websites, and computer software provide a more diverse and engaging learning environment for students. This significantly improves the educational process, as the use of digital tools increases the interaction between the student and the content, which in turn enhances students' motivation and facilitates the acquisition of new skills. Also, the flexibility of online education provides teachers and learners with more freedom, as well as a wide variety of learning contents and easy access. However, among its disadvantages, the lack of humanistic care and supervision for students and their learning effects stand out [11]. On the other hand, traditional learning is more focused on the information transfer paradigm: the teacher transfers information to the students, who act solely as passive consumers. This traditional approach centred on passive instruction, requiring little or no reaction from students beyond listening, watching, and taking notes [14, 15].

Studies have shown that nowadays there are some professors who still attach to traditional educational methods. However, it's rare to find professors who don't utilize any form of modern technology or equipment in the classroom. Consequently, various devices have been created to assist teachers in the classroom, helping to reduce desk work by replacing textbooks and reports with workstations or tablets containing all necessary data for the class. Furthermore, research highlights that student's homework assignments, with the exception of cases where specific teacher guidance is needed, can naturally be facilitated by software tools, such as Google, Wikipedia, and YouTube, which are easily accessible [16, 17].

In other ways, studies have shown that the way students learn can influence their academic performance. Research has compared how traditional education and modern education influence students' literacy skills, including reading and writing. Digital education platforms of various kinds were utilized, enabling teachers and students to discuss and access educational content, as well as the use of tablets. At the end of both studies, it was demonstrated that students who completed tasks through a digital environment, as well as with the use of tablets, had better skill performance than students who did in the traditional environment [14, 18].

2.3 New Technologies and Gamification

The development of the technologies accelerates the transformation of the education industry, leading to the implementation of new technologies aimed at enhancing and dynamically conveying the concepts of academic subjects [16]. For instance, the schools are trying to implement some online activities that are designed for improving the participation of the students, such as discussion forums. In fact, much research has been conducted that shows the positive impact of participation by students in some e-learning activities [21].

Not only have technologies been implemented to enhance communication between students and teachers, but there are also various technologies that are used to transform classroom instruction, making teaching more dynamic for students. For instance, studies focused on mobile learning have shown that, overall, the use of this technology enhances students' academic performance by providing rich learning resources, educational accessibility, personalized learning, and facilitating time management. However, like everything else, it has its downside. There is a minority of students over 30 years old who have expressed discomfort in using mobile devices for learning. Additionally, the main problems identified in studies include distractions, device failures, and inadequate supervision [20, 21].

Digitalization in schools plays a transformative role in education, offering more personalized and engaging learning experiences for students. Digital tools empower educators to cater to diverse student needs, making learning more flexible and interactive. This personalization fosters not only academic success but also encourages lifelong learning by equipping students with essential digital skills for the future [24]. However, teachers are critical to the success of digital integration. They must develop both pedagogical and technical competencies, and their attitudes toward technology greatly influence how effectively digital tools are incorporated into classroom practice [25].

Furthermore, the digitalization process requires strong leadership and support structures within schools. The importance of distributed leadership, where responsibility for technology integration is shared across various levels, from teachers to students. Collaboration and innovation are key to creating a culture that embraces technology [26]. Likewise, the need for instructional coaches to support and guide teachers through the complexities of integrating new technologies [27]. By addressing challenges like resource limitations and fostering teacher confidence, schools can fully leverage digitalization to enhance both teaching practices and student outcomes.

2.4 HWID and Serious Games

HWID is an emergent approach that aims at connecting studies of work and the workplace with interaction design [28]. Also, is a comprehensive approach in HCI, and to provide an easy understanding based on a revised version of the general HWID, we reproduce the characteristics of humans and work domain contents and the interaction during their tasks and decision activities, individually and collaboratively.

Nowadays, it is a true challenge to design games that support users of technology in complex and emergent organizational and classroom environments. As previously presented, various factors such as school infrastructure, and classroom interactions can influence the performance of students, such as the complexity and its relationships between extensive HCI designs [29].

Human Work Interaction Design (HWID) and Serious Games are fields that interconnect in significant ways, especially in terms of user-centred design and the application of games in non-play contexts such as education, training and healthcare. Both HWID and Serious Games emphasize the importance of user-centred design [30]. Exploring how principles of Human-Work Interaction Design (HWID) can be translated into the design of serious games for workplace training and other professional environments, we can argue that in serious games for workplace training User-Centered Design (UCD) ensures that games are designed with a focus on user characteristics, such as their experience level, preferred working style, and cognitive capabilities. According to [31], UCD principles can be adapted to work environments to design intuitive interfaces and processes that make tasks more manageable for workers. For example, games designed for healthcare, such as those used for medical training, benefit from UCD by tailoring the gameplay to simulate complex medical procedures while ensuring the design is approachable for medical professionals at various stages of their careers [32]. These games allow for an effective transfer of skills, much like the training methods described by [33] in serious games for educational purposes.

Simulating real-world tasks in a controlled environment is a key principle of HWID and serious games. By mimicking workplace tasks, serious games can prepare workers for real-world challenges in a low-risk environment. For example, simulation games in emergency medical response allow users to practice protocols in realistic scenarios without the risk of harm [34]. In manufacturing, serious games can simulate the production line, allowing employees to practice improving efficiency, troubleshooting issues, and optimizing workflows without disrupting actual operations [35].

As we argue before, HWID focuses on understanding how people interact with work systems [36], while Serious Games uses game design principles to create engaging experiences that can educate or train users.

In a holistic way Serious Games are designed to motivate and engage users in activities that may be difficult or monotonous. HWID seeks to optimize the user experience, and gamification can be a powerful tool to achieve this goal. HWID also, emphasizes the importance of collaboration between humans and systems in work contexts. Serious games can replicate these team dynamics, fostering collaboration and improving communication skills, such as using collaborative serious games, that allow employees to simulate teamwork in different work scenarios. In a study by [37], multiplayer games were used in a corporate setting to improve team communication and problem-solving skills. These games simulated real-world work situations, such as project management or crisis communication, where employees needed to interact and collaborate to reach a common goal [37].

Both fields use continuous feedback to improve interaction. In Serious Games, feedback is often incorporated into game mechanics, while in HWID, usability evaluations are crucial to understanding how users interact with systems [38].

Continuous feedback, integral to both HWID and serious games, plays a significant role in improving interactions and task performance. It encourages users to adapt, learn, and refine their skills during training. Real-time feedback in serious games for workplace training is designed to guide users in improving their skills, much like the feedback loops used in HWID studies to optimize systems for users [39]. For example, in a customer service training game, real-time feedback could assess whether employees are responding appropriately to customer queries, guiding them to better communication strategies. Usability evaluations in serious games ensure that the games are not only engaging but also functional. Studies by [40] emphasize the importance of feedback in gamified systems to ensure users remain engaged while also receiving critical insights into their performance [40].

Gamification can transform routine tasks into competitive or rewarding activities. For example, a warehouse employee might earn points for accuracy and speed in sorting inventory, encouraging improvement through game-like elements [41]. This aligns with principles of engagement from HWID, which seeks to make work systems more enjoyable and less monotonous for users. According to [42], gamification has been successfully applied in several workplace training programs to improve performance. Gamification not only motivates employees but also makes learning more fun, which ultimately contributes to better retention of knowledge and skills [42].

By applying the principles of HWID to the design of serious games, the development of workplace training tools can be significantly enhanced. Serious games, rooted in UCD, gamification, and task simulation, can provide a rich, interactive learning experience that prepares workers for real-world challenges. The incorporation of feedback loops, collaboration simulations, and adaptability ensures that these tools are not only engaging but also effective in fostering skill development in various professional contexts. The references provided illustrate the integration of HWID and serious games, demonstrating their value in both educational and workplace environments.

On the reflection on the state, we can identify several opportunities for HCI research to impact serious games and work domain in educational environments. The principles of Human-Work Interaction Design (HWID) and serious games, though often associated with workplace training, are highly relevant to educational games as well. Just as HWID emphasizes user-centered design (UCD), educational games similarly prioritize creating engaging, intuitive experiences for learners, ensuring that the game's structure and interface meet students' cognitive needs [31].Task simulation in educational games mirrors how workplace training games simulate real-world scenarios, allowing students to practice complex concepts in a risk-free environment, such as virtual labs or historical reenactments [35]. Collaboration and communication, key aspects of HWID, are also emphasized in educational games, where multiplayer scenarios help students improve teamwork and problem-solving [37]. Continuous feedback in educational games, like in workplace training games, provides real-time guidance, helping students learn from their mistakes and refine their skills [33]. Similarly, gamification in educational games introduces rewards, progression systems, and competitive elements, motivating students to engage more deeply with the material and improving their learning outcomes [42]. Finally, just as serious games adapt to different work contexts, educational games can be customized to meet the diverse needs of learners across various disciplines, ensuring the content is both relevant and engaging [43]. Through these elements, the design of educational games can be deeply informed by HWID principles, making learning more effective, immersive, and enjoyable.

3 Materials and Methods

For the study, a prototype was developed to test how using serious games in the classroom environment could potentiate the learning process and mitigate boredom. Taking into consideration the aim of the study, the prototype was designed to focus first on how to make the game enjoyable and only afterward introduce the content of the subject. With this in our heads during the development process, it was easier to stay tuned on the main objective of the game, help students learn but also be motivated to learn and want to pursue new information about the topic.

3.1 Prototype

The development of the prototype occurred after the research of what was taught in history classes, more particularly in the 10th grade about the subject of ancient Athens. Not only the content was analysed, but also some tests were taken into consideration so that not only did the students enjoy learning the subject but also helped them as a study tool for future tests.

The team decided that a 3D game was the better solution for what we wanted to achieve since it provided a greater sense of presence than a 2D game and didn't have the limitations that VR still has such as motion sickness and technical difficulties. The primary genre selected for the game was Role Playing Game (RPG), as it offers an effective means of presenting the subject matter. Through this genre, players assume the role of a character rooted in the location and era relevant to the topic being taught. This approach fosters immersion, enabling players to actively engage with the environment and events, thereby deepening their understanding. RPGs are particularly well-suited for creating dynamic, choice-driven experiences, where players can explore the narrative and directly connect with the material in an interactive and meaningful way. In that way, it was easier for a non-gamer to still have fun with the game.

The prototype followed a path where the user played minigames along the way learning specific parts of Athens. In the minigames, the player had to collect coins, build columns, and visit locations and statues while a narrator explained parts that were considered important to the students.

3.2 Narrative

The player starts in the habitational zone of Athens and is immediately tasked with their first mission: to head to the Acropolis to find hidden treasures. As the player explores the

Acropolis and collects these treasures, a narrator provides historical context, explaining its significance and usage in ancient Greece.

Once all the treasures are collected, a new mission directs the player to the Agora, the marketplace and administrative centre of ancient Greece. Upon arrival, the narrator explains the importance of the Agora, and two missions are triggered:

- Race Minigame: The player competes in a race against two other characters
- Important People: The player locates statues of two prominent historical figures, Pericles and Clisthenes, and the narrator explains who these men were and their contributions to ancient Greek society.

Finally, the last mission, Escape Puzzle, the player needs to open a gate to escape the zone. To do this, they must solve a puzzle involving the reconstruction of Doric, Ionic, and Corinthian columns. The narrator briefly explains the characteristics of each column style, and the player must correctly assemble a column of each type to unlock the gate and complete the mission (Fig. 1).

Fig. 1. Prototype of the serious game

3.3 Methods

To evaluate the motivation of the students in the classroom environment, the user testers were divided into two groups: the first one had a typical history class with a teacher teaching the subject, while the other group went into a room where all the students would play the prototype. Although the main objective of the study was to understand if the students had an increase in motivation in a different environment we had still to understand if they still learned the subject. Because of that, the study was divided into three: analyse the knowledge obtained between the serious game and the normal class, the motivation from each group, and gather insights into the prototype for further development. The game took between 15 to 20 min to finished, where participants had to complete several minigames inside the game. Those minigames were collection of coins, build columns, visit buildings and statues while a narrator in the game explained the topic. To investigate these three points, two questionnaires were used, one before playing the game/having the class, and the other after the test.

1. To determine the knowledge obtained in the study the pre- and post-questionnaires had questions about the topic determined by the teacher. Having the measurements before and after the test we can then compare if the serious game could be used in the classroom environment as a tool to help the teacher provide the content.
2. To investigate the motivation the user tester had during the test and to compare a normal class and a serious game, some questions were in the post-questionnaire regarding using the Intrinsic Motivation Inventory scale [44].
3. To gather feedback from the participants a short version of the scale called the Game User Experience Satisfaction Scale (GUESS), was used on the post-questionnaire to give the possibility of improvements of the prototype for future research and also to see what is already well implemented [45].

3.4 Procedure

To collect the data necessary to analyse how the serious game could influence the environment in the classroom, each user had their participation divided into three main parts. All participants were randomly assigned to each environment. The first part was to fulfil a pre-questionnaire to gather basic information about the user and their knowledge about the topic. The following part was playing the serious game or being in the normal class. The last part consisted of doing a post-questionnaire where the same questions about the topic were made to check the knowledge obtained, a motivation questionnaire to check the participant's motivation to learn new information about the topic in that environment, and finally, some feedback about the prototype to improve for future research. The pre and post questionnaire were filled on paper and since all participants spoke better in Portuguese, the questionnaires were translated.

Knowledge Questions

The pre- and post-questionnaires used in the research were comprised of five multiple-choice questions that served to measure the level of participants' knowledge related to Ancient Greece. These questions had been designed in such a way as to reflect the purpose of the research properly and included three main spheres: the term ancient Greeks called their city-states, Polis, famous historical personalities, and the architecture of the classical Greek style. The order of the questions was switched between pre- and post- on purpose to prevent a reliance on memory for answers. In that way, participants considered the content rather than merely recalling specific answers.

The first part of the questionnaire concerned the concept of Polis, the very focal point of political and social life in ancient Greece and had the purpose of testing the knowledge about specific places within the structure of these city-states. The questions of the section read as follows: "What is the Acropolis?" and "What is the Agora?" The

Acropolis-a high point in the centre of a Greek city, typically containing the most crucial temples and monuments-and the Agora-a large area in the centre of ancient Greek cities where people congregated, commerce was undertaken, and where political matters were deliberated-played a vital role for the Greek cities' understanding. In fact, these questions tried to examine whether these subjects were able to identify these prominent places and understand their individual purposes relating to everyday Greek life. We want to know really if the participants could identify the places they had navigated in the game and their purposes according to the in-game interaction and visual display.

The second part of the questionnaire referred to the main historical personalities, including such figures as Cleisthenes and Pericles, two great men of Ancient Greece. Cleisthenes is considered the father of Athenian democracy, whereas Pericles played an important role in the politics of Athens during its Golden Age. With Cleisthenes and Pericles, we asked if players could recall and then repeat information about the roles of these two key figures after having played the game.

The final section of the questionnaire concerned ancient Greek architecture. We asked about the three types of columns which were used on classical Greek buildings: Doric, Ionic, and Corinthian. Participants were then asked to match various parts of these architectural styles with their correct descriptions. These columns are some of the most iconic features of Greek architecture: the Doric, Ionic, and Corinthian, each representing different levels of complexity and decoration. By this question, we tried to understand whether players would be able to tell these styles correctly and identify their characteristic features having encountered the representation during the gameplay.

Put differently, the questionnaires were designed to test players' knowledge in key elements from Ancient Greece, such as city layout and important locations, historical figures, and style of architecture, through both visual and auditory interactions throughout the game. The pre-questionnaire compared with the post-questionnaire allowed us to assess if the game experience improved participants' retention and understanding of the mentioned cultural and historical knowledge.

3.5 Participants

Taking into account the inclusion criteria that require the participants to be students, at least 15 years old, and have some prior experience with video games, 20 students from the 10th grade of Apel's school [46] were selected. Through the study, due to technical and time problems, only 14 students were able to enter the study. The main issue was the incapacity of school computers to play the prototype. Not only that, five students didn't answer the full post-questionnaire, meaning that from those students only a few data will be analysed.

Considering all mentioned before, the study ended up with 5 students that tested the prototype, 4 males and 1 female aged between 15 and 16 years old ($M = 15{,}20$; $SD = 0{,}44$), and 9 students had the normal class, 4 males, 4 females, and 1 undefined aged between 15 and 17 years old ($M = 15{,}89$; $SD = 0{,}601$).

4 Results

The presentation of the results of the study in this section follows the three points discussed in the methods section. First will be presented the comparison of the knowledge obtained before and after the test, followed by the results of the motivation, and finally the results of the usability scale gathered from the participants about the implementation of the serious game.

4.1 Knowledge

The knowledge results were obtained after participants answered five questions about the topic in the pre- and post-questionnaire (Fig. 2).

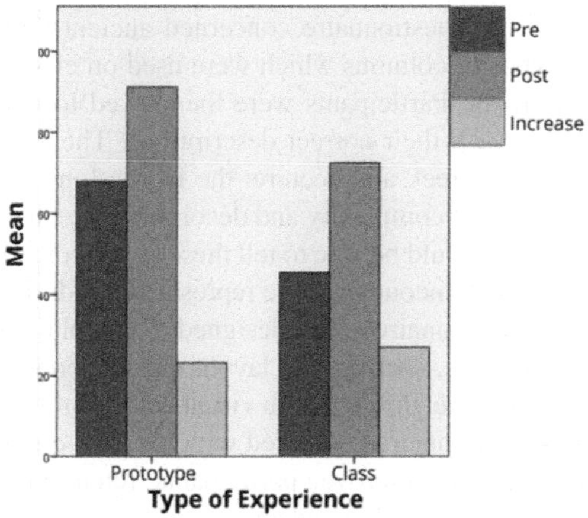

Fig. 2. Comparison between prototype and normal class

Considering the table presented before, the participants that had a normal class had an increase of knowledge for about ($M = 27{,}00$; $SD = 36{,}08$), while the users that played the prototype had an increase of ($M = 23{,}20$; $SD = 26{,}21$).

4.2 Motivation

The data obtained from the motivation scale is shown in the next tables. The data gathered was from only 10 participants since 4 that experimented in the class didn't answer all the questions (Tables 1 and 2).

Table 1. The four subscales from the Intrinsic Motivation Scale. 1 – Prototype; 2 – Normal class

Type of Experiment	Interest	Competence	Choice	Tension
2	35	24	33	18
2	26	31	16	22
2	37	17	33	17
2	20	17	23	8
2	15	17	11	7
1	43	35	17	23
1	39	14	27	13
1	49	31	35	6
1	38	26	30	11
1	17	19	7	6

Table 2. The means and standard deviations of each subscale of the Intrinsic Motivation Scale for each type of experience. 1 – Prototype; 2 – Normal class.

Type of Experiment	Interest	Competence	Choice	Tension
2	$M = 26{,}60$; $SD = 9{,}45$	$M = 21{,}20$; $SD = 6{,}26$	$M = 23{,}20$; $SD = 9{,}91$	$M = 14{,}80$; $SD = 6{,}06$
1	$M = 37{,}20$; $SD = 12{,}09$	$M = 25{,}00$; $SD = 8{,}57$	$M = 23{,}20$; $SD = 11{,}19$	$M = 11{,}80$; $SD = 6{,}98$

4.3 Usability

The usability scale used, the Game User Experience Satisfaction Scale – 18 (GUESS-18), was only measured by the participants who experimented with the prototype. Not only that, one of the participants didn't answer all the questions and because of that was excluded from these analyses. The results were as follows (Table 3):

Table 3. Overall GUESS Score for the four participants that did the prototype test.

Overall GUESS Score
58,5
36
55,5
32

5 Discussion

To understand if the change of the environment of the classroom to a more game focus could be possible, it was necessary to understand if the game might still provide the required content and students could learn from that. Looking at the results shown before, the students who played the prototype learned the subject similarly to the ones who had a normal class. The average increase was lower compared to students that had a normal class (23,20 vs 27,00) it was found that students who played the game had already on average a better result on the pre-questionnaire, becoming the possibility of an increase of knowledge smaller than the ones who had a normal class. Not only that, but students also who were in the study learned two weeks before the themes that were going to be evaluated, resulting in a higher classification on the pretest than expected. The participants had previously studied the topic of Ancient Greece a few weeks before the study, which led to a higher-than-expected percentage of correct answers in the pre-questionnaire. As a result, the improvement between the pre- and post-questionnaires was less pronounced than anticipated. Additionally, participants who engaged with the game prototype performed better overall, with a higher average number of correct answers (68) compared to those who received traditional classroom instruction (45.55). This made it more challenging for them to show a significant increase in the post-questionnaire results.

Considering the motivation results, there was an increase in interest, the participants felt more competent and with less tension when using the prototype in comparison to a normal class. These results showed that a change in the classroom environment with the usage of games as a teaching method could potentiate the student's motivation to learn the subject. Also, it was possible to verify this possibility because when the participants were assigned to have a normal class or play the prototype, some students that were going to have the normal class started grumbling when they knew which environment they would be in.

The GUESS-18 scale is evaluated from a minimum of 9 and a maximum of 63. The results showed an $M = 45{,}50$ and $SD = 13{,}43$. After the check of normality was used the t-test, where it can be concluded that it was statistically significant, $t(3) = 6{,}773$, $p = 0{,}007$. Considering these results and further supported by qualitative results, it's possible to assume that the participants felt the prototype was usable and easy to an extent of being possible to learn the topics expected.

Although the results showed a positive impact of the serious game, future research must address the preservation of knowledge obtained so that this method can be used on a long-term issue.

6 Conclusion

In summary, the classroom environment plays a crucial role in shaping how students engage with learning. A well-designed classroom can enhance engagement, collaboration, and creativity among students.

Furthermore, serious games offer a promising path for enhancing classroom engagement and learning outcomes. By integrating game mechanics and interactive storytelling, serious games can transform the learning process more enjoyable, immersive, and effective. These games can be designed to align with educational objectives, providing opportunities for students to consolidate their knowledge. As technology continues to advance and affordable computers become more accessible, transitioning to a more digital classroom environment becomes increasingly feasible. Studies that explore the integration of these new teaching methods could help schools and parents become more open to adopting them.

The study evaluated a game prototype's effectiveness in a classroom setting, finding that students using the game had similar knowledge gains (23.20) as those in traditional classes (27.00), despite having higher pre-test scores. Participants scored an average of 68 correct answers compared to 45.55 for traditional students and reported increased motivation and lower anxiety. The GUESS-18 scale showed a mean score of 45.50, with significant results (t (3) = 6.773, p = 0.007), indicating the game was effective and user-friendly for learning.

The results of the pilot study showed that an educational game designed focusing primarily on the game part and then including the subject alongside the narrative of the game motivated more the students than the ones who had a normal class, without compromising the learning part.

The questionnaire results can guide future research and spark discussions about the use of serious games in education and how they might evolve. Future studies could involve conducting the experiment with a larger group of participants to gain more reliable data, or implementing the game over an extended period to assess how knowledge retention compares between the two teaching methods.

Acknowledgements. We would like to thank to the teacher Dina Gonçalves who participated in this research. The institutional support from Escola da APEL was generously provided by the director Pe. Fernando Gonçalves, by the pedagogical director Gonçalo Faria and by the administrative secretary Rubina Mendonça. This research was funded by the Portuguese Recovery and Resilience Program (PRR), IAPMEI/ANI/FCT under Agenda C645022399-00000057 (eGamesLab).

References

1. Cheng, Y.C.: Classroom environment and student affective performance: an effective profile. J. Exp. Educ. **62**, 221–239 (1994). https://doi.org/10.1080/00220973.1994.9943842
2. de Borba, G.S., Alves, I.M., Campagnolo, P.D.B.: How learning spaces can collaborate with student engagement and enhance student-faculty interaction in higher education. Innov. High. Educ. **45**, 51–63 (2020). https://doi.org/10.1007/s10755-019-09483-9
3. Hanaysha, J.R., Shriedeh, F.B., In'airat, M.: Impact of classroom environment, teacher competency, information and communication technology resources, and university facilities on student engagement and academic performance. Int. J. Inf. Manag. Data Insights **3**, 100188 (2023). https://doi.org/10.1016/j.jjimei.2023.100188
4. Wahyuddin, W.: Headmaster leadership and teacher competence in increasing student achievement in school. Int. Educ. Stud. **10**, 215–226 (2017)
5. Laamarti, F., Eid, M., Saddik, A.E.: An overview of serious games. Int. J. Comput. Games Technol. **11**, 11 (2014). https://doi.org/10.1155/2014/358152

6. Zhonggen, Y.: A meta-analysis of use of serious games in education over a decade. Int. J. Comput. Games Technol. **2019**, e4797032 (2019). https://doi.org/10.1155/2019/4797032
7. Bellotti, F., Berta, R., Gloria, A.D.: Designing effective serious games: opportunities and challenges for research. Int. J. Emerg. Technol. Learn. (iJET) **5** (2010)
8. Naul, E., Liu, M.: Why story matters: a review of narrative in serious games. J. Educ. Comput. Res. **58**, 687–707 (2020). https://doi.org/10.1177/0735633119859904
9. Irkinovich, N.R.: The importance of role-playing game in teaching english in a non-linguistic university. Int. J. Pedagogics **2**, 29–32 (2022). https://doi.org/10.37547/ijp/Volume02Issue09-07
10. Rote, V., Clemmensen, T.: Designing Interactive Systems for Work Engagement (2018)
11. Barricelli, B.R., Clemmensen, T., Campos, P., Abdelnour-Nocera, J., Lopes, A.: Motivation, participation, and engagement in human work interaction design literature. In: CoPDA 2016. Cultures of Participation in the Digital Age: Proceedings of the Fourth edition of the International Workshop on Cultures of Participation in the Digital Age. «Have to» to «Want to» Participate co-located with the 9th Nordic Conference on Human-Computer Interaction (NordiCHI 2016), pp. 8–13. CEUR (2016)
12. Fredricks, J.A., Filsecker, M., Lawson, M.A.: Student engagement, context, and adjustment: addressing definitional, measurement, and methodological issues. Learn. Instr. **43**, 1–4 (2016). https://doi.org/10.1016/j.learninstruc.2016.02.002
13. Begnaud, D., Coenraad, M., Jain, N., Patel, D., Bonsignore, E.: «It's just too much»: exploring children's views of boredom and strategies to manage feelings of boredom. In: Proceedings of the Interaction Design and Children Conference. pp. 624–636. Association for Computing Machinery, New York (2020)
14. Paik, J.H., Himelfarb, I., Yoo, S.H., Yoo, K., Ha, H.: The relationships among school engagement, students' emotions, and academic performance in an elementary online learning. In: Proceedings of the 14th Learning Analytics and Knowledge Conference, pp. 219–230. Association for Computing Machinery, New York (2024)
15. Martins, J., Cunha, J., Lopes, S., Moreira, T., Rosário, P.: School engagement in elementary school: a systematic review of 35 years of research. Educ. Psychol. Rev. **34**, 793–849 (2022). https://doi.org/10.1007/s10648-021-09642-5
16. Runtian, Z.: The game and integration between online education and traditional school education. In: Proceedings of the 2020 11th International Conference on E-Education, E-Business, E-Management, and E-Learning, pp. 121–124. Association for Computing Machinery, New York (2020)
17. Zhao, H.: Introducing ICT in a traditional higher education environment. In: Lin, S. e Huang, X. (eds.) Advances in Computer Science, Environment, Ecoinformatics, and Education. pp. 129–132. Springer, Heidelberg (2011)
18. Yarychev, N.U., Mentsiev, A.U.: Impact of digital education on traditional education. J. Phys.: Conf. Ser. **1691**, 012132 (2020). https://doi.org/10.1088/1742-6596/1691/1/012132
19. Alneyadi, S., Abulibdeh, E., Wardat, Y.: The impact of digital environment vs. traditional method on literacy skills; reading and writing of emirati fourth graders. Sustainability **15**, 3418 (2023). https://doi.org/10.3390/su15043418
20. Patronis, M.: The effect of using the ipad on students' performance in writing and reading comprehension: pilot study report. Arab World English J. (2014)
21. Kew, S.N., Tasir, Z.: Analysing students' cognitive engagement in e-learning discussion forums through content analysis. Knowl. Manag. E-Learn. **13**, 39–57 (2021)
22. Wang, X.: Mobile learning in Chinese higher education: student perspectives, advantages and challenges. In: Proceedings of the 14th International Conference on Education Technology and Computers, pp. 207–211. Association for Computing Machinery, New York (2023)

23. B. Guruge, D., Paudel, K., Kadel, R., Aziz, S., Karagiannidis, V.: Analysing student expectation on mobile technologies to enhance student learning experience. In: Proceedings of the 2021 2nd International Conference on Education Development and Studies, pp. 45–49. Association for Computing Machinery, New York (2021)
24. Rakha, N.A.: Revolution in learning through digitization: how technology is changing the landscape of education. Int. J. Cyber Law **1** (2023). https://doi.org/10.59022/ijcl.38
25. Wohlfart, O., Wagner, I.: Teachers' role in digitalizing education: an umbrella review. Educ. Tech. Res. Dev. **71**, 339–365 (2023). https://doi.org/10.1007/s11423-022-10166-0
26. Siljebo, J.: Leading learning through digitalization in Swedish schools: beyond school leaders? (2023)
27. Caneva, C., Monnier, E., Pulfrey, C., El-Hamamsy, L., Avry, S., Delher Zufferey, J.: Technology integration needs empowered instructional coaches: accompanying in-service teachers in school digitalization. Int. J. Mentor. Coach. Educ. **12**, 194–215 (2023). https://doi.org/10.1108/IJMCE-04-2022-0029
28. Clemmensen, T.: A human work interaction design (HWID) case study in e-government and public information systems. Int. J. Public Inf. Syst. **7** (2011)
29. Campos, P., Clemmensen, T., Nocera, J.A., Katre, D., Lopes, A., Ørngreen, R.: Human work interaction design. work analysis and HCI: Third IFIP 13.6 Working Conference, HWID 2012, Copenhagen, Denmark, 5–6 December 2012, Revised Selected Papers. Springer, Heidelberg (2013)
30. Fuchsberger, V., et al.: Human work interaction design (HWID): design for challenging work environments. In: Abascal, J., Barbosa, S., Fetter, M., Gross, T., Palanque, P., e Winckler, M. (eds.) Human-Computer Interaction – INTERACT 2015, pp. 659–660. Springer, Cham (2015)
31. Norman, D.: The design of everyday things: Revised and expanded edition. Basic books (2013)
32. van Gaalen, A.E.J., Brouwer, J., Schönrock-Adema, J., Bouwkamp-Timmer, T., Jaarsma, A.D.C., Georgiadis, J.R.: Gamification of health professions education: a systematic review. Adv. Health Sci. Educ. **26**, 683–711 (2021). https://doi.org/10.1007/s10459-020-10000-3
33. Shute, V.J., Becker, K.W.: Advances in Game-Based Learning. Educational Technology Research and Development (2010)
34. Sitzmann, T.: A meta-analytic examination of the instructional effectiveness of computer-based simulation games. Pers. Psychol. **64**, 489–528 (2011). https://doi.org/10.1111/j.1744-6570.2011.01190.x
35. Gee, J.P.: What video games have to teach us about learning and literacy. Comput. Entertain. **1**, 20 (2003). https://doi.org/10.1145/950566.950595
36. Gonçalves, F., Campos, P., Clemmensen, T.: Human work interaction design: an overview. In: Abdelnour Nocera, J., Barricelli, B.R., Lopes, A., Campos, P., e Clemmensen, T. (eds.) Human Work Interaction Design. Work Analysis and Interaction Design Methods for Pervasive and Smart Workplaces, pp. 3–19. Springer, Cham (2015)
37. Johnson, D.W., Johnson, R.T.: Cooperation and Competition: Theory and research. Interaction Book Company, Edina (1989)
38. Gonçalves, F., Clemmensen, T., Molka-Danielsen, J., Campos, P.: Drifting towards a new HCI field: a review of 10 years of HWID research. In: Bhutkar, G., et al. (eds.) Human Work Interaction Design. Artificial Intelligence and Designing for a Positive Work Experience in a Low Desire Society, pp. 3–33. Springer, Cham (2022)
39. Fogg, B.J.: Persuasive technology: using computers to change what we think and do. Ubiquity **5**, 2 (2002). https://doi.org/10.1145/764008.763957
40. Lazzaro, N.: Why We Play Games: Four Keys to More Emotion Without Story (2004)
41. Werbach, K., Hunter, D.: For the Win: How Game Thinking Can Revolutionize Your Business. Wharton Digital Press (2012)

42. Does Gamification Work? -- A Literature Review of Empirical Studies on Gamification | IEEE Conference Publication | IEEE Xplore. https://ieeexplore.ieee.org/document/6758978
43. Michael, D.R., Chen, S.L.: Serious Games: Games That Educate, Train, and Inform. Muska & Lipman/Premier-Trade (2005)
44. Oudeyer, P.-Y.: What is intrinsic motivation? A typology of computational approaches. Front. Neurorobot. **1**, (2007). https://doi.org/10.3389/neuro.12.006.2007
45. Phan, M.H., Keebler, J.R., Chaparro, B.S.: The development and validation of the game user experience satisfaction scale (GUESS). Hum. Factors **58**, 1217–1247 (2016). https://doi.org/10.1177/0018720816669646
46. APEL. https://www.escola-apel.com/web/

Empowering Expertise: A Digital Twin for Supporting Practical Shooting Coaches

Stefano Morzenti[1,2(✉)]

[1] Università degli Studi di Brescia, Brescia, Italy
stefano.morzenti@unibs.it
[2] Fabbrica d'Armi Pietro Beretta, Gardone Val Trompia, Italy
stefano.morzenti@beretta.com

Abstract. Human Digital Twins (HDTs) offer several opportunities when applied to sports. Our research explores the adoption of Digital Twins to create a system to monitor athletes, enhance performance, and prevent injuries. We focus on Practical Shooting, a discipline demanding speed, accuracy, and strategic decision-making. The proposed system is a digital coaching aid that provides real-time insights to coaches and athletes. This paper outlines our preliminary implementation plan. We detail the project's core themes, a system architecture tailored for the shooting range, an interaction design informed by coach and athlete collaboration, developed with the involvement of 19 athletes and 35 trainers, and the planned future developments.

Keywords: Digital twin · Coaching Assistant · Human Work Interaction Design

1 Introduction

Through Digital Twin technologies, a physical system can be modeled into a virtual counterpart and employed for various applications, comprising monitoring, optimization, simulation, and management [2], often employing Artificial Intelligence (AI) techniques to adjust the model alongside the evolution of the physical entity. Despite being first introduced in the Product Life-cycle Management field and finding diffusion in industrial applications, Digital Twins are more recently being extended to human modeling for the simulation of organs and physiological functions and monitoring physical activity [2,12]. In this case, we talk about the Human Digital Twin. In this application domain, we find Digital Twin Coaching, which refers to Digital Twin applications whose objective is monitoring athletes performing sports disciplines with various purposes, including performance enhancement and injury prevention [6]. Digital Twins, applied to coaching, inherently aligns with UN Sustainable Development Goal[1]

[1] UN SDGs: https://sdgs.un.org/goals.

Published by Springer Nature Switzerland AG 2026
B. R. Barricelli et al. (Eds.): HWID 2024, IFIP AICT 751, pp. 127–139, 2026.
https://doi.org/10.1007/978-3-031-95334-7_8

(SDG) 3: Good Health and Well-being by promoting a preventative approach to training and potentially reducing sports-related injuries, and also (SDG) 8: Decent work and Economic growth by providing tools that enhance the trainer's effectiveness and professionalism.

In scientific literature, examples of such applications are available where the authors developed semi-autonomous systems across a variety of disciplines, like football [3], tennis [4], swimming [7], weightlifting [16], and cycling [10], among others. Our project specifically evaluates Digital Twin Coaching in Practical Shooting, a sports discipline where coaching relies heavily on personal experience, with limited technological support beyond recording and replaying sessions.

The objectives of our project are to develop a digital training system based on a Digital Twin model of the Practical Shooting athlete, and in doing so, to study the concept of Digital Twin Coaching and its open issues. Our digital training system is meant to enhance the work of the trainer (SDG 8) by providing a tool for the analysis of the athletes' gesture and a database of historic data, and by providing a suggestion model. For the athlete, the system is meant to improve the effectiveness of the training and the safety of the discipline (SDG 3) through customized physical training and through verification of the safety procedures. In this context, Human Work Interaction Design (HWID) [5,13] plays a crucial role by focusing on the interaction between the coach and the AI system. The project is designed to assist the professional coach who requires guidance in evaluating athletes' performances. Through HWID, the AI-generated suggestions support the coach's professional judgment without imposing decisions. This design ensures that the AI informs the coach's advice process, enhancing their expertise while allowing them to control the final decisions regarding training and feedback.

This paper introduces our Digital Twin architecture and the preliminary design of a mobile interactive system. This system empowers coaches by supervising athletes in real time, assisting with training strategy decisions, and providing personalized guidance and feedback to athletes. The first section summarizes the major results of a literature review through which we evaluated the state of the art of Digital Twin Coaching and gathered the open issues and research opportunities. Then, the description of the user research that culminated in the design, development, and evaluation of an Android application for the interaction between athletes and the training system is presented. Finally, an architecture for a measurement system designed around the characteristics of the Practical Shooting discipline and of the shooting field is described.

2 Research Background

The research project began with a literature review concerning the state of the art for Digital Twins and their application to sports training. We searched in the most common scientific repositories for keywords such as "digital twin", "human digital twin", "digital twin coaching", in concatenation with "sport" and "training". A portion of the research also concerned training applications for specific shooting disciplines that did not appear in the previous, broader research. By this process we identified the following themes for further research to meet the requirements for an adequate system for our application and to address the open issues that affect the human-digital twin concept in general.

Acquisition of Physical and Physiological Quantities: To accurately model trainee performance, a suite of measurement instruments that capture both physical [1] and physiological data is needed. This project includes wearable inertial and physiological sensors and an on-field stereo camera for tracking user trajectories. The selection process prioritized capturing the necessary information while minimizing interference with the athletes' training.

Design, Implementation, and Evaluation of User-System Interaction: Scientific literature emphasize the importance of well-designed user interaction in returning clear and actionable insights, fostering user engagement (especially when additional input is needed), and building trust in the system's feedback [2,9]. To achieve this, we are developing a mobile graphical user interface (GUI) as a dashboard for both athletes and coaches. We surveyed 19 expert athletes and 35 trainers through user research on their training habits, technology preferences, and understanding of common chart types. These same experts will evaluate the user experience of our high-fidelity prototype.

Selection and Training of a User-Model: The athletes' modeling will be performed with machine learning algorithms because of the necessity to keep the model up to date with the athletes at each additional input data. In similar coaching applications, various algorithms were employed, even if focused on different sports disciplines. However, in the case of digital twin coaching, the most common are SVM, CNN, KNN, and Decision Tree [6].

Data Storing and Elaboration: Raw data collected on the field must be processed and stored. For example, feature extraction is necessary for the algorithms for user modeling but is also helpful in reducing the data we need to store and compute. We will also evaluate the possibility of employing sensor fusion algorithms to improve the quantity of information in our data. Examples from the literature also show the necessity of reconstructing missing samples [3], which can be performed with various methods, but among the most common is the KNN algorithm [6]. Finally, for Human Digital Twins, the privacy and security of the data must be guaranteed during the whole process [3,9].

3 Interaction Design of the Digital Twin

For the design of the interaction between users and the digital training system, we follow a user-centered approach, where athletes and coaches are involved in the design process to obtain a training system that fits their necessities. More specifically, we developed two tablet applications for athletes and coaches, given the different needs the two users have, for example, athletes may have a vast difference in age, occupation, and instruction level and need to access their data in an intuitive manner, insert additional information and receive the coach's feedback and instructions, while coaches are trained professionals and can have a more in-depth view of their athlete's statistics but also need an intuitive way to compare multiple athletes or multiple executions of a stage. Although the design of the interaction involved both an application for the coach and one for the athlete, our focus was primarily on studying the needs and expectations of the coach, as a professional and an expert user of the application domain. Our design process followed a Human Work Interaction Design [5] approach, with direct involvement of domain experts both during the design phase and in the evaluation phase.

The following sections detail the development of the athletes' application, while the coaches' counterpart is currently being developed following a similar process.

3.1 User Research

The development began with a competitor analysis, in which we gathered information from the competitors on the Android and iOS stores. While not having a proper direct competitor, we searched applications that monitor physical activity and coaching across multiple sports and applications related to score tracking in shooting disciplines. Our research concerned the nature of information and functionalities provided to the user, the arrangement of the data, and the types of graphical representation most commonly employed.

A survey was then distributed to the group of nineteen athletes to characterize them regarding shooting and training habits, personal background, and technological proficiency. The survey was shared as a Google Form through which athletes anonymously provided the following information:

- *Personal information* such as age range, gender, education, occupation, and proficiency with smart devices.
- *Technical information* concerning Practical Shooting, such as discipline, division, years of experience, their opinion on the most affecting factors, the types of training they perform, and their propensity to receive suggestions from an automated system.
- *Graphics questions* regarding which types of graphical representation they're most familiar with and which type of graph would best represent certain data types.

From the surveys, we determine athletes are mainly male (84.2%) with a high school diploma (57.9%), but they are a heterogeneous group in terms of age and occupation.

In Fig. 1 are reported some of the results we collected. Users manifested familiarity with mobile devices, with only 15.8% of them using smartphones or tablets for less than an hour a day, and 10.5% of athletes using them for more than 6 h a day, both for work and personal use. Interestingly, 68.4% of the athletes positively view the inclusion of suggestions generated by an AI, and only 5.3% would refuse to follow them, although no significant relation was found between the propensity to trust AI and shooting experience.

In terms of athletic capabilities, the most common type of weapon is the handgun (76.3%) and the most popular division is *Production*. It appears that our sample comprised mainly experienced athletes, with 73.7% of them having performed this sport for at least 4 years, and 10% of them being experts with more than 12 years of activity.

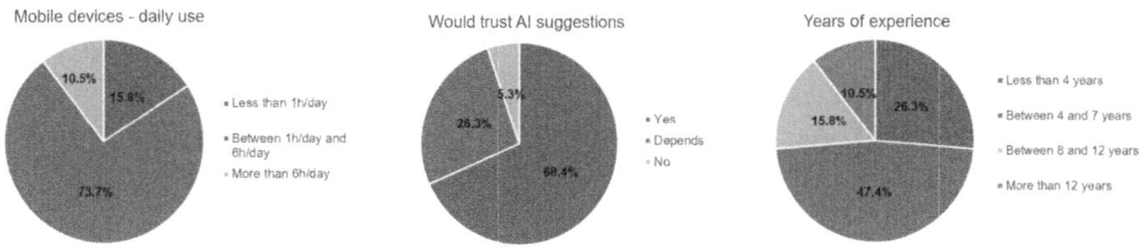

Fig. 1. Extract of results of the user research

3.2 Development of the Application Prototype

The development of a prototype interface revolved around the concept of personas and scenarios that were built to synthesize the nineteen answers we collected in our survey in three significant use cases. The application prototyping was performed through several iterative steps of design of a navigation map and implementation of a mock-up interface in Figma (Fig. 2) until a satisfactory state was reached.

The Figma mock-up was then implemented in an actual Android tablet application in the Android Studio environment and Kotlin language. The prototype application was developed around the data collected on the field in collaboration with a subset of expert shooters, although some of the information displayed was hypothesized since a part of the training system is still under development. The main functionalities that were provided are:

- Personal profile, with the possibility to edit a catalog of personal equipment that can be assigned to the training sessions.
- Digital Twin screen, in which the athlete can have an overview of their own model and its statistics, divided into different groups
- Training calendar, with the possibility to access past training experiences and have an overview of its performance,
- training page, with the possibility to manage new training sessions and executions and to insert additional information manually
- Stage database, to access and review the characteristics of a specific stage and its own executions of said stage (Fig. 3)
- Suggestion page, with a list of suggestions relayed from the coach

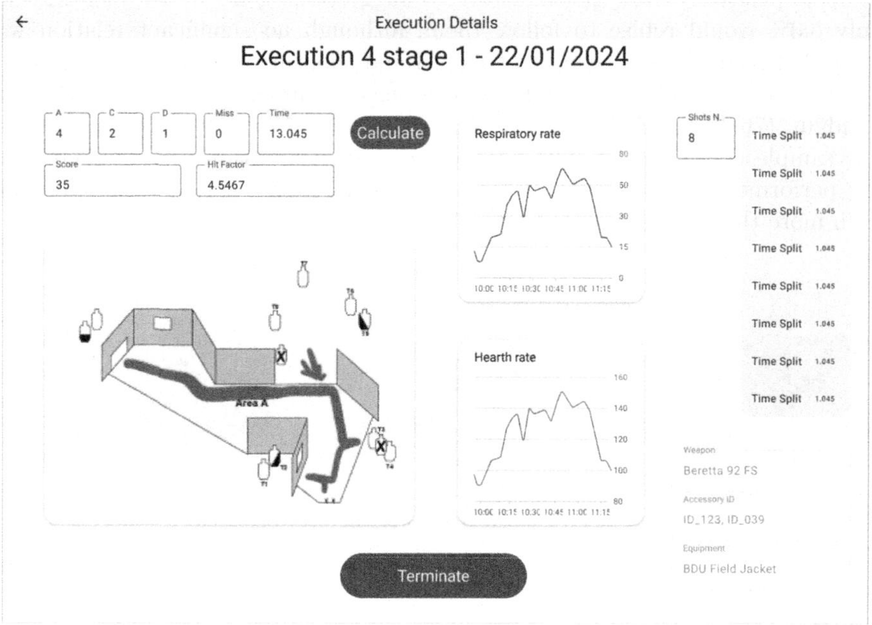

Fig. 2. Example of a screen of the Figma mock-up, with the data of a single stage execution.

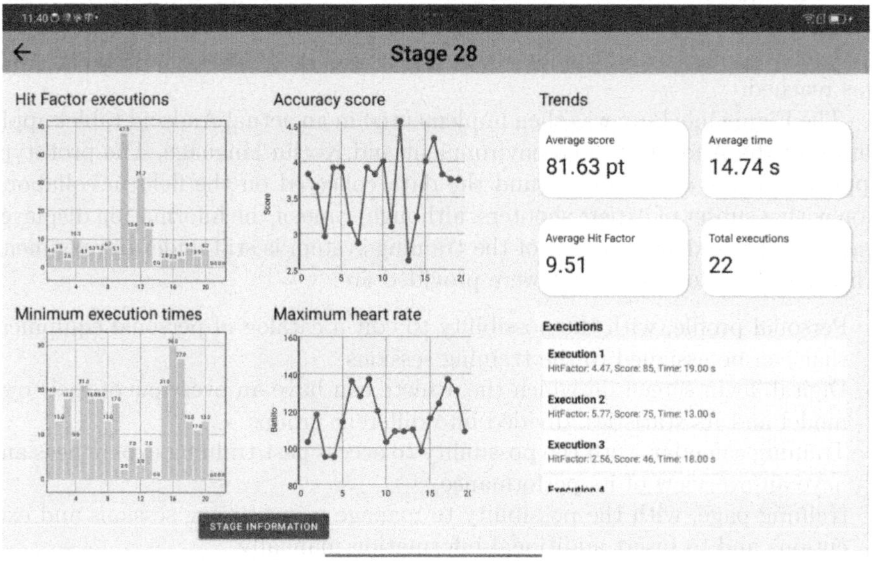

Fig. 3. One screen of the final application providing an overview of past executions of a stage

3.3 Testing and Validation

The effectiveness and usability of the user interface we designed were finally tested with the intention of quantifying the users' opinions of the application and identifying eventual weaknesses in the user experience. Out of the 19 athletes who participated in the user research, five users also participated in the validation. The sample size, while being scientifically not optimal, was constricted by the availability of the athletes, their geographical location, and the necessity to perform the test in their presence. For this reason we tried to maximize the information collected during the test by also including open questions and an unstructured interview.

To validate the user experience, the task and observation methodology was employed, where users were required to perform certain specific tasks, and researchers observed their behavior and collected quantitative data. The tasks presented to the athletes varied from very simple actions, such as logging into the application, to more complex operations, such as gathering specific information or performing a complete training session cycle.

While the users performed their tasks, researchers observed their behavior and recorded the time elapsed, number of taps, number of errors, and feedback from the user. The users were also tasked to complete two surveys, one for introductory information before the test, and one about their personal evaluation of the application after. The questions in the second survey were structured following three standard tests: System Usability Scale (SUS), Computer System Usability Questionnaire (CSUQ), and User Experience Questionnaire (UEQ).

System Usability Scale. The first part of the questionnaire, related to the SUS test, required users to indicate on a scale between 1 and 5 how much they agreed with the ten proposed statements. The answers were elaborated per the SUS standard and resulted in a score of **89.5/100**, where a result is considered "sufficient" if superior to 68/100.

Computer System Usability Questionnaire. In the second section of the survey were 19 statements related to the CSUQ test, divided between three themes: system usefulness, information quality, and interface quality. Once again, users answered how much they agreed with the statements on a scale of 1 to 5, and the results were computed to obtain synthetic scores per the CSUQ test. The application was positively evaluated as follows:

- System Usefulness: 4.27/5
- Information Quality: 4.11/5
- Interface Quality: 4.20/5
- Overall: 4.20/5

User Experience Questionnaire. In the last portion of the survey, 26 couples of counterpoising adjectives describing the application were presented, and users indicated for each couple a degree of adherence to one adjective or the other on a scale of 1 to 7. The twenty-six couples are meant to quantify the user's opinion across six themes: attractiveness, perspicuity, efficiency, dependability, stimulation, and novelty. The answers are computed in order to obtain a score for each category between –3 and +3, where a result greater than 1.5 is considered satisfactory. The scores obtained by our dashboard are as follows:

- Attractiveness: +2.33
- Perspicuity: +2.35
- Efficiency: +1.80
- Dependability: +2.00
- Stimulation: +2.15
- Novelty: +2.30

The results were also bench-marked against a database containing the scores of 468 studies over several software, web pages, web shops, and social media. The results were categorised as *bad* if below 25%, *below average* if in the range 25–50%, *above average* in the range 50–75%, *good* between 75–90% or *excellent* if higher than 90% Fig. 4 shows the comparison results, which were very positive across all themes.

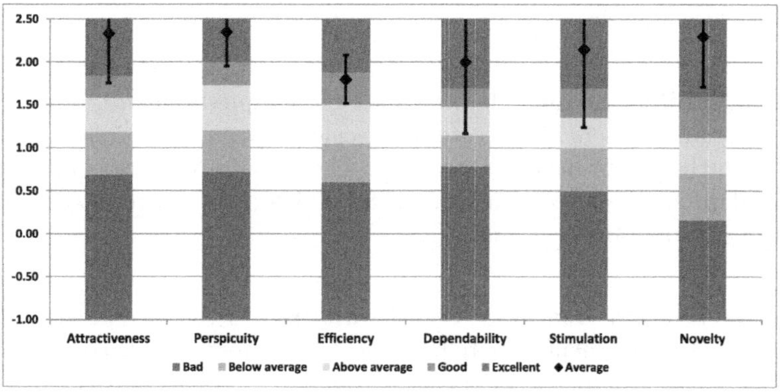

Fig. 4. UEQ bench-marking of the athlete's dashboard

4 System Architecture

The overall training system we are developing can be summarised into three main entities as in Fig. 5. Firstly, the training environment, in which users practice their discipline while being monitored by a combination of wearable and on-field sensors; secondly, the training system, which will model the user, produce customized suggestions, and optimize the training routine; and finally, a feedback system whose task is to format the system's output and making it intelligible for the target user. The three components are bound by a network connection to transfer the collected data to the training system and relay the results to the user.

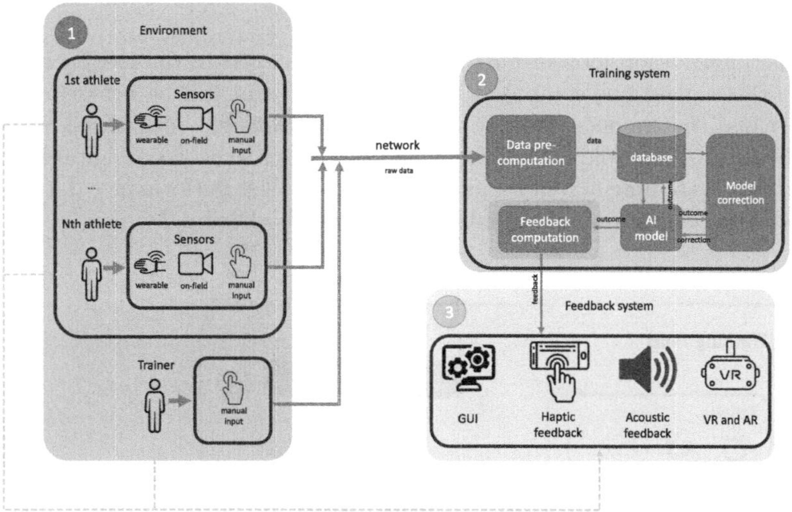

Fig. 5. Schematic representation of overall training system

4.1 On-Field System for Athlete and Coach

In our system architecture, a shooting field is equipped with some measurement instruments to monitor the athletes, an on-field computing unit and a local network to communicate between the agents. As represented in Fig. 6, each athlete is also equipped with a compact Single Board Computer (SBC), such as a Raspberry Pi, and some wearable measurement instruments. The field computer works as an acquisition master, acquires the on-field measurement instruments, communicates with the users' devices and bridges the commands received from the system server to the devices on the shooting field. The athlete's SBC interacts with the wearable instruments, controlling and acquiring them, with the acquisition manager, receiving commands and sharing the collected data, and with the user, providing an acoustic signal to indicate the start of the shooting session. This design was derived by criteria given by the sports discipline, by safety concerns, by practical necessities, and by the scientific literature. For example, through user research, by observing the athletes on the field and with unstructured interviews, we could identify the aspects we needed to monitor and the functionalities we needed to provide the users. We could also place the measurement instruments to be as little invasive as possible, and to not interfere with the athletic gesture and the natural execution of the training. Other significant examples are the practical necessity to collect information on the athlete's movement and behaviour to feed the user's digital model, that dictated the measured quantities, or the necessity to maintain robust communication with the wearable devices, which is one of the typical issues in Human Digital Twin and dictated the inclusion of the user's SBC.

The information loop of our Digital Twin is closed in the feedback system, where the suggestions computed by the Digital Twin will be bridged with the trainer and the trainees. We are developing solutions for both based on mobile dashboards for Android tablets, allowing the trainer to access a digital library of the athlete's training activity and an overview of their performance data, and to receive and relay training suggestions based on the Digital Twin.

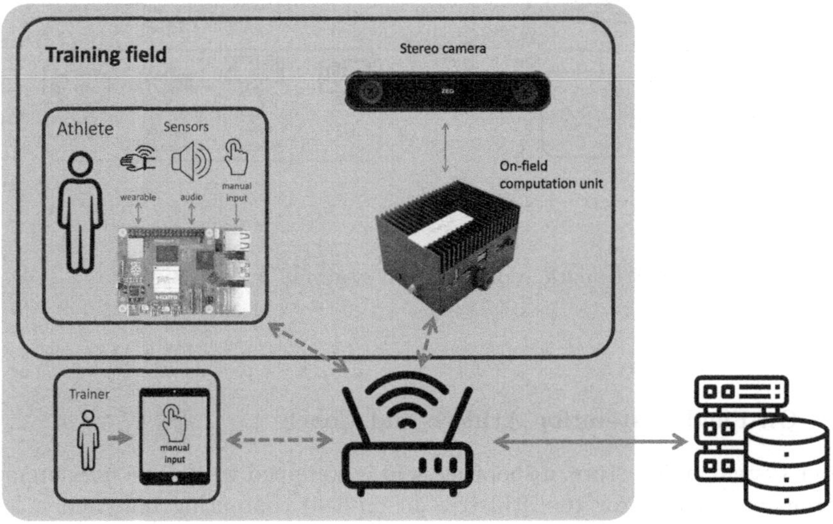

Fig. 6. Schematic representation of the portion of the system to be installed on the shooting field

4.2 Collection of User Data

In order to model the athlete's behavior and performance, we collect a multitude of information during the training session. The user is equipped with a set of wearable measurement instruments (Fig. 7). In particular:

Inertial Measurement Units: Inertial units are placed on the pelvis (belt), on the wrists, and on the weapons and are used to measure 3D accelerations, angular velocities, and orientation at 200 Hz. The Muse sensor package manufactured by 221e was selected for this application because of its compact size, battery operation, BLE communication, the capability of storing recorded data, and the capability to compute orientation autonomously through a motion processing library.

Some of the uses of these instruments, beyond the raw accelerations and angular velocities values, are a more robust shot detection, improved user tracking through sensor fusion, and the measure of the weapon's orientation as a safety measure.

Hearth Rate Monitor: A chest strap with a heart rate monitor is used to monitor hearth-related quantities that correlate with stress and fatigue. In our application, the Movesense Flash is a single-channel ECG with reliable data quality [14], BLE communication and internal storage in case of connection loss, capable of measuring and streaming the raw ECG value, HR, R-R interval, and also an integrated IMU. We are employing this instrument to stream the raw ECG value, from which we then calculate Hearth Rate and R-R interval statistics through the neurokit2 [11] Python package.

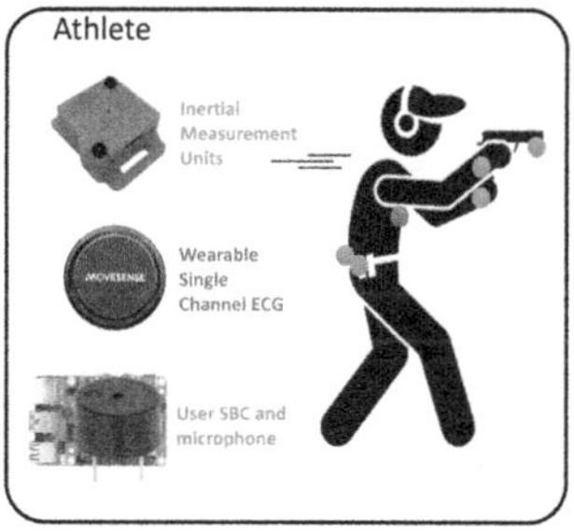

Fig. 7. Position of the wearable instruments on the athlete

Shooting Timer: A shooting timer is the standard instrument for Practical Shooting. It produces an acoustic signal as "start", detects the shots and records their timestamp, and gives the athlete or coach the number of shots, the overall time between the start signal and the last shot, and the *split time* between each shot. In our case, a simple shooting timer was implemented in a custom PCB connected to the Raspberry pin header.

Stereoscopic Camera: Another significant source of information is installed on the shooting field. In our application, we employ a single stereoscopic camera ZED X manufactured by Stereolabs [8,15], and acquired with the Stereolabs ZED Box, which is a repackaged NVIDIA Jetson Orin NX, which also serves as acquisition Master. With this camera, we can track the 3D position of the athlete and collect information on its trajectory and pose, processing the video with a neural network for the fit of an 18-point human model (Fig. 8).

Additional Information: The last source of information is the athlete itself, which is required to manually insert some information about their daily life, such as nutrition and sleeping quality. For this, a dedicated screen in the tablet application was designed.

Fig. 8. Athlete's joints detection and tracking

4.3 Information System

The Digital Twin system will be implemented on a server and comprise computational capability and storage. The training system will receive formatted training data from the on-field computing units and will cover feature extraction on the data, storage of historical data, implementation of a machine learning model of the user, and the capability to adjust the model to follow the trainee's performance evolution. Similar applications in literature also suggest other necessities, such as the fill-in of missing data, especially if manual input is required, or the employment of sensor fusion techniques to improve the informational content of the data. The computed suggestions will then be sent to the user and trainer dashboards.

5 Conclusion

This paper explores the design and development of a digital twin system to enhance practical shooting coaching. We detail the system's architecture and showcase initial results in the interaction design of two mobile applications: one for athletes and another for coaches. Moving forward, we will collaborate with field experts to collect physical data to refine the digital twin model, test various implementations for the training system components, and terminate the development of the trainer's mobile applications. Future efforts will concentrate on developing the server-side infrastructure of the coaching system. The project will culminate in testing and validating a high-fidelity prototype encompassing the entire system.

References

1. Adesida, Y., Papi, E., McGregor, A.H.: Exploring the role of wearable technology in sport kinematics and kinetics: a systematic review. Sensors **19**(7) (2019). https://doi.org/10.3390/s19071597. https://www.mdpi.com/1424-8220/19/7/1597
2. Barricelli, B.R., Casiraghi, E., Fogli, D.: A survey on digital twin: definitions, characteristics, applications, and design implications. IEEE Access **7**, 167653–167671 (2019). https://doi.org/10.1109/ACCESS.2019.2953499
3. Barricelli, B.R., Casiraghi, E., Gliozzo, J., Petrini, A., Valtolina, S.: Human digital twin for fitness management. IEEE Access **8**, 26637–26664 (2020). https://api.semanticscholar.org/CorpusID:211210870
4. Bačić, B., Hume, P.: Computational intelligence for qualitative coaching diagnostics: automated assessment of tennis swings to improve performance and safety. Big Data **6**(4) (2017)
5. Clemmensen, T.: Human Work Interaction Design. HIS. Springer, Cham (2021). https://doi.org/10.1007/978-3-030-71796-4
6. Gámez Díaz, R., Yu, Q., Ding, Y., Laamarti, F., El Saddik, A.: Digital twin coaching for physical activities: a survey. Sensors **20**(20) (2020). https://doi.org/10.3390/s20205936. https://www.mdpi.com/1424-8220/20/20/5936
7. Jensen, U., Prade, F., Eskofier, B.: Classification of kinematic swimming data with emphasis on resource consumption. In: 2013 IEEE International Conference on Body Sensor Networks, pp. 1–5 (2013). https://doi.org/10.1109/BSN.2013.6575501
8. Kim, P., Kim, J., Song, M., Lee, Y., Jung, M., Kim, H.G.: A benchmark comparison of four off-the-shelf proprietary visual–inertial odometry systems. Sensors **22**(24) (2022). https://doi.org/10.3390/s22249873. https://www.mdpi.com/1424-8220/22/24/9873
9. Lauer-Schmaltz, M.W., Cash, P., Hansen, J.P., Maier, A.: Designing human digital twins for behaviour-changing therapy and rehabilitation: a systematic review. Proc. Des. Soc. **2**, 1303–1312 (2022). https://doi.org/10.1017/pds.2022.132
10. Lukač, L., Fister, I., Fister, I.: Digital twin in sport: from an idea to realization. Appl. Sci. **12**(24) (2022). https://doi.org/10.3390/app122412741
11. Makowski, D., et al.: NeuroKit2: a python toolbox for neurophysiological signal processing. Behav. Res. Methods **53**(4), 1689–1696 (2021). https://doi.org/10.3758/s13428-020-01516-y
12. Miller, M.E., Spatz, E.: A unified view of a human digital twin. Hum.-Intell. Syst. Integrat. **4**(1), 23–33 (2022)
13. Abdelnour Nocera, J., Barricelli, B.R., Lopes, A., Campos, P., Clemmensen, T. (eds.): HWID 2015. IAICT, vol. 468. Springer, Cham (2015). https://doi.org/10.1007/978-3-319-27048-7
14. Rogers, B., Schaffarczyk, M., Clauß, M., Mourot, L., Gronwald, T.: The movesense medical sensor chest belt device as single channel ECG for RR interval detection and HRV analysis during resting state and incremental exercise: a cross-sectional validation study. Sensors (Basel) **22**(5) (2022)
15. Sosa-León, V.A.L., Schwering, A.: Evaluating automatic body orientation detection for indoor location from skeleton tracking data to detect socially occupied spaces using the kinect v2, azure kinect and zed 2i. Sensors **22**(10) (2022). https://doi.org/10.3390/s22103798. https://www.mdpi.com/1424-8220/22/10/3798
16. Yasser, A., Tariq, D., Samy, R., Hassan, M.A., Atia, A.: Smart coaching: enhancing weightlifting and preventing injuries. Int. J. Adv. Comput. Sci. Appl. **10**(7) (2019). https://doi.org/10.14569/IJACSA.2019.0100789

Collaboration with Intelligent Artificial Team Members at Work

AI and Work Engagement: A Study of IT Professionals Through the Lens of Self-Determination Theory

Åsa Cajander[1(✉)], Andreas Bergqvist[1], Tony Clear[2], Mats Daniels[1], Niklas Humble[1], Marta Larusdottir[3], Maria Normark[1], and Sofia Ouhbi[1]

[1] Uppsala University, Uppsala, Sweden
asa.cajander@it.uu.se
[2] Auckland University of Technology, Auckland, New Zealand
[3] Reykjavik University, Reykjavik, Iceland

Abstract. Artificial intelligence (AI) is reshaping work, presenting new challenges and opportunities for professionals across industries. This study, grounded in Self-Determination Theory (SDT), examines the impact of AI integration on work engagement among IT professionals. Through qualitative investigation, our research reveals that AI both augments and complicates professionals' work lives, providing opportunities for growth while also demanding ongoing adaptation. Key findings indicate that AI tools like UiPath and GitHub Copilot enhance work efficiency by automating routine tasks, enabling professionals to concentrate on more complex aspects of their work and enhancing their perceived competence. However, this efficiency gain requires continuous learning and adaptation, posing challenges in maintaining engagement and mastery. These findings illuminate the complex balance between leveraging AI for increased efficiency and maintaining the intrinsic human elements of IT design, offering some insights for navigating AI integration in the workplace.

Keywords: Work Engagement · Artificial Intelligence (AI) · User Experience (UX) Professionals · Professional Development · Self-Determination Theory

1 Introduction

Work practices are undergoing a profound transformation due to the advent of artificial intelligence (AI), with significant changes particularly evident within the information technology (IT) sector [6, 14, 16]. This technological revolution is reshaping task management, promising efficiency gains while introducing challenges in adapting to new workflows. As pioneers in technology adoption, IT professionals are uniquely positioned to assess AI's impact on work practices and engagement. Self-Determination Theory (SDT) offers a valuable framework for this exploration, emphasising how AI integration might affect basic psychological needs—autonomy, competence, and relatedness—crucial for high work engagement [8, 9, 11]. This study focuses on the need

Published by Springer Nature Switzerland AG 2026
B. R. Barricelli et al. (Eds.): HWID 2024, IFIP AICT 751, pp. 143–157, 2026.
https://doi.org/10.1007/978-3-031-95334-7_9

for competence, exploring how AI's role in automating tasks might alter professionals' perceptions of their effectiveness and mastery, thus impacting their motivation to engage in work.

While traditional workplace automation primarily aimed to improve efficiency and safety, introducing AI systems suggests a broader scope, encompassing tasks that were once difficult to automate, such as professional judgement, creativity, and imagination [21]. This shift toward advanced AI and automation raises essential questions about work motivations, particularly how to preserve meaningful and healthy work experiences while fostering new opportunities for fulfilling and enjoyable work. To enhance the resilience and sustainability of work, the European Commission envisions a "fifth industrial revolution" centred around human-focused automation, where employee well-being takes priority in industrial processes [35]. These changes highlight the need for research into a future of human-centred work, even in an AI-driven world. Hence, our research seeks to understand the consequences of AI on competence and overall work engagement through qualitative interviews with IT professionals. In this study, we have chosen to concentrate on the competence aspect of SDT, since such a focus is suitable for unravelling the complex interplay between technological changes and their psychological effects. This focus is essential for unravelling the complex interplay between technological changes and their psychological effects.

Responding to academic calls for more detailed exploration of AI's workplace impact, such as those by Zirar et al. [34] and Simsek et al. [26], this study aims to bridge gaps in understanding how AI influences worker competencies and work engagement. Given this backdrop, this study's research question is: "How does the integration of artificial intelligence in IT design work influence professionals' perceptions of competence and overall work engagement?" Our findings aim to provide a more comprehensive understanding of AI's role, highlighting the importance of creating work environments that support performance and well-being.

As an example of current industrial work interpreting the impacts of AI on IT Professionals' work, the SFIA (Skills Framework for the Information Age) foundation has produced a BETA framework for AI skills, which highlights a set of challenges in defining a set of often cross-cutting AI skills and an overview of AI skills incorporated into SFIA version nine [24]. Challenges in the framework include pace of change; breadth and depth; integration with existing skills; industry variation; ethical and legal considerations; and SFIA user needs.

In the field of Human-Data Interaction (HDI) [31], researchers have suggested that HCI should broaden its scope to include "how people interact with data, much like how HCI explores the relationship between people and computers" [31]. This view highlights the importance of "actively engaging with data rather than simply consuming it" [31]. Building on this perspective, the study investigates how individuals experience and interpret their interactions with AI data in their contexts.

This study contributes to HCI and to human-work interaction design (HWID) by providing empirical insights into the impact of AI on work engagement and perceived competence, using the competence aspect of self-determination theory as a framework. In this paper, results from four semi-structured interviews are described and interpreted. The findings highlight how AI tools like UiPath and GitHub Copilot [12, 33] enhance task efficiency and require continuous learning, influencing professionals' sense of competence and motivation. The research also expands the understanding of AI as a collaborative tool in IT work, offering insights into how AI supports decision-making and problem-solving. Finally, the study provides design implications for AI-integrated systems, emphasising the need to support user autonomy and competence to maintain engagement in technology-driven work environments.

2 Background

2.1 Evolution and Integration of AI in the Workplace

Integrating AI from its developing stages to its current pervasive role in workplace tools and processes marks a significant evolution in how work is conducted, especially within the IT and design sectors. The journey of AI began with the development of artificial neural networks in the mid-20th century and formalised as a distinct discipline in the 1950s [4]. Today, driven by advancements in machine learning, big data, and computational power, AI is deeply integrated into modern workplaces, fundamentally transforming job roles and tasks [3].

Applying AI technologies has changed software development, data analysis, and cybersecurity in the IT sector [29]. These innovations require specialised skills, and addressing the knowledge gap between business managers and data scientists is critical for successful AI implementation [17]. Similarly, the IT sector has witnessed a shift from manual tasks to more strategic and creative roles facilitated by AI, enabling rapid prototyping and trend prediction, thus reshaping the creative process [10, 15].

AI is transforming the workplace by automating repetitive tasks and enhancing human intelligence, improving efficiency and experiences while raising concerns about job loss and AI dominance [5]. AI's dual impact in the workplace is evident in its capacity to enhance efficiency and foster innovation while challenging traditional job roles and skill requirements. This paradigm shift underscores the need for continual learning and adaptation among professionals to leverage AI's benefits fully. This continual learning could benefit from AI technology through personalised, hands-on, and simulation-based approaches [32].

Bainbridge's paper on the ironies inherent in the automation process, published in the eighties yet still relevant to this day [27], provides a pertinent framework for understanding the paradoxes presented by AI in the workplace. One of the core ironies identified is that while automation aims to reduce the need for human labour, it simultaneously creates a demand for higher-order human skills to oversee, manage, and intervene in automated systems. This irony highlights a paradox in AI's role in competence development: the displacement of routine tasks by AI necessitates a shift towards more complex, abstract competencies that are harder to define, acquire, and assess [1].

The integration of AI also raises ethical considerations and safety risks, including concerns related to data privacy and algorithmic biases, which are pivotal in navigating the sustainable deployment of AI technologies in the workplace [30]. As AI evolves, organisations must balance the technological benefits against socio-technical and ethical considerations. This balance is crucial for fostering environments that support performance and holistic well-being. The future workplace will likely be characterised by a hybrid model where AI augments human capabilities, requiring a re-examination of job roles, skills, and the nature of work [7, 13].

2.2 Work Engagement and Self-Determination Theory

Work engagement, characterised by vigour, dedication, and absorption, is essential to employee motivation and productivity. According to the job demands-resources (JD-R) model, work engagement is driven by the balance between job demands, which require effort and lead to physical and psychological strain, and job resources, which help employees manage these demands while fostering learning and development [2]. Research by Schaufeli, Bakker, and Salanova [22, 23] provides a foundational understanding of this construct, emphasising its significance in fostering a motivated and committed workforce. Work engagement is closely linked to SDT [8, 9, 11], a psychological framework for understanding human motivation and personality in social contexts. SDT, developed by Deci and Ryan, emphasises the role of intrinsic and extrinsic motivations in driving human behaviour and highlights three basic psychological needs: autonomy, competence, and relatedness [8].

Autonomy refers to feeling in control of one's actions and decisions. Autonomy is associated with a sense of choice and freedom in performing tasks. When employees feel autonomous, they are more likely to be engaged in their work, perceiving their actions as self-endorsed and aligned with their values and interests.

Competence reflects the desire to feel adequate and capable within one's environment. At work, feeling competent involves the perception that one can successfully meet job demands and challenges. When employees feel competent, they are more likely to experience work engagement, as they feel a sense of accomplishment and efficacy in their roles. The workplace context magnifies this need, as employees yearn to meet and excel in their job requirements and challenges. This research mainly focuses on competence given the unique inflexion point provided by the integration of AI in IT design work. As AI technologies assume roles traditionally filled by humans, they redefine the landscape of tasks and, subsequently, the avenues through which employees experience mastery and effectiveness. This shift harbours profound implications for work engagement, hinging on the perceived competence of employees. Exploring how AI integration impacts this psychological need is poised to uncover insights into maintaining and fostering engagement in the evolving workplace.

Relatedness involves feeling connected to others and having a sense of belonging. In the workplace, relatedness refers to the quality of relationships with colleagues, managers, and the organisation. When employees experience high levels of relatedness, they are more likely to be engaged, as they feel supported, valued, and part of a community.

According to SDT, fulfilling the needs for autonomy, competence, and relatedness fosters intrinsic motivation, which is a key driver of work engagement. Hence, the analysis in this paper focuses on analysing the fulfilling of autonomy, competence and relatedness, how that fosters intrinsic motivation, and how that affects work engagement. Intrinsic motivation occurs when individuals engage in an activity for the inherent satisfaction and enjoyment it brings rather than for some separable consequence. Figure 1 illustrates the main psychological needs of SDT and the effect that fulfilling those has on intrinsic motivation, described in the text above.

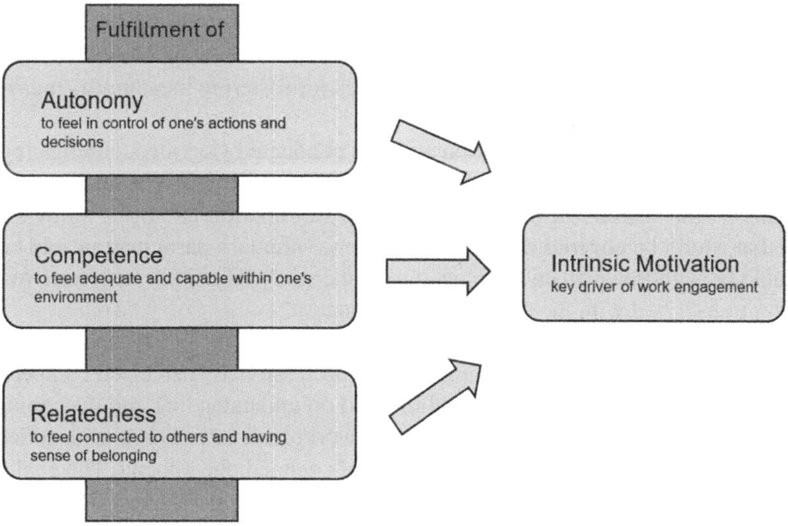

Fig. 1. Fulfilment of Autonomy, competence and relatedness leads to intrinsic motivation.

3 Method

This paper delivers initial findings from a qualitative investigation focusing on work engagement among IT professionals within AI-integrated environments. Although the broader study is expected to encompass at least 60 participants, this report focuses on four initial exploratory interviews. It sheds light on how artificial intelligence shapes work engagement dynamics in professional settings. In line with exploratory research's aim of producing new and interesting findings on a research topic [28], this interview study hopes to provide the reader with initial and interesting findings on a research topic that is becoming increasingly important for many IT professionals.

Table 1. Overview of demographic data of interviewees

Participant ID	Age	Gender	Years working in IT	Type of organisation
P1	45	M	6	Consulting organisation > 250
P2	34	M	8	Consulting organisation > 250
P3	48	M	27	Consulting organisation > 250
P4	28	F	1	Consulting organisation > 250

As detailed in Table 1, the participants were selected through purposeful sampling to provide information-rich cases that could be studied in depth [19]. They are IT professionals working in environments where AI tools are in active use. The semi-structured interviews, guided by an interview guide, explored various AI-related topics in professional settings. These topics ranged from the participants' daily work routines with AI, the degree to which AI has been integrated into their daily work tasks, how they perceived potential shifts in work engagement attributable to the integration of AI, as well as potential associated challenges and opportunities for fostering meaningful engagement at the workplace with AI.

Each interview lasted 30 to 60 min and was conducted via videoconferencing tools like Zoom. Before the interviews, participants received information about the study. This information was shared via email and included information about the study's intent, topics that would be covered during the interview, voluntary participation, and consent that could be withdrawn at any moment during the study. The interviews were recorded and later transcribed with the participants' consent.

A phenomenological analysis [20], informed by SDT [8, 9, 11], was employed to deepen our understanding of AI's impact on IT professionals' perceived competencies. The phenomenological analysis applied focused on understanding and describing how individuals experience and make sense of their workplace, interactions with colleagues, job roles, organizational culture, and overall work-related phenomena. The goal was to uncover the core meanings, structures, and experiences that define how people perceive their work environment.

The analysis used three main themes, further described in Table 2.

Table 2. Themes used in the analysis of the results

Theme	Description
Perceived Competence in AI-Enhanced Tasks	Understanding how AI impacts IT professionals' sense of competence, skill, and mastery
Learning and Competence Development	The respondents' perceptions on learning, and the need to keep pace with new technologies
Implications for Work Engagement	The respondents' views on the impact and implications of AI on work engagement

For clarity, quotes from these interviews have been edited and translated into English when included in this paper. Importantly, this study has been approved by the Swedish National Ethical Authority (2023–06103-01), ensuring compliance with ethical standards.

The deductive use of theory-based measurement methodologies, such as psychometric scales in Self-Determination Theory (SDT) and work engagement research, could limit the depth of understanding by focusing on predefined variables and quantifiable aspects. While these methods provide structured and reliable data, they may overlook the nuanced, subjective experiences of individuals that aren't easily captured through fixed scales.

4 Results

Reflecting the predefined themes based on SDT, our analysis targeted the impact of AI on work engagement among IT professionals. The themes—Perceived Competence in AI-enhanced Tasks, Learning and Competence Development and Implications for Work Engagement—were chosen to explore how AI integration aligns with or challenges the SDT competence component.

4.1 Perceived Competence in AI-Enhanced Tasks

This theme relates to understanding AI's impact on IT professionals' sense of competence, skill and mastery. AI tools, especially automation technologies like UiPath and GitHub Copilot, are frequently mentioned as augmenting work efficiency by automating routine tasks.

AI Allows us to Focus on More Complex Work. These tools allow professionals to focus on more complex aspects of their work, potentially enhancing their perceived competence and efficiency. This quote highlights how UiPath, as a robust RPA tool, has evolved to include AI functionalities, improving the automation of simple, rule-based processes. Thus, IT professionals can focus on more complex tasks and enhance their perceived effectiveness and competence: "*UiPath is the most robust and largest RPA tool. [...] Initially, RPA was about automating simple, rule-driven processes. These RPA tools have become better and better and UiPath is probably at the forefront of the world around its development [...] where, among other things, AI is a large part that has been invested in recently.*".

AI as a Valuable Assistant. IT professionals increasingly integrate AI into their workflows, utilising these technologies for various tasks, from debugging and code suggestions to automating video editing and documentation. These AI tools are generally perceived as valuable assistants that enhance efficiency by handling time-consuming tasks. For instance, one professional describes their use of AI technology: *"I use a tool called Descript which allows you to do video and sound editing with transcript. You upload a video and transcript and then you can remove O, Ä, Us and so on and it is removed from the video"*. This quote illustrates how AI tools simplify complex editing processes, enabling professionals to focus on more strategic aspects of their work.

Nuanced Impact on Perceived Competence. However, others do not see themselves as AI experts and do not see their skills beyond what AI can automate. They see their current implementation of AI in companies as a minor part of their work, as a tool in their toolbox, suggesting a nuanced impact on self-perception of competence.*"So far, not many companies are far ahead in their digital journey, which makes it a little difficult to start introducing complex AI models. [...] I am not some kind of AI expert in my field, but I overall work with automation, where AI is just a tool in the box"*. This is further nuanced by how the participants describe that some of their skills are possible to automate: "*I really believe that low coding will be replaced, so to speak, by some form of AI model instead [...] here you have, you describe to the AI model what you want to do and it writes the code for you*" and "*Yes, but there is probably a lot that can be replaced or automated. But maybe not like whole pieces*".

Pressure to Deepen AI Knowledge. In today's landscape, where AI is a buzzword that resonates across various media, there is significant pressure on professionals to deepen their understanding of AI technologies. This necessity stems from the need to stay informed due to AI's immense hype. Many clients and colleagues within their organisations may need a deeper understanding of the technology. Professionals are responsible for bridging this knowledge gap, ensuring that AI implementations are effective and appropriately leveraged within their projects. This ongoing learning is crucial, as it allows them to provide accurate insights and guidance in an environment where misconceptions about AI capabilities and applications are expected, which is illustrated by the following quote: "*For me who meets a lot of new customers and stakeholders, AI is something they often ask about. Because it is AI, they hear about it actually every single day if you watch TV or read newspapers or articles so to speak. AI is a term that is used so frequently. So for our part, we must be updated on the topic in all our relationships really, both internally and externally as well*".

4.2 Learning and Competence Development

This theme captures how professionals view AI in two distinct ways; as a reason for the need for them to develop as well as a tool in their own overall learning. Their own development is commonly described as continuous while stressing their individual responsibility in staying up to date.

Continuous Learning. The integration of AI requires continuous learning and adaptation. Several respondents discussed the importance of continuously updating their skills to keep pace with new technologies. This constant need to learn new tools can be both an opportunity and a challenge, affecting their engagement and sense of mastery over their work. This quote reflects the ongoing process of learning and adapting to new AI technologies, which is both a challenge and an opportunity for personal and professional development: *"I learn about them by reading different things on the internet. In our community, on Slack or on Mastodon or Hacker News, different websites or podcasts, people talk about different things and then just go ahead and try it out"*. And as previously stated, another interviewee expressed it like this: *"We must be updated on the topic in all our relationships really, both internally and externally as well. Otherwise, we risk falling behind"*.

Self-directed Learning. Since formal training on AI discussed in the interviews is minimal, it is often on the IT professionals to stay informed and adapt to AI technologies through self-directed learning and practical application. This approach reflects a broader trend in the interviews where professionals must often take the initiative to keep their skills relevant in a rapidly advancing technological landscape, as in this quote and that they learn through using the technology: *"I had some internal training. But, it wasn't very big. [...] I am interested so there is a lot that I read on my own. Then there's a lot of using products and solutions"*. Another participant refers to *"own-world monitoring"* and reading up on AI and automation topics as part of their development, stating, *"I limit my AI learning to what I can use in my work"*.

AI as a Competence Development Tool. Several interviewees express how they use AI not only as a work tool but also for learning. One describes using AI to generate new ideas and validate thoughts before taking action, explaining that they use it as a *"second opinion"* to ensure their ideas are aligned with other possible solutions. Another uses AI to quickly grasp unfamiliar IT concepts, noting that *"you know this; so I can still use it as a tool in the process if I don't understand"*. In contrast, another one notes that it probably will be such a tool soon but is not fully there yet, stating: *"You can't google your way to experience. You may be able to google your way to understanding, but practice makes perfect"*. In addition, IT professionals use tools like ChatGPT or access educational content on platforms provided by their companies to stay up to date. One participant notes *"Yes, we see [ChatGPT] as a new source for me to not only search for information but also to process what I might be stuck with and pondering"*.

4.3 Implications for Work Engagement

Integrating AI in IT work influences professionals' perceptions of competence and overall work engagement. The perceptions in this theme showed that the respondents had differing views on the impact of AI on work engagement. This multifaceted impact presents opportunities for enhanced efficiency and challenges related to personal interaction and technological dependency. The findings suggest that the balance between these factors is critical in shaping the overall engagement of IT professionals in their work environments.

Resource for Engagement: AI as Providing Support: All participants described ways that AI helps them as employees in their work and tackling complex tasks. One interviewee says, *"It simplifies things a lot, it does. It's not an encyclopedia, it's more of a place you go to actually hold a conversation and work out what you might want to get an answer to"*. Another starts describing how it allows them to save time by not manually having to find sounds in video files before also commenting on how it helps them work between different projects: *"But also that I can change a little easier between different projects and tasks. It helps me to remember the context better"*. A third participant describes how it helps them face challenging tasks as *"the barrier might be lowered a little because you know this; so I can still use it as a tool in the process if I don't understand, for example"* before agreeing to feel more confident about doing things that they know little about. This suggests that AI empowers workers by functioning as a job resource that supports employees in their work and can reduce the anxiety related to challenging assignments and boost engagement.

Resource for Engagement: AI as a Facilitator of Autonomy: AI tools also enable greater independence. As an example, one participant mentions, *"But maybe I'll spare them that so I don't disturb them in their work and just turn quickly to ChatGPT instead. This bit of me doing the work myself before I get help from someone else so I've done my research"*. This reflects the idea that AI fosters a sense of autonomy, which is often a critical job resource in motivating engagement.

Demand limiting Engagement: Uncertainty and Limitations of AI: However, concerns about AI's accuracy can lead to hesitation. For example, as one participant explains, *"it may give wrong answers, incomplete answers. Sometimes you might have wanted to have the source for something"*. Another participant echoes similar sentiments: *"I don't really want to use them for fact-finding, nor for counsel. So there goes my limit"*. This highlights a potential job demand that can decrease engagement when the tools do not meet expectations and require extra effort to verify AI output.

Impacts on Collaboration and Team Dynamics: AI is seen as reshaping colleague interactions and using social support resources. One participant explained that using colleagues was the secondary choice for help: *"So if ChatGPT hadn't existed, I would still have been able to go to like an actual colleague and ask instead."*. Similarly, another participant notes, *"it might have taken me much longer with just basic web searches or having to talk to colleagues"*, indicating that AI can streamline internal communications but may also reduce direct collaboration in certain contexts.

Increased Engagement through AI Usage. Two respondents report increased engagement due to AI tools' support and efficiency gains. One participant stated that it did so and described how AI supports them in completing challenging tasks as an example, *"Yes, but if I'm going to come up with something, it might be that I can get quite challenging tasks sometimes [...] I myself might take the plunge now, it's like this, if I can check with ChatGPT"*. While the other participant stated that they did not perceive that their engagement had increased, but then also repeatedly discussed how much it affected them and their work: *"So mainly to save time. But as I said, I think that it will increase the quality more and more before long, because then we will have more time for quality-raising work"*. These sentiments underscores the positive impact that AI could have on work engagement, where the adoption of advanced tools is not only a matter of enhancing capabilities but also a source of professional pride and curiosity.

No Influence on Work Engagement. On the other hand, another sentiment regarding integrating AI in their roles is that it has little to no impact on work engagement. While the participants recognise the advantages of AI, such as increased efficiency and the ability to focus on more complex tasks, some do not attribute any significant changes in their perceived engagement to AI. For instance, one respondent stated, *"No, I don't think it has been affected in any way, it's unaffected"* while another elaborated more on what drives them:

> *"I don't think it has affected my engagement at all. I am rather driven by the idea of helping businesses have a smoother everyday life, enabling people to perform more value-creating tasks. That is what has driven me in this."*

Though AI was perceived as promoting motivation, efficiency and innovation, none of the interview participants indicated that it had extensively altered their engagement. Instead, they remain motivated by the intrinsic aspects of their roles, such as contributing to business improvements or addressing customer needs. Additionally, concerns about reduced human interaction and over-reliance on automation exist in broader discussions of AI. However, these themes did not emerge in the interviews, further reinforcing that AI has not had a major effect on their sense of engagement at work.

5 Discussion

Integrating AI in IT professionals' work influences their engagement in some cases and perceptions of competence, which we analysed through SDT. Our study identified several themes, which are discussed below.

Efficiency and Competence Enhancement Through AI. AI tools such as UiPath and GitHub Copilot enhance work efficiency by automating routine tasks, aligning with the historical evolution of AI integration in the workplace, which began with developments in artificial neural networks and has now become fundamental in transforming job roles and tasks [3]. This automation allows IT professionals to engage more deeply with complex challenges, enhancing their perceived competence. This finding aligns with SDT's emphasis on feeling effective and capable within one's environment and reflects historical shifts from manual tasks to more strategic and creative roles facilitated by AI [10, 15].

Continuous Learning and Professional Adaptation. As AI technologies evolve rapidly, IT professionals face the dual challenge and opportunity of continuous skill updating This dual aspect resonates with SDT's principles, which highlight integrating new experiences into one's competency framework. The dynamic pace of technological advancements thus represents a significant professional growth opportunity, even as it poses challenges in maintaining current competencies. Our findings align with Ebert and Louridas' observations [10] regarding the need for new competencies among software developers in the age of generative AI. Moreover, participants expressed a need to enhance their competencies, which echoes Ebert and Louridas' caution against marketing hype that may oversimplify the capabilities of generative AI [10], suggesting that a deeper, more critical understanding of AI technologies is essential.

Work Engagement and Motivational Implications. Automating routine tasks boosts efficiency and affects IT professionals' work engagement. In the context of work engagement and motivation, Roto et al. [21] emphasise the diversity in defining engagement, highlighting a spectrum from short-term, task-focused absorption to long-term attributes like vigour and dedication. This framework is relevant to our findings where IT professionals report varying impacts of AI on their work engagement. For example, the automation of routine tasks by AI technologies such as UiPath and GitHub Copilot enhances professionals' absorption by freeing them up to concentrate on more complex and engaging tasks. This shift fosters short-term absorption and supports long-term vigour and dedication by enabling professionals to tackle more challenging and meaningful work, enhancing their sense of significance, enthusiasm, and pride in their roles.

Furthermore, as discussed by Sharp et al. [25], the concept of motivation in the software engineering context points out that motivation is heavily influenced by context, including individual personality and the environment. Our study extends this notion by illustrating how the integration of AI reshapes the professional environment, thereby influencing motivation. AI tools modify the context in which IT professionals operate by changing the nature of their tasks and altering the skills required and how these professionals engage with their work.

Our results indicate that while AI can enhance competence and efficiency, IT professionals must also engage in continuous learning and adaptation, impacting both their motivation and engagement. This is consistent with Sharp et al.'s emphasis on the complex interplay between individual characteristics and environmental changes [25]. As AI technologies evolve, so does the context in which these professionals work, demanding a dynamic response to maintain high levels of motivation and engagement.

Navigating AI Paradoxes and Enhancing Professional Competence. Navigating the paradoxes of AI in competence development requires an understanding of the complex interplay between technology and human skill. Drawing on the insights provided by Bainbridge's "Ironies of Automation," [1] professionals and organisations can begin to address the challenges of AI integration in a manner that enhances, rather than undermines, professional competence and knowledge. As the field of IT continues to evolve in response to advancements in AI, embracing the lessons learned from these paradoxes will be crucial for fostering a resilient, adaptable, and equipped workforce to leverage AI's potential responsibly and effectively.

6 Limitations

While this study provides insights into AI's impact on work engagement among IT professionals through the lens of SDT, it is subject to several limitations. First, the exploratory nature and the small sample size of four interviews limit the transferability. This constraint also impacts the depth and variety of perspectives on how AI influences perceived competence and engagement. Additionally, the study's focus on perceived competence within SDT, while offering a targeted exploration of this critical aspect, leaves other components of SDT, such as autonomy and relatedness, less examined in the context of AI integration. Finally, using a theory-driven design introduces specific limitations. The reliance on SDT might lead to theoretical bias, potentially overlooking insights beyond the theory's scope. Acknowledging these constraints is essential for understanding the study's scope and guiding future research to address these gaps.

7 Future Work

As noted previously, this study has reported the preliminary findings of a subset of participants in a more extensive qualitative study aimed at exploring work engagement among IT professionals in AI-integrated workplaces. The overall international study will employ an extensive interview study, where purposeful sampling [18], with criterion sampling, will be used to select participants, identified based on their grouped or specific ICT professional roles as classified within the Skills Framework for the Information Age [24] and in addition based on their appropriateness for the research question, such as people who have used AI in their work.

Future studies could adopt a longitudinal approach to examine the long-term effects of AI integration on work engagement and perceived competence. This would enable an understanding how continuous adaptation to AI affects professional motivation and engagement over time.

This study concentrates on the competence aspect of SDT; future work could explore how AI integration affects the need for autonomy and relatedness. This would provide a more holistic view of how AI influences overall work engagement.

Future studies could complement the qualitative findings with quantitative methods, such as surveys or large-scale assessments, to systematically measure the relationship between AI usage and work engagement. This would allow for greater generalizability and validation of the findings.

Finally, future research could explore the role of organisational culture, leadership, and training in shaping the adoption of AI and its effects on work engagement. Understanding how organisations facilitate AI integration through support structures could provide valuable insights into fostering positive engagement outcomes.

8 Conclusion

This study explored the impact of AI integration on work engagement and perceived competence among IT professionals through the lens of SDT. Our findings suggest that AI tools such as UiPath and GitHub Copilot enhance efficiency by automating routine tasks, which can increase professionals' perceived competence. However, the continuous learning required to adapt to evolving AI technologies introduces opportunities and challenges for maintaining engagement. While AI offers new ways to augment productivity and support decision-making, it also underscores the need for careful system design to support autonomy, competence, and ongoing skill development.

These insights provide valuable implications for the design of AI-integrated work environments. To foster sustained engagement, organisations must focus on task automation and creating environments where professionals can maintain and enhance their competence. This will be critical in ensuring that adopting AI technologies leads to positive outcomes for both productivity and employee well-being. Future research could extend this study by exploring the long-term effects of AI integration on work engagement and examining other psychological factors, such as autonomy and relatedness within different professional contexts.

Acknowledgements. The authors thank the interviewees for their valuable contributions to this study. Afa Försäkringar, Sweden [grant number 220244], and the EDU-AI project from The Department of Information Technology supported the project financially.

Disclosure of Interests. The authors have no competing interests to declare relevant to this article's content.

References

1. Bainbridge, L.: Ironies of automation. IFAC Proc. **15**, 129–135 (1982). https://doi.org/10.1016/S1474-6670(17)62897-0
2. Bakker, A.B., Demerouti, E.: The job demands-resources model: state of the art. J. Manag. Psychol. **22**, 309–328 (2007)

3. Benbya, H., Davenport, T.H., Pachidi, S.: Artificial intelligence in organizations: current state and future opportunities. SSRN Electron. J. (2020). https://doi.org/10.2139/ssrn.3741983
4. Benko, A., Lányi, C.S.: History of artificial intelligence. In: Encyclopedia of Information Science and Technology, 2nd edn, pp. pp 1759–1762. IGI global (2009)
5. Bhutkar, G., et al.: Human work interaction design. In: Artificial Intelligence and Designing for a Positive Work Experience in a Low Desire Society: 6th IFIP WG 13.6 Working Conference, HWID 2021, Beijing, China, 15–16 May 2021, Revised Selected Papers. Springer, Heidelberg (2022)
6. Brynjolfsson, E., Li, D., Raymond, L.R.: Generative AI at Work (2023)
7. Chatterjee, S., Jemima, A.G., Ray, S., Kumar, M.S., Ahluwalia, G.: A systematic review of artificial intelligence (AI) and impact on human resource management (HRM): challenges, risks and opportunities. Nat. Camp. **28**, 558–591 (2024)
8. Deci, E.L., Olafsen, A.H., Ryan, R.M.: Self-determination theory in work organizations: the state of a science. Ann. Rev. Organ. Psychol. Organ. Behav. **4**, 19–43 (2017). https://doi.org/10.1146/annurev-orgpsych-032516-113108
9. Deci, E.L., Ryan, R.M.: Intrinsic Motivation and Self-Determination in Human Behavior. Springer, Heidelberg (2013)
10. Ebert, C., Louridas, P.: Generative AI for software practitioners. IEEE Softw. **40**, 30–38 (2023)
11. Gagné, M., Deci, E.L.: Self-determination theory and work motivation. J. Organ. Behav. **26**, 331–362 (2005). https://doi.org/10.1002/job.322
12. Harding, W., Kloster, M.: Coding on Copilot: 2023 data shows downward pressure on code quality. GitClear (2024). Accessed 1 Mar 2024
13. Khuwaja, B., Katper, N., Azhar, S.D., Chanar, P.H., Shaikh, S.: Beyond traditional methods: harnessing AI for employee engagement in Karachi's multinationals. Remit Rev. **9**, 1771–1793 (2024)
14. McAfee, A., Brynjolfsson, E.: Human work in the robotic future policy for the age of automation. Foreign Aff. **95**, 139–150 (2016)
15. Möllers, M., Berger, B., Klein, S.: Contrasting human-AI workplace relationship configurations. In: Research Handbook on Artificial Intelligence and Decision Making in Organizations, pp 282–303. Edward Elgar Publishing (2024)
16. Noponen, N., Feshchenko, P., Auvinen, T., Luoma-aho, V., Abrahamsson, P.:) Taylorism on steroids or enabling autonomy? A systematic review of algorithmic management. Manag. Rev. Q. (2023). https://doi.org/10.1007/s11301-023-00345-5
17. Pachidi, S., Huysman, M.: Addressing the knowledge gap between business managers and data scientists: the case of data analytics implementation in a sales organization. In: Research Handbook on Artificial Intelligence and Decision Making in Organizations, pp 179–194. Edward Elgar Publishing (2024)
18. Palinkas, L.A., Horwitz, S.M., Green, C.A., Wisdom, J.P., Duan, N., Hoagwood, K.: Purposeful sampling for qualitative data collection and analysis in mixed method implementation research. Adm. Policy Ment Health Ment. Health Serv. Res. **42**, 533–544 (2015)
19. Patton, M.Q.: Qualitative Research & Evaluation Methods: Integrating Theory and Practice. Sage publications, Thousand Oaks (2014)
20. Polkinghorne, D.E.: Phenomenological research methods. In: Valle, R.S., Halling, S. (eds.) Existential-Phenomenological Perspectives in Psychology, pp. 41–60. Springer, Boston (1989)
21. Roto, V., Palanque, P., Karvonen, H.: Engaging automation at work: a literature review. In: Human Work Interaction Design: Designing Engaging Automation, HWID 2018, pp. 158–172. Springer, Heidelberg (2019)
22. Schaufeli, W., Salanova, M.: Work engagement. Manag. Soc. Ethical Issues Organ. **135**, 177 (2007)

23. Schaufeli, W.B., Salanova, M., Gronzalez-Roma, V., Bakker, A.B.: The measurement of work engagement and burnout: a comparative analytic approach. J. Happiness Stud. **3**, 1–92 (2002)
24. SFIA. The global skills and competency framework for a digital world. SFIA. https://sfia-online.org/en. Accessed 1 Apr 2024
25. Sharp, H., Baddoo, N., Beecham, S., Hall, T., Robinson, H.: Models of motivation in software engineering. Inf. Softw. Technol. **51**, 219–233 (2009)
26. Simsek Caglar, P., Roto, V., Vainio, T.: User experience research in the work context: maps, gaps and agenda. Proc. ACM Hum.-Comput. Interact. **6**, 1–28 (2022)
27. Strauch, B.: Ironies of automation: still unresolved after all these years. IEEE Trans. Hum.-Mach. Syst. **48**, 419–433 (2018). https://doi.org/10.1109/THMS.2017.2732506
28. Swedberg, R.: Exploratory research. In: Elman, C., Gerring, J., Mahoney, J. (eds.) The Production of Knowledge, 1st edn., pp. 17–41. Cambridge University Press, Cambridge (2020)
29. Tyagi, A.K., Fernandez, T.F., Mishra, S., Kumari, S.: Intelligent automation systems at the core of industry 4.0. In: Abraham, A., Piuri, V., Gandhi, N., Siarry, P., Kaklauskas, A., Madureira, A. (eds.) Intelligent Systems Design and Applications, pp. 1–18. Springer, Cham (2021)
30. Verma, S., Bhalla, P.: Sustainable development and AI: navigating safety and ethical challenges. In: Demystifying the Dark Side of AI in Business, pp 174–184. IGI Global (2024)
31. Victorelli, E.Z., Dos Reis, J.C., Hornung, H., Prado, A.B.: Understanding human-data interaction: literature review and recommendations for design. Int. J. Hum.-Comput. Stud. **134**, 13–32 (2020). https://doi.org/10.1016/j.ijhcs.2019.09.004
32. Viterouli, M., Belias, D., Koustelios, A., Tsigilis, N., Papademetriou, C.: Time for change: designing tailored training initiatives for organizational transformation. In: Organizational Behavior and Human Resource Management for Complex Work Environments, pp 267–307. IGI Global (2024)
33. Ziegler, A., et al.: Measuring GitHub copilot's impact on productivity. Commun. ACM **67**, 54–63 (2024). https://doi.org/10.1145/3633453
34. Zirar, A., Ali, S.I., Islam, N.: Worker and workplace Artificial Intelligence (AI) coexistence: emerging themes and research agenda. Technovation **124**, 102747 (2023)
35. Industry 5.0 - European Commission (2024). https://research-and-innovation.ec.europa.eu/research-area/industrial-research-and-innovation/industry-50_en. Accessed 4 Oct 2024

Who is Responsible? Roles of Future Pilots in Single Pilot Operations

Elodie Bouzekri[1(✉)], Benjamin Berton[2], and Philippe Doyon-Poulin[2]

[1] McGill University, Montréal, Canada
elodie.bouzekri@mail.mcgill.ca
[2] Polytechnique Montréal, Québec, Canada
benjamin.berton@polytml.ca, philippe.doyon-poulin@polymtl.ca

Abstract. Despite the development of the technology required to support single pilot operations (SPO) in civil aviation, the definition of roles of the single pilot and the diffusion of responsibilities between the human and the autonomous system are still under study. In this paper, we propose a critical analysis of existing SPO concepts involving a highly autonomous teammate in the cockpit. We show that not all facets of responsibility are addressed. In an attempt to solve this issue, we propose to extend a framework to support the analysis of authority, responsibilities, resources shared between roles and permissible control transitions when designing collaboration with autonomous systems.

Keywords: single pilot operations · meaningful control · responsibility · Human Work Interaction Design

1 Introduction

Current civil aviation operations require two pilots. Typically, a captain and a first officer act as pilot flying (PF), who must always fly the aircraft, or as pilot monitoring (PM) also refereed as pilot-non flying, who monitors systems and assists the pilot flying. For economic reasons, the industry is moving towards single pilot operations (SPO), where the number of human operators in the cockpit is reduced to one. Aviation has a long history of decrewing the flight deck. However, having only one pilot supported by a highly-autonomous system in the cockpit poses unique challenges concerning skill degradation, isolation, first officer training, pilot incapacitation, public and pilot acceptance, certification, and the definition of a new task allocation in the flight deck and on the ground [21]. In connection with this last challenge, the role of the single pilot will change significantly. Even in today's cockpit, some authors argue that pilots are no longer 'pilots', but rather "*automation managers*" or "*exception handlers*" [29]. The move to single pilot operations seems to feed the expectation that pilots will be further and further removed from their piloting tasks [8].

In alignment with the conference theme, specifically the social dimension of sustainability (decent and safe work), this paper proposes an examination of the

Published by Springer Nature Switzerland AG 2026
B. R. Barricelli et al. (Eds.): HWID 2024, IFIP AICT 751, pp. 158–173, 2026.
https://doi.org/10.1007/978-3-031-95334-7_10

responsibilities of future single pilots when operating with highly autonomous aircraft systems. This work is part of Human Work Interaction Design (HWID) [7], as it aims to contribute to the efficiency, awareness, and satisfaction of future pilots, to their involvement in decision-making, and to their engagement in stimulating activities in the cockpit. It is posited that a clear definition of future single pilots' role and their responsibilities is not only essential for safe operations but also for the acceptance of SPO (see current rejection of SPO by pilots' associations [1,12]).

We propose to explore the concept of meaningful control of future pilots over autonomy in order to fulfill their responsibilities. The concept of meaningful control has gone beyond the domain of autonomous weapons for which the concept was introduced. It is now being applied to various sectors involving safety-critical autonomous systems, including AI-based hiring, autonomous vehicles [5], and aviation [17]. To have meaningful control, human operators must "ultimately remain in control", so that they can be held morally responsible for the outcome of decisions during operations [17]. More precisely, Holford [17] proposed two required conditions to enable meaningful control: "actual decision-making authority" and "ability to detect relevant cues and take relevant actions". These conditions influence the way in which operators can be held morally responsible (i.e., moral obligation or morally significant actions), causally responsible (i.e., performing or ordering someone to do a task), legally responsible (i.e., accountable regarding the law), or in relation to their professional duties (e.g., today's Captains are responsible for safe operation) [17].

This work forms part of our ongoing reflections within the ADvanced AIRspace Usability (ADAIR) research project. While it does not present finalized results, its purpose is to share our current inquiries and foster discussions on designing workplaces in which responsibility is shared with autonomy in critical contexts. Specifically, we propose to study pilot roles in SPO in 'aircraft-centric' configuration where the single pilot is supported by an autonomous teammate. We will discuss the allocation of responsibilities as well as the underlying authority and possible control changes allowed in the different concepts. Finally, we propose a framework to support such analysis when designing for SPO and an illustrative example of its implementation.

2 Existing Aircraft-Centric SPO Concepts and Pilots' Roles

Today, single pilot operations in civil aviation exist only for small aircraft such as very light jets (Very Light Jets, part 21 [10]). Such operations for large civil aircraft require an evolution regulation that has yet to be defined. Interested readers may wish to refer to the work of Harris [16], who has detailed the challenges to be addressed (e.g., new certification including ground-based elements, aircraft design, and new training), particularly with regard to human factors. However, several SPO Concept of operation (ConOps) have been proposed. These concepts can be divided into two categories: aircraft-centric and distributed [22,31]. Distributed concepts involved on-ground human assistance to support the single on-board pilot. Such distributed team on-ground can be classified into four categories: remote pilot, harbour pilots, hybrid ground operator, and specialist ground operator. A remote pilot can take control of the aircraft in case of single pilot incapacitation [16,22]. A harbour pilot is similar to marine ship pilots who take over the vessel command when approaching the harbour. A harbour pilot is responsible for supporting single pilots during the take-off, approach, and landing phases. A hybrid ground operator may provide support to a particular aircraft in case of abnormal situations or emergencies. The hybrid ground operator also perform dispatch and support multiple aircraft. Specialist ground operators are divided into two categories: ground associates and ground pilots. The first is dedicated to dispatch and support multiple aircraft, the second assist a single pilot during abnormal situations or emergencies and can take over control of the aircraft. A distributed team of human operators on ground introduces redundancy and reduces the burden in the cockpit by distributing the workload between several roles on the ground. These arguments in favor of increased safety for distributed concepts mean that they are favored by researchers [22]. These solutions require increased collaboration and cooperation between ground operators and the flight deck. Consequently, the main assumption and constraint of these solutions is a stable, fast, and secure data connection between cockpit and ground operators. Beyond this assumption, the required infrastructure and additional ground staff may undermine the initial objective of cost reduction [16].

At this stage of our research project, we chose to investigate aircraft-centric solutions. This approach allows us to avoid making strong assumptions about future datalink technologies while addressing the need for on-board assistance that will be required even in distributed solutions.

Aircraft-centric concepts focus on providing single pilot support within the aircraft [22,31]. One option is to rely solely on the single pilot. However, allocating all the tasks only to the single pilot is not a viable solution due to overload in complex flight phases (i.e., take-off, approach, landing) and boredom during cruise [22]. Indeed, the single pilot suffers from high workload during landing, approach, and take-off impairing safety. Similarly, concept proposing the involvement of on-board personnel (e.g., cabin crew or flight attendants) to support the single pilot during operations have been ruled out as detrimental to safety [22]. In consequences, we only consider solutions involving an autonomous agent to support the single pilot.

Existing literature reviews [22,31] classify the concepts shown in Table 2 in this category. From these reviews, we have reduced our selection to concepts for civil aviation. SATS [23] and the naturalistic flight deck [26] propose SPO solutions for small aeroplanes for which safety requirements are lower. This type of solution could form the basis of a solution for larger aircraft, but the operational requirements differ between these aircraft types and have an impact on SPO design. As we want to analyze the roles and responsibilities of the airline single pilot and autonomous systems, we will focus only on solutions for civil aviation and large aeroplanes. We also exclude CAMMI [18] that proposes an adaptive automation to assist the crew and not a single pilot (Table 1).

Table 1. Aircraft-centric SPO concepts for civil aviation [22,31]

Civil aviation	Small/Large aeroplane
Cognitive Adaptive Man Machine Interface (CAMMI) [18]	large
Small Aircraft Transportation System (SATS) [23]	small
Naturalistic Flight Desk [26]	small
Digital Copilot [13]	large
Electronic standby pilot ACROSS [20]	large
Cognitive Pilot-Aircraft Interface (CPAI) [19]	large
SAFEdeck [25]	large

In the following, we describe aircraft-centric SPO concepts for large aeroplanes and the single pilot's roles within these concepts. We detail responsibilities allocation when describes by the authors. The Table 2 recaps this analysis. These aircraft-centric SPO concept can be divided into two categories: substitution or machine based function allocation and role-based function allocation.

2.1 Substitution-Based and Machine-Based Function Allocation

A first category of aircraft-centric solutions follows a substitution or machine-based approach. In substitution-based approaches, the entire set of tasks is considered, and each task is allocated either to the pilot or the autonomous system [25]. Autonomous systems are assumed to perform certain tasks better, and those tasks are automated. The pilot is responsible for performing the remaining tasks [25]. These approaches often retains the current roles in the flight deck: PF and PM. The primary task of the PF is to always fly the aircraft. They are also in charge of navigation tasks, initiating procedures, and reading and confirming messages. The PM's is responsible for monitoring the aircraft and its systems, performing checklists under the PF's supervision, and communicating with Air Traffic Control (ATC). Additionally, the PM assists the PF in flying by monitoring flight parameters. Some SPO solutions consider the PM's tasks suitable candidates for automation.

Digital Copilot. For example, the Digital Copilot [13] assists the single pilot by performing tasks of pilot monitoring. However, the digital copilot only covers part of PM's tasks. The digital copilot helps the single pilot by offering speech recognition and replying to questions related to the destination, approach, airport of arrival. It can also read checklists. The digital copilot also provides notifications based on context. Depending on the destination or flight phase, it can notify the right radio frequency to obtain weather, for example. The human pilot remains the pilot-in-command flying the aircraft with the help of the digital copilot. The human pilot keeps their actual decision-making authority as the automated system only provides information. However, the remaining PM tasks will probably be performed by the single pilot. This is likely to result in a mismatch between the pilot's responsibilities and their ability to perform these tasks, due to the increased effort and workload involved, especially during high-workload phases (i.e., take-off, approach, and landing). The single pilot role is not defined and will differ from the current pilot flying role. In consequence, the single pilot new causal, legal, and moral responsibilities are not defined.

Cognitive Pilot-Aircraft Interface. The Cognitive Pilot-Aircraft Interface (CPAI) [19] assesses the physiological states, fatigue level, and cognitive workload of the single pilot, as well as external conditions. It then infers the pilot's cognitive state and adapts the level of automation of CPAI, from full task load allocated to the pilot to full allocation of this load to the automation systems. The automation is adaptive, but the authors have not detailed how each level of automation is implemented. In addition, they describe the automation systems responsible for the actions undertaken within a high level of automation. This may conflict with the single pilot's role as captain [16], who is responsible for the safety of operations.

The single pilot role and causal responsibility are directing the aircraft, managing automation and taking decisions. However, the single pilot new legal, and moral responsibilities are not defined. This solution considers a "ground-based flight crew" but emphasizes the CPAI functions that assist the single pilot. They demonstrated technical feasibility of CPAI.

Both Digital Copilot and CPAI introduce technologies (i.e., notification system and pilot health and workload monitoring system) to support SPO. The ACROSS Global Operational Concept provides solutions to reduce crew workload in current operations. This concept covers configurations where one-pilot or both are incapacitated, and can be used as a starting point for SPO design.

ACROSS - Global Operational Concept. The ACROSS Global Operational Concept [20] introduces a system that can replace the copilot in the event of an intentional or unintentional crew reduction. In this way, the system supports the single pilot only when one of the pilots takes a break, or one of the pilots is incapacitated. In the first case, the system monitors the remaining pilot and can take the control of the aircraft momentarily. In the second case, the system monitors the remaining pilot, helps for aviate tasks, reconfigures the aircraft for automatic descent and landing, and aids select the nearest airport. Full crew incapacitation is also described by introducing auto-landing function. In case of false detection of full incapacitation, the crew can veto the decision and takeover control. The current pilot monitoring and flying roles are considered. Consequently, the current responsibilities allocation will apply. However, the autonomous systems have increased abilities and authorities, such as monitoring the crew and taking over control of the aircraft. The underlying impact on pilots' additional tasks and causal, legal, and moral responsibilities are not discussed. Finally, the pilot's role is not designed to be a single pilot. This concept describes a solution to manage single pilot situations in current operations.

2.2 Role-Based Function Allocation: *Complemation*

SAFEdeck. The SAFEdeck [25] is designed following *Complemation* approach. *Complemation* approach proposes first to identify the purpose of the single pilot in the cockpit, in order to define their role. Then, the role of the autonomous system must support the role of the single pilot. SAFEdeck uses the semi-autonomous car analogy. The responsibilities of the single pilot are to fly the aircraft, make high-level decisions, manage risk, and serve as a backup if automation failed. To this aim, the single pilot can exercise their authority by controlling the stick and throttle. SAFEdeck provides envelope protection (i.e., avoid unsafe aircraft state), danger avoidance, self-preservation, precision assistance, and active flight control to the single pilot. The SAFEdeck does not require certification of new technologies such as artificial intelligence or significant changes in cockpit instrumentation. Rather, it modifies the way there are implemented, allowing the single pilot to engage in fly and navigation tasks while preserving their skills and situation awareness.

Although they claim to be focused on the human role, the system's functions are more detailed than the tasks of the future pilot. However, the author defines the pilot as the actual decision-maker and provides them the means to exercise this authority (i.e., through stick, inceptors, automation disengagement button, and notifications) and takeover at any time. Roles and causal responsibilities are defined for normal situations. In abnormal situations, the aircraft enters in self-preservation and full autonomous mode. ATC and other pilots are responsible for providing clear space for the autonomous aircraft. However, the responsibilities associated with fully autonomous decision-making without the control of a human operator on the ground or onboard still need to be addressed.

3 Towards a Framework to Support Design of Meaningful Control for Future Pilots

In previous section, we detailed the observation of Neis et al. [22] regarding the lack of definition of allocation of responsibilities and authorities in the description of SPO concepts, focusing on aircraft-centric solutions for civil aviation. We also pointed out that none of the proposed concepts detailed all the moral, causal, legal, and roles responsibilities of the single pilot. In the following, we will propose a first step towards tackling this issue by extending a framework offering support for analyzing authorities, responsibilities, resources shared between roles and allowed control transitions when designing for SPO.

Rooted in definitions of Flemisch [15] of responsibility, authority, control, and ability, RCAFT framework [3] refines these definitions for fine-grained analysis, and details resources sharing and cooperative tasks. It thus enables their description in task models [2,3]. We propose to extend this framework to decompose the complexity of designing meaningful control for single pilot.

Table 2. Pilot' roles in SPO.

Concept	Pilot' roles	Resp. causal	Resp. legal	Resp. moral	Resp. role
Digital Copilot [13]	PF/Captain	All to the pilot	–	–	Captain
Cognitive Pilot-Aircraft Interface [19]	PF/Captain	Flying the aircraft, Managing systems, Taking decisions	–	–	Captain
ACROSS [20]	PF and PM	Same as today	–	–	Captain and FO
SAFEdeck [25]	High-level decision maker, Risk manager and Backup	All to the human except when incapacitated	–	–	Captain

3.1 Role Definition, Legal, Moral, Role Responsibilities and Goals

Based on operational requirements, roles for human and autonomous actors must be defined as well as their responsibilities. This first phase enables to cover the first property of meaningful control defined by [5] stating that the conditions under which the autonomy "is designed to operate" (called the *envelope* in the aviation domain) must be explicit and include moral aspects. Here, we will focus on clarifying not only the moral aspects, but also the roles and legal aspects. Each human role pursues a goal for which a particular result is expected (e.g., the aircraft arrive in time and safely at destination). Beyond defining the purpose of the pilot in the cockpit, when the pilot cannot be held responsible, other actors who may be responsible must be identified. This means that for any autonomous actions leading to a significant deviation from the goal when the pilot cannot be held accountable (e.g., incapacitation), another human or organizational entity must be identified. In addition, both the roles of the pilot and the autonomous teammate must be designed for mutual support, backup and redundancy within the team [27]. A possible pathway is to follow an approach similar to *Complemation* [25] approach, in which each autonomy role supports the human roles in achieving their goals. This approach would align with current effort for a regulatory framework proposed by EASA for Human-AI cooperation and collaboration [11]. The responsibilities defined in this phase guide design decisions in subsequent steps in accordance with Flemisch [15].

3.2 Authority and Initiative

In order to control the aircraft and achieve the goal, each role must perform tasks and cooperate in order to exercise authority and initiate control transitions when necessary (e.g., takeover control to manage an unforeseen event). Designers need to carefully allocate decision-making tasks, those limiting the scope of action of other roles, or those performing manual actions, to ensure that the pilot has the "actual decision-making authority" (e.g., the pilot should be able to regain control of the flight at any time if an autopilot function is active) in accordance with their responsibilities [5] defined at step 1. Such activity can be supported by methods for function allocation focusing on effective cooperation. For guidance, the reader can refer to [24], for example. Using the appropriate method can help designers focusing on dynamic pilot-autonomy interactions and encouraging strong interdependent teams incorporating feedback mechanisms and pilot-led authority [30].

3.3 Sharing Resources

Both the human and the autonomy must share a compatible mental model to enable meaningful control [5]. Bi-directional communication and transparency are components of effective teamwork with autonomy [4,28] and participate in building a shared mental model. We propose to describe resources manipulated during the interactions between the pilot and the autonomy. A resource can be information or an object that may or may not be exchanged between roles. These resources are manipulated by the pilot or the autonomy to exercise control. For example, flight path information can be shared between the pilot and the autonomy via the cockpit interface and modified by the pilot on ground operator's recommendation. In this step, choices for interface design must be compliant with required authority (e.g., provide a button to disengage automation at any time, as in SAFEdeck [25]) and information needed by the responsible role.

3.4 Causal Responsibility

Finally, these actions will modify resources that may impact the expected result of the activity (e.g., modification to the flight path). The underlying responsibility for deviation from the expected result must be compliant with the responsibilities defined in step 1. As each task leading to causal responsibility is formally described [3], this step identifies the human tasks that lead to the actual result (i.e., "Backward link") [5]. For example, if the single pilot is incapacitated and the autonomy activates auto-landing thus impacting the flight path, underlying responsibilities must be identified as the single pilot does not have the ability to exercise control. Distributed solutions propose a human operator on-ground to control the aircraft in such situations.

4 Illustrative Example

In this section, we detail the framework on a concrete example[1] considering a single pilot who collaborates with an autonomous system by making a joint

[1] This illustrative example does not describe the final design choices made during the ADAIR project, but is intended to illustrate the on-going work on design collaboration with autonomy with responsibilities in mind.

decision on the actions to be performed to resolve a complex abnormal situation and monitoring it.

4.1 Scenario

We propose the following working scenario to illustrate the framework.

The captain collaborates with an autonomous system to fly the aircraft. The captain is the flyer of the aircraft and macro-mange the autonomy for their first flight of the day. The weather is sunny without any perturbations. They are in cruise phase and the autopilot is on. The captain monitors the flight parameters and the autonomy. Suddenly, the captain perceives that the left engine failed and suspects an engine failure. The autonomy also detects the issue. Shortly after that, an alarm raises. The captain notices and reacts to the chime and the caution light. The captain looks at the page detailing current state of the engines and the active alarm. The autonomy displays a message indicating that the left engine failed and the related checklist is proposed. The captain can choose to perform a detailed diagnosis with the autonomy, by confirming the sensed information (i.e., information the system is able to acquire) and providing contextual information to agree a solution. The captain confirms the diagnosis and asks the autonomy to start the checklist. The autonomy starts the procedure. The autonomy announces that the procedure to shutdown the left engine must be accomplished and waits for the captain's confirmation. The captain confirms. The autonomy starts the procedure to shutdown the left engine. At any time, the captain can intervene and stop any recovery action to be executed. The captain must confirm actions that: are irreversible, explicitly ask to be confirmed, ask questions, ask to confirm the start or end of the procedure. The captain must also acknowledge notes and caution messages.

4.2 Role Definition, Legal, Moral, and Role Responsibilities

Distinguishing between responsibility and accountability is essential. The allocation of responsibility serves to determine the actor to blame after an undesired outcome [15]. To eliminate any potential ambiguity, it must be noted that an autonomous system cannot be held accountable for undesired outcomes generated by autonomous actions. This responsibility is delineated by the organization, legislation, or law and is subject to analysis in investigations subsequent to aircraft accidents. It is important to emphasize that the work presented in this paper is indissociable from work analysis encompassing societal and organizational constraints, as the allocation of responsibilities must comply with these constraints [5].

Role Responsibilities. Regarding their role, we assumed that all pilots would possess the captain's responsibilities [16]. In accordance with today's captain's responsibilities [14], a single pilot is granted final authority, must ensure safety, initiate checklists and procedures, assess situations at any time, and determine the task distribution for flight.

In abnormal situations, the goal of a single pilot is to ensure the safety of the aircraft and come back to a nominal situation, which includes addressing the issues indicated by alarms, among other critical tasks. This subgoal (i.e., to resolve alarms) is achieved when no further Crew Alerting System (CAS) messages are displayed in the cockpit. Therefore, in accordance with European Union Aviation Safety Agency (EASA) recommendations for collaboration with an autonomous system [11], the single pilot monitors autonomy (e.g., approves and checks autonomy's actions when irreversible, confirms autonomy's actions when asked), must be able to take over control of each autonomy's actions (e.g., cancel, restart, or override checklists, pause, override, or cancel or manually perform any autonomous actions), and must maintain a shared situation awareness with autonomy (e.g., acknowledgment of alarms, co-assessment, analysis, and decision-making with autonomy in complex situations). Autonomy acts as complementary visual, motor, and cognitive support for a single pilot. The autonomy must support the single pilot's goals while maintaining bi-directional communication and understanding, reducing the single pilot's workload, and without undermining the final authority of the single pilot, who is ultimately responsible for all outcomes during the flight.

Role responsibilities of the pilot and autonomy can be summarized as presented in Table 3.

Table 3. Managing alarms in SPO - Role responsibilities

Single Pilot	Autonomy
Cooperates and collaborates with autonomy	Determine the most suitable checklist to perform with the information provided by the single pilot
Approves and checks autonomy irreversible actions	Perform the checklist
Must confirm actions when asked	Cross-check irreversible actions with the single pilot
Co-decides with autonomy the checklist to be performed	Ask the single pilot to perform recovery actions that the autonomy cannot handle
Directs the autonomy to perform the checklist	
Performs actions the autonomy cannot handle	
Takeover control when necessary	
Informs ground operator when necessary	
Can delegate part of flying task to the autonomy	

Legal Responsibilities. Currently, the pilot-in-command[2] is legally responsible for ensuring flight safety [14]. As the single pilot will be the single human crew member, these responsibilities may be allocated to them. Specifically, the pilot is "directly responsible for, [...], the operation of that aircraft" [14]. In the event of an emergency, they may "deviate from any rule of this part to the extent required to meet that emergency" and subsequently inform the competent persons of that deviation [14]. To be certified, autonomous aircraft systems must fulfill the requirements defined by certification authorities. For example, CS-25 [9] states that pilots should be able to plan and prepare tasks for an autonomous system without any confusion or impact on the current task, avoid mode confusion or uncertainty regarding the current controlling entity over a resource, and take over control of any action of autonomy.

Moral Responsibilities. From the definition of moral responsibility [5,6] and current pilots' obligations (see above sections), the pilot is responsible for any outcomes of actions allocated to them over which they were able to exercise sufficient control or could have acted differently during alarm resolution. Furthermore, to be held morally responsible, the pilot must act of their own free will, in accordance with their training and a mental model shared with autonomy, which includes an understanding of the abilities of the systems with which they collaborate, as well as their own. Consequently, domain experts, designers, and developers must design an autonomy that avoids situations of complacency or situations analogous to coercion, enables the appropriate level of control for the pilot (contingent upon the current pilot's capacity, workload, and the current context), and supports an appropriate level of situation awareness.

Moral responsibilities of the pilot and autonomy can be summarized as presented in Table 4.

Table 4. Managing alarms in SPO - Moral responsibilities

Single Pilot	Autonomy
Outcomes over which they were able to exercise sufficient control	Avoid situations of complacency
Outcomes over which they had the ability and opportunity to act otherwise	Enable the appropriate level of control to the pilot depending on the current pilot's capacity and the current context
Actions performed of their own free will based on an appropriate shared mental model	Support appropriate level of situation awareness

[2] The captain is a rank, while the pilot-in-command is the pilot ultimately responsible for flight safety, according to the FAA's legal definition. In general, the captain is the pilot in command.

4.3 Authority and Initiative

We propose to follow the process defined in [3] to systematically describe the authority and initiative of control transitions in task models. Due to space constraints, we will not present the resulting models but a summary of authority and control transitions distribution at a fine grained of description when managing alarms in SPO.

The single pilot as defined above has the authority to decide on the immediate actions, approve result of the co-diagnosis, confirm, cancel, override checklist, perform actions, suspend, resume, cancel, override, revert action, verify and check actions. The autonomy as defined above has the authority to display messages (e.g., an alarm), compute associated checklists, recommend checklists and alternatives, allow the pilot to confirm, override, cancel, reset checklists, perform action, allow the pilot to stop, revert, resume, cancel, override actions. For each of these tasks, we identify the constraints defined by the entity to influence the situation. For example, when the single pilot 'approves result of the co-diagnosis', they define the checklist to be performed and initiate the checklist execution (see Table 5).

Table 5. Managing alarms in SPO - Authority

Single Pilot Task	Constraint
Approve result of the co-diagnosis	Define appropriate checklist for the situation

Similarly, we identify each control transitions between the autonomy and the pilot. For example, regarding the checklist, the autonomy allows the pilot to confirm or not the checklist, after confirming, autonomy takeover control and perform the reversible actions and allow the pilot to takeover control at any moment (suspend, cancel, override, or revert the action). For example, when the autonomy allows the pilot to cancel a checklist by displaying and activating the CANCEL button, the pilot can takeover control over the checklist execution by canceling it (see Table 6).

Table 6. Managing alarms in SPO - Control transitions

Transmitter	Receiver
Autonomy: Display Cancel checklist	Pilot: Perceive Cancel checklist btn
Pilot: Cancel checklist	Autonomy: Receive cancel checklist

4.4 Sharing Resources

Then, we propose to detail how information or objects are exchanged or not between the single pilot and the autonomy to help analysis of bidirectional communication and transparency [3]. These resources are related to alarms, checklists and procedures, recovery actions (i.e. checklist lines), aircraft system states, and strategies related to filtering alarms or checking procedure suitability for a particular situation. Each of these resources can required rules or knowledge, can be manipulated using buttons, mental processing and communicated through sounds, displays, light, or colors.

For example, the states of the aircraft systems are shared between the pilot and the autonomy through two different pages called SYNOPTIC and STATUS pages and controllable through buttons dedicated to these pages. Filtering and verification strategies of the system and of the pilot are not currently shared between them in our work-in-progress design.

4.5 Causal Responsibility

Finally, following the process of [3], we can identify tasks performed that modify resources and may impact the expected result of the activity. The underlying causal responsibility for deviation from the expected result must be compliant with the responsibilities defined during the first step.

For example, when the pilot confirms the checklist following the co-diagnosis process, this action significantly shaped the course of the next actions to be performed. This causal responsibility is compliant with some defined legal responsibilities (i.e., initiate appropriate actions), role responsibilities (i.e., the pilot has the final authority over checklist selection and direct the autonomy to perform that checklist), and moral responsibilities as the pilot have the opportunity to select this checklist or not.

5 Conclusion

In this paper, we highlighted that the set of solutions for large aircraft-centric SPO solutions is limited. Furthermore, we concur with the observation of Neis et al. [22] on the lack of precise definition of responsibility and authority allocations in these concepts. We proposed to extend an existing framework to support the design of meaningful control of future pilots working with an autonomous teammate. The applicability of this framework is not limited to aviation and SPO, but to any safety-critical domain where operators work closely with autonomous systems. We argue that a clear definition of roles and responsibilities, along with systematic verification of compliance with actual control and the contextual capacity to apply this control, is a mean of avoiding mismatch with the moral and legal responsibilities of the actors. However, this framework has limitations as it offers only limited guidance to consider moral and legal responsibilities. In future work, we will detail our extension of the framework and define an SPO concept following the proposed framework as part of ADAIR project.

Acknowledgments. The research described here was supported by funding of the ADvanced AIRspace Usability (ADAIR) research project through the Consortium for Research and Innovation in Aerospace in Québec (CRIAQ) and the Natural Sciences and Engineering Research Council (NSERC, Canada).

References

1. ALPA: A gamble with safety: Reduced-crew operations. white paper, ALPA (2024). https://www.alpa.org/-/media/ALPA/Files/pdfs/news-events/white-papers/white-paper-reduced-crew-operations.pdf
2. Bouzekri, E., Canny, A., Martinie, C., Palanque, P., Gris, C.: Using task descriptions with explicit representation of allocation of functions, authority and responsibility to design and assess automation. In: Barricelli, B.R., Roto, V., Clemmensen, T., Campos, P., Lopes, A., Gonçalves, F., Abdelnour-Nocera, J. (eds.) HWID 2018. IAICT, vol. 544, pp. 36–56. Springer, Cham (2019). https://doi.org/10.1007/978-3-030-05297-3_3
3. Bouzekri, E., Martinie, C., Palanque, P., Atwood, K., Gris, C.: Should i add recommendations to my warning system? The RCRAFT framework can answer this and other questions about supporting the assessment of automation designs. In: Ardito, C., et al. (eds.) INTERACT 2021. LNCS, vol. 12935, pp. 405–429. Springer, Cham (2021). https://doi.org/10.1007/978-3-030-85610-6_24
4. Brandt, S.L., Lachter, J., Russell, R., Shively, R.J.: A human-autonomy teaming approach for a flight-following task. In: Baldwin, C. (ed.) AHFE 2017. AISC, vol. 586, pp. 12–22. Springer, Cham (2018). https://doi.org/10.1007/978-3-319-60642-2_2
5. Cavalcante Siebert, L., et al.: Meaningful human control: actionable properties for AI system development. AI Ethics **3**(1), 241–255 (2023). https://doi.org/10.1007/s43681-022-00167-3
6. Chevarie-Cossette, S.P.: Responsabilité morale (A), chap. Responsabilité morale. Maxime Kristanek (dir.), l'Encyclopédie philosophique (2017). https://encyclo-philo.fr/responsabilite-morale-a
7. Clemmensen, T.: Sketching for Digital Human Work. In: Clemmensen, T. (ed.) Human Work Interaction Design. HIS, pp. 281–292. Springer, Cham (2021). https://doi.org/10.1007/978-3-030-71796-4_11
8. Cummings, M.L., Stimpson, A., Clamann, M.: Functional requirements for onboard intelligent automation in single pilot operations. In: AIAA Infotech @ Aerospace. American Institute of Aeronautics and Astronautics, San Diego (2016). https://doi.org/10.2514/6.2016-1652
9. EASA: CS-25 Amendment 28 (2023). https://www.easa.europa.eu/en/document-library/certification-specifications/cs-25-amendment-28
10. EASA: Part 21 - Airworthiness and Environmental Certification (2023). https://www.easa.europa.eu/en/document-library/acceptable-means-of-compliance-and-guidance-materials/group/part-21---airworthiness-and-environmental-certification
11. EASA: EASA Artificial Intelligence Concept Paper Issue 2 - Guidance for Level 1 & 2 machine-learning applications | EASA (2024). https://www.easa.europa.eu/en/document-library/general-publications/easa-artificial-intelligence-concept-paper-issue-2

12. ECA: The human and the concepts of extended minimum crew operations (EMCO) and single pilot operations (SIPO). white paper, ECA (2021). https://safetystartswith2.com/Portals/8/Documents/emco-sipo-position-paper-eca.pdf
13. Estes, S., Burns, K., Helleberg, J., Long, K., Stein, J., Pollack, M.: Digital copilot: cognitive assistance for pilots. In: 2016 AAAI Fall Symposium Series (2016)
14. FAA: Pilot/Controller Roles and Responsibilities (2024). https://www.faa.gov/air_traffic/publications/atpubs/aim_html/chap5_section_5.html
15. Flemisch, F., Heesen, M., Hesse, T., Kelsch, J., Schieben, A., Beller, J.: Towards a dynamic balance between humans and automation: authority, ability, responsibility and control in shared and cooperative control situations. Cogn. Technol. Work **14**(1), 3–18 (2012). https://doi.org/10.1007/s10111-011-0191-6
16. Harris, D.: Single-pilot airline operations: Designing the aircraft may be the easy part. Aeronaut. J. **127**(1313), 1171–1191 (2023). https://doi.org/10.1017/aer.2022.110
17. Holford, W.D.: An ethical inquiry of the effect of cockpit automation on the responsibilities of airline pilots: dissonance or meaningful control? J. Bus. Ethics **176**(1), 141–157 (2020). https://doi.org/10.1007/s10551-020-04640-z
18. Keinrath, C., Dorneich, M., Vašek, J.: Designing for the future: a cognitive-adaptive-man-machine-interface. In: Annual Meeting of Human Factors and Ergonomics Society Europe Chapter, pp. 14–16. Citeseer (2009)
19. Liu, J., Gardi, A., Ramasamy, S., Lim, Y., Sabatini, R.: Cognitive pilot-aircraft interface for single-pilot operations. Knowl.-Based Syst. **112**, 37–53 (2016). https://doi.org/10.1016/j.knosys.2016.08.031
20. Mosquera Benitez, D., del Corte Valiente, A., Lanzi, P.: A novel global operational concept in cockpits under peak workload situations. Saf. Sci. **102**, 38–50 (2018). https://doi.org/10.1016/j.ssci.2017.09.028
21. Myers, P.L., Starr, A.W.: Single pilot operations IN commercial cockpits: background, challenges, and options. J. Intell. Robot. Syst. **102**(1), 1–15 (2021). https://doi.org/10.1007/s10846-021-01371-9
22. Neis, S.M., Klingauf, U., Schiefele, J.: Classification and review of conceptual frameworks for commercial single pilot operations. In: 2018 IEEE/AIAA 37th Digital Avionics Systems Conference (DASC), pp. 1–8. IEEE, London (2018). https://doi.org/10.1109/DASC.2018.8569680
23. Rong, J., Spaeth, T., Valasek, J.: Small aircraft pilot assistant: onboard decision support system for SATS aircraft. In: AIAA 5th ATIO and16th Lighter-Than-Air Sys Technology and Balloon Systems Conferences. American Institute of Aeronautics and Astronautics (2005). https://doi.org/10.2514/6.2005-7382
24. Roth, E.M., Sushereba, C., Militello, L.G., Diiulio, J., Ernst, K.: Function allocation considerations in the era of human autonomy teaming. J. Cogn. Eng. Decis. Making **13**(4), 199–220 (2019). https://doi.org/10.1177/1555343419878038
25. Schutte, P., Goodrich, K., Williams, R.: Synergistic allocation of flight expertise on the flight deck (SAFEdeck): a design concept to combat mode confusion, complacency, and skill loss in the flight deck. In: Stanton, N.A., Landry, S., Di Bucchianico, G., Vallicelli, A. (eds.) Advances in Human Aspects of Transportation. AISC, vol. 484, pp. 899–911. Springer, Cham (2017). https://doi.org/10.1007/978-3-319-41682-3_74
26. Schutte, P.C., et al.: The naturalistic flight deck system: an integrated system concept for improved single-pilot operations (2007)
27. National Academies of Sciences, E., Medicine: Human-AI Teaming: State-of-the-Art and Research Needs. National Academies Press, Washington, D.C. (2022). https://doi.org/10.17226/26355

28. Shively, R.J., Lachter, J., Brandt, S.L., Matessa, M., Battiste, V., Johnson, W.W.: Why human-autonomy teaming? In: Baldwin, C. (ed.) AHFE 2017. AISC, vol. 586, pp. 3–11. Springer, Cham (2018). https://doi.org/10.1007/978-3-319-60642-2_1
29. Sprengart, S.M., Neis, S.M., Schiefele, J.: Role of the human operator in future commercial reduced crew operations. In: 2018 IEEE/AIAA 37th Digital Avionics Systems Conference (DASC), pp. 1–10 (2018). https://doi.org/10.1109/DASC.2018.8569803. ISSN 2155-7209
30. Stensrud, R., Mikkelsen, B., Valaker, S.: Exploring human-autonomy teaming methods in challenging environments: the case of fighter pilots and loyal wingmen. Hum.-Intell. Syst. Integr. (2024). https://doi.org/10.1007/s42454-024-00050-y
31. Wang, G., Li, M., Wang, M., Ding, D.: A systematic literature review of human-centered design approach in single pilot operations. Chin. J. Aeronaut. (2023). https://doi.org/10.1016/j.cja.2023.07.026

Humans in the Group, Computers in the Coop. Comparison of Individual and Collective Improvement in Cognitive Tasks in Adjunct AI Settings

Chiara Natali[1,2(✉)], Luca Marconi[1], Caterina Fregosi[1], and Federico Cabitza[1,3]

[1] Department of Computer Science, Systems and Communication, Università degli Studi di Milano-Bicocca, Milan, Italy
chiara.natali@unimib.it

[2] University of Applied Sciences and Arts of Southern Switzerland, Dalle Molle Institute for Artificial Intelligence, Lugano, Switzerland

[3] IRCCS Ospedale Galeazzi-Sant'Ambrogio, Milan, Italy

Abstract. This paper explores how different human-AI collaboration protocols (HAI-CPs) influence performance in individual human+AI 'centaur' settings as well as in 'computer in the group' settings. Establishing effective HAI-CPs is essential to advancing Human Work Interaction Design (HWID), especially as industries move from the question of AI adoption to the challenge of integrating AI sustainably and effectively into collaborative workflows. Based on an experiment with logic puzzles supported by a simulated GPT-like AI, this study assesses AI's impact on decision-making, particularly regarding automation bias (the degree to which AI misleads users) and algorithmic aversion (the rejection of accurate AI recommendations). Our findings reveal that AI significantly enhances the cognitive performance of both centaurs and groups ('Bigae'), acting as a performance leveler by improving outcomes for lower performers more than high performers. Centaurs and Bigae's reported perceptions and observed error rates suggest that collective intelligence leads to less reliance on AI in group settings, relegating the machine to a more peripheral (adjunct) role in the decision-making process. While collectives are still improved by adding AI systems as additional average-performing teammates, deliberation with peers still appears to be the most powerful booster of human performance, and collective intelligence still outperforms individual intelligence, even when this is supported by AI.

Keywords: Human-AI Interaction · Group Decision-Making · Hybrid Intelligence · Technology Dominance · Kasparov's Law · Frictional AI

1 Introduction

Recent research has consistently confirmed the benefits of Artificial Intelligence (AI) in individual decision-making, where AI-based support is leveraged for

Published by Springer Nature Switzerland AG 2026
B. R. Barricelli et al. (Eds.): HWID 2024, IFIP AICT 751, pp. 174–191, 2026.
https://doi.org/10.1007/978-3-031-95334-7_11

cognition- and knowledge-intensive tasks in single-user settings [22]. This body of work has strengthened the legitimacy of the 'centaur' model (human-AI hybrid intelligence) in Human-AI Interaction (HAII) [19].

The centaur model symbolized a synergistic collaboration in which the complementary strengths of human and machine intelligence are integrated to achieve superior outcomes. The model gained prominence through the experiences of Chess Grandmaster Garry Kasparov, whose widely publicized defeat against IBM's chess-playing system *Deep Blue* in 1997 marked a pivotal moment in the evolving narrative of human versus machine intelligence. Rather than framing this as a zero-sum competition, Kasparov envisioned a new paradigm for collaboration.

This vision led to his creation of *Advanced Chess*, a format where human players enhance their decision-making by partnering with AI. It was in this context that the term 'centaur' emerged, describing the *Advanced Chess* player who blends AI's computational efficiency with their own intuition and creativity.

This term has been previously used in workplace studies, with Dell'Acqua et al. [19] defining as 'centaurs' those workers who strategically delegate tasks between AI and themselves, leveraging the strengths of each.

While the centaur model has demonstrated success in individual settings, achieving effective and sustainable integration into broader work environments presents an ongoing challenge.

Extending this concept to group deliberations, where decisions are made collectively, introduces added complexity in the interactions between humans, AI, and group members in collaborative settings [23]. This complexity, however, presents opportunities for richer outcomes [14] as it can be mitigated through collective sense-making, where team members jointly interpret and understand the AI system, enhancing group cohesion and performance [23].

This paper contributes to this nascent strand of research by exploring how different human-AI collaboration protocols (HAI-CPs) [8] influence group performance in hybrid human-AI decision-making settings, particularly in the context of solving logic puzzles collaboratively.

Understanding and establishing optimal HAI-CPs is crucial for advancing Human Work Interaction Design (HWID). As industries shift their focus from adopting AI to integrating it effectively into collaborative workflows and complex analytic tasks [19], it becomes clear that the quality of human-AI interactions is as critical—if not more so—than the quality of AI itself for decision-making and performance. This requires a detailed investigation of the dynamics that characterize human-machine interactions [34], resonating with Malone's call for a deeper understanding of how human intelligence and computational power can together address complex cognitive challenges effectively [27].

Integrating AI into collaborative decision-making must be approached as a matter of sustainability, not only due to the environmental costs of AI but also in consideration of its potential long-term impacts on human skills, responsibility, and workforce inclusion.

This broader view on sustainability aligns with HWID's commitment to fostering the UN Sustainable Development Goal of 'Decent Work' (SDG 8) by prioritizing skill-preserving and meaningful work environments [15]. This includes addressing "cognitive work environment problems", defined by Sandblad et al. as "when properties of the work environment hinder the workers to use their skills efficiently" [36]. Tackling the complex cognitive challenges in technology-intensive workplaces requires careful design and are thus less frequently addressed than physical and psychosocial factors, with Bouzekri et al. [5] admitting in 2023 that (until then) "little HWID research has so far addressed [...] social dimensions of sustainability".

In this study, we use the mythological and historical terms 'Centaurs' and 'Bigae' to metaphorically describe three different HAI-CPs, as detailed Sect. 3. The centaur (1), a mythological hybrid, represents a system where humans and AI collaborate as a single unit, blending human intuition with AI's computational power. The Roman two-horse chariots, named 'Bigae', represent instead the group collaboration setting, further categorized into Group-first Bigae (2) and AI-first Bigae (3). Historically, Bigae are driven by charioteers named 'Aurigae': here, we use this term to refer to the individuals within the group making their autonomous decision during the pre-group deliberation phase.

This study is also a first of its kind in assessing *technology dominance* [1] in group deliberation settings. This refers to the impact of AI on decision-making in terms of automation bias (the extent AI misleads users or groups) and algorithmic aversion (the extent humans reject AI recommendations) [7].

By examining these phenomena, we aim to shed light on how AI shapes decision-making in collaborative environments, offering insights that are critical for understanding and optimizing Human-AI interaction in workplace settings for their long-term sustainability.

2 The Adjunction Perspective to the Computer in the Group

The integration of AI into decision-making processes offers a dual perspective: AI acting as an agent that can either collaborate with or supplant human users, or AI serving as a powerful tool enhancing human capabilities, positioned as "supertools and active appliances" that amplify human capabilities to achieve masterful outcomes, rather than as teammates or collaborators [39]. Further emphasizing group dynamics, Malone suggests shifting from placing humans in the loop to integrating AI systems within the human group [27], a sentiment driven further by Shneiderman's mantra, "Humans in the group; computers in the loop" [38].

Elaborating on these proposals, we propose the concept of *adjunct* AI [12], likening it to a computer "in the *coop*", that is, relegated to an ancillary and peripheral position and function, especially so for decision-support systems based on Large Language Models (LLM) that have recently been equated to "stochastic parrots" by Bender et al. [4]. This isolation "in the coop", stems from reflections on the potentially adverse effects of AI on individual cognition, including automation bias, complacency, and algorithm aversion [25].

Adjunct AI can be considered an instance of Frictional AI [31], in that it ensures that decision support systems stimulate user cognitive activation, countering the motivational dip observed when humans collaborate with high-productivity AI [18]. When adjunct, AI acts as a post-consultation or second opinion mechanism which requires initial human decision-making. This aims at mitigating both anchoring bias [2,14] and possibly groupthink phenomena [3]. Anchoring bias, where initial AI recommendations heavily influence subsequent deliberations, risks constraining decision-makers' perspectives [14]. For example, it has been observed that many groups often commence their deliberative process by discussing topics related to AI recommendations [14]. While this direct initiation of discussions based on AI recommendations might anchor decisions, the diversity of opinions within a group can serve as a counterbalance, diluting the anchoring effect through exposure to varying viewpoints [14]. Still, the absence of individual pre-deliberation decisions may lead to a homogenization of thought, known as *groupthink*, where dissent and innovation are stifled [3]. This dynamic interplay suggests that the structure of interaction with AI—whether initiating discussion or following individual deliberation—significantly influences the cognitive biases at play within group decision-making processes. By encouraging initial independent decision-making, followed by AI consultation, Adjunct AI can facilitate a balance between leveraging AI insights and preserving individual and collective critical thinking.

Previous research underscores the advantage of group decision-making where AI contributes to group discussion (Bigae) over human-AI dyads (Centaurs) [10]. Rather than serving as oracles [30], AI systems should be catalysts for collective discourse, leveraging human transactive memory and social skills to mitigate the biases associated with AI-dominated decision-making, or agential AI [10]. The impact of AI in decision-making is difficult to understate, as Decision Support Systems posited as "structuring the cognitive process latent to the decision-making" even when providing access to the necessary information sources [37]. Our approach advocates for positioning AI as an enabler of enhanced cognitive engagement and collective intelligence, shifting its role from a dominant agent to a supportive, consultative entity [12]. This reimagined interaction seeks to amplify the benefits of human-AI collaboration, leveraging the unique strengths of both while mitigating known cognitive biases and fostering a more dynamic, thoughtful, and hybrid [20] decision-making environment.

3 Methods

3.1 Participants

Forty-six Master's students from a 'Communications and Technology' degree participated, forming 22 human-AI pairs, or 'Centaurs', and six teams, or 'Bigae' (i.e., chariots), who act as a collective, expressing a single decision. We chose this term to represent the enhanced collective dynamics through human-AI teamwork as sort of 'super minds', in Malone's terminology [27]. Bigae are composed of four participants named 'Aurigae' (i.e., charioteers), who are individual decision-makers in the initial step. We further categorized Bigae in two different HAI-CPs based on the timing of AI advice: Group-first teams discussed potential solutions before AI consultation, while AI-first teams received AI input before deliberation (see Fig. 3). These two HAI-CPs have been previously studied in the literature focusing on identifying and studying cognitive biases only in individual decision-making processes arising from interaction with AI support systems (see, for example, [6] and [8]). Finally, Centaurs are human-AI pairs where an individual works directly with the AI support. All three participants configurations are illustrated intuitively in Fig. 2.

The composition of these groups, albeit random, ensured gender diversity with a majority of women (on average, 2.71 women and 1.28 men per four-person group), possibly aligning with Woolley et al.'s observations on ideal group composition for team performance [42] albeit the significance of gender for team cooperation has been debated in the HWID literature [44]. The variation in experimental protocol according to the assigned HAI-CP are detailed in Sect. 3.3 and in Fig. 3.

3.2 Materials

Interface. We employed a simulated 'Wizard-of-Oz' [16] GPT-like interface developed via *Figma*, as shown in Fig. 1. The system appeared to respond to images of pattern reasoning tasks or transcriptions of word logic puzzles, to which it provided both answers and accompanying rationales.

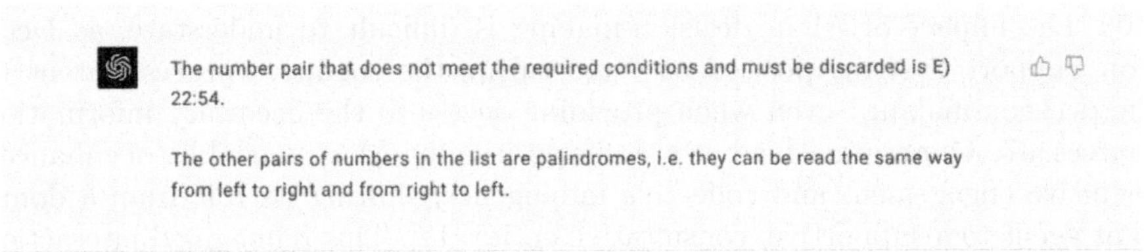

Fig. 1. Simulated interface shown to the participants, with an example of an erroneous AI suggestion in response to the puzzle *"Deduce the pair of numbers to discard from those proposed below: A) 11:22; B) 01:11; C) 15:51; D) 16:61; E) 22:54"* (screenshot translated from Italian).

To assess group and individual performance in terms of accuracy and examine the influence of AI, even when providing incorrect answers, we designed the 19 responses of the simulated AI so that would be 13 correct and 6 incorrect, resulting in an accuracy rate of 68.42%.

This accuracy rate closely aligns with, but exceeds, the 62.5% accuracy rate set by Chen et al. [13] in their study on human-AI decision-making with explanations. The authors chose this rate to oversample incorrect AI predictions, where oversampling incorrect predictions enabled deeper investigation into participant reliance on AI.

Furthermore, selecting a clearly less-than-perfect accuracy rate mirrors realistic scenarios reflecting the limitations of LLMs. Given the well-documented struggles of LLMs with logical tasks [35], the chosen accuracy rate could be considered generous, especially considering the period of experimentation, which occurred before the release of more advanced GPT systems like *ChatGPT-4o*. This design choice aimed to present the AI as a realistic tool, with strengths and weaknesses, to provide participants with an authentic experience of interacting with current AI limitations.

To minimize the risk of negative priming due to inaccurate answers and foster user trust in the AI system, we designed the initial sequence of responses to include 9 consecutive correct answers. The first 2 answers displayed highly relevant and compelling explanations, while lower-quality explanations were deliberately included in answers 3, 5, 7 and 9. Wrong answers were introduced later at questions 10, 12, 14, 16, 18 and 19, with all other responses being correct. This design choice allowed us to investigate the level of user trust in an AI that makes mistakes, as well as to verify potential automation biases.

This strategy aimed to create an initial positive impression of the AI as a reliable, though not infallible, tool. This positive priming could subsequently influence user willingness to accept AI suggestions even when incorrect.

While alternative response patterns might foster a more dynamic trust-building experience, the use of an initial sequence of correct answers as a trust-building strategy has been documented in the literature on interactive XAI systems [32,33]. This approach was chosen for its effectiveness in enabling cross-comparison of trust formation among different groups, allowing us to study automation bias in a controlled and consistent manner.

Pre- and Post-test Assessments. We also conducted both pre- and post-test assessments of perceived trust and utility regarding AI interaction, with questionnaires drawing from validated scales such as the Artificial Intelligence Anxiety Scale [41] and the Technology Acceptance Model [17]. These questionnaires included questions on trust in AI and the perceived benefits of AI support and allowed us a comprehensive view of participants' attitudes towards AI. We aggregated the TAM-related questions to construct a UTILITY score, which were associated with a .85 Cronbach's Alpha.

3.3 Procedure

In this study, we investigated the effects of AI on decision-making accuracy and cognitive biases in both individual and group contexts. The experiment involved administering 19 logic puzzles, including numerical and alphanumeric logic, deductive reasoning, graphic interpretation, and anagrams from the website *Youmath*[1]. The 19 items were selected and extracted from higher-level quizzes so that the task would be challenging for the subjects, thus evoking the need to include the AI's opinion and support. The rationale behind choosing these types of puzzles was to simulate tasks that individuals commonly face alone but could benefit from collaborative problem-solving and AI support. While the puzzles are generally solved individually, our aim was to examine how transitioning from individual to collective, AI-augmented problem-solving could reveal shifts in cognitive reliance and performance. This setup allowed us to analyze whether group deliberation could mitigate the influence of automation bias or algorithmic aversion typically observed in solitary decision-making.

Fig. 2. On the left, a representation of the Centaur configuration (human - upper body, AI system - lower body). On the centre, the AI-first Biga configuration (four humans - the 'Aurigae', AI system - the horse). On the right, the Group-first Biga (Aurigae first deliberate together: only then will they take the reins of the AI system).

Having introduced in Sect. 3.1 the general concept of the different collaboration protocols used in our study, we now provide a more detailed description of each of specific configuration within the experiment procedure. In our experiment, we tested three different HAI-CPs to better understand their influence on decision-making outcomes:

- **Group-First Bigae:** In this configuration, group members (Aurigae) discussed potential solutions within their groups before consulting the AI system. This protocol aimed to observe the natural flow of group deliberation and the influence of AI when introduced after an initial group decision was made. This allowed us to measure how AI input could alter or refine group consensus.
- **AI-First Bigae:** Conversely, in this protocol, group members (Aurigae) first received the AI's suggestion before engaging in group discussions. The goal here was to understand how AI could prime discussions, potentially influencing group dynamics by anchoring initial deliberations to the AI's suggestion.
- **Centaurs:** In this individual-focused collaboration model, each participant worked directly with the AI system, aiming to combine human decision-making skills with AI's computational power. This setting allowed us to isolate the impact of AI on individual performance without the complexities introduced by group interactions.

[1] https://www.youmath.it.

These protocols were chosen to explore the dynamics of human-AI collaboration beyond its outcomes in terms of accuracy, emphasizing the process of how decisions are made within different collaborative settings.

The experimental phase took place in-person, within university spaces. It began with an initial questionnaire (via *Google Forms*) to gauge the participants' predispositions towards teamwork and AI interaction, followed by six collaborative sessions (plus one centaur-specific session), and concluded with a post-test questionnaire. Each session lasted approximately 1 h and 30 min, including the initial and final questionnaires.

Phase 1: Initial Questionnaire. The initial questionnaire involved completing 18 questions on Google Forms to assess the predisposition to interaction with AI systems and, for aurigae participants, to teamwork. The questions can be divided into two subcategories: a section of 3 questions on the perceived usefulness of using artificial intelligence; a section of 9 questions on the predisposition to group work. Users were asked to indicate their degree of agreement along a six-point Likert scale-like semantic differential where 1 corresponded to (totally disagree) and 6 to (totally agree), to mitigate central tendency bias.

Phase 2: Collaborative Sessions. Following the initial questionnaire, participants were then sequentially shown 19 logic puzzles with four answer options ('Case presentation' in Fig. 3) and asked to provide anonymous individual answers via LimeSurvey[2], including their confidence level for each response on a 4-value ordinal scale, where 1 corresponded to the minimum confidence and 4 to the maximum confidence (Step 1, 'First Individual Answer' and 'Confidence Collection', 60″).

The collaborative session protocol then varied by HAI-CP, as illustrated in Fig. 3. Specifically:

- **Group-First Bigae**: Participants discussed possible solutions together and were asked to provide a first group decision, denoted as the 'auriga' decision (Step 2, '1° Group Deliberation', 60″). After that, participants consulted the AI advice and together developed the final 'biga' (group+AI) answer (Step 3, 'FHD collection', 60″). Both responses were manually marked by the moderators.
- **AI-First Bigae:** Participants consulted the AI before having the opportunity to talk to each other, and after two minutes of group discussion were asked to provide a final 'biga' answer (Step 2, 'FHD collection', 120″). This response was manually marked by the moderators.
- **Centaurs:** The participant consulted the AI system and provided their final answer (Step 2, 'FHD collection', 120″). This response was marked independently by the participants on the LimeSurvey platform.

In all configurations, the total time allocated for each logic puzzle was 180″.

[2] http://limesurvey.org.

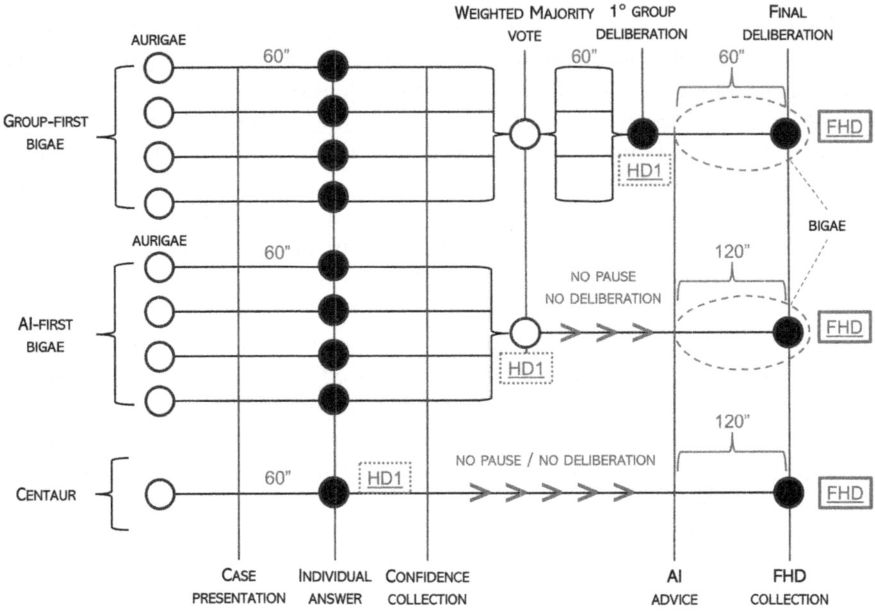

Fig. 3. Group deliberation scheme for Group-First Bigae, AI-First Bigae and Centaurs.

Phase 3: Final Questionnaire. A final questionnaire assessed participants' attitudes towards AI post-experiment, mirroring the initial questionnaire but with varied question order and phrasing to ensure participants would not mindlessly replicate the answers provided before the experiment.

3.4 Reliance Patterns

Reliance patterns have been proposed as a critical framework for evaluating the influence of Artificial Intelligence within AI-enhanced decision-making processes [7]. These patterns are rooted in the theory of technology dominance [1] and, as outlined in Table 1, they describe how humans interact and rely on AI systems during the decision-making process through a sequence of decision stages: an initial, unassisted human decision (HD1), the subsequent AI advice (AI), and the final AI-supported human decision (FHD). By analyzing the correctness (and/or incorrectness) of decisions at each stage, reliance patterns offers a structured method to quantify the impact of AI on human decision-making, that allows to assess the extent to which individuals might adjust their initial judgments after considering AI input. For example, AI advice enhances decision-making by encouraging the rejection of initially incorrect human decisions (HD1) in favor of correct AI advice, or conversely, AI support may detrimentally lead individuals to discard their correct initial decisions for incorrect final decisions (FHD) based on erroneous AI recommendations. We elaborated these reliance patterns via the open-access tool *Human - AI Interaction Assessment*[3] to assess the levels of automation bias and conservatism bias displayed by the responders. The collection of HD1, AI and FHD is illustrated in Fig. 3. Notably, for Group-First Aurigae, HD1 refers to the first, pre-AI Group (Bigae) Deliberation. For AI-First Aurigae, instead, HD1 was the weighted average of individual, pre-AI responses, according to the responder's confidence. Weighted averages were considered in place of HD1 in order to isolate the effect of group deliberation in a cross-HAI-CP comparison (Group First vs. AI-First) as well an intra-HAI-CP comparison (Weighted Average vs. Group Deliberations in Group-First Bigae).

Table 1. Definition of Automation Bias and Conservatism Bias as reliance patterns between human decision makers and their AI system. In the first three columns, 0 denotes an incorrect decision, and 1 a correct decision.

Human judgment (HD1)	AI support (AI)	Final decision (FHD)	Reliance pattern
1	0	0	Detrimental Over-reliance **(Automation Bias)**
0	1	0	Detrimental Self-reliance **(Conservatism Bias)**

4 Results and Discussion

4.1 Centaurs vs. Bigae: *Kasparov's Law* in Action

Initial human group performance was 57.89% for AI-first Bigae and 50% for Group-first Bigae, compared to the AI performance of 68.42%. To guide our analysis, we built on the study by Cabitza et al. [9] on radiological double reading, which explored Kasparov's law [24]. This law posits that 'Weak *[sic]* human + machine + better process is superior to a strong computer alone'. In their study, the researchers found that groups of humans who initially perform worse than AI can significantly outperform it when their judgments are aggregated via majority voting. We observed a similar phenomenon in our study, as both Group-first and AI-first HAI-CPs showed marked improvements in group performance after deliberation.

Final group performance reached 78.95% for AI-first Bigae and 75% for Group-first Bigae, representing gains of +21.06% and +25%, respectively, compared to their initial performance. Notably, these final performances also exceeded AI performance, though not statistically significant, with AI-first Bigae outperforming AI by +10.53% ($t(56) = 1.6$, $p = .109$) and Group-first Bigae by +6.58% ($t(75) = 1$, $p = .300$). In contrast, Centaurs, who did not aggregate

[3] https://haiiassessment.pythonanywhere.com, last accessed 29/12/2024.

their judgments with others, achieved a final performance of 69.14%, comparable to AI albeit marginally higher (+0.72%), and this difference not statistically significant ($t(417) = 0.3$, $p = .756$). As these findings suggest alignment with Kasparov's law, further studies are needed to robustly validate this trend with a larger sample to further support the idea that a 'better process' emerges through collaborative human efforts, rather than relying solely on individual human-AI pairings.

Moreover, we observed that the AI acted as a performance leveler, as shown graphically in Fig. 4: global performance variance decreased and the average performance of the low-performers increased. This means that the low-performers (at pre-support step), both individuals and teams, improved more than high-performers at the post-support step. This phenomenon was analytically confirmed through a negative (−0.55) and statistically significant Pearson Correlation Coefficient ($p = 0.002$), as well as by the angular coefficient of the regression line (−0.43).

As for Automation Bias, it was lower for Aurigae as expected, while for Conservatism Bias we did not observe any statistically significant difference, though Aurigae had higher variance (Fig. 5). Despite these differences, both Aurigae and Centaurs reported increased trust in AI, with Aurigae showing a significantly higher trust level post-test ($p = 0.028$, effect size = 0.31).

4.2 Deep Dive Into Group Deliberation: AI-First vs. Group-First

We found no statistically significant difference in teamwork predisposition between the Aurigae in Group-first and AI-first Bigae ($p = 0.2258$, effect size = 0.23), suggesting that our findings on group performance were not inadvertently skewed by this variable.

While in AI-first Bigae we could not decouple the collective intelligence effect (that is the power of discussion) from the AI influence, this was possible in the Group-first Bigae. In fact, the first group deliberation of AI-first Bigae necessarily followed exposure to AI advice and could as such be influenced by it. Instead, the initial group decision of the Group-first Bigae was the result of the collective deliberation of the members preceding any exposure to AI advice.

We observed no significant difference in the perceived utility of AI between the AI-first and Group-first HAI-CPs ($p = 0.2114$, effect size = 0.17), although Group-first Aurigae experienced lower Automation Bias and higher Conservatism Bias (Fig. 5), thus relying less on AI.

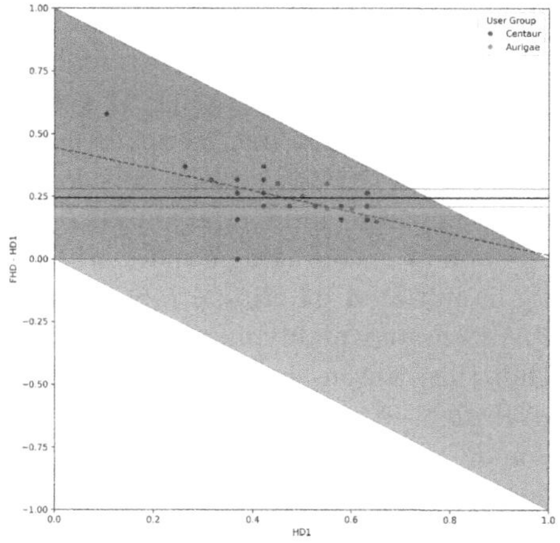

Fig. 4. Benefit Diagram for Aurigae and Centaurs, showing an increase in performance for both types of users.

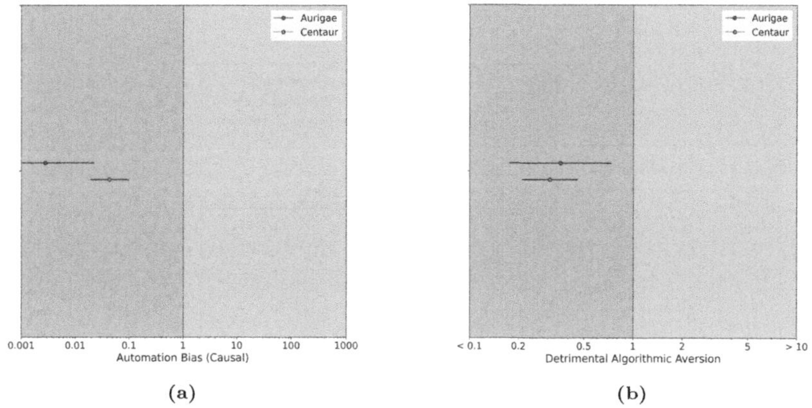

Fig. 5. (a) Automation Bias Diagram for Aurigae and Centaurs, showing a significantly lower automation bias for Aurigae and (b) Conservatism Bias Diagram for Aurigae and Centaurs, showing similar levels for Centaurs and Aurigae.

For AI-first groups, the average of 8.3 errors at Weighted Average became 3.7 errors after exposure to AI advice (FHD), a 58% decrease. Group-first Bigae exhibited a lower basal Weighted Average accuracy, averaging at 9.5 HD1. However, their transition from Weighted Majority (38 errors) to Group Deliberation (32 errors) marked a 16% error reduction, while the final error count post-AI exposure dropped by 41% compared to Group Deliberation (and 50% relative to Weighted Majority). This provides a more granular description of the difference in final accuracy observed in Sect. 4.1 which was 3.95% lower for Group-First Bigae.

Our conjecture is that, within the Group-first setting, discussions that precede AI consultation risk entrenching groupthink phenomena and marginalizing AI input due to a pronounced algorithmic aversion. Specifically, Group-first configurations face the challenge of integrating AI advice within a constrained timeframe—having only a minute to incorporate AI perspectives following earlier group deliberation. Conversely, AI-first groups benefit from two minutes of deliberation time in light of the AI advice, allowing for a comprehensive evaluation of AI suggestions alongside individual initial decisions. This structure may curb groupthink as well as encouraging a more critical engagement with AI input, where discussion is initiated by critical reflections on AI's contributions [14]. While group deliberation undeniably influences and enhances outcomes, the integration of AI within these discussions emerges as powerful a determinant of group performance. In light of the critical role of the initial private decision [3], we advocate for a model where humans remain at the core of the group, with AI serving as an adjunct 'in the coop', acting as a trigger to group deliberation that also allows for its suggestions to be doubted and discussed by the human team. This approach balances AI's role in stimulating dialogue and ensuring that human intelligence remains at the forefront of collective decision-making (Fig. 6).

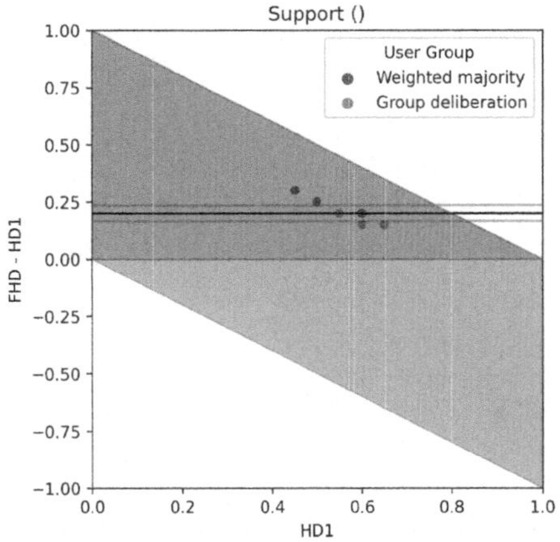

Fig. 6. Benefit Diagram for Weighted Majority vs Group Deliberation Aurigae, showing the higher basal performance for group deliberation and clear improvement for both WM and GD following exposure to AI advice.

5 Conclusion

Our findings reveal AI's potential in augmenting group intelligence and facilitating productive deliberation, suggesting the importance of integrating AI into collaborative settings through sustainable, human-centred approaches. This study on HAI-CPs aligns with HWID's goal to foster working environments that prioritize human skill, intuition, and well-being, in line with the Sustainable Development Goal of "decent work for all" (SDG 8) [15]. By tailoring effective HAI-CPs for specific work environments, we can support more resilient teams where individuals benefit from AI support without experiencing dependency or skill erosion.

The various HAI-CPs studied in this work can contribute to the identification and understanding of new human-AI interaction patterns in collaborative work environments. Specifically, these protocols illustrate how different approaches to AI integration—whether AI-first, human-first, or adjunct—can shape user experience in ways that either enhance or inhibit effective collaboration. This insight complements HWID's emphasis on the careful design of interaction models that are adaptive to the specific needs of users and their work environments [21,29,40], and further develops the research on the validity of *Kasparov's Law* [10,24].

Sustainability, as understood by Kuhlman and Farrington's, extends beyond environmental preservation to include other essential resources as legacies for future generations [5,26]. In this context, recent concerns about over-reliance on AI highlight the importance of safeguarding human skill and intuition as integral to sustainability at large. Specifically, we have shown how the use of AI in an auxiliary role has been shown to enhance the ability to maintain consistent performance among participants, particularly benefiting those with initially lower performance levels by promoting a more equitable distribution of cognitive load within the group.

However, we acknowledge certain limitations in our study's methodology and scope. Specifically, the formation of groups did not account for individual performance levels or internal leadership dynamics. In addition, our use of logic tasks does not adequately reflect current capabilities of LLMs [43], so we chose to simulate these ones as a proxy to explore AI-enabled 'hybrid intelligence' in a non-professional setting, preferring it to notion-driven tasks such as trivia. Another potential limitation of this study is related to the choice of task types. Although our study focused on logic puzzles typically used for individual cognitive training, we acknowledge that different types of tasks could potentially have influenced the outcomes. Tasks that require more explicit collaboration, such as problem-solving that benefits from diverse skill sets or tasks involving creativity, might yield different group dynamics and AI reliance patterns.

Future research should then investigate the differences between AI contributions that are limited to simple 'advice and explanation' (as in our study) and more complex, interactive scenarios facilitated by advanced LLMs.

The study was designed with a high degree of control, including specific tasks (logic puzzles), a fixed sequence of correct and incorrect AI responses, and predefined collaboration protocols. These choices were necessary to isolate variables like automation bias and trust-building. While the study's controlled design allows for rigorous exploration of HAI-CP dynamics, its generalizability to real-world work environments is inherently limited by the specificity of tasks and experimental conditions.

Despite these constraints, the findings offer a foundational understanding of HAI-CP dynamics, providing hypotheses for how similar patterns might manifest in professional settings. Future research should test these hypotheses in diverse and realistic contexts, incorporating varied task types, AI capabilities, and organizational constraints to validate and refine their applicability.

Ultimately, our study contributes to broader research on AI's potential to enhance group intelligence and stimulate human discussion, thus ensuring that AI does not merely act as *deus ex crowd* for challenging tasks [28]. Instead, the adjunction approach exemplifies what has been termed *frictional AI* [11,31] by intentionally incorporating elements of resistance - in this instance, positioning AI in an ancillary role. This 'friction' encourages deeper engagement, critical thinking, and more comprehensive evaluation among decision-makers, ultimately enhancing the decision-making process.

This leads to the provocative statement of the title: *Humans in the group, computers in the coop*, as to motivate and call for further research into sustainable Human-AI interaction configurations where AI is moved to an ancillary role. Such configurations, or HAI-CPs, hold the potential to reinforce and elevate human intelligence in workplace settings, advancing both performance and collaboration.

Acknowledgements. C. Natali gratefully acknowledges the PhD grant awarded by the Fondazione Fratelli Confalonieri, which has been instrumental in facilitating her research pursuits. Chiara Natali gratefully acknowledges the financial support provided by the Federal Commission for Scholarships for Foreign Students in the form of the Swiss Government Excellence Scholarship (ESKAS No. 2024.0002) for the academic year 2024–25.

F. Cabitza and C. Fregosi acknowledge funding support provided by the Italian project PRIN PNRR 2022 InXAID - Interaction with eXplainable Artificial Intelligence in (medical) Decision making. CUP: H53D23008090001 funded by the European Union - Next Generation EU.

References

1. Arnold, V., Sutton, S.G., et al.: The theory of technology dominance: understanding the impact of intelligent decision aids on decision maker's judgments. Adv. Acc. Behav. Res. **1**(3), 175–194 (1998)
2. Bach, A.K.P., Nørgaard, T.M., Brok, J.C., Van Berkel, N.: "if i had all the time in the world": ophthalmologists' perceptions of anchoring bias mitigation in clinical AI support. In: Proceedings of the 2023 CHI Conference on Human Factors in Computing Systems, pp. 1–14 (2023)
3. Bahrami, B., Olsen, K., Bang, D., Roepstorff, A., Rees, G., Frith, C.: What failure in collective decision-making tells us about metacognition. Philos. Trans. Roy. Soc. B: Biol. Sci. **367**(1594), 1350–1365 (2012)
4. Bender, E.M., Gebru, T., McMillan-Major, A., Shmitchell, S.: On the dangers of stochastic parrots: can language models be too big? In: Proceedings of ACM FA, pp. 610–623 (2021)
5. Bouzekri, E., Barricelli, B.R., Clemmensen, T., Hertzum, M., Masoodian, M.: Sustainable human-work interaction designs. In: IFIP Conference on Human-Computer Interaction, pp. 674–679. Springer (2023)

6. Buçinca, Z., Malaya, M.B., Gajos, K.Z.: To trust or to think: cognitive forcing functions can reduce overreliance on AI in AI-assisted decision-making. Proc. ACM Hum.-Comput. Interact. **5**(CSCW1), 1–21 (2021)
7. Cabitza, F., Campagner, A., Angius, R., Natali, C., Reverberi, C.: Ai shall have no dominion: on how to measure technology dominance in AI-supported human decision-making. In: Proceedings of the 2023 CHI Conference on Human Factors in Computing Systems, pp. 1–20 (2023)
8. Cabitza, F., Campagner, A., Ronzio, L., et al.: Rams, hounds and white boxes: investigating human–AI collaboration protocols in medical diagnosis. Artif. Intell. Med. **138**, 102506 (2023)
9. Cabitza, F., Campagner, A., Sconfienza, L.M.: Studying human-AI collaboration protocols: the case of the Kasparov's law in radiological double reading. Health inf. sci. syst. **9**, 1–20 (2021)
10. Cabitza, F., Campagner, A., Simone, C.: The need to move away from agential-AI: empirical investigations, useful concepts and open issues. Int. J. Hum Comput Stud. **155**, 102696 (2021)
11. Cabitza, F., Natali, C., Famiglini, L., Campagner, A., Caccavella, V., Gallazzi, E.: Never tell me the odds: investigating pro-hoc explanations in medical decision making. Artif. Intell. Med. **150**, 102819 (2024)
12. Cabitza, F., Natali, C., et al.: Open, multiple, adjunct. decision support at the time of relational AI. FAIA **354** (2022)
13. Chen, V., Liao, Q.V., Wortman Vaughan, J., Bansal, G.: Understanding the role of human intuition on reliance in human-AI decision-making with explanations. Proc. ACM Hum.-Comput. Interact. **7**(CSCW2), 1–32 (2023)
14. Chiang, C.W., Lu, Z., Li, Z., Yin, M.: Are two heads better than one in AI-assisted decision making? Comparing the behavior and performance of groups and individuals in human-AI collaborative recidivism risk assessment. In: Proceedings of the 2023 CHI Conference on Human Factors in Computing Systems, pp. 1–18 (2023)
15. Clemmensen, T., Clemmensen, T.: HWID policymaking. Human Work Interaction Design: A Platform for Theory and Action, pp. 237–266 (2021)
16. Dahlbäck, N., Jönsson, A., Ahrenberg, L.: Wizard of OZ studies: why and how. In: Proceedings of the 1st International Conference on Intelligent User Interfaces, pp. 193–200 (1993)
17. Davis, F.D., et al.: Technology acceptance model: Tam. In: Al-Suqri, M.N., Al-Aufi, A.S. (eds.) Information Seeking Behavior and Technology Adoption, pp. 205–219 (1989)
18. Dell'Acqua, F., Kogut, B., Perkowski, P.: Super mario meets AI: experimental effects of automation and skills on team performance and coordination. Rev. Econ. Stat. 1–47 (2023)
19. Dell'Acqua, F., et al.: Navigating the jagged technological frontier: field experimental evidence of the effects of AI on knowledge worker productivity and quality. Harvard Business School Technology & Operations Management Unit Working Paper (24-013) (2023)
20. Dellermann, D., Ebel, P., Söllner, M., Leimeister, J.M.: Hybrid intelligence. Bus. Inf. Syst. Eng. **61**, 637–643 (2019)
21. Gonçalves, F., Campos, P., Clemmensen, T.: Human work interaction design: An overview. In: Abdelnour Nocera, J., Barricelli, B.R., Lopes, A., Campos, P., Clemmensen, T. (eds.) Human Work Interaction Design. Work Analysis and Interaction Design Methods for Pervasive and Smart Workplaces, pp. 3–19. Springer, Cham (2015)

22. Jarrahi, M.H.: Artificial intelligence and the future of work: human-AI symbiosis in organizational decision making. Bus. Horiz. **61**(4), 577–586 (2018)
23. Karvonen, H., Heikkilä, E., Wahlström, M.: Artificial intelligence awareness in work environments. In: Human Work Interaction Design. Designing Engaging Automation: 5th IFIP WG 13.6 Working Conference, HWID 2018, Espoo, Finland, 20–21 August 2018, Revised Selected Papers 5, pp. 175–185. Springer (2019)
24. Kasparov, G.: Deep thinking: where machine intelligence ends and human creativity begins. Hachette UK (2017)
25. Kliegr, T., Bahník, Š, Fürnkranz, J.: A review of possible effects of cognitive biases on interpretation of rule-based machine learning models. Artif. Intell. **295**, 103458 (2021)
26. Kuhlman, T., Farrington, J.: What is sustainability? Sustainability **2**(11), 3436–3448 (2010)
27. Malone, T.W.: Superminds: The Surprising Power of People and Computers Thinking Together. Little, Brown Spark (2018)
28. Malone, T.W., Bernstein, M.S.: Handbook of Collective Intelligence. MIT Press (2022)
29. Miao, X., Hou, W.J.: Research on the integration of human-computer interaction and cognitive neuroscience. In: Bhutkar, G., et al. (eds.) Human Work Interaction Design. Artificial Intelligence and Designing for a Positive Work Experience in a Low Desire Society, pp. 66–82. Springer, Cham (2022)
30. Miller, R.A., Masarie, F. E., J.: The demise of the "Greek oracle" model for medical diagnostic systems. Methods Inf. Med. **29**(01), 1–2 (1990)
31. Natali, C., et al.: Per aspera ad astra, or flourishing via friction: stimulating cognitive activation by design through frictional decision support systems. In: CEUR Workshop Proceedings, vol. 3481, pp. 15–19 (2023)
32. Nourani, M., King, J., Ragan, E.: The role of domain expertise in user trust and the impact of first impressions with intelligent systems. In: Proceedings of the AAAI Conference on Human Computation and Crowdsourcing, vol. 8, pp. 112–121 (2020)
33. Nourani, M., et al.: On the importance of user backgrounds and impressions: Lessons learned from interactive AI applications. ACM Trans. Interact. Intell. Syst. **12**(4), 1–29 (2022)
34. Peng, A., Nushi, B., Kiciman, E., Inkpen, K., Kamar, E.: Investigations of performance and bias in human-AI teamwork in hiring. In: Proceedings of the AAAI Conference on Artificial Intelligence, vol. 36, pp. 12089–12097 (2022)
35. Plevris, V., Papazafeiropoulos, G., Jiménez Rios, A.: Chatbots put to the test in math and logic problems: a comparison and assessment of chatGPT-3.5, chatGPT-4, and Google bard. AI **4**(4), 949–969 (2023). https://doi.org/10.3390/ai4040048, https://www.mdpi.com/2673-2688/4/4/48
36. Sandblad, B., et al.: Work environment and computer systems development. Behav. Inf. Technol. **22**(6), 375–387 (2003)
37. Seymoens, T., Ongenae, F., Jacobs, A., Verstichel, S., Ackaert, A.: A methodology to involve domain experts and machine learning techniques in the design of human-centered algorithms. In: Human Work Interaction Design. Designing Engaging Automation: 5th IFIP WG 13.6 Working Conference, HWID 2018, Espoo, Finland, 20–21 August 2018, Revised Selected Papers 5, pp. 200–214. Springer (2019)
38. Shneiderman, B.: Human-centered artificial intelligence: three fresh ideas. AIS Trans. Hum.-Comput. Interact. **12**(3), 109–124 (2020)
39. Shneiderman, B.: Human-centered AI. Issues Sci. Technol. **37**(2), 56–61 (2021)
40. Vicente, K.J.: Cognitive Work Analysis: Toward Safe, Productive, and Healthy Computer-Based Work. CRC Press (1999)

41. Wang, Y.Y., Wang, Y.S.: Development and validation of an artificial intelligence anxiety scale: An initial application in predicting motivated learning behavior. Interact. Learn. Environ. **30**(4), 619–634 (2022)
42. Woolley, A., Malone, T., et al.: What makes a team smarter? More women. Harv. Bus. Rev. **89**(6), 32–33 (2011)
43. Zhang, H., Huang, J., Li, Z.,et al.: Improved logical reasoning of language models via differentiable symbolic programming. arXiv preprint arXiv:2305.03742 (2023)
44. Zhi, X., Zhou, R.: The influence of automation and culture on human cooperation. In: IFIP Working Conference on Human Work Interaction Design, pp. 123–140. Springer (2021)

Innovating Sustainable Healthcare with Humanoid Robotics

Judith Molka-Danielsen[1](✉), Carl Hayden Smith[2], and David Hanson[3]

[1] Department of Logistics, Molde University College, Britvn. 2, 6402 Molde, Norway
j.molka-danielsen@himolde.no

[2] School of Arts and Creative Industries, University of East London, London E16 2RD, UK
c.smith7@uel.ac.uk

[3] Hanson Robotics, Unit A, 25/F Block 2, Superluck Industrial Centre, 57 Sha Tsui Road, Tsuen Wan, Hong Kong
david@hansonrobotics.com

Abstract. Global trends of increasing human lifespans and decreasing birth rates are at present having an impact in the "care" related services domains, such as healthcare that have traditionally required a human touch. The availability of the workforce in the healthcare domain is predicted to be deficient to meet the needs of an aging population. Humanoid robots have the potential to take up the shortcomings left by a diminishing workforce, and provide improved efficiency, increase accuracy of diagnosis, and better overall care and wellbeing for humans in society. In this paper we describe the distinguishing characteristics of a humanoid robot. We review the state of the art in this area. This paper explores human work analysis in the healthcare sector. We present theories in Human Work Interaction Design and reflect on design approaches that can contribute to future designs of humanoid robots that may better aid human work in healthcare services and better achieve sustainability goals. The main contribution of this paper is that it presents the transformative potential of humanoid robots regarding how they can impact sustainability in the workplace in care industries with focus on the healthcare sector.

Keywords: humanoid robots · healthcare work · sustainability

1 Introduction: Implications of an Ageing Population

Presently one-fifth of the population in Europe are over the age of 65 [1] and by 2060 this will be one-third [2]. An aging population combined with decreasing fertility rates will mean a diminished available workforce. This for healthcare workers is combined with often unfavourable working conditions in the healthcare sector such as dangerous exposures, serving higher numbers of patients, and low pay. Such factors have been shown to lead to burn-out and increasingly a lack of availability of healthcare workers [2]. Robotics with Artificial Intelligence (AI) have for some decades made inroads into industrial settings. In manufacturing, for example, the benefits of robotics are reputed for offering higher precision and safety for workers. Little explored are the opportunities for robotics in the care related services industry such as healthcare.

Published by Springer Nature Switzerland AG 2026
B. R. Barricelli et al. (Eds.): HWID 2024, IFIP AICT 751, pp. 192–207, 2026.
https://doi.org/10.1007/978-3-031-95334-7_12

Population ageing is a general shift of the median age of the overall population that is an effect of increasing longevity and declining fertility rates. The UN reports that developed countries have increased median age, from 28 in 1950, predicted to be 44 by 2050 [3]. The total fertility rate (TFR) is the average number of children born to a woman in a lifetime. The rate for global TFR has decreased by half from 1950 from 5 to 2.4 in 2021 [4]. The TFR for 2023 in Europe average 1.615 [1, 5].

What does an ageing population mean for human wellbeing? Areas of concern include being at higher risk for debilitating disease and reduced income security. Cases of dementia are expected to double in Europe within the next 30 years [6]. Dementia symptoms are caused by various diseases, it disrupts the individual's memory and/or other cognitive functions. It can impede the individual from performing daily tasks and as such can diminish self-reliance, autonomy, and quality of life. The implications of pensioner poverty are that pensioners rely on a fixed income while annual inflation may lead them to living in material deprivation. As a result, older people are tending to work longer. Europe's health workforce in particular is ageing. In Europe, 30% of the doctors are over 55, while in Italy 60% of the doctors are over 55 [7]. However, even with a healthcare workforce that is working longer, this is not enough to meet the future needs of care in the sector. Europe and global society in general require a strategy for improving sustainability in the workplace within the healthcare sector.

Robotics with AI have potential to contribute to improvements of efficiency, increase accuracy of diagnosis, and better overall care and wellbeing for humans in society [8]. The care related service industries may benefit especially from humanoid robots. Humanoid robots are machines that are designed to act and look to some extent like a human. Humanoid robots may elicit higher emotional investment and thus evoke higher engagement from its human stakeholders. The human may in turn be better served by a robot that resembles a human or another character that can represent a human persona (e.g. placing human personas on robots that appear as pets). Moreover, the design of the robot could have added benefit if it has a humanoid form because it can share the human locomotion perspective and learn through reenforced learning and interaction points with the external environment as a human would experience it.

The research objective of this paper is to review the current state of the art on humanoid robotics in the healthcare sector. We explore the research question, what is the transformative potential of emergent humanoid robot technology, and its implications on sustainability of work and services in the healthcare sector?

2 Sustainability in Healthcare

The United Nations in 2015 adopted a 2030 agenda for sustainability that included seventeen sustainability goals. These goals provide "a shared blueprint for peace and prosperity for people and the planet, now and into the future" [9]. This paper seeks to support the 3rd UN sustainability goal, to "ensure healthy lives and promote well-being for all at all ages".

The term sustainability means in general to maintain capital where the category of capital can be economic, environmental, human, or social [10]. Sustainability in the healthcare sector encompasses environmental sustainability, efficient resource consumption, reducing emissions, that includes factors such as managing efficient use of lights and ventilation systems in hospitals, and reduction of waste [11]. However, environmental sustainability must be achieved alongside positive health outcomes. Positive health outcomes require social equity and accessibility, and a resilient health care environment that supports stakeholder communities over time. To achieve positive health outcomes, health care strategies also need to aim for preventive healthcare, keeping populations healthy to alleviate stress on the health care systems, reducing needs and length of stays in facilities (e.g. in hospitals, rehabilitation centres, elderly care homes) [11]. Healthcare systems are under increasing pressure throughout Europe and globally. In this environment, robotics offers opportunities in numerous ways, such as in post-operation therapy for rehabilitation or as a social assistant. Human-like robots have the potential to bring about positive interventions in care services to promote sustainability.

Some key areas where robots can contribute to sustainability improvements are:

1. Enhanced Efficiency - Robots can take on tasks such as distributing medication monitoring vital signs and delivering meals. This frees up healthcare professionals to focus on care, leading to greater efficiency.
2. Tireless Assistance - Robots can work tirelessly without getting tired, ensuring round the clock care and monitoring. This can help prevent caregiver burnout whilst enhancing safety.
3. Companionship - Social robots with behaviours can provide companionship to individuals facing isolation by reducing feelings of loneliness and improving wellbeing.
4. Cost Effectiveness - By automating multiple tasks the long-term costs of care can be reduced, making it more affordable for both patients and institutions.
5. Training Opportunities - Robots can help simulate scenarios which can be a valuable training tool for healthcare workers and students.
6. Data Collection – With appropriate hardware and sensors robots are capable of collecting health data to track trends, predict conditions, and customise care plans.
7. Accessibility Features - Equipping robots with features can aid individuals with mobility challenges which help promote independence and enhance overall quality of life.

These advantages have the potential to revolutionize healthcare services by providing quality care at a low cost while also boosting the wellbeing of caregivers and those under their care.

3 Robots in the Healthcare Sector

Robots in the healthcare sector are often categorized under their type of functionality. These categories are surgical, rehabilitation, and social [12]. Surgical robots are used by staff, typically surgeons, have limited autonomy (require human control), and aim to assist and enhance performance of the surgeons [13]. Rehabilitation robots are usually used after medical procedures to help patients recover. They assist both patients and medical staff in working with patients. They can in some cases be used from outside of medical facilities (at home). They also have limited autonomy, can initiate movement, and can react to the actions of the user (e.g. exoskeletons and smart walker) [14].

The third category is social robots. These typically interact with users through conversation or touch. They can be used in many ways, such as in preventive medicine (e.g. reminders to take medication), support physical impairments such as limited mobility (e.g. robotic cleaners, collecting items- called "fetch and carry") and mental impairments such as dementia (e.g. reminders, guidance to locate items, companionship) [15]. The research by [12] provided a systematic review of robots used in health facilities and by patients in-house from 1990–2020. They found a stagnation of functionalities and a disconnect between robotic-platforms and designs for intervention. Typical problems were underestimation of the complexity of tasks (e.g. indoor navigation, fine manipulation of objects) and a need for a larger technological types of sensors).

Table 1 provides examples of some recent humanoid robots that are applied in the healthcare sector. While some robots are providing assistance to patients, e.g. offering support for cognitive functions; others are aimed at assisting health workers directly, e.g. collecting components and charts to assist nurses. These examples are largely not available on a commercial scale and are therefore not available for home use.

Table 1. Examples of humanoid robots applied in healthcare.

Robot name	Main function	Manufacturer	Source (Video)
Garmi	Physical assistant and service robot for elderly	Technical University, Munich Germany	[16]
Pepper	Service robot for patients	Aldebaran Robotics and Softbank Mobil Corp	[17]
Moxi	Service robot, assisting healthcare worker	Diligent Robotics	[18]

The above examples are task focused humanoid robots and were trialled over the past decade in healthcare facilities. Of the robots in Table 1, Pepper has function to provide autonomous speech interaction with patients. It acquires cultural competence through interactive dialogue and remembering past dialogue with for example elderly patients [45]. Examples of Pepper interacting with elderly patients can be found in videos associated with the CARESSES EU-Japan project of whom many seemed engaged and admittedly satisfied [46]. This indicates a contribution for humanoid robots is that they have the potential to provide companionship in situations where humans assistants are perhaps not available or where the human could not provide the same level of care. Companion robots are designed with intention to support a sense of companionship for the patients. Other examples of companion robots that have been in use in both homes and in structured living spaces (lab-homes) have often had the appearance of cartoon characters or pets (e.g. Paro – dog [19], Lovot – fictional animal [20] and Huggable - bear [21]. These examples are all soft to touch and hug and request attention and engagement from the user. One advantage of the pet appearance robots is that when the robot is not intended to replicate with fidelity the appearance of human or animal in real life, it can reduce the complexity of producing such product. The pet robots may be smaller, and users may have lower expectations regarding how they should look and interact.

For example, a pet robot could meet expectations of providing tactile interaction (e.g. hugging) but not be expected to hold an autonomous dialogue [48]. This can reduce the cost of units and increase accessibility to the product. Further, the form of a pet is sometimes chosen over humanoid form to avoid the feeling of the "uncanny valley" that can stir feelings of uneasiness in cases where the robot closely resembles humans but is unconvincing, although the authors experiments do demonstrate that good designs can overcome un-canny effects in realistic humanoid robots [63– 69].

One may ask, why design robots to resemble humans at all? Early research on design principles examining the effects of physical embodiment on human-robot interaction supports that physical embodiment is an essential dimension that affords proper social interaction. Additionally, support for tactile interaction (e.g. handshakes, hugs) in interpersonal relationships is important to facilitating meaningful social interaction [49]. This is an argument that design of humanoid robots should consider not only the fidelity of human-like appearance, but also consider touch-input capabilities. Another argument to be made for robots that resemble humans in size and form is that they may be better suited to replicate tasks that must be done by humans. Recent research found that human-likeness is not the only factor in modulating trust and acceptance of interactions with humanoid robots. The study found that humans were more likely to partner with a virtual agent after they have shared a mildly stressful experience together [47].

Table 2 identifies recent and mostly experimental products in humanoid robotics. Ameca for example, engages through conversation and facial expressions but is not mobile [22, 23]. A critical point of these products is that they are not designed for specific tasks or industries such as healthcare. These may however be positioned to better integrate into smart homes and health facilities to support patients and help healthcare communities to operate more sustainably.

Table 2. Recent examples of humanoid robots.

Robot name	Main function	Manufacturer	Source (Video)
Sophia Robot	Social interaction, assisting humans	Hanson Robotics (since 2016)	[26, 27]
Ameca	Social interaction	Engineered Arts (2023)	[22, 23]
Figure 01	Assisting humans, supplement the labour force	Figure AI Inc. (since 2022)	[28, 29]

One sustainable benefit of companion robot assistants is that they can help elderly in care facilities or to prolong their ability to stay at home longer [12]. Studies have shown that elderly who are entering into healthcare facilities can experience the situation as traumatic and distressful, and the patients can experience depression and other emotional problems [24, 25]. These studies find that a favourable strategy for elderly healthcare has been to implement systems for allowing elderly to live at home as long as possible, to "age in place" [24, 25].

4 User Perceptions of Robots in Healthcare and Human Work Analysis

In the recent COVID-19 crisis healthcare systems around the world struggled to provide services to support patients. A study by [31] explored patients' perspectives on robotic systems and AI regarding healthcare automation within the context of high pressure on the health system as experienced during the pandemic. They interviewed 13 patients (ages 53–83) that had been hospitalized with COVID-19 in Catalonia Spain, regarding their feelings of the hospitalization experience and asking about what specific tasks could be carried out by a robot. The interviewed patients had not interacted with any robot and were not aware of the use of robots in the hospital where they were admitted. The patients marked experiences of overcrowding and lack of resources. They reported stress associated with waiting for admissions, diagnosis, lack of communication during stay and isolation from relatives. Patients recognised and found it desirable that robotics could help assist medical staff. However, the research could not establish which tasks or functions could be specifically automated. They reported that patients valued the face-to-face contact with healthcare workers. Several described that the "nurse enters and smiles at you" and that the "smile of a nurse cures you". They reflected that delegating tasks to a robot was acceptable and even desirable for helping the healthcare worker, but that the robot could not replace the human. Patients expressed a link between the relationship with humans, wellbeing and the perception of good care. When talking about the "health system" this research concluded that patients identified a "responsibility repertoire" that are actions a robot could do would be associated with procedures, queuing, organization of services, responses and resources.

The nature of work activities that could be performed by care robots is further explored in [32]. Their research is based on the premise in [33] that practice-oriented activities should be left to humans, but goal-directed activities could be done with the assistance of a robot. The findings of [32] further suggest that activities can be broken down into components of which some components are practice-oriented with goals internal to the activity (e.g. chatting with a nurse) and some are goal-oriented components with goals external to the activity (e.g. exchanging information). They identify design requirements of a "wee-bot" robot (e.g. the activity is to take a urine sample) which identifies the external goal where the robot can assist in the safe collection of a sample, and the internal goal is to allow for the attentiveness and interaction of the healthcare worker during the procedure.

A comprehensive scoping review was conducted by [34] on the thoughts, views and attitudes of healthcare workers on the use of social assistive humanoid and animal-like robots in healthcare. Views on specific robots were discussed in the review. In general, the workers were positive about the use of robots in their work settings. They reported on the positive impact the robots could have on their patient's physical and psychological health and safety. The positive assistive intervention for older adults could include monitoring vital signs, aiding mobility, and rehabilitation. They also highlight the social and emotional potential of robots in helping fulfil patients' needs with cognitive impairments. Robots could monitor changes in mood, be a calming tool for agitation and confusion (e.g. Paro [35]). The robots could potentially encourage social interaction between residents, offering a new avenue for communication. Concerns of workers centred on ethics and the possibilities for breaches of patient privacy, such that technology should not be used as a method for surveillance or policing of patients.

5 HWID Principles to Inform Design for Humanoid Robots in Elderly Healthcare Workplace

In this paper we focus on the informed design of humanoid robots for better elderly healthcare. Research has shown that robots support elderly in addressing declining physical healthcare, declining cognitive capabilities and psychologically health (e.g. supporting social interactions and reducing loneliness) [48]. But how do we inform the design of the workplace based on Human Work Interaction Design (HWID) principles?

At present there is little research on framework design specifically for robotics in healthcare. A HWID framework will need to emphasize the need for workplace analysis. The prior section emphasized that understanding the nature of workplace activities can be a starting point for understanding complex workplace context, particularly the interaction process in the workplace environment. In a case study of work and workplace analysis in an elderly healthcare centre with the goal of agility improvements, it recommended a work analysis process to understand the interaction process in the workplace environment. [36] Their initial Data Analysis Framework identifies factors of (1) the Workplace– characteristics of the organization (e.g. goals, mission) and what people do; (2) People– users or stakeholders; (3) Work Analysis– task, procedures; and (4) Technology– devices, information artifacts, software systems, methods and procedures. [36] We relate these factors to HWID principles and actionable areas in Table 3.

Table 3. HWID principles to inform robotics in healthcare workplace

Principle(s)	Actionable areas
• Prioritize healthcare worker safety and worker wellbeing • Prioritize user-centred design for target stakeholders • Work-crafting – understand and redefine the role of the worker • Technology integration – prioritize adoption of technology that support sustainability goals of improving efficiency, assistance, accessibility and wellbeing [9]	• Workplace – apply standards on worker well-being for physical and psychological hazards, include upholding individuals' information security and privacy (EU OSH) [50] • People – apply sensemaking methodology to understand the appropriateness of the technology for workers and patients, what is intimidating [51] or useful [52] • Work – apply cognitive crafting to analysis, understand and redefine the relationship between the healthcare worker and patient using robotics; address pragmatic and ethical concerns of when and how to use robots [38] • Technology – explore stakeholder acceptance through models such as Technology Acceptance Model (TAM) [53] or Unified Theory of Acceptance and Use of Technology Model (UTAUT) that considers technology performance expectations, effort expectations, convenience, social influence [54]

A similar approach to [36] could be taken to obtain a holistic understanding of healthcare work within a specific case of (1) Workplace - that is a workplace analysis of the hospital, assisted living or other facility. For example, in the [36] case study the approach is recommended that collected data are needed to complete a holistic understanding of the institution's known and unknown situations. Regarding the principle of user-centred design, research by [37] point out the challenges in assessing the (2) People in the healthcare context. They explain how patients and healthcare professionals collaborate with robots in the healthcare industry. They state, "Many obstacles stand in the way of human robot interaction in healthcare, including safety concerns, acceptability issues, appropriateness, usefulness, and worry that robots may replace human carers. These difficulties result in a poor adoption rate for robotic technology".

What factors need to be considered in (3) Work Analysis? Clemmensen denotes in [38] that the goal of (HWID) is to support organizations and individuals in problem-solving for technology-interaction based job design, productivity and wellbeing of workers for digitalization of work with digital technologies including AI and robotics. HWID supports job-crafting, where workers proactively change their work and tasks, "that is the idea that people (workers) can revise their work identities and increase and improve the meaning of their work through crafting their job tasks, the way they think about their job (cognitive crafting)" [38, p. 14]. So, although prototyping technologies such as robotics, might be a part of solutions within healthcare to improve worker productivity and well-being, the technology itself or digital artifacts can only be part of the solution. Rather the solutions are comprehensively social-technical solutions. Further, that the aim of HWID is not only for, "product design that aims to create novel products but about design as psychological 'UX crafting' for productivity and well-being in the age of AI and robotics" [38, p. 15].

A starting point for UX crafting in healthcare would be to understand the essential elements, characteristics and attributes of the discipline that the social-technical solution is intended to support. Watson [39] and Tanioka [40, p. 98, 41], define for example, the role of nurse as "a human science of persons and human health-illness experiences that are mediated by professional, personal, scientific, aesthetic and ethical human transactions." Tanioka further expands, "Nursing is a knowledgeable practice provided within a human-to-human relationship in which caring is expressed in a continuous process. To understand persons, it is essential to enter into their world, recognize, understand, and appreciate who and what they are as whole persons." [40, p. 98]. In brief, a nurse expresses technology competence as caring, can enter the patient's world, empathically distinguish the patient's situation, and offer wholistic care.

AI Technology (4) will be at the core of applied social humanoid robotics solutions that could serve the healthcare sector. How will the use of AI reshape service provision and how will it support the work tasks provided in the sector? Both human intelligence (HI) and artificial intelligence (AI) can be categorized into four types of intelligence: mechanical, analytical, intuitive and empathetic. AI and robotics have increasing difficulty in providing services within each successive category of intelligence. Because jobs often require a composite of these types of intelligence, jobs are often broken down into tasks. AI can replace some human labour for some types of tasks, e.g. can provide easier mechanical tasks, but current products have not yet achieved higher levels of empathic intelligence. Research on AI in service have categorized AI skills needed with, types of skills needed, and AI applications [42]. This represented for the category of empathetic intelligence is in Table 4.

Table 4. Empathic Intelligence, Nature of Task, Service/App [42, p. 157]

Empathetic Intelligence	Skills Required	Nature of Task	Service/App (Goal)
• Learn and adapt empathetically based on experience • Emotion recognition, affective computing, and communication style learning • Decision-making incorporates emotions	• Soft empathetic professionals that require social, communication, and relationship building skills • Thinking jobs requiring people skill, for example, politicians and negotiators or feeling jobs, for example, psychiatrists	• Social, emotional, communicative, and highly interactive service • Tasks that require empathy, emotional labor, or emotional • High-touch service	• Chatbots communicate with customers and learn from the users • Hanson's humanoid Sophia robot interacts with users as employees would

6 Transformative Potential in Social Humanoid Robots – Case of Sophia Robot

Sophia Robot is the creation of Hanson Robotics led by David Hanson. Sophia is classified as an intelligent humanoid robot and was introduced first in 2016 and is today still an ongoing work in progress [26, 27]. The developers consider her experimental, symbolic and by no means the most advanced AI. Sophia is running chatbot type software and can respond with facial expressions and generative answers. Sophia is different from Alexa or Siri. She is an embodied social robot, in human form, intended to mirror human expressions and movements. Hanson Robotics view that social robots are art and performance medium, intended to evoke emotional responses that mirror human attributes and characterizations. Social robots can provide social assistance such as suggestions (of selection alternatives), supportive feedback, or expressed emotionally as a sense of companionship. How is this possible? In the case of Hanson Robots, the skin-like material used to create human expression on the Hanson robots is the application of a patented lightweight polymer called Frubber. This allows for smooth movements and more natural expressions. Hanson Robots aim for believability. David Hanson states the goal is to humanize robots, to seek to create assistants and guides for humans. He sees social robots as built to serve and augment the abilities of humans and as new kinds of performers. In the same way that immersion in VR environments allows the user to somehow suspend belief of the external real world and to become engaged in the virtual one, the aim of Hanson's creations is to be equally engaging. How well robots can take on the characteristics of humans may play a role in building trust and avoiding unwanted emotional responses like the "uncanny valley". We humans use verbal and non-verbal language to express ourselves, including facial expressions, gestures, non-formulated words (e.g. grunts). These need to be integrated in human-robot interactions as well.

During Covid-19 there were at least four to five versions of Sophia in action. In more recent versions the chatbot is a database in which Sophia can draw on from her proprietary language processing algorithm to answer questions. This contrasts with performances where she is drawing on pre-scripted text. Sophia is still considered weak-AI and cannot respond as dynamically as Chat-GPT 4 (does in text). Although the AI algorithms in the background of Sophia can still have room for advancement, the transformative potential of Sophia is in the social communicative goals of what she was made for: a companion, aid, and helper for humanity.

However, transforming Sophia the robot, from a humanoid into a healthcare aide would involve a process that spans hardware enhancements, software upgrades and ethical considerations. More specifically Sophia would require improvements in her hardware setup, such as advanced sensors to monitor health indicators like body temperature and heart rate. Ideally, she would also need to handle instruments and aid in procedures. In terms of software Sophia would need to be equipped with a medical knowledge database and diagnostic algorithms to assist with healthcare tasks like evaluating symptoms and interacting with patients (although this would always need a second opinion from a human). Improving her communication skills is crucial for conveying information and engaging empathetically with patients and healthcare professionals. This may involve communicating in a variety of languages to cater to populations.

Crucially adhering to regulations and cybersecurity standards is essential to protect information and ensure safe operations. Collaboration with healthcare specialists is key for Sophia to receive training that aligns her abilities with processes and ethical guidelines in patient care. Addressing concerns about interactions between robots and humans in healthcare environments as privacy issues is equally important requiring careful planning and execution to build trust and acceptance. Through testing, validation procedures and continuous enhancements Sophia can evolve into a healthcare assistant capable of supporting various medical tasks while upholding ethical principles and improving patient care outcomes.

7 Future Directions for Social Humanoid Robotics

How can humanoid social robotics technologies transition to better serve the healthcare sector? David Hanson of Hanson Robotics, responded to this question with insights into the state of the art and indicated future directions. He pointed out that there are several models that are already in use in the healthcare sector. Sophia's design already adheres to a number of the principles of interaction design including making the human-robot interactions as natural and comfortable as possible, which is in line with the strategies of user-centred design and emotional engagement. The design of Sophia also includes facial recognition and expression capabilities whereby Sophie is able to perceive and emulate human feelings, hence creating a good user experience [55, 63]. For example, Sophia robot has been used in guided meditation session with elderly users. A case study highlighting Sophia's performance is the "Loving AI" project. In this study, Sophia engaged participants in dialogues focused on meditation and relaxation, this demonstrated her ability to adapt to users' emotional states and provide supportive companionship. The findings suggest that such interactions can positively impact human emotional well-being, showcasing Sophia's potential in therapeutic settings [56, 60, 61].

Another model of Hanson Robotics, Grace, has been used in autism therapy. Grace was developed during Covid-19, and is equipped with sensors, such as a thermal camera to detect a patient's temperature and pulse, she can partake in talk therapy, and can speak in three languages, English, Mandarin, and Cantonese. [43] Based on the Sophia 2020 platform that uses the Hanson-AI SDK [58, 59], the AI in Grace enables the robot to interact with users, and can converse with users, and respond to their needs. Through talk therapy and disease analysis programs the AI robotic based personality can detect and respond appropriately to patients based on both what they say and the emotional context. The AI can assess awareness and cognitive performance of patients. For some patients the humanoid robot is appropriate for those who respond better to the humanoid face. That is some users they feel more comfortable responding to the humanoid robot, rather than just to audio-only AI [44].

While it has been a goal of Hanson Robotics to mass produce robotics and thereby offer them at a lower development cost, Hanson recognizes the potential of developing and offering virtual robots. Virtual robots ("bots") can be animated through apps, can be virtual representations of the same character that exists in physical robot form (made to look like the physical representations). These can be developed as characters that human individuals have a connection to the characters or developed personalities. This integrative cross-platform approach to developing characters, that people have a relationship with, can be very powerful. The physical and virtual representations across one integrative platform, can offer potential benefits of both representations, as applied within the needed context. Virtual robots can have a low-cost deployment, animated through apps, where users can have an actual face-to-face encounter for that sense of a personal relationship.

Hanson's vision of the future designs of robotics are grounded in our human-centric connections to characters through storytelling. He expresses that, "often, we forget the power of humanities, of character, of fiction, and how that actually reconnects us, the power of storytelling, and character connects us back with humans. It doesn't dehumanize us. I'm interested in how we can humanize the technologies in this way, by bringing them together as a greater humanity. The science, the technology, the therapeutic applications and clinical approaches that AI, robotics, can be combined with the senses of humanities to do what humanities do well, and achieve what science and technologies do not do well yet. You cannot engineer your way into a loveable animated feature film, or you cannot engineer a children's book. It has to be from the heart. This fusion of technology with the humanitarian arts has a power".

8 Concluding Remarks and Ethical Implications

Rapid changes in state-of-the-art robot technology are expected to have a hugely significant and growing impact throughout society. We are already seeing transformative changes in the application of OPEN AI foundational models with the emergence of new robots that are in industry workplaces. These can achieve tireless manipulation of objects with fluidity and precision. For example, Digit bipedal robots by Amazon [30] are replacing human workers in Amazon warehouses. More recently, Figure AI Inc. Has developed a robot model they call Figure01 that can interact in conversation with little delay and integrate experience [28, 29]. Industry partners such as Nvidia are providing foundational hardware and software. The use of generative AI algorithms is accelerating the coding of new robots that can perform more functions and perform more effectively. For example, robots can more rapidly train or learn mobility through virtual simulations and are able to hold real-time conversations through these ever-improving natural language processing algorithms.

Yet the scope of future humanoid robotics in healthcare applications raises some complex ethical issues especially on data privacy, consent and autonomy. These are the issues of data control and use, which are important to avoid the wrong use of data as well as to ensure the patients' data transparency. Also, the physical contact with the human-like robots creates difficulties; on the one hand, they can be helpful in providing companionship; on the other hand, they may create emotional reliance or disappointment especially among the vulnerable groups. This may lead to the development of unrealistic expectations by the users on what the robots can do and when these expectations are not met, there is tendency of losing trust. This is why it is crucial to develop ethical frameworks and empathetic design to ensure that humanoid robots enhance human's welfare rather than compromise it [57].

While robotic technology is advancing quickly, with increased capability to hold convincing social conversations, improved mobility and interoperability, and have the potential to be less expensive and more accessible for purchase because they are designed for general purposes; this leaves society still in the need of "warm hands" in healthcare. Human caregiving goes beyond what robots can do, by incorporating connections, flexibility, critical thinking, communication skills and ethical judgment. In a care facility while robots like 'Robbie' efficiently handle tasks such as grooming and meal preparation, human caregivers, like 'Sarah' offer emotional support and personalized care. Sarah interacts meaningfully with residents evaluates their being and adjusts care according to their individual needs and preferences. Unlike robots she navigates situations makes decisions and fosters dignity and a sense of community through compassionate communication. Her role goes beyond completing tasks to ensuring the emotional wellbeing of residents advocating for their rights and creating an environment that improves their quality of life. This underscores the nature of human caregiving in delivering empathetic care that surpasses mere functional assistance. In this paper we impressed that there are rapid changes in AI that are already impacting the robotics industry [28]. We anticipate that lower cost products will soon be widely available with the functionally that are relevant for the support of healthcare workers and patients. However, the greatest potential of robotics for sustainability in healthcare work will be to assist and augment the capabilities of humans to provide patient care.

References

1. Eurostat. Online database (2024). https://ec.europa.eu/eurostat/statistics-explained/index.php?title=Population_structure_and_ageing
2. Creighton, H.: Europe's Ageing Deography, ILC-UK2014 EU Factpack (2014). https://ilcuk.org.uk/wp-content/uploads/2019/11/Europes-Ageing-Demography.pdf
3. United Nations. World Ageing Population 2013 (2013). https://www.un.org/en/development/desa/population/publications/pdf/ageing/WorldPopulationAgeing2013.pdf
4. UN. UN World Population Prospect (2022). OurWorldInData.org/fertility-rate | CC BY
5. Yeon-woo, L.: Fertility rate falls to historic low of 0.65 in Q4 2023. The Korean Times, Finance, 5/7 (2024). https://www.koreatimes.co.kr/www/biz/2024/04/602_369678.html
6. Fleck, A.: Dementia cases are expected to double in many countries over the next 30 years. Health and Healthcare Systems. World Economic Forum. 9/26, 2022 (2022). https://www.weforum.org/agenda/2022/09/europe-is-facing-a-dementia-problem/
7. Anderson, S.: Europe is Struggling to Keep its Health, Systems Afloat. Health Policy Watch. 28/09 (2023). https://healthpolicy-watch.news/europe-struggles-to-keep-health-systems-afloat/
8. Hyde, T.: How humanoid robotics are making an impact in the healthcare market. 29-6 (2023). https://barringtonjames.com/post/how-humanoid-robotics-are-making-an-impact-in-the-healthcare-market
9. United Nations. Ensure healthy lives and promote well-being for all at all ages (2015). https://sdgs.un.org/goals/goal3
10. Goodland, R.: Sustainability: human, social, economic and environmental. In: Encyclopedia of Global Environmental Change, vol. 5, pp. 481–491. Wiley, Hoboken (2002)
11. AMA. Environmental Sustainability in Health Care - 2019, Australian Medical Association, Position Statement, 20/3 (2019). https://www.ama.com.au/position-statement/environmental-sustainability-health-care-2019
12. Bardaro, G., Antonini, A., Motta, E.: Robots for elderly care in the home: a landscape analysis and co-design toolkit. Int. J. Soc. Robot. **14**(3), 657–681 (2022). https://doi.org/10.1007/s12369-021-00816-3
13. Le, H.M., Do, T.N., Phee, S.J.: A survey of actuators-driven surgical robots. Sens Actuat. A **247**, 323–354 (2016)
14. Cheng, L., Chen, M., Li, Z.: Design and control of a wearable hand rehabilitation robot. IEEE Access **6**, 74039–74050 (2018)
15. Abdi, J., Al-Hindawi, A., Ng, T., Vizcaychipi, M.P.: Scoping review on the use of socially assistive robot technology in elderly care. BMJ Open **8**(29), e018815 (2018)
16. News Australia, Garmi. 03/19, news.com.au (2023). https://www.youtube.com/watch?v=zNwatRfLaQs
17. CBS Evening News. 8/30 (2022). https://www.youtube.com/watch?v=AQn8RuKcGII
18. ChristianaCare. Health Care (2022). https://www.youtube.com/watch?v=2iGrdX_kjuY
19. Kidd, C.D., Taggart, W., Turkle, S.: A sociable robot to encourage social interaction among the elderly. In: Proc IEEE International Conference on robotics and automatin, ICRA, pp. 3972–3976 (2006)
20. Yasu, J.M.: In: love with LOVOT Japan's new robot pet - LOVOT cafe. In: Japan Go! This Week in Japan, Posted 2/13 (2021). https://www.youtube.com/watch?v=yeTTl333hY8
21. Stiehl, W., et al.: The huggable: a therapeutic robotic companion for relational, affective, touch. In: ACM SIGGRAPH 2006 emerging technologies, pp. 15–19 (2006)
22. Engineering Arts: Ameca. The Future Face of Robotics (2024). https://www.engineeredarts.co.uk/robot/ameca/

23. This Morning. Meet Ameca! The World's Most Advance Robot, 18 May 2023. Phillip and Holly (2023). https://www.youtube.com/watch?v=vE9tIYGyRE8
24. Melrose, S.: Reducing relocation stress syndrome in long term care facilities. J. Pract. Nurs. **54**(4), 15 (2004)
25. Šabanovi, S., Chang, W.L., Bennett, C.C., Piatt, J.A., Hakken D.: A robot of my own: participatory design of socially assistive robots for independently living older adults diagnosed w/ depression. In: International Conference on Human Aspects of it for Aged Population, pp. 104–114. Springer (2015)
26. Riccio, T., et al.: Sophia robot: an emergent ethnography. TDR 65:3 (T251). Cambridge University Press for Tisch School of the Arts/NYU (2021). https://doi.org/10.1017/S1054204321000319
27. Hanson Robotics (2024). https://www.hansonrobotics.com/
28. Figure AI Inc. (2024). https://www.figure.ai/
29. ColdFusion Music. 3/25 (2024). https://www.youtube.com/watch?v=VAtoqAQ2aEg
30. Dresser, S.: Amazon. Amazon announces 2 new ways it's using robots to assist employees and deliver for customers (2023). https://www.aboutamazon.com/news/operations/amazon-introduces-new-robotics-solutions
31. Vallès-Peris, N., Barat-Auleda, O., Domènech, M.: Robots in healthcare? What patients say. Int. J. Environ. Res. Public Health **18**, 9933 (2021). https://doi.org/10.3390/ijerph18189933
32. Santoni de Sio, F.; van Wynsberghe, A.: When should we use care robots? The nature-of-activities approach. Sci. Eng. Ethics **22**, 1745–1760 (2016). https://doi.org/10.1007/s11948-015-9715-4
33. Santoni de Sio, F., Robichaud, P., Vincent, N.A.: Who should enhance? Conceptual and normative dimensions of cognitive enhancement. Humana. Mente J. Philos. Stud. **26**, 179–197 (2014)
34. Papadopoulos, I., Koulouglioti, C., Ali, S.: (2018) Views of nurses and other health and social care workers on the use of assistive humanoid and animal-like robots in health and social care: a scoping review. Contemp. Nurse **54**(4–5), 425–442 (2018). https://doi.org/10.1080/10376178.2018.1519374
35. Robinson, H., Broadbent, E., MacDonald, B.: Group sessions with Paro in nursing home: structure, observations and interviews. Aust. J. Ageing **35**(2), 106–112 (2016)
36. Lopes, A.G.: The work and workplace analysis in an elderly centre for agility improvement. In: Abdelnour Nocera, J., Barricelli, B., Lopes, A., Campos, P., Clemmensen, T. (eds.) Human Work Interaction Design. Work Analysis and Interaction Design Methods for Pervasive and Smart Workplaces. HWID IFIP Advances in Information and Communication Technology, vol. 468. Springer, Cham (2015). https://doi.org/10.1007/978-3-319-27048-7_11
37. Weerarathna, I.N., Raymond, D., Luharia, A.: Human-robot collaboration for healthcare: a narrative review. Cureus **15**(11), e49210 (2023). https://doi.org/10.7759/cureus.49210
38. Clemmensen, T.: Human Work Interaction Design: A Platform for Theory and Action. Springer, Frederiksberg, Demark (2021). https://doi.org/10.1007/978-3-030-71796-4
39. Watson Caring Science Institute. Core Concepts of Jean Watson's Theory of Human Caring/Caring Science (2010). https://www.watsoncaringscience.org/files/Cohort%206/watsons-theory-of-humancaring-core-concepts-and-evolution-to-caritas-processes-handout.pdf
40. Tanioka, T., Osaka, K., Locsin, R., Yasuhara, Y., Ito, H.: Recommended design and direction of development for humanoid nursing robots perspective from nursing researchers. Intell. Control. Autom. **8**, 96–110 (2017). https://doi.org/10.4236/ica.2017.82008
41. Nursing Research. Nursing Theories: Jean Watson's Philosophy of Nursing (2012). http://currentnursing.com/nursing_theory/Watson.html
42. Huang, M.-H., Rust, T.: Artificial intelligence in service. J. Serv. Res. **21**(2), 155–172 (2018). https://journals.sagepub.com/doi/10.1177/1094670517752459

43. Cairns, R., Tham, D.: Meet Grace, the ultra-lifelike nurse robot, CNN (2021). https://edition.cnn.com/2021/08/19/asia/grace-hanson-robotics-android-nurse-hnk-spc-intl/index.html
44. HHM Global. Awakening Health Launches Humanoid Robot Healthcare Assistant Named Grace, Hospital and Healthcare Management Global (2020). https://www.hhmglobal.com/knowledge-bank/news/awakening-health-launches-humanoid-robot-healthcare-assistant-named-grace
45. Sgorbissa, A., et al.: CARESSESS: the flowere that taught robots about culture. In: 2019 14th ACM/IEEE International Conference on Human-Robot Interaction (HRI), Daegu, Korea (South), p. 371 (2019). https://doi.org/10.1109/HRI.2019.8673086
46. CARESSES. CARESSES, A robot for the elderly that knows about different cultures (featuring Pepper) (2020). https://www.youtube.com/watch?v=0at2oZt_rag
47. Bing, R., Michael, J.: Overcoming the uncanny valley through shared stressful experience with a humanoid robot. J. Emerg. Invest. 1–6 (2018). https://emerginginvestigators.org/articles/18-001. ISSN 2638–0870
48. Petrie, H., Samaddar, S.: measuring older people's attitudes towards personal robots. In: Proceedings of the 10th International Conference on ICT for Ageing Well and e-Health, ICT4AWE, pp. 108–118 (2024). https://doi.org/10.5220/0012740400003699. ISBN 978-989-758-700-9; ISSN 2184-4984
49. Lee, K., Jung, Y., Kim, J., Kim, S.: Are physically embodied social agents better than disembodied social agents? The effects of physical embodiment, tactile interaction, and people's loneliness in human–robot interaction. Int. J. Hum.-Comput. Stud. **64**, 962–973 (2006)
50. EU OSH. The OSH Framework Directive. 89/391. European Agency for Safety and Health at Work (2021). https://osha.europa.eu/en/legislation/directives/the-osh-framework-directive/the-osh-framework-directive-introduction
51. Frennert, S.: Expectations and sensemaking: older people and care robots. In: Gao, Q., Zhou, J. (eds.) Human Aspects of IT for the Aged Population. Technology and Society (HCII 2020). Lecture Notes in Computer Science, vol. 12209. Springer (2020)
52. Eftring, H., Frennert, S.: Designing a social and assistive robot for seniors. Zeitschrift Gerontologie Geriatrie 1–8 (2016)
53. Davis F.D.: A technology acceptance model for empirically testing new end-user information systems: theory and results. Thesis (Ph. D.). MIT, Cambridge (1986)
54. Venkatesh, V., Morris, M.G., Davis, G., Davis, F.D.: User acceptance of information technology: toward a unified view. MIS Q. **27**(3), 425 (2003). https://doi.org/10.2307/30036540
55. Hanson, D.: The making of Sophia: facial recognition, expressions and the loving AI project. Hanson Robotics (2019). https://www.hansonrobotics.com/the-making-of-sophia-facial-recognition-expressions-and-the-loving-ai-project/?utm_source=chatgpt.com
56. Goertzel, B. Mossbridge, J. Monroe, E., Hanson, D., Yu, G.: Loving AI: humanoid robots as agents of human consciousness expansion. arXiv (2017). https://doi.org/10.48550/arXiv.1709.07791
57. Parviainen, J., Coeckelbergh, M.: The political choreography of the Sophia robot: beyond robot rights and citizenship to political performances for the social robotics market. AI Soc. **36**, 715–724 (2021). https://doi.org/10.1007/s00146-020-01104-w
58. Shen, Y., Mo, X., Krisciunas, V., Hanson, D., Shi, B.E.: Intention Estimation via Gaze for Robot Guidance in Hierarchical Tasks. Neurips 2022, Gaze Meets ML @NeurIPS 2022, @Gaze_Meets_ML, Dec 4, Best Paper Award (2022)
59. Hanson, D.: AAAS-21 poster: human emulation robotics and AI: recent experiments and results. AAAS Annual meeting for Science Magazine (2021)
60. Mossbridge, J., et al.: Emotionally sensitive AI-driven android interactions improve social welfare through helping people access self-transcendent states. In: AI for social good workshop poster, NIPS (2018). https://aiforsocialgood.github.io/2018/acceptedpapers.htm

61. Goertzel, B., Mossbridge, M., Monroe, E., Hanson, D.: Humanoid robots as agents of human consciousness expansion. arXiv: (2017). https://arxiv.org/pdf/1709.07791.pdf
62. Hanson, D.: The need for creativity, aesthetics, and the arts in the design of increasingly intelligent humanoid robots. In: ICRA Workshop on General Intelligence for Humanoid Robots, (2014)
63. Habib, A., Das S., Bogdan, I.C., Hanson, D., Popa, D.: Learning human-like facial expressions for the Android Phillip K. Dick. In: ICRA 2014, Hong Kong, AGI for Humanoid Robotics, Workshop Proceedings (2014)
64. Hanson, D., Mazzei, D., Garver, C., De Rossi, D., Stevenson, M.: Realistic humanlike robots for treatment of asd, social training, and research; shown to appeal to youths with asd, cause physiological arousal, and increase human-to-human social engagement. In: PETRA (PErvasive Technologies Related to Assistive Environment) (2012)
65. Hanson, D.: Robotics in the World of Entertainment, American Physical Society (APS) March Meeting, 2011 adsabs.harvard.edu, March 21–25 (2011)
66. Hanson, D.: Expanding the design domain of humanoid robots. In: Proc. ICCS CogSci Conference, special session on Android Science. Vancouver (2006)
67. Oh, J.H., Hanson, D., Kim, W.S., Han, Y., Kim, J.Y., Park, I.W.: Design of android type humanoid robot albert HUBO, In: Proc. IEEE/RJS IROS Robotics Conference, Beijing, 2006. Int. Conf. on Intell. Robots and Sys., IEEE/RSJ, pp. 1428–1433 (2006)
68. Hanson, D., et al.: Upending the uncanny valley. In: Proc. AAAI's National Conference, Pitts-burgh, (2005)
69. Hanson, D.: The neural basis of the uncanny valley, graduate research paper for Alice O'Toole in UTD Brain Sciences. Sept (2003). Published online at https://www.humanrobot.org/

Empowering Worker-Robot Collaboration: Leveraging LLMs for Extracting and Visualizing Robot Task Metrics

Luigi Gargioni(✉) and Daniela Fogli

Department of Information Engineering, University of Brescia, Brescia, Italy
{luigi.gargioni,daniela.fogli}@unibs.it

Abstract. In the context of Industry 5.0, which is characterized by a close integration between digital technology, industrial production, and human-centered design, collaborative robots emerge as key players. These robots are no longer isolated machines but an integral part of an interconnected ecosystem, where the fluidity of data plays a crucial role. Collaborative robots facilitate flexibility, efficiency, and safety in operations. However, this also introduces novel programming and data management challenges. A distinctive feature of collaborative robots is their ability to be programmed and used by non-expert users. This democratization of access to robotics offers significant advantages but also requires careful design of tools and interfaces to enable easy access to the data generated by the robots. In this context, the user interface assumes a pivotal role in ensuring that even those lacking programming expertise can fully benefit from the capabilities of collaborative robots and the data they produce. This study exploits Human Work Interaction Design principles to examine the problems encountered by individuals lacking programming skills when attempting to obtain data about robot performance. A solution that exploits Large Language Models is proposed.

Keywords: Meta-Design · Large Language Model · Human-Robot Interaction · Collaborative Robot · Data Visualization

1 Introduction

Data has become a valuable resource in the digital era, driving innovation and guiding strategic decisions across various sectors. Among these data, those generated by the use of collaborative robots can provide important information for decision-making, thus entailing a significant impact on human work and well-being. Collaborative robots are robots that can stay in close contact with humans thanks to technologies and sensors designed to ensure the physical safety of the operator [24]. They are usually employed beyond the traditional industrial production lines, to carry out tasks in close collaboration with human operators [21]. Collaborative robotics is a research field with significant potential impacts

Published by Springer Nature Switzerland AG 2026
B. R. Barricelli et al. (Eds.): HWID 2024, IFIP AICT 751, pp. 208–222, 2026.
https://doi.org/10.1007/978-3-031-95334-7_13

on industries, services, and societies at large, fostering an economic development model that is sustainable and respectful of the environment and people [19]. Indeed, collaborative robotics is a central element of Industry 5.0 [5], which in turn pays attention to creating collaborative, interconnected, and adaptable industrial settings, where a meaningful interaction between workers and technology contributes to achieving higher efficiency, effectiveness, and customization of manufacturing and production processes [11,26]. Industry 5.0 strongly emphasizes sustainable workplaces aiming to optimize processes and consumption, reduce waste materials, and improve human safety and well-being at work [2,22]. Collaborative robotics represents one of the technologies that can contribute to achieving these goals by supporting a safe collaboration between robots and humans and ensuring that workers' expertise is properly valued in production processes.

The literature reports that there are various types of data that may be of interest when performing tasks with collaborative robots. The paper [18] underlines the importance of productivity-related metrics, such as the average time taken to complete a specific category of tasks and the relative completion frequency. In [7], the efficiency of robot usage also comes into play in terms of the robot's up-time compared to the total available time. This is also an important indicator in terms of the economic viability of the investment in an automated solution. Another interesting factor, as reported in [14], is resource usage: this refers to monitoring the usage of tools and materials required during task execution to obtain an indicator for predictive maintenance. Another factor, probably the most important, is work safety, which includes monitoring of safety issues while interacting with the robot (e.g., stop due to collision) [13,18].

Usually, data of interest for robot users are represented in dashboards that aggregate them in different ways. The problem is that these dashboards statically show only the data and the visualization that the developer decided to include when creating it. Therefore, accessing and analyzing the data generated by collaborative robots remain challenging activities, often reserved for technical experts and industry specialists. Different workers with different roles in the company may need different data aggregated or presented differently. It becomes necessary for each worker to obtain customized data visualization simply by requesting the data and the visualization format they prefer, without the developer having to provide this combination at design time.

The application of Human Work Interaction Design (HWID) methods to work analysis led us to propose a natural language-based approach to democratize access and analysis of robot usage data. This approach would make data available and understandable even for people without specific technical training, facilitating the engagement of a broader base of interested users. In particular, the adoption of Large Language Models (LLMs) to obtain and analyze robot usage metrics will be explored in this paper. It will focus on the importance of extracting and analyzing usage data in a simple and accessible manner for end users, regardless of technical expertise.

The paper is organized as follows. Section 2 provides an overview of the related works; Sect. 3 details the user-system interaction assumed for the proposed solution; Sect. 4 presents the technical implementation of the proposed solution with two different approaches; Sect. 5 describes a use case to show how the different solutions would be applied; and, finally, Sect. 6 provides concluding remarks and discusses future works.

2 Related Work

The capability of LLM systems to comprehend natural language and discern users' intentions has prompted an investigation into their potential applications in various domains. Recent proposals have been put forth to use LLMs to enhance the easiness and naturalness of web development, such as generating mock-ups of web interfaces [10] or snippets of HTML, Javascript, and CSS [12], on the basis of textual descriptions. To address potential shortcomings of LLMs, such as generating unnecessary or inaccurate content, these tools provide end users with several controls: 1) displaying multiple output options, 2) allowing editing of the model's output, and 3) facilitating transitions to external resources via web searches. As a further advancement, the prompt engineering technique explored in [3] enables end users to refine LLM outputs through iterative input refinements, thereby allowing them greater influence over the generated web pages. However, users must be familiar with web terminology to effectively convey their design intentions to the LLM. A similar approach has been experimented in the field of robot programming, as highlighted by the system described in [23], which uses OpenAI ChatGPT. Here, users are tasked with providing feedback on the quality and safety of Python or C++ code generated by ChatGPT. However, this requires that users comprehend the generated code and are capable of suggesting appropriate corrections, thereby requiring programming proficiency. In an attempt to address this challenge, the approach described in [6,8] explores the use of a graphical visualization of the program generated by a Natural Language Processing (NLP) interface. This interface also enables users to directly manipulate the program through its graphical representation.

As far as the problem considered in this paper, namely, fostering access and analysis of robot-generated data by workers without programming competencies, natural language understanding might be exploited to construct Structured Query Language (SQL) queries. The automatic generation of SQL queries is not a novel concept. For instance, in [17], a rule-based NLP approach is employed to interpret the query description provided by the user. With the advent of LLMs, a series of analyses have been conducted to evaluate the effectiveness of the SQL queries produced in accordance with the user request [25] and their efficiency during execution [20]. Thus far, the outcomes have been promising but still far from an optimal solution [16]. Furthermore, additional research is required to facilitate end users' usage of data.

This paper proposes the adoption of HWID in the design of an LLM-based application that can address the aforementioned need, considering the data generated by collaborative robots as a case study. As previously underlined, these robots are designed for use in environments beyond the traditional factory setting. Consequently, the retrieving of data and metrics associated with the robot tasks should be performed by workers who lack programming expertise. Interrogation of databases should, therefore, be made as simple as possible, potentially using natural language.

3 Interaction Design

HWID promotes the integration of work analysis and human-centered interaction design to develop better workplaces and sustain improved work practices [1, 4]. Following the methods and principles of HWID, we studied how to make dashboards related to the use of collaborative robots more flexible and suitable for different human workers.

We observed and interviewed healthcare professionals in the frame of a project about supporting the preparation of personalized medicines with cobots [9]; on that occasion, we gathered workers' needs related to data visualization and exploration tasks that require personalized dashboards. Specifically, we developed healthcare worker personas to better frame their goals and frustrations. In particular, we found that in the healthcare sector, current technologies are often imposed by manufacturers without taking into account the needs of the end users. As a result, it is the user who has to adapt to the proposed functionalities rather than the tools that are tailored to real workers' needs. The same argument can be applied to data visualization features provided in commercial dashboards.

A conventional dashboard typically displays the most important metrics, commonly called Key Performance Indicators (KPIs). However, guessing all the information that any user might require is challenging. Furthermore, data of interest may change over time, even partially (e.g., the time interval), and users who utilize these tools may also change. The proposed interaction is designed to facilitate the extraction of information, avoiding the necessity for a developer to predict it within a pre-defined dashboard.

In accordance with the HWID principles, the initial stage of the interaction design process entails the development of preliminary mock-ups. The user interface mock-up in Fig. 1 presents a possible interaction scenario between the user and the system. The interface includes a chat panel on the left and a data visualization panel on the right. In the chat panel, the user can express their requests by writing or even speaking. In the considered scenario, the user needs to obtain the robot usage time in the current month in comparison with the previous month. This statistic could be useful to determine the robot's up-time compared to the total available time. If the user does not express any specific preference for data visualization, the assistant will take care of this aspect based on the results obtained from the query executed on the database. Once the extracted data has been displayed using the chosen or suggested visualization type, it can be further refined in terms of both the data itself, namely editing the proposed query, and the representation type. Figure 2 illustrates an example where the user requests a change of visualization and a different comparison metric.

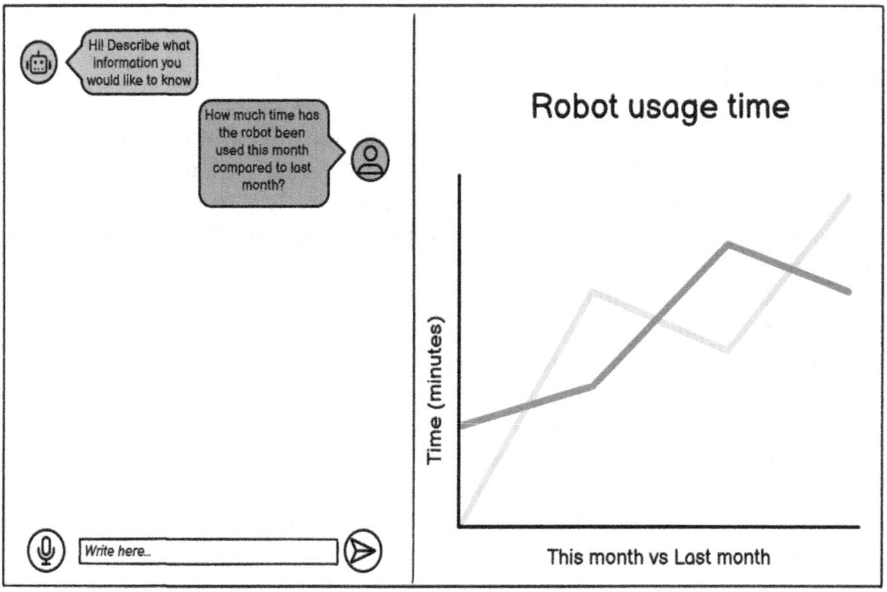

Fig. 1. The interface mockup.

4 The Implemented LLM-Based Solution

The proposed solution is based on a web application that employs the client-server paradigm. Specifically, the database used is PostgreSQL, and therefore the query examples presented later will adhere to PostgreSQL syntax. To exploit the functionalities of an LLM, the APIs provided by the LLM service provider will be used. In this context, OpenAI ChatGPT offers an easily integrated API service and a model that is currently one of the most powerful (*GPT-4o*).

The solution can be implemented in two ways: with a workflow that includes two model instances or with a workflow that includes only one model instance The main difference is whether to have a single model instance or two separate model instances to i) create the extraction query based on the user intent and ii) suggest the most appropriate visualization for the extracted data.

The two approaches are outlined below, and a subsequent analysis will be presented, evaluating the advantages and disadvantages of each of them.

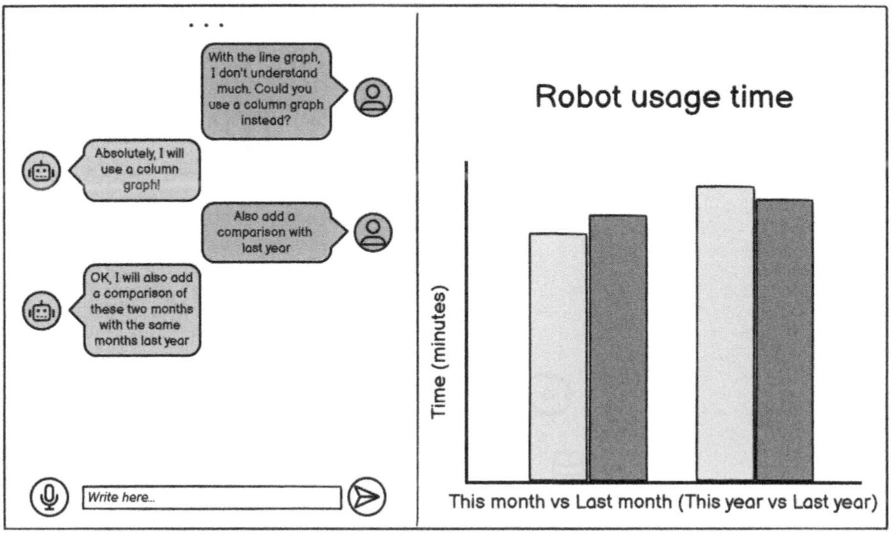

Fig. 2. The refinement interaction.

4.1 Interaction Workflow Based on Two Model Instances

In this workflow (Fig. 3), two distinct instances of the model are used, each one appropriately instructed:

- *First instance*: to recognize the user request and produce the SQL query to access the database;
- *Second instance*: to suggest the recommended data visualization based on the extracted data.

To instruct the first instance of the model, which is responsible for query creation, it is necessary to provide it with a specific instruction set. These directives will inform the model about the context and the specific task. The instructing process, namely *prompt engineering*, is conducted in natural language by the developer of the application and includes phrases such as *"You are an assistant who must help the staff of a laboratory to extract information from a database about their robots and their tasks. If the user's request is not clear, ask for more details before proposing an SQL query. Return an SQL query that can be executed on this database schema."*. In addition to contextual information, it is essential to provide the model with the structure of the database to enable it to propose formally correct queries. Furthermore, the inclusion of some example queries among the most common ones that might be asked helps the model considerably in its task. The latter will not constrain the model to respond only to those queries, but rather assist it in developing a more nuanced understanding of how to respond. Before execution on the database, the query proposed by the model is subjected to a formal syntax check to ensure that it adheres to the correct

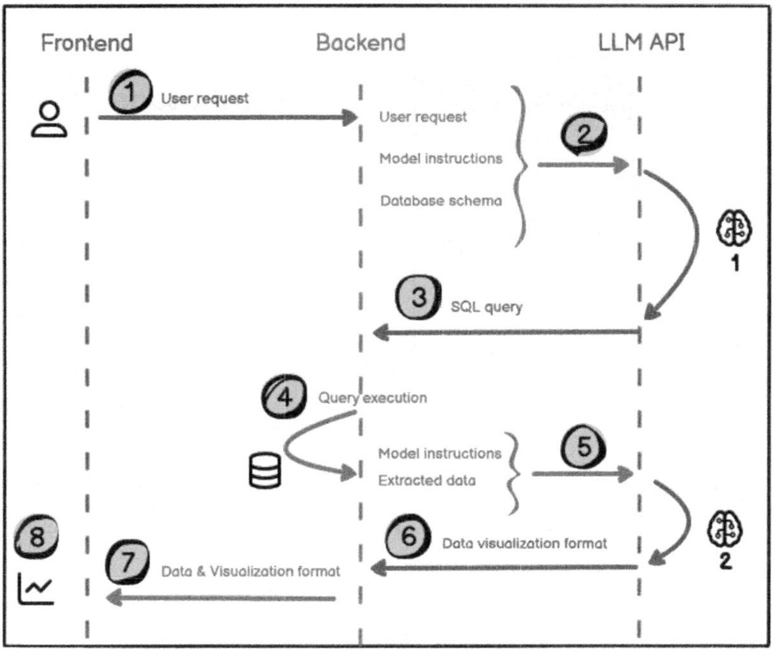

Fig. 3. The workflow based on two model instances.

SQL syntax and that it only contains data selection operations (*SELECT* statements), and not edit or delete operations (*UPDATE* or *DELETE* statements), thus preventing any potential security breaches.

In contrast, for the initialization of the second model instance, the one designed to suggest a proper data visualization based on the retrieved data, it is sufficient to provide contextual information such as *"Based on the data the user will provide, reply with how they might be represented so that they are usable and understandable in the best way possible."*.

For both instances, it is crucial to minimize the parameter that regulates the variation of the responses to the same input, called *temperature*, to obtain answers that are as deterministic as possible.

Figure 3 shows the workflow during user interaction, also making the parts of the architecture involved explicit. The process starts with the user's request (*Step 1*) in natural language, as illustrated in Fig. 1. This is sent to the back-end server and then sent, along with the model initialization instructions, the history of the previous messages in this conversation, and the database structure, to the LLM (*Step 2*) through its API. The first instance of the model will interpret the user's request and, given the database structure, will reply with a specific SQL query to extract the requested information (*Step 3*). The query is then executed on the database (*Step 4*), and the data are obtained. An additional request containing the extracted data (*Step 5*) is sent to the LLM using the second model instance to retrieve the recommendation of the most appropriate data representation (*Step 6*). Then, the data and the recommended representation are then sent to the front-end (*Step 7*) for the final visualization (*Step 8*). Depending on the result, the user may refine their request to correct or improve the information obtained. This can be easily done through a conversational interaction as illustrated in Fig. 2.

4.2 Interaction Workflow Based on One Model Instance

Figure 4 reports the workflow based on a single model instance. It is quite similar to the one based on two model instances: the only differences are in *Step 3*, where the model provides both the SQL query and the data visualization format to the backend devoted to query execution, and in *Step 5*, where the data are passed directly to the frontend to be visualized, rather than to the second model instance. The model instance prompt is also quite similar to the prompt of the first model instance in the other workflow. This prompt has been modified simply by adding an instruction to provide the data visualization format suggestion in addition to the SQL query, relying only on the user's request. All the rest of the parameters and supporting functions are the same.

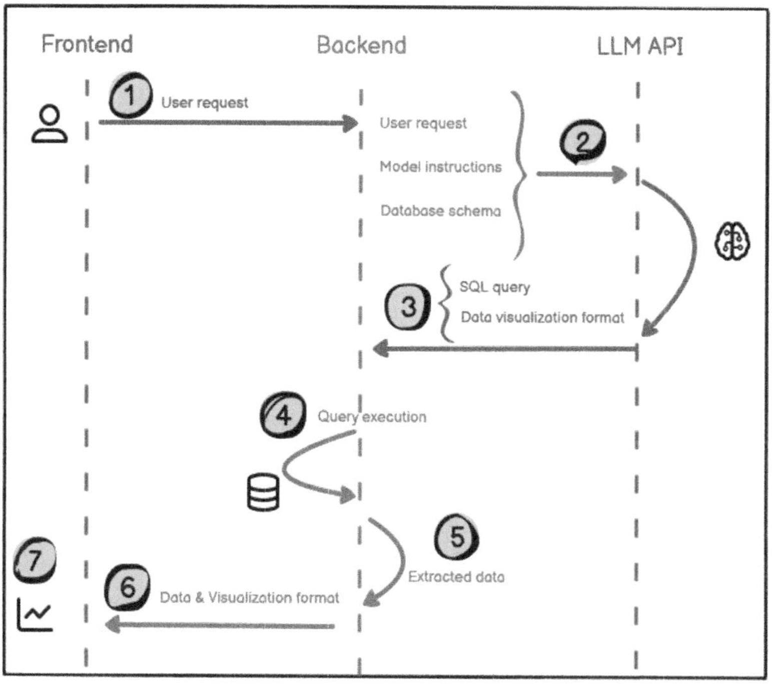

Fig. 4. Alternative workflow based on a single model instance.

4.3 Comparing the Two Interaction Workflows

Both approaches have advantages and disadvantages that should be taken into consideration to make the best choice based on the situation at hand.

The workflow comprising two model instances offers an effective representation of the extracted data, and the user is not required to define a representation explicitly. On the other hand, this approach does not consider the user's preference, as the visualization relies only on the extracted data. In addition, the use of a proprietary model, such as the one provided by OpenAI, raises privacy issues, as the extracted data is transmitted in plain text to the model and the company.

In the alternative workflow, there is a single model instance that takes care of both creating the query and proposing the graphical visualization. This approach has the advantage of being faster and cheaper since only one API call for each request is performed. Another advantage is that users are free to choose their preferred data visualization format by including such information in their request. However, this workflow does not rely on the extracted data to suggest the most suitable visualization; it can rely only on the user's request and the database schema. Such an approach may result in visualizations that are not adequate to the actual extracted data.

5 Use Case

This section presents a use case to demonstrate the proposed system's applicability in supporting workers in an analysis laboratory where collaborative robots are used to handle test tubes with the help of reagents and specific manipulations to obtain desired preparations and solutions. The main objective of this use case is to illustrate how the system can cater to different types of users, based on their roles and the complexity of their requests, by offering tailored visualizations.

The laboratory staff faces diverse challenges depending on their responsibilities. On the one hand, management personnel require customized metrics on production, performance, and economic aspects, often presented in specific visualization formats. On the other hand, operational staff are focused on quality control and product monitoring, seeking information such as how many products meet quality standards, how many products have been rejected, or how often a particular reagent is used.

To address the variety of needs, users can be classified according to their data requirements and their role within the organization:

- *(a1)* **Management Level:** Users interested in tailored metrics and specific visualizations related to production, performance, or economic efficiency.
- *(a2)* **Operational Level:** Users primarily concerned with product control and quality, focusing on metrics such as compliance with standards or reagent usage.

Additionally, users' requests can be categorized based on their complexity:

- *(b1)* **Simple Data Request:** Requests for straightforward data, typically in table format or as a single value, reflecting what is directly available in the database (e.g., task lists, average task duration, or tasks completed during a day).
- *(b2)* **Complex Data Request:** Requests for more advanced metrics that involve aggregating data from various database tables and sources (e.g., products discarded due to specific reagent batches, production chain efficiency, or reagent quality based on supplier data) or that should be displayed in a specific visualization format.

The combination of user role and request complexity is shown in Table 1, which outlines the most suitable workflow for each scenario:

Table 1. User/Data Request Matrix

USER/DATA REQUEST	*(b1)* **SIMPLE**	*(b2)* **COMPLEX**
(a1) **MANAGEMENT**	*(1)* Equivalent	*(3)* ONE model instance
(a2) **OPERATIONAL**	*(2)* Equivalent	*(4)* TWO model instances

This matrix illustrates that simple requests are handled similarly across user types, while complex requests necessitate different workflows based on the user's role. The following examples illustrate the practical applications of each combination:

- **Example** *(1)*: A manager requests data on how many orders were processed in the previous month. Since this is a simple data request, both workflows would provide an equivalent result.
- **Example** *(2)*: A worker at the operational level asks for data on how many products were rejected during yesterday's quality control checks. Similar to the first case, this is a simple data request that can be handled equivalently by both workflows.
- **Example** *(3)*: A manager requests the number of completed and failed tasks for each robot over the past three months, including the average duration of both completed and failed tasks. The manager adds that the requested output should be displayed in a bar chart with one bar for each robot showing the number of completed and failed tasks, as well as additional bars for the average task duration. Since the manager knows the exact visualization format they need, the one model instance is more suitable to deliver the requested bar chart. Figure 5 shows a screenshot of the application for this example, while the SQL query generated on the user's request is reported in Listing 1.1. However, if the manager had been unsure of the best way to present the data, the two model instances could have suggested a more appropriate visualization.

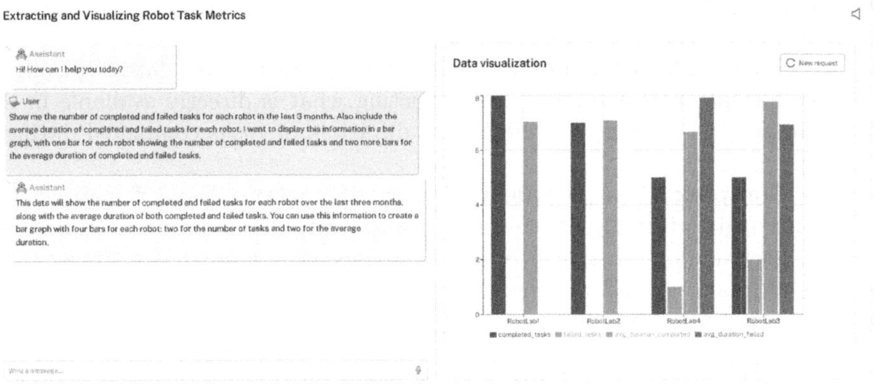

Fig. 5. A production manager requests the number of completed and failed tasks for each robot over the past three months, along with the average task durations.

```
SELECT
    robot_name,
    COUNT(case when status = 'COMPLETED' then 1 end) as completed_tasks,
    COUNT(case when status = 'ERROR' then 1 end) as failed_tasks,
    AVG(case when status = 'COMPLETED' then duration end) as
     avg_duration_completed,
    AVG(case when status = 'ERROR' then duration end) as
     avg_duration_failed
FROM
    robot_tasks_execution
WHERE
    start_time between '2024-06-19' and '2024-09-19'
GROUP BY
    robot_name
ORDER BY
    completed_tasks desc;
```

Listing 1.1. Showing a bar graph with last three months production in the laboratories

- **Example** *(4):* A laboratory technician needs to determine how frequently new pH sensors should be ordered, and requests data on the use of pH sensors in tasks performed over the past six months. In this case, the workflow with two model instances is more suitable. The first model instance initially suggests a table as the visualization format. However, the second instance, which has a more comprehensive understanding of the data, recommends a line chart as a more suitable way to represent the data over time. Figure 6 reports a screenshot of the application for this example, while the generated SQL query is reported in Listing 1.2.

```
SELECT manipulated_objects, start_time
FROM robot_tasks_execution
WHERE tool ILIKE '%pH sensor%'
    AND start_time >= NOW() - INTERVAL '6 MONTH';
```

Listing 1.2. Showing the use of a pH sensor as tool in the tasks performed during last 6 months

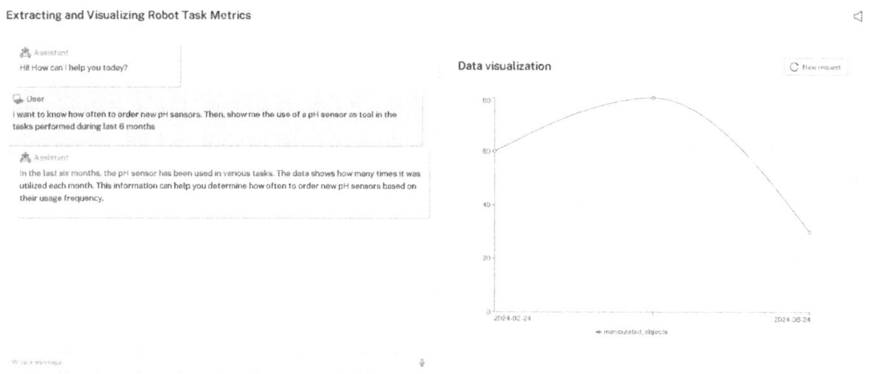

Fig. 6. A laboratory technician requests information on how often pH sensors are used, in order to decide how frequently to reorder them.

This use case has shown how the proposed system can effectively support both management and operational staff in a laboratory environment by providing tailored workflows based on the complexity of their data requests. The one model instance is best suited for users with specific visualization needs, while the workflow with the two model instances excels in situations where users benefit from system-generated suggestions about data visualization.

It is important to remark that examples and results reported in this section are based on the testing we have done by executing different types of requests with different workflows, and that extensive experimentation with real users is reserved for future work.

6 Discussion and Conclusion

The prioritization of easy-to-use interfaces to access robot data paves the way for seamless human-robot collaboration, thus ensuring that the transformative potential of collaborative robots can be exploited in different work environments. In an era where knowledge is power, the capacity to comprehend and exploit robot usage data can be a pivotal factor in the success and sustainability of organizations and societies.

This paper explores how LLMs can help designers achieve the goals of HWID, using AI to improve workers' wellbeing. Specifically, it elaborates on how human workers can retrieve information from a database with the assistance of an LLM-based system, aiming to obtain more effective exploitation of collaborative robots in work contexts.

Nevertheless, only once the prototype has been tested with users will it be possible to validate the efficacy of the proposed approach and which of the two workflows is best suited to users' requests in different cases. In this sense, the examples analyzed in the use case can be a good starting point for a user study.

A further dimension of analysis for the developed prototype will be that of query optimization. This includes an examination of the proposed query efficiency in terms of execution speed. It is also crucial to assess the model's comprehension of the database structure in the context of large databases. The database structure description may influence the *context window* of the model, which determines the amount of information that the model can take into account before ignoring older messages of a conversation, thereby losing some contextual information.

An additional extension is to train the model further by performing an initial fine-tuning with different queries. Additionally, also the subsequent interactions with users, which are appropriately marked as correct, can be used to further train the model to enable gradual improvement with use. To facilitate a more comprehensive understanding of the context and the interconnection of data by the model, it will be interesting to examine the use of specific domain knowledge using the Retrieval-Augmented Generation (RAG) [15]. Using RAG, the LLM can be trained with the provision of documents and information, which will increase its ability to make connections between data and provide more accurate queries. It is important to note that this documentation should not be limited to technical information about the data itself. Rather, it must also include information about the real applications of the data. Finally, as a prospective development, it would be of interest to investigate the extension of this approach to the analysis of NoSQL databases, in which there is no predefined data structure.

In summary, this study aims to provide insights for developing tools and methodologies that enhance transparency, comprehension, and data usage by leveraging natural language interaction. The approach can be generalized and applied to other work environments beyond computing metrics for collaborative robots. This will just require changing the initial context of the LLM and its database schema, thus making the proposed solution flexible and dynamic.

References

1. Abdelnour-Nocera, J., Baricelli, B.R., Lopes, A., Campos, P., Clemmensen, T.: Human Work Interaction Design: Analysis and Interaction Design Methods for Pervasive and Smart Workplaces: 4th IFIP 13.6 Working Conference, HWID 2015, London, UK, June 25–26, 2015, Revised Selected Papers, vol. 468. Springer, Cham (2015)
2. Bi, Z.M., Luo, C., Miao, Z., Zhang, B., Zhang, W.J., Wang, L.: Safety assurance mechanisms of collaborative robotic systems in manufacturing. Robot. Comput.-Integr. Manuf. **67**, 102022 (2021)
3. Calò, T., De Russis, L.: Leveraging large language models for end-user website generation. In: Spano, L.D., Schmidt, A., Santoro, C., Stumpf, S. (eds.) IS-EUD 2023. LNCS, vol. 13917, pp. 52–61. Springer, Cham (2023). https://doi.org/10.1007/978-3-031-34433-6_4
4. Clemmensen, T.: Human Work Interaction Design: A Platform for Theory and Action. Springer, Cham (2021). https://doi.org/10.1007/978-3-030-71796-4
5. Doyle-Kent, M.: Collaborative robotics in industry 5.0. Ph.D. thesis, Technische Universität Wien (2021)

6. Fogli, D., Gargioni, L., Guida, G., Tampalini, F.: A hybrid approach to user-oriented programming of collaborative robots. Robot. Comput.-Integr. Manuf. **73**, 102234 (2022)
7. Galin, R.R., Meshcheryakov, R.V.: Human-robot interaction efficiency and human-robot collaboration. In: Kravets, A.G. (ed.) Robotics: Industry 4.0 Issues & New Intelligent Control Paradigms. SSDC, vol. 272, pp. 55–63. Springer, Cham (2020). https://doi.org/10.1007/978-3-030-37841-7_5
8. Gargioni, L., Fogli, D.: Integrating chatGPT with blockly for end-user development of robot tasks. In: Companion of the 2024 ACM/IEEE International Conference on Human-Robot Interaction, pp. 478–482 (2024)
9. Gargioni, L., Fogli, D., Baroni, P.: Designing human-robot collaboration for the preparation of personalized medicines. In: Proceedings of the 2023 ACM Conference on Information Technology for Social Good, pp. 135–140 (2023)
10. Huang, F., Li, G., Zhou, X., Canny, J.F., Li, Y.: Creating user interface mock-ups from high-level text descriptions with deep-learning models (2021)
11. Huang, S., Wang, B., Li, X., Zheng, P., Mourtzis, D., Wang, L.: Industry 5.0 and society 5.0—comparison, complementation and co-evolution. J. Manuf. Syst. **64**, 424–428 (2022)
12. Jiang, E., Toh, E., Molina, A., Donsbach, A., Cai, C.J., Terry, M.: GenLine and GenForm: two tools for interacting with generative language models in a code editor. In: Adjunct Proceedings of the 34th Annual ACM Symposium on User Interface Software and Technology, UIST 2021 Adjunct, pp. 145–147. Association for Computing Machinery, New York (2021). https://doi.org/10.1145/3474349.3480209
13. Kanazawa, A., Kinugawa, J., Kosuge, K.: Adaptive motion planning for a collaborative robot based on prediction uncertainty to enhance human safety and work efficiency. IEEE Trans. Rob. **35**(4), 817–832 (2019)
14. Kolvig-Raun, E.S., Kjærgaard, M.B., Brorsen, R.: Joint stress estimation and remaining useful life prediction for collaborative robots to support predictive maintenance. IEEE Robot. Autom. Lett. (2024)
15. Lewis, P., et al.: Retrieval-augmented generation for knowledge-intensive NLP tasks. Adv. Neural. Inf. Process. Syst. **33**, 9459–9474 (2020)
16. Li, J., et al.: Can LLM already serve as a database interface. A big bench for large-scale database grounded text-to-sqls. CoRR abs/2305.03111 (2023)
17. Mahmud, T., Hasan, K.A., Ahmed, M., Chak, T.H.C.: A rule based approach for NLP based query processing. In: 2015 2nd International Conference on Electrical Information and Communication Technologies (EICT), pp. 78–82. IEEE (2015)
18. Proia, S., Carli, R., Cavone, G., Dotoli, M.: A literature review on control techniques for collaborative robotics in industrial applications. In: 2021 IEEE 17th International Conference on Automation Science and Engineering (CASE), pp. 591–596. IEEE (2021)
19. Rahman, M.M., Khatun, F., Jahan, I., Devnath, R., Bhuiyan, M.A.A.: Cobotics: the evolving roles and prospects of next-generation collaborative robots in industry 5.0. J. Robot. **2024**(1), 2918089 (2024)
20. Rajkumar, N., Li, R., Bahdanau, D.: Evaluating the text-to-SQL capabilities of large language models. arXiv preprint arXiv:2204.00498 (2022)
21. Rozo, L., Calinon, S., Caldwell, D.G., Jimenez, P., Torras, C.: Learning physical collaborative robot behaviors from human demonstrations. IEEE Trans. Rob. **32**(3), 513–527 (2016)
22. Sahoo, S., Lo, C.Y.: Smart manufacturing powered by recent technological advancements: a review. J. Manuf. Syst. **64**, 236–250 (2022)

23. Vemprala, S., Bonatti, R., Bucker, A., Kapoor, A.: ChatGPT for robotics: design principles and model abilities. Technical report, Microsoft (2023). https://www.microsoft.com/en-us/research/uploads/prod/2023/02/ChatGPT_Robotics.pdf
24. Wannasuphoprasit, W., Gillespie, R.B., Colgate, J.E., Peshkin, M.A.: Cobot control. In: Proceedings of International Conference on Robotics and Automation, vol. 4, pp. 3571–3576. IEEE (1997)
25. Zhang, X., Khedri, K., Rawassizadeh, R.: Can LLMs substitute SQL? Comparing resource utilization of querying LLMs versus traditional relational databases. arXiv preprint arXiv:2404.08727 (2024)
26. Zizic, M.C., Mladineo, M., Gjeldum, N., Celent, L.: From industry 4.0 towards industry 5.0: a review and analysis of paradigm shift for the people, organization and technology. Energies **15**(14), 5221 (2022)

Working With Complex Data and Data Visualization

Mapping Context-Dependent Dimensions of Human-Data Viz Interaction

Sara Beschi(✉) and Angela Locoro

Dip. di Economia e Management, Università degli Studi di Brescia, Brescia, Italy
{sara.beschi,angela.locoro}@unibs.it

Abstract. This paper attempts to identify and characterize some context-dependent dimensions of Human-Data Visualization Interaction that are crucial to estimate the complexity of data-driven decision making. These dimensions are only partly related to off-line considerations such as the kind of charts, the data represented, and the like, and are mapped with operationalization constructs for their characterization and assessment. A what-if scenario in an industrial company is the starting point to reflect upon living constraints, such as the level of expertise in visual analytics of managers (the so-called Visual Information Literacy), the strategy that drives the decision process, and the flexibility and adaptability of the technology design to the data characterizing the decisions and both the previous aspects. How can we relate these three aspects for a better estimate of the data-driven decision-making flaws and complexity? Some hypotheses are proposed here.

Keywords: Data Visualization · Visual Information Literacy · Human-Data Interaction · Evaluation Methods · Pragmatic Framework

1 Introduction and Background

Enterprises are increasingly immersed in the data-driven revolution and need to align with innovative corporate process management. This change is closely related to the fast development of big data technologies, the imperative for digital transformation, and the vast volume of data that companies have access to [20]. Data analysis offers a new opportunity to uncover hidden values among the vast array of available information, improve understanding of business processes, develop predictive capabilities, and facilitate issue detection.

The use of information and data through the adoption of Business Intelligence (BI) and Analytics systems yields *Business Value* in Organizations, directing processes towards increased productivity, enhanced decision-making efficiency, and deeper insights into customers and markets to foster innovation. This corporate value translates into tangible performance enhancements, such as cost reduction, identification of growth opportunities, and maintenance of competitive advantage in the market [10].

Published by Springer Nature Switzerland AG 2026
B. R. Barricelli et al. (Eds.): HWID 2024, IFIP AICT 751, pp. 225–240, 2026.
https://doi.org/10.1007/978-3-031-95334-7_14

To effectively measure *Business Value* and the impacts arising from the adoption of these systems, it is important to predict and identify the various professional roles and competencies necessary to grasp the business context, formulate suitable analytical solutions and data visualizations, understand data sources and data formats, and be familiar with data collection and transformation systems [8].

These professional figures, dedicated to uncovering the most significant insights, emerge as key users of Data Visualization systems. Throughout their interaction, various factors impact the analysis activity and subsequent interpretation of results.

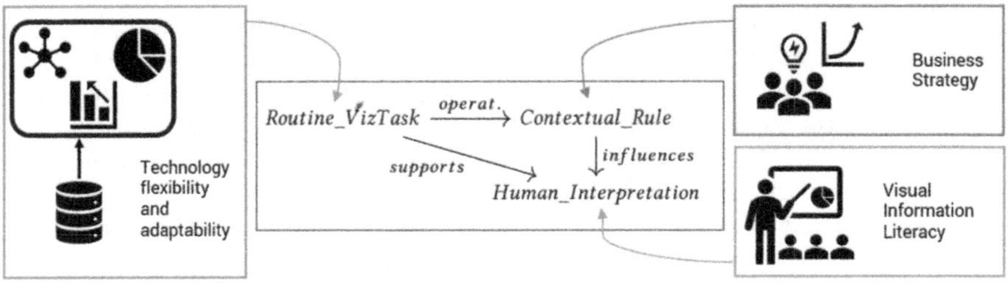

Fig. 1. The diagrammatic sketch of a pragmatic framework for human-data viz interaction at the center of the figure was proposed by one of the authors in [7] (the abbreviation "operate." stands for "operationalizes"), and extended with the current hypothesized dimensions (Technology flexibility and adaptability; Visual Information Literacy; Business Strategy) emerging from and applied to a Business Case.

These factors not only concern the type of visualization presenting the data, but also how the professional figure reads and interprets the charts, their familiarity with the system, their approach to daily professional practices, and the impact of context and experience on the decisions and questions arising during data analysis and *Business Strategy* definition.

This work contributes to the Human-Work Interaction Design (HWID) domain by investigating how users interact with data visualization tools within specific organizational contexts. Aligning with HWID principles, our framework emphasizes the socio-technical interplay between user skills, tasks, and system usability, providing a structured approach to understanding these interactions.

In our previous work, presented at AVI in 2020 [7], we introduced a pragmatic framework for Human-Data visualization interaction [21], which we report in the center of Fig. 1. This schema aimed at capturing, from a category-theoretic perspective, structural elements and their structure-preserving interactions during data visualization activities in the wild.

From this schema, it was clear that each interaction property should be contextualized, and different "concretions" can emerge among the elements of the framework. For example, the same Data Visualization may be interpreted differently, based on the task, the role, and the background knowledge of the user interacting with it. The same task may include the interaction with very different, sometimes opposite, data visualizations, depending on the rules that each organization has for defining their routine interactions with data and, again, based on the level of expertise of its members. The three dimensions of the framework—Technology Flexibility and Adaptability, Visual Information Literacy, and Business Strategy—are interrelated. While each dimension addresses a distinct aspect of Human-Data Visualization Interaction, their interdependence becomes evident in practical applications. For instance, usability (linked to Technology Flexibility) must account for user needs, abilities, and expertise, which are inherently tied to the context and task at hand (Visual Information Literacy). Furthermore, usability is closely related to data complexity, as more complex data requires interfaces that enhance interpretability without overwhelming the user. To clarify the first dimension, Technology Flexibility and Adaptability refers to the system's ability to accommodate varying levels of data complexity and user expertise. This includes features like customizable visualizations, interactive elements, and adaptive feedback mechanisms that adjust to user behavior and context. For example, in scenarios involving high data complexity, the system should provide advanced filtering and drill-down options to facilitate sense-making for experienced users, while simplifying views for less experienced ones. Other studies in the same domain [5] witnessed and highlighted the consolidated importance of characterizing and strengthening the connection between visualization tasks and data management optimization techniques, hence developing research directions for visualization interactions and optimization techniques for data management. The major gaps that 30 years of studies explored with the above review let emerge were related to the lack of mechanisms in data visualization interactions to:

- provide semi-automatic means to visually encode data, especially in routine data analysis
- allow the annotation and labeling of visualizations, in order to improve sense-making, intra-personal and inter-personal communication
- recording the interactions with data visualization, to enhance longitudinal patterns finding among other dimensions that are related to history of interactions

In the present study, we want to reinforce this framework in two directions: the former is to show its instantiation through a business experience made by one of the authors, which allowed the translation of some structure-preserving relations of the framework into accurate what-if analysis dimensions of interactions in the company (Sect. 3); the latter aims at mapping the theoretic dimensions of our framework into context-dependent ones, emerging from the concrete case explained, to characterize measurable constructs (Sect. 4).

Mapping this framework with concrete dimensions, and illustrating an example of a *Business Scenario*, we highlight the significant influence of the following factors on data interpretation and the resulting *Business Value*: interaction with data visualizations, experience with the system, and the business context.

2 A Business Scenario Context

Among the various data-driven decision-making processes that emerge in the business context, one of the key sectors is marketing. Specifically, *Customer Relationship Management* (CRM) systems represent a fundamental data source for generating value from customer information. Effectively leveraging this data can provide meaningful insights into marketing performance, enabling marketers to optimize campaigns, increase sales, enhance customer engagement, and improve relationships with customers to better meet their needs [1].

The various widely used CRM systems in the market offer a range of tools for chart creation and data exploration. This enables the development of dashboards that provide marketers with a constant overview of key indicators derived from data sources such as social media, website interactions, sales, and email campaigns.

Depending on marketers' level of experience in using the systems, they can create increasingly sophisticated visualizations, starting from simple metrics like click-through rates and conversions, all the way to customer segmentation. This enables them to extract increasingly detailed information, which can then be transformed into targeted and strategic actions.

An example of using data analysis tools integrated into the CRM could involve monitoring marketing campaigns. To assess their effectiveness, measures such as conversion rates, click-through rates, and revenue generated are utilized. This approach allows for the rapid identification of less effective campaigns and enables data-driven adjustments to optimize performance.

The presented scenario focuses on a real-life case where professionals interact with these systems to address a business question. We will see how users' level of experience and the type of visualization chosen to represent performance metrics significantly influence the level of understanding and analysis of the data, as well as the overall experience quality.

3 A What-if Business Scenario from Observation of Business Practices

Alpha Manufacturing is a manufacturing company based in Northern Italy, specialized in the production of consumer goods. Alpha Manufacturing is focused on improving *internal data analytics*, with a focus on *marketing campaigns performance*. During the direct observation of business activity by one of the authors, the what-if user scenario named "Unexperienced User with Complex Graph and First Interaction" was identified. In this scenario, User1 had no experience with the system but she was a domain expert, and she was asked to answer a question: *"What is the impact of our latest marketing campaign on customers?"*. User1 was interacting with the CRM dashboard and came across a three-dimensional scatterplot showing email open rate concerning variables such as the day of the week, time-sent stamp, and content type (Fig. 2a). She had many interpretation difficulties. These were related to understanding the meaning of the three-dimensional graph, also due to the lack of suggestions from the interface on how to interact with the graph, which further confused her.

A second observation during a routine activity brought to identify the second what-if user scenario named "Expert User Scenario with a Simple Graph as First Iteration". Here, User2 was a system and domain expert, and should answer the question: *"Which user segments showed the most engagement in the latest marketing campaign?"*. Interacting with a chart as simple as the one required by User1 limited User2's initial interaction experience, as she wanted to derive detailed information where she had only bars showing email open rate by day of the week (Fig. 2b). The interpretation difficulty lying in the current interface did not allow User2 to explore specific details or identify relevant customer segments. The methodology used to develop the framework involved direct observations in business scenarios, focusing on capturing user interactions and challenges in real-world contexts. The observations were conducted through direct monitoring of user interactions within a CRM environment. Data were collected using think-aloud protocols, where participants verbalized their thought processes while navigating the system. This method provided insights into their challenges and decision-making strategies, revealing usability gaps and areas for improvement in the design of complex visualizations. For example, the "Inexperienced User with Complex Graph" scenario emphasized the importance of adaptive interfaces and usability in systems, while the "Expert User with Simple Graph" scenario highlighted the need for custom tools tailored to varying levels of VIL. Future studies could incorporate controlled experiments or surveys to validate these findings and further strengthen the framework's empirical foundation.

4 Mapping the Three Dimensions to the Pragmatic Framework and Characterizing Them

Once recognized that concrete dimensions exist and are mappable in our framework, there is the need to characterize and operationalized them. Some hypotheses of how to characterize them and assess them are outlined.

Usability, Never too Much Usability! The visual inspection step above is an instantiation of the *Routine_VizTask* structure of our framework, which concerns the need to interact with data visualization *Technology* that (should be) flexible and adaptable enough for doing visual analytics as often as the user's role may require. Characterizing this context-dependent dimension means providing evidence of the users' difficulties in the scenarios depicted, in terms of usability of the data visualization interface. This may have led to introducing explanatory feedback making sense of each element for User1 scenario, which may have improved the experience of User1 with the Data visualization system. For User2, an advanced control panel may have allowed her to select and combine dimensions to create custom views. Drill-down tools may have let her explore specific details without losing the big picture. Advanced filters may have

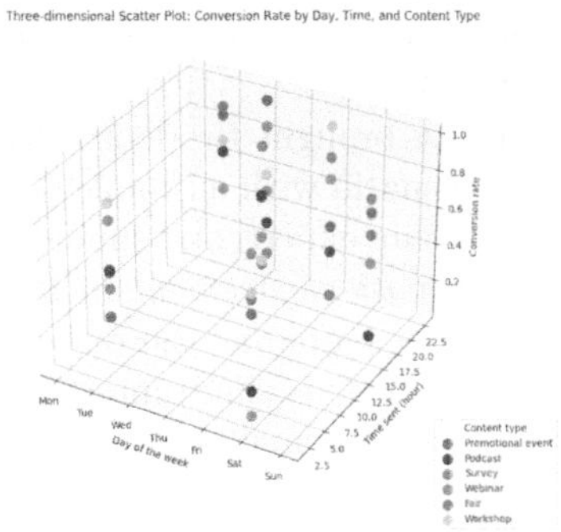

(a) An example chart similar to the one utilized in the what-if user scenario titled "Unexperienced User with Complex Graph and First Interaction".

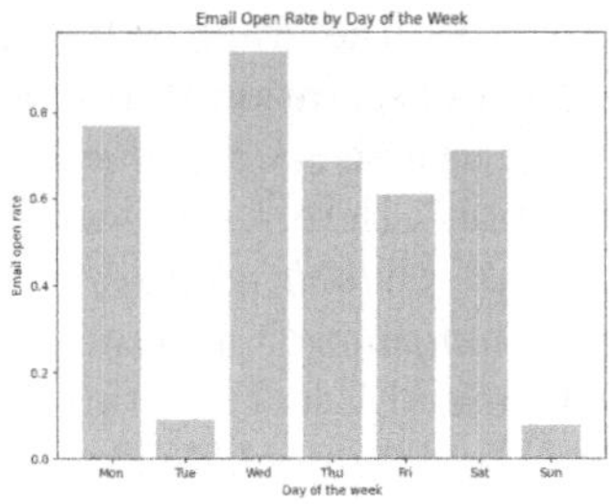

(b) An example chart similar to the one utilized in the what-if user scenario titled "Expert User Scenario with a Simple Graph as First Iteration".

Fig. 2. In the What-if Business Scenario two different data visualizations are involved, both aimed at representing frequent measures of interest in the analysis of marketing campaign performance.

allowed User2 to apply specific conditions to isolate relevant data, optimizing the process of finding specific segments of users. Besides the need to assess usability through traditional tests to measure interaction efficiency, an open challenge may be how to relate usability to the user's behaviors need that depend on the level of literacy and expertise in routinely using data visualization. Going beyond usability has been advocated in other domain such as the EUD one, where the notion of EUDability came to the scenes [4] and new assessment dimensions were devised. As affirmed by studies on data visualization usability [5] [7], it is evident that a data visualization interface is a specific kind of interface, whose "ability to be used" depend on at least two dimensions: the *complexity* of the data and its *interpretability*, e.g., the difficulty of the data and the ability of the user [17]. The former can be strictly related to the query posed by users upon the data and, hence, to the data complexity. A classification of data properties contributing to their complexity is depicted in Fig. 3, where each single dimension of complexity is put in relation with the others, and an order of magnitude of complexity is emerging from the picture.

For example, if data are composed of multiple entities (e.g., thousands of e) and each entity have multiple properties (e.g., tenths of p) of multiple data type and aggregation type, the order of complexity would be maximum, e.g.,

$$O(|e| * |p| * |type| * |aggr|) \tag{1}$$

would be the magnitude of the complexity to keep into account.

The complexity of the data raises connected problems of:

- what are the best visualization that enact sense making for data with those characteristics

- what is the best interaction that should be provided with data of such complexity
- what is the level of expertise of the user for data of such complexity and what are techniques to simplify the complexity and optimize understanding

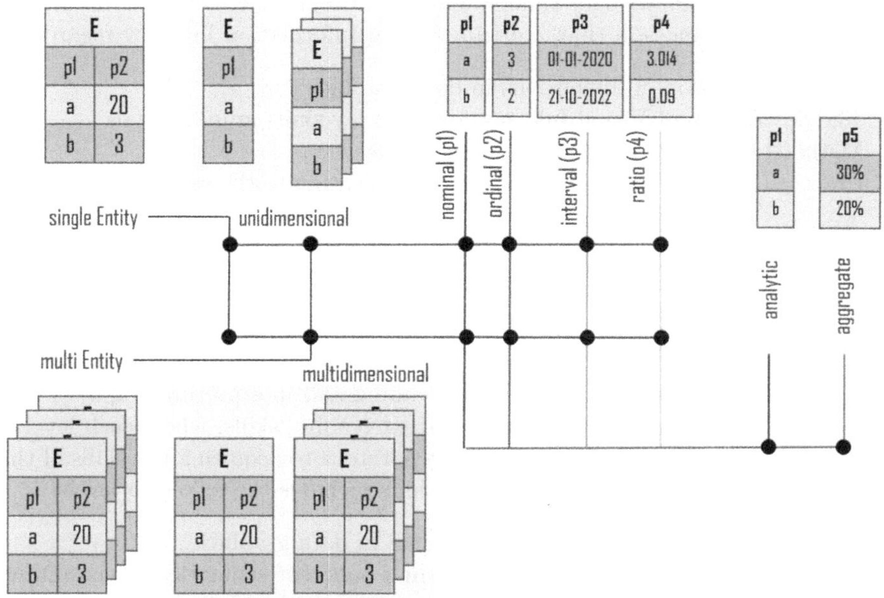

Fig. 3. The schematic overview of how complexity can be seen as a multi-dimensional construct, where each dimension (entity dimensionality, type of data, type of aggregation) belongs to data properties $(p_1, p_2, ..., p_n)$, and the complexity of data emerges as an "operationalization" of data characteristics and number of dimensions, through an order of magnitude of complexity that grows as the number of data properties grow.

Assessing the Visualization Literacy of Individuals. The visual inspection should boost the *Human_Interpretation* of the data at hand to answer the questions about the marketing campaigns. This step regards the second structure in our framework. The context-dependent characterization of this dimension may concern the *Visual Information Literacy* of the user, besides her domain of expertise. Visual Information Literacy has been defined as "the ability to properly process information related to data graphics, i.e., encoding information into data graphics and decoding information from data graphics" [18].

The importance of characterizing conceptual and practical skills in data visualization stems from the fact that this ability is deemed as crucial as textual literacy and numeracy. Many challenges arise from the need to characterize Visual Information Literacy of individuals. For example, the "information" aspect is a challenging one, in that what and to which extent the informational aspects should be considered in the definition of individual skills is far from being clarified. This issue points to the need to consider whether to include in the Literacy also the abilities to work well with information sources, using strategies to locate, compare, evaluate, organize, apply, and synthesize data, to communicate, explain, and instruct people about abstract concepts and ideas towards constructing new knowledge, understanding and refining communication skills.

Some main stances in characterizing Visual Information Literacy regard:

1. The identification of dimensions in data graphics
2. The description of Visual Information Literacy skills in individuals
3. Methods to assess Visual Information Literacy
4. Practical solutions to adjust visual communication to the skills of individuals

The first point has been addressed in the section on usability, where the concept of complexity of data dimensions was explored and depicted in Fig. 3.

An example of Visual Information Literacy characterization and assessment was given in [18]. The model of Visual literacy presented in this paper consists of six cognitive levels, which are seen in progression, from the first to the last one, as an evolution of people's skills in reading and interpreting graphics. The model was partly borrowed by models of text reading skills, where each level is characterized by specific skills that are preparatory to acquiring the skills of the next level. The model for visual literacy skills includes the following levels:

1. Map: basic recognition of syntax elements in data graphics.
2. Integrate: relate visual elements to form a coherent semantic understanding of the graphic.
3. Compute: quantification of relationships within the visual data (e.g., computations over numerical data).
4. Reason: draw conclusions based on visual information.
5. Infer: add new knowledge to proper beliefs from the data.
6. Explain: provide rationales for the design of data graphics and exhibit critical thinking skills about the efficacy and the effectiveness in conveying information.

As said above, the model showed a progressive increase in complexity at each level. Participants' ability to correctly interpret data graphics decrease as the complexity of the visualizations increases. The study in [18] found that the levels of the designed model align well with the participants increasing cognitive demands. Simple visualizations were processed more accurately than complex ones, with a higher rate of correct answers for lower-level tasks.

In the current scenarios, for example, where the User1 Visual Information Literacy is scarce, replacing the graph with a bar graph that shows the email open rate by day of the week, may have facilitated User1 in identifying the days that registered the highest email opening rate and obtain an immediate indication of the positive or negative impact of the campaign on the various days. User1 may have found the new interface more accessible and may have become capable of answering her questions more efficiently, improving her confidence in analyzing marketing data.

An improved experience for User2 may have taken into account her higher Visual Information Literacy, and the full advantage of the complexity of an advanced graph, able to answer her analytical questions quicker and more thoroughly and, overall, improving her marketing data analysis experience. For example, a more complex chart such as an interactive heatmap may have improved the visualization of customers engagement based on demographic (age, gender, geographic location), behavior (frequency of interaction with emails), and temporal variables. This new view may have given User2 the ability to customize data presentation and explore specific details.

Besides models of visual literacy like the ones presented above, there are new scenario of research that try to go beyond rigid constructs for characterizing visual literacy to appeal to contextual evidences [14]. Starting from the considerations that various aspects of visual literacy were already targeted, what is yet to be fully captured is how define, study, and improve visualization literacy with the lenses of measurement, interventions, and pedagogy.

In the scenarios above presented, we need to cope with two different kind of literacy: the one acquired in the past, which can be based on previous learning and education curricula, and can be thought as a quite standard baggage of notions; the one acquired during individual experiences of tools, interfaces, visualization kinds, and ways of more or less creatively re-combine the knowledge acquired into new, creative and personalized practices (e.g., pragmatic knowledge in the domain of semiotics seeding and re-seeding of experiences and knowledge, see for example [9,12]). We need to keep into account, in the words of [12], that "evolutionary processes [...] are determined through an iterative process of collaboration among multiple stakeholders, rather than being completely specified before system development occurs; they must evolve because they cannot be completely designed prior to use; they must evolve to some extent at the hands of the users, and; they must be designed for evolution".

Tracing the Behaviors of Users. The visual inspections step also supports a precise *Business Strategy*, which is concretely rendered as highly-customized query related to the marketing campaigns. This step may be seen as an instantiation of the *Contextual_Rule* in our framework. This third context-dependent dimension may be characterized as the capability of the Data Visualization to reflect the users' strategies. In terms of interactions, these strategies concern the two aspects outlined above: the information quantity (complexity) contained in the data and the users' behavior (interpretation) during interactions with visualizations [11,16]. The former requires a classification of data visualization information from the least to the most complex, depending on the number of entities represented in the data, the number of properties depicted for each entity, the type of data of each represented property (being nominal, ordinal, numeric discrete, and numeric continuous), and the level of details (e.g., aggregated or not aggregated) [15].

Analyzing users' systematic behavior can help identify the areas of interest they focus on, based on their confidence with the visualization, their current strategy, and their literacy level. Recurring interaction patterns often emerge, shaped by these factors. For instance, users with higher Visual Information Literacy tend to leverage advanced tools and techniques, as demonstrated in our case studies. This identification is essential for acquiring knowledge of data more effectively and efficiently, and for providing a more customized experience. Furthermore, behavioral aspects in users depend on related concepts such as literacy level, usability of the tools, and complexity of the data. In line with the socio-technical approach to Human Computer Interaction, it is essential to consider both technical and social factors in designing interactive visualizations, as this dual perspective facilitates a more contextual analysis of user behavior and interaction [2]. This higher level of customization may be reached, for example, by tracing users' behaviors with Data Visualizations in search of systematic biases or recurrent patterns of visual analysis. Some tools already exist for exploration paths and analytics history storage [13,19]. Assessing the information complexity, the usability, and the literacy of individuals for comprehending the users' behavior may advance data visualization tools. These tools may reach a personalized level such as being able to formulate on-the-fly query-answering and personalized charts interactions that could improve both the *Business Strategy* requirements and the *Human-Interpretation* aspects.

5 The Impact of Augmented Analytics and the Quest for Explainability

The challenges observed in user interactions, such as the need for adaptive interfaces and better interpretability, highlight the importance of integrating advanced tools like Augmented Analytics (AA) and Explainable AI (XAI) to bridge usability gaps and enhance decision-making processes. In recent years, BI software has integrated Artificial Intelligence (AI) into various functions, leading to the rise of Augmented Analytics (AA). This approach combines machine intelligence with human intuition to accelerate insights, uncover discoveries, and enhance data literacy across organizations [3].

The integration of AA introduces a significant opportunity to enhance both the usability and interpretability of data visualizations within BI systems. By automating insights and providing explainable outputs, AA can supports users with varying levels of VIL in understanding and leveraging complex data.

While some AI applications are fully automated, complex business problems require human involvement. AI enhances human-machine collaboration, surpassing individual capabilities, facilitating modern analytics for different types of users, and increasing confidence in outcomes.

AA systems are significantly transforming BI software by integrating AI, fundamentally changing how users interact with these advanced tools. This integration leads to a drastic shift in user interaction, necessitating new skills to utilize the enhanced features effectively [6]. Some of the main features are:

- Facilitating smart discovery by assisting managers and analysts in generating automated insights directly within the dashboard;
- Automating and guiding data preparation, transformation, and integration, thereby minimizing manual effort and expediting the analysis process;
- Enabling users to easily create charts, visualizations, and dashboards for quick and efficient preliminary data exploration;
- Allowing users to ask questions in plain language through natural language interaction, making data analysis accessible to users of all expertise levels, automating routine tasks, and freeing up human resources;
- Empowering users to incorporate complex analytics into their decision-making processes through Automated Machine Learning;
- Accelerating the analysis process and uncovering hidden patterns through automated data analysis and anomaly detection, providing valuable insights for process optimization;
- Enabling agile decision-making through real-time data processing, allowing businesses to respond swiftly to changing market conditions and emerging trends;
- Integrating tools for analyzing and visualizing unstructured data such as social media, news, and cyber intelligence.

Utilizing AA significantly enhances sustainability across various industries. For example, automating data preparation, data analysis, and reporting, reduces the need for extensive manual data handling, minimizes resource consumption, reduces costs, helps to make predictions and anticipate phenomena, and saves valuable time for analysts and managers allowing them to focus on strategic activities. The proposed framework also aligns with sustainability goals by promoting efficient use of data visualization tools. Simplifying user interactions reduces cognitive load and resource consumption, while fostering a better understanding of complex data ensures informed and sustainable decision-making.

While current research has highlighted the benefits of AI-powered insights and automation, the ways in which users interact with these advanced tools require further investigation. Understanding how different user roles and skill levels impact interaction with enhanced BI systems can reveal crucial insights into user adoption and satisfaction. Additionally, examining contextual factors, such as organizational culture and industry-specific challenges, can provide a more complete understanding of how these platforms can be optimized to meet different user needs.

5.1 Explainable AA and Visual Explanatory Information

There remains a need for a more in-depth exploration of the implications of user interaction with these systems. AA raised the problem of explainability of AI and visual explainability. Both are crucial in the user scenario that we were analyzing and are considering for improvements.

AA systems are now integrated in various scenarios, where their decisions can have profound impacts on human lives. Despite their success, one of the critical challenges their "black-box" nature, which makes them nor transparent nor fully understandable. The need for explainability should become a major concern in the development of AA models. Transparent and interpretable models are essential for fostering trust in AA, ensuring fairness, and facilitating accountability. The field of Explainable Artificial Intelligence (XAI) aims to address these concerns by creating models that not only perform well but also provide understandable explanations for their decisions. This is particularly fitting the problem of providing the right degree of usability, understandability and explainability that enterprises stakeholders need to trust and evolve with the use of tools for supporting decision making.

By providing reasons or explanations for the decisions made by AA models, users can develop trust in the system. If users understand how a decision was made, they are more likely to trust its outcome, which is especially important in high-stakes fields such as healthcare, finance, or autonomous driving. Trustworthiness of models is a crucial goal of explainable AI, as it enables both technical and non-technical users to gain confidence in the system's outputs.

Explanations help users, particularly those affected by the AA's decisions, engage more with the process. Users can assess whether a decision is justifiable and align it with their expectations, leading to more informed decision-making. This is important in applications where user interaction with the AA would benefit by more user engagement, such as decision support systems.

Explanatory information enables users to assess the fairness of AA models. By understanding how inputs are processed to produce outputs, users can spot potential biases or unethical decisions. Fairness and ethics are vital for ensuring that AA does not perpetuate discrimination or other unfair practices.

Explanations lower the barrier for non-expert users to interact with and utilize AA systems. By making the internal workings of models understandable, XAI can help product owners, managers, and non-technical users leverage AI without needing deep technical knowledge, hence improving accessibility. For example, interactive explanations within dashboards can help non-expert users like User1 decode complex visualizations, while expert users like User2 can leverage advanced features to drill down into specific insights, enhancing their strategic analysis.

In an interactive workflow, explanatory information can guide users toward refining models. For developers, understanding how a model behaves in different scenarios can suggest ways to improve performance. Providing transparency through explanations allows for better refinement of the AI systems, particularly when users can see how different inputs lead to various outcomes.

Interactive refinement and optimization are an outcome and a goal of better visual interactions, and open challenges are those which address these new topics emerging with the possibility of introducing aware and trustworthy AA tools into the visual analytics routines.

Visual explanatory information may enter this picture by:

- providing a system for interactive visualization with visual feedback and explanatory annotations;

- providing a system of diagnosing automatic decisions, visual feedback and exploration of complex reasoning by machines and identification of relevant points, nodes, or features for the decision made;
- allow higher-level abstractions upon algorithms and data, in order to interpret even more complex patterns in data, identify which data properties impact more on observed outcomes and
- tracking the interaction history and the data provenance, as well as tracking the visual explainers used. In this way a log of insights and findings may help refine and optimize models and decisions based upon them.

6 Addressing Limitations and Expanding Applications

The proposed framework has successfully outlined key dimensions of Human-Data Interaction, yet certain practical limitations highlight opportunities for further development. One pressing challenge is balancing the complexity of visualizations with their usability, particularly for non-expert users. Although advanced tools offer powerful insights, they risk alienating users with lower levels of VIL. To address this, future studies could explore interaction designs that adapt dynamically to user expertise, leveraging modular interfaces or customizable levels of detail to cater to diverse user groups.

Another critical limitation lies in system scalability and workflow integration. As datasets grow in size and complexity, ensuring the framework's adaptability across industries and organizational contexts becomes crucial. Future work could investigate approaches to optimize data handling, such as integrating cloud-based analytics or developing AI-driven tools that streamline workflows without compromising performance.

Beyond marketing and CRM scenarios, the framework's adaptability to other industries offers an exciting avenue for exploration. For instance, in healthcare, the interpretability of clinical dashboards could support timely and accurate decision-making, while in finance, adaptive visualizations could enhance real-time investment analyses. These domain-specific applications may reveal unique challenges, such as the need for higher granularity in data interpretation or stricter usability requirements, thereby enriching the framework's versatility.

To advance this field, establishing standardized evaluation methods for dimensions like VIL, usability, and complexity is essential. Future research should aim to design context-specific tasks and metrics that assess user interaction across varying domains, ensuring consistent benchmarks for system performance.

By addressing these challenges and broadening its applications, the framework can evolve into a robust tool that supports diverse industries, offering a foundation for more intuitive and effective Human-Data Interaction systems.

7 Conclusion and Future Work

Context-dependent dimensions of Human-Data Interaction are related to individuals and their tasks, role level, and tools usability dimensions composing the environmental conditions where big data interpretations and decisions based upon them take place. Despite the desire to provide timely and useful information, there are still gaps in technology design and margins for improvement in their intrinsic quality and in the quality of communication through them.

A dedicated study on this matter would give the possibility of characterizing and assessing the main dimensions of Human-Data Interaction with the aim to:

- identify the nature and the complexity of problems and data underlying the solution of problems through visual analytics practices and explanations;
- identify criteria of rightness of information visualization with respect to the Visual Information Literacy of individuals, in combination with further dimensions such as the data to be represented, the decisions to be made, and the context of information (routine, critical and fast, strategic, and the like);
- investigate the interaction dynamics and properties of visual tools for the proper communication of data, towards the identification of high-level requirements for their effective and efficient design;
- provide suggestions to the design, customization, and adoption of visual information systems for visual analytics and comprehension of big data in new and emerging data-driven scenarios in organizations
- let visual explanatory information become one of the major issues when AA tools are pervading the routine practices of analysis, prediction, and understanding of business trends, processes, and strategies

Mapping hypothesized dimensions with their operational counterpart may bring light on how to boost the business processes and practices towards a more aware and sized use of big data, and on how to improve the daily practice of people in different work scenarios, still providing a rigorous method of investigation through and decision driven by data.

Artificial Intelligence may support the process of providing customized data visualization as long as the context of practices becomes routinized and well-defined patterns of visual analytics and users' behavior are identified. For example, users' profiles may be designed and prompted by the AI to obtain different visualizations for the same dataset, depending on constraints about the role, task, and visualization literacy levels of individuals. Practices of explainable AI and AA may become routine tasks supporting trust and transparency, and may benefit from the visual means to become part and parcel of the visual analytics related to business.

Acknowledgments. Research funded by the European Union Next-Generation EU, with project: "Characterizing and Measuring Visual Information Literacy" n. 2022JJ3PA5, CUP D53D23008690006.

References

1. Abbott, J., Stone, M., Buttle, F.: Integrating customer data into customer relationship management strategy: an empirical study. J. Database Mark. Custom. Strategy Manage. (2001)
2. Abdelnour-Nocera, J., Clemmensen, T.: Theorizing about socio-technical approaches to HCI. In: 5th IFIP Working Conference on Human Work Interaction Design (HWID), pp. 242–262 (2018)
3. Alghamdi, N.A., Al-Baity, H.H.: Augmented analytics driven by AI: a digital transformation beyond business intelligence. Sensors (2022)
4. Barricelli, B.R., Fogli, D., Locoro, A.: EUDability: a new construct at the intersection of end-user development and computational thinking. J. Syst. Softw. **195** (2023)
5. Battle, L., Scheidegger, C.: A structured review of data management technology for interactive visualization and analysis. IEEE Trans. Vis. Comput. Graph. **27**(2), 1128–1138 (2020)
6. Bharadiya, J.P.: Machine learning and AI in business intelligence: trends and opportunities. Int. J. Comput. (IJC) (2023)
7. Buono, P., Locoro, A.: Modelling data visualization interactions: from semiotics to pragmatics and back to humans. In: Proceedings of the International Conference on Advanced Visual Interfaces, pp. 1–5 (2020)
8. Chen, H., Chiang, R.H.L., Storey, V.C.: Business intelligence and analytics: from big data to big impact. JSTOR (2012)
9. de Souza, C.S.: The semiotic engineering of user interface languages. Int. J. Man Mach. Stud. **39**(5), 753–773 (1993)
10. Dignity, P. and Olawande, D.: Business intelligence and business value in organisations: a systematic literature review. mdpi.com (2021)
11. Dimara, E., Franconeri, S., Plaisant, C., Bezerianos, A., Dragicevic, P.: A task-based taxonomy of cognitive biases for information visualization. IEEE Trans. Vis. Comput. Graph. 1413–1432 (2018)
12. Fischer, G.: Seeding, evolutionary growth and reseeding: constructing, capturing and evolving knowledge in domain-oriented design environments. Autom. Softw. Eng. **5**, 447–464 (1998)
13. Furmanova, K., et al.: Taggle: scalable visualization of tabular data through aggregation. Inf. Vis. **19**(2), 114–136 (2019)
14. Ge, L.W., et al.: Toward a more comprehensive understanding of visualization literacy. In: Proceedings of the CHI Conference on Human Factors in Computing Systems. ACM (2024)
15. Holliman, N.S., Coltekin, A., Fernstad, S.J., McLaughlin, L., Simpson, M.D., Woods, A.J.: Visual entropy and the visualization of uncertainty. arXiv preprint arXiv:1907.12879 (2019)
16. Kahneman, D., Sibony, O., Sunstein, C.R.: Noise: A Flaw in Human Judgment. Hachette, UK (2021)
17. Knauper, B., Belli, R.F., Hill, D.H., Herzog, A.R.: Question difficulty and respondents' cognitive ability: the effect on data quality. J. Off. Stat. **13**, 181–199 (1997)
18. Locoro, A., Fisher, W.P., Mari, L.: Visual information literacy: definition, construct modeling and assessment. IEEE Access 71053–71071 (2021)

19. Menin, A., et al.: Using chained views and follow-up queries to assist the visual exploration of the web of big linked data. Int. J. Hum. Comput. Interact. 224–240 (2024)
20. Raguseo, E.: Big Data Technologies: An Empirical Investigation on Their Adoption, Benefits and Risks for Companies. Elsevier (2018)
21. Shneiderman, B.: The eyes have it: a task by data type taxonomy for information visualizations, pp. 364–371. Elsevier (2003)

Introducing an Innovative Approach to Archaeological Data Management, Visualization, and Intelligent Analysis

Alice Bezzolato, Giovanna Bagnasco Gianni, Lorenzo Marcolli, Matilde Marzullo, Sara Micheletti, Alberto Rizzi, Eleonora Rossi, and Stefano Valtolina(✉)

University of Milano, Milan, Italy
{alice.bezzolato,giovanna.bagnasco,lorenzo.marcolli,matilde.marzullo, sara.micheletti,alberto.rizzi,eleonora.rossi,stefano.valtolina}@unimi.it

Abstract. This article explores how domain experts involved in the archaeological field are transforming their working practices through the advanced tools available to them for data storage and analysis, including the use of conversational chatbots. It introduces an innovative approach to data management in archaeology. The focus is on the implementation of information management techniques that take contextual requirements into account and promote interoperability through standardised models. A flexible and customised database schema is proposed. Functionalities are presented to support data analysis through a graph-based environment and an intuitive visual interface for querying the database even for non-technical users. The aim is thus creating a new dashboard with valuable tools and methodologies for archaeological research, facilitating its practical use also for non-technical users. Our work aligns with the UN's Sustainable Development Goals, emphasizing innovation in digital tools (Goal 9) and fostering sustainable preservation practices to benefit cities and communities (Goal 11).

Keywords: Archaeology · Data management · Data analysis · Visual interface · Data interoperability

1 Introduction

The digitalisation of archaeological data has radically transformed how researchers manage, analyse, and interpret the information generated from excavations. In today's ICT (information and Communication Technology) era, archaeological projects often produce complex, heterogeneous datasets that require advanced tools for efficient processing and analysis. To address these challenges, archaeologists increasingly integrate sophisticated digital platforms, such as data management systems, visualisation tools, and artificial intelligence (AI), into their workflows. This shift has enhanced research outcomes and improved

Published by Springer Nature Switzerland AG 2026
B. R. Barricelli et al. (Eds.): HWID 2024, IFIP AICT 751, pp. 241–257, 2026.
https://doi.org/10.1007/978-3-031-95334-7_15

the overall work experience for archaeologists, making daily tasks more manageable and satisfying. This research integrates design strategies that resonate with the UN's Sustainable Development Goals, particularly Goal 9, by promoting innovation in archaeological tools, and Goal 11, by advancing sustainable management of cultural heritage within communities.

1.1 Technical Innovations in the Tarquinia Project

At the heart of the innovations proposed in this paper is the Tarquinia Project, a pioneering collaboration between archaeologists and computer scientists at the University of Milan. Over the last two decades, the project has significantly modernised archaeological workflows with tools like ArchMatrix, a system for efficient data management, visualisation, and analysis. ArchMatrix leverages flexible data modelling techniques and graph-based visualisation, making it easier for technical and non-technical users to interact with complex datasets. These advancements have profoundly changed how archaeological research is conducted, enabling more profound insights into ancient civilisations while fostering a more efficient and satisfying work environment.

1.2 Sustainability and Workplace Transformation

Sustainability in the context of archaeology extends beyond preserving historical sites and data. It also encompasses the well-being and job satisfaction of the professionals working in the field. Introducing advanced digital tools contributes to a more sustainable work environment by alleviating the mental and physical burdens often associated with traditional archaeological practices. For example, archaeologists previously relied on labour-intensive, manual methods for recording and analysing excavation data, which could be time-consuming and prone to error. The advent of automated systems like ArchMatrix, capable of handling large amounts of data quickly and accurately, has streamlined these processes, significantly reducing stress and increasing productivity. After a description of the background of the Tarquinia Project and related literature review in Sect. 2, Sect. 3 explores how our innovative approach to data modeling and the user-friendly design of the tools developed for the Tarquinia Project enables a more inclusive working environment. In addition, Sect. 4 discusses how our framework aims to provide tools to support "domain experts" studies by introducing innovative database query functionality and graph-based visualisation. The idea is to allow non-technical users, such as archaeologists, historians, and cultural heritage experts, to engage with complex databases without requiring advanced programming skills [1–3], enabling democratised access to data. This solution promotes collaboration and communication across disciplines, reducing frustration and increasing satisfaction among team members who may have previously felt excluded from digital processes. Section 5 examines the use of artificial intelligence as a conversational agent, facilitating natural language queries and promoting accessibility to research data. Using intuitive visual interfaces and AI-powered query systems enables a more inclusive working environment. This agent broadens the possibilities of data discovery and understanding by providing a direct and intuitive means of interacting with databases, making information accessible to experts and non-experts [1,4,5]. In this way, our work aims to contribute significantly to advancing archaeological research by adopting advanced and innovative tools and improving access to and use of data. This solution aligns with HWID[1] (Human Work Interaction Design) research on the impact of AI on work experience, as highlighted in HWID publications on artificial intelligence technologies in workplaces [6]. The basic idea of enhancing job satisfaction through technology also stems from the ability to interact more meaningfully with the data. Instead of spending time on repetitive or tedious tasks, archaeologists can focus on higher-level analysis and interpretation, which are often the most intellectually rewarding aspects of their work. Moreover, integrating AI-driven tools such as conversational agents allows for natural language queries, streamlining the retrieval of relevant data and empowering users to conduct more thorough and efficient analyses. These systems save time and reduce cognitive load, leading to greater focus and well-being in the workplace. Section 6 describes the impact of archaeological research and the transmission of knowledge about our work. Specifically, we present how our system has improved daily archaeological workflows, favouring interdisciplinary collaboration between computer scientists and archaeologists and democratising access to archaeological data for non-experts. In conclusion, Sect. 7 succinctly summarises the achieved objectives and how the collaboration among archaeologists and computer sciences improves research outcomes and promotes a more dynamic and satisfying workplace where professionals can work together toward a common goal. Significant enhancements in efficiency and depth of analysis have been realised by harnessing advanced data modelling tech-niques, database query functionalities, and AI integration. Additionally, the section outlines potential future developments, highlighting the ongoing commitment to innovation and continuous improvement within archaeology.

2 Background on the Tarquinia Project

2.1 History and Objectives of the Tarquinia Project

The "Tarquinia Project", which began 40 years ago in the ancient Etruscan city of Tarquinia in Italy (UNESCO 2004), benefits from previous research from the 19th and first half of the 20th century, as well as excavations carried out by the Università degli Studi di Milano since 1982 in two sacred areas of the ancient city: the "monumental complex" and the Ara della Regina sanctuary [7], along with the fortifications [8]. Since 2015, the project has been directed by Professor Bagnasco Gianni, a professor of Etruscology at the Università di Milano. The

[1] Human Work Interaction Design (HWID) is a research group within the International Federation for Information Processing (IFIP) that focuses on the integration of work analysis and interaction design to enhance user experience in intelligent workplaces.

significance of the research results has led to a series of interpretations regarding visible and invisible Etruscan cultural traits, particularly focusing on the material aspects of rituals based on the recurrence of cultic practices in these sacred areas, as revealed by organic and inorganic remains [9].

Tarquinia presents a complex challenge for researchers, encouraging the exploration of unconventional and underexplored topics. Its multifaceted heritage encompasses inhabited areas on the Civita plateau (150 hectares), the necropolises (approximately 6,000 tombs, 400 of which are painted), and the surrounding territory. Researchers must navigate the intertwined connections between people from different regions of the ancient Mediterranean, the Near East, and Europe, as well as a stratification of activities spanning over eight centuries, from the city's founding to its Romanization, and its lasting impact on scholars and artists inspired by its remarkable heritage. Additionally, the indirect literary sources must also be taken into account [10].

2.2 Evolution of Data Management Tools in the Project Comparing Solutions in Other Projects and from Early Systems to ArchMatrix

The research within the "Tarquinia Projec" aligns with broader challenges in archaeology, focusing on interdisciplinary and technological tools for historical reconstruction.

Reconstructing historical and cultural contexts is complex, requiring various expertise and a deep understanding of interacting realities. The rise of digital resources has transformed the way information is studied and shared. Information and Communication Technologies (ICTs) and geo-spatial technologies (GIS, LiDAR, laser scanning) are now central to creating virtual reconstructions [11]. However, users often encounter either inaccessible databases or simplified reconstructions over which they have no control.

Our research challenges this paradigm by proposing a new cognitive framework that bridges disciplines such as archaeology, geoarchaeology, architecture, and ICT, offering more intelligent, creative solutions for understanding ancient communities [10].

Building on the innovative use of technology in archaeology, as discussed earlier in relation to the "Tarquinia Project", the long-standing collaboration between the Etruscology Department and the Department of Computer Science at the University of Milan has further demonstrated the potential of interdisciplinary efforts. This partnership has not only advanced the understanding of historical contexts but has also developed cutting-edge tools for managing and disseminating archaeological data.

The synergy between these disciplines has produced impactful projects, such as T.Arc.H.N.A. and the ArchMatrix database, which highlight how digital solutions can enhance archaeological research and make complex data more accessible to both specialists and the general public. These initiatives continue to push the boundaries of how we preserve, analyze, and share knowledge about ancient communities. The T.Arc.H.N.A. (Towards Archaeological Heritage New

Accessibility) project, conducted between 2004 and 2007 as part of the European Culture 2000 Program, aimed to virtually reunite the dispersed cultural heritage of Tarquinia and create a knowledge network to better contextualize these artifacts historically and culturally. This initiative was led by the University of Milan, with contributions from the Department of Ancient Sciences, the Etruscology chair, and the Department of Informatics and Communication.

One of the project's main goals was the creation of a Virtual Museum to bring together artifacts from Tarquinia that had been scattered across various museums in Europe, often losing their original context. By systematically cataloging materials from the National Museum of Tarquinia and recovering artifacts from major institutions like the Cinquantenaire Museum in Brussels, the Louvre in Paris, and the British Museum in London, the project allowed for a more comprehensive understanding of these objects within their original Etruscan framework [12].

The project also resulted in the development of a new system for managing and disseminating scientific content. This system was designed to be flexible and innovative, offering tools that are useful for both scholars and accessible to a wider public audience. A key achievement was the creation of a bilingual Virtual Museum, funded by the Cariciv Foundation, which allows for widespread, innovative dissemination of Tarquinia's cultural heritage. This platform not only preserves and presents valuable archaeological data but also makes it more engaging and accessible to a broader audience, including non-specialists, thereby enhancing public understanding of the ancient Etruscan civilization [13].

One of the most significant outcomes of the Tarquinia Project is the development of an updated archaeological database through a collaboration between the Department of Cultural Heritage and the Department of Informatics. Building on the foundations of the ArchMatrix database, this new platform integrates excavation data with findings from various scientific disciplines involved in the research at Tarquinia's monumental complex. Notably, the new database will feature advanced tools such as automated virtual generation of Harris Matrix, facilitating the visualization of stratigraphic unit relationships. This represents a major improvement in data management, enabling archaeologists to intuitively access both quantitative and qualitative information from excavations.

As part of the PRIN (Progetti di Ricerca di Rilevante Interesse Nazionale[2]), 2022 initiative, the goal is to innovate approaches to the study of rituals at the Tarquinia complex. The updated database will be a crucial tool for students and researchers, allowing them to easily navigate complex layers of data, from stratigraphy to material culture, and enhance understanding of the rituals at the ancient Etruscan site of Civita. In other words, the aim of our contribution is to develop robust interdisciplinary tools and services to mitigate the risk of fragmentation within archaeology-oriented disciplines. A key challenge we face is fostering collaboration among experts from diverse disciplines and organizations [10].

[2] https://prin.mur.gov.it/.

2.3 Overview of Archaeological Excavations and Findings at Tarquinia, Focusing on the Etruscan Sacred Area

To better understand the archaeological significance of the ancient Etruscan city of Tarquinia and its rich historical context, it is essential to explore the findings and methodologies of the ongoing "Tarquinia Project". The excavated areas of this project, ongoing for over forty years on the Civita plateaux, are situated at the site of the ancient Etruscan city of Tarquinia. Research focuses on two primary locations: the 'monumental complex' and the Ara della Regina sanctuary [14]. The findings from this extensive research have been disseminated through various publications, including volumes, supplements, articles, exhibitions, and conferences.

The project aims to contextualize the archaeological remains within the broader framework of the ancient city. Since 2012, the research scope has expanded to encompass the entire plateau, investigating the territory surrounding the archaeological sites, including all sites excavated over the past century. This effort culminated in the production of the Archaeological Map of the Civita of Tarquinia in 2018 [15].

Excavations at the monumental complex have revealed its antiquity, tracing the city's foundation back to the early Villanovan period (9th-8th century BC) and illuminating the cult practices and memorials of the ancient community. The earliest phase of settlement, dating to the 10th century BC, highlights the emergence of a natural cavity that served as the focal point for sacred-institutional activities, as supported by written sources indicating Tarquinia's central role in Etruscan religion.

During the Orientalizing period, a temple-altar was constructed beside the cavity, dedicated to a goddess by a priest-king. This structure featured pilaster walls influenced by Near Eastern architectural styles. In the 6th century BC, the monumental complex adopted a more imposing appearance while retaining its function as a site for communal gathering and remembrance.

Recent discoveries have also illuminated the history of Tarquinia during the mid-2nd century BC, coinciding with Rome's expansion. Research on the Ara della Regina sanctuary, initiated in 2012, revealed that the temple was visible from afar due to its height and monumental structure, spanning four main phases [16].

The architectural characteristics of the two Archaic phases (Temple I and II), dating to the 6th century BC, reflect a blend of designs from contemporary Magna Graecia and Sicilian temples, integrated with Etruscan high podiums raised on a tall basement to enhance the terrain on which the sanctuary stands.

Temple III, datable to the early 4th century BC, saw the addition of a monumentally proportioned terrace that retained earlier, differently oriented Archaic structures and featured a pediment decoration, including the renowned 'Winged Horses.' Temple IV, corresponding to the 3rd century BC, underwent further renovations, showcasing the evolving architectural significance of the sanctuary through its various phases.

Overall, the ongoing excavations and research not only enhance the understanding of Tarquinia's historical and cultural development but also contribute to the broader comprehension of Etruscan civilization and its religious practices, particularly the evolution of the important female deity Uni [17].

3 Innovative Data Modeling and Management Techniques

3.1 Use of CIDOC CRM Conceptual Model for Interoperability in Cultural Heritage Data

The CIDOC CRM conceptual model has been adopted as a standard to ensure interoperability and data integration in the cultural heritage sector, facilitating the representation and exchange of information between various organizations. This model provides a shared semantic language that enables the mapping and connection of heterogeneous data, allowing for a broader and more contextual understanding of cultural resources.

The MongoDB database for the new dashboard was chosen for its flexibility and scalability. The database modeling took the CIDOC CRM conceptual model as a reference, a widely used standard for representing Cultural Heritage (CH) data, which is essential for ensuring conceptual conformity across different organizations and sectors [18].

The new database model operates through an innovative semantic integration strategy based on the methodology developed by the "Tarquinia Project" over the last 20 years [19]. This approach fosters scientific collaboration with the common goal of creating new strategies and developing innovative systems for research, aiming to reconstruct the cultural dimension of the ancient city—from the materiality of archaeological findings to the invisibility of past daily life.

3.2 Flexible Data Modeling Tailored for Archaeologists and Non-technical Users

In archaeological contexts, the collection and analysis of excavation data is of fundamental importance for understanding past history and culture. Considering the changing nature of discoveries and the diversity of experts involved in the process, it becomes essential to adopt an approach to data modelling that is highly flexible and easily adaptable over time. Such an approach aims also to enable non-technical users (e.g. the archeologists) to be able to modify the logical schema of the database, either by adding new fields or in an intuitive manner without having to modify the code with each change, thus making the tool more scalable and maintainable.

In technical terms, a new collection has been created in which to save the new fields, we can see in Fig. 1 the schema, specifying the *type*, the *label* and the reference entity (e.g. *archeological find*). Archaeologists or other domain experts can create these new fields through simple forms, avoiding the intervention of a person with technical knowledge.

At this point, all data entry forms of the dashboard will automatically be extended with this new field, thus giving the possibility to save new information. Furthermore, when adding the new field, it is possible to define whether the field is mandatory.

Participatory design [20] has played a pivotal role in developing these flexible and user-centric data modeling tools. Early requirements gathering involved workshops and brainstorming sessions with archaeologists and historians to understand their workflows, challenges, and specific needs for the system. During development, prototypes and mockups were iteratively shared with domain experts, whose feedback guided adjustments to features and interface design. Collaborative testing, even in informal settings, allowed archaeologists to interact with early versions of the system, providing valuable insights that influenced the final interface and functionality. This co-design approach not only fosters usability but also strengthens the alignment of the system with the everyday challenges faced by domain experts [21].

```
{
        "collection": "dig",
        "additionalInformation": {
                "label": "Latitude",
                "type": "string",
                "required": true,
        }
}
```

Fig. 1. The MongoDB schema shows how new fields are saved in the database. In particular, a new "Latitude" field is pointed out for the "dig" collection.

3.3 Uploading Data with CSV File

An additional feature developed was the possibility to upload data using CSV files. In fact, archaeologists and the other domain experts involved use several spreadsheets for their internal sharing and for data collection during excavation. This new functionality addresses the problem of having to upload data individually to the database, which would be very time-consuming, thus favouring digitisation and standardisation by allowing the bulk upload of many data.

Therefore, a section was created from which the file could be uploaded and a mapping between the CSV columns (Fig. 2) and the fields in the database could be made, also taking into account the new fields inserted and explained in Sect. 3.2, thus favouring continuous integration and flexibility.

4 Visualisation and Data Analysis Tools

As well as offering solutions for data storage and management, the project focuses on supporting archaeologists and other domain experts in the interpretation of data, developing functionalities for interactive data visualisation and

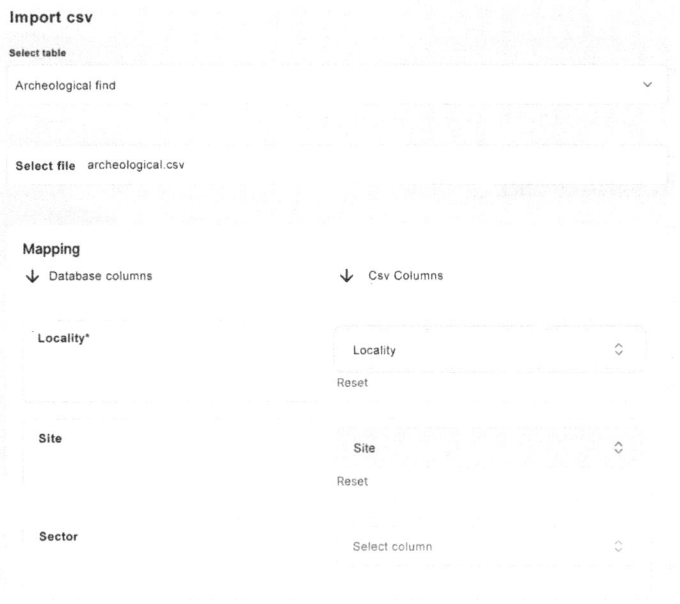

Fig. 2. The figure shows how you can upload a CSV file and select, in the right input, which column corresponds with the relevant field on the database.

the possibility of advanced data consultation to better understand the meaning of the entire data set available.

Compared to the previous version of ArchMatrix, a new graphical solution was developed that allows stratigraphic units to be explored and analysed more intuitively and effectively. This approach makes it possible to discover new relationships and gain a deeper understanding of the historical and cultural dynamics associated with archaeological finds [22].

The Harris Matrix system, which is commonly used in archeology to schematically represent the stratigraphic sequences [23], is represented as a directed graph ($G = (V, E)$), where nodes represent stratigraphic units (US) and arcs reflect different types of stratigraphic relationships.

Based on this model, the graphs illustrated in Fig. 3 part *b* are generated, which include all observable relationships within the stratigraphy.

As ArchMatrix has demonstrated, including all these relations in a single graph may result in an overly complex and difficult-to-read representation, as well as introducing considerable computational complexity in the presence of a large number of nodes (US) and arcs (relations). Although all the relationships between the layers are effectively recorded in the database, in the visualization, it is necessary to minimise the non-essential relations, thus reducing the computational complexity and obtaining a "simplified" version of the Matrix. Transitive reduction produces a subgraph of the original graph that retains the

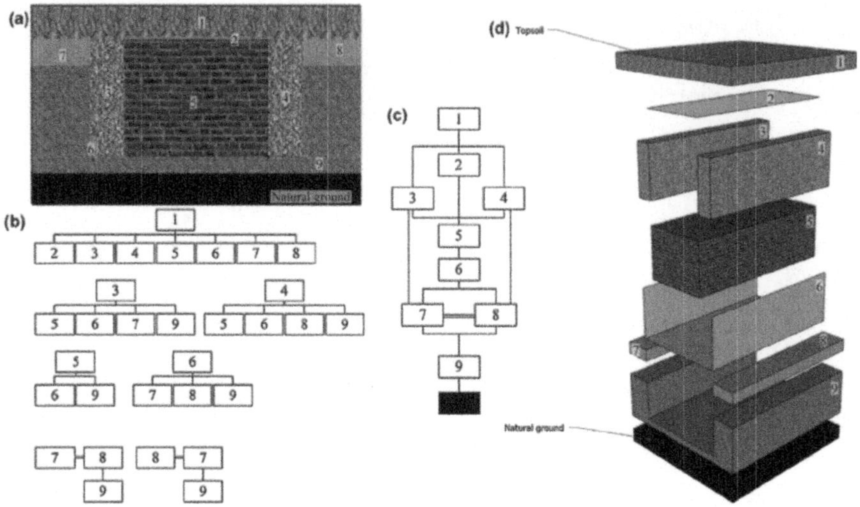

Fig. 3. Representation of a Harris Matrix: a) example stratigraphy, b) complete Harris Matrix, c) simplified Harris Matrix, d) three-dimensional view of the stratigraphy [24].

same connectivity between nodes, but with as few arcs as possible [25], realised through the use of the Graphviz library[3] (Figs. 4 and 5).

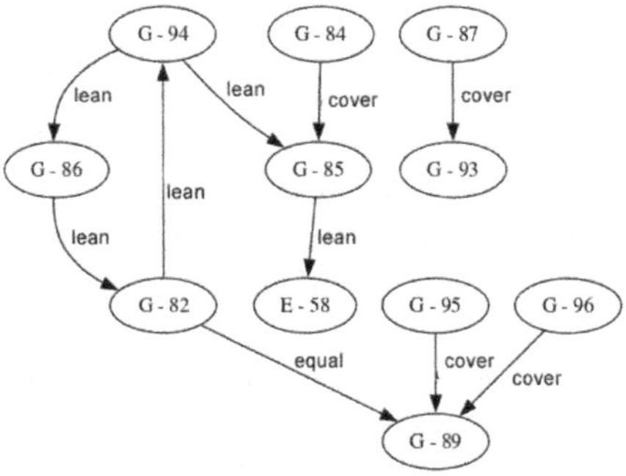

Fig. 4. Viewing a Harris Matrix via the Graphviz library.

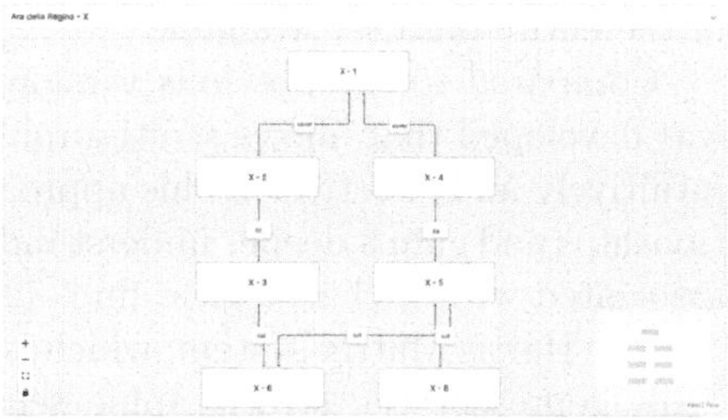

Fig. 5. Viewing a Harris Matrix via the React Flow library.

[3] Graphviz is an open source suite of tools for creating graphical representations of data structures, networks and directed graphs.

Once the graph has been calculated using the ReactFlow library[4], archaeologists can interact with and edit nodes and arcs, enabling interesting exploration, analysis and collaborative interaction.

Finally, to make querying the database accessible also to those without specific computer skills, such as archaeologists and humanities scholars, a query builder was developed to retrieve data from the database using a visual and interactive language, abstracting the technical complexity [26]. Users can then specify exactly what data they want to extract. An archaeologist, for example, can select one or more desired research field, thus creating a query to filter the data in the MongoDB database without needing to know its specific syntax. The advantages of using query builders, as described in the article "*Criteria Builder for Query Builders*" [27], include:

- **Simplification of query creation:** the system eliminates the need to handle complex parentheses or to know the syntax of query languages in depth, making query construction simpler and more intuitive.
- **Intuitive and visual user interface:** offers a visual method for composing queries, making the process more accessible and reducing errors, especially for non-technical users.
- **Democratic access to data:** particularly useful in specialised fields, the system allows users with various skills to access and analyse complex data easily.
- **Flexibility and customisation:** allows users to easily change the order and grouping of query criteria, as well as choose between logical connectors, thus adapting the query to their specific needs.
- **Error Reduction:** the graphical approach to query construction decreases the probability of syntactic or logical errors, improving the efficiency and accuracy of database queries.

Participatory design [20] played a key role in shaping the visual and interactive tools, as archaeologists and domain experts provided direct input during the development process, ensuring the solutions meet their analytical requirements. The query builder, an example of which is shown in Fig. 6, acts as a translator, converting the visual query set by the user into a structured MongoDB query.

Figure 6, for example, illustrates a research in the database for all archaeological finds having the term "pozzo" in the description of the stratigraphic unit, with a functional form containing the term "olla", a rim thickness between 0 cm and 20 cm, and being a "capofila".

Thanks to this functionality, archaeologists can query the database to improve and speed up their research.

[4] ReactFlow is a JavaScript library for building user interfaces for visualising and interacting with graphs and data flows. It provides responsive components that facilitate drag-and-drop, zoom, pan, and customisation of nodes and arcs. Its flexibility and ease of use make it ideal for creating interactive and customised graph visualisations in web applications.

Fig. 6. Visual and interactive queries.

5 Artificial Intelligence Integration

5.1 The Role of AI and Natural Language Queries in Archaeological Research

Artificial Intelligence (AI) plays a pivotal role in modern archaeological research by enhancing data accessibility and usability, particularly through natural language processing. AI-driven systems, like conversational agents, allow non-expert users to interact with complex archaeological databases using simple, intuitive queries. These tools are especially useful in facilitating access to research data for individuals without technical expertise, thereby democratizing the retrieval process and making data accessible to a broader audience. For instance, users can ask questions in natural language about specific artifact types or historical events, and the AI will interpret and process these queries to provide relevant results. This functionality not only streamlines data exploration for archaeologists but also supports interdisciplinary engagement and knowledge sharing.

5.2 Case Study of the AQ4AI Project: Using AI for Zooarchaeological and Stratigraphic Data

Understanding ancient communities' cultural activities and practices presents a complex challenge for modern scholars. In this case study, our research endeavours aim to explore innovative approaches for archaeological interpretation and historical-cultural reconstruction through the Archaeological Questions for Archaeological Intelligence project (AQ4AI) [28,29].

This project employs an IT system to streamline data recording, analysis, and processing, focusing on correlations between zooarchaeological data and broader datasets. An Artificial Intelligence (AI) tool, in the form of a conversational agent, facilitates natural language queries, promote accessibility to research data.

This agent expands the scope for discovering and understanding data and offers a direct and intuitive means to interact with databases, making information more accessible to experts and non-experts alike. We aim to leverage this technology to help the researchers to access the information stored within databases.

For the design of the conversational agent, we utilised Large Language Models (LLMs) and Retrieval-Augmented Generation (RAG) models [30], emphasising their advantages in enhancing answer accuracy and minimising misinformation. Specifically, we integrated the Cheshire Cat AI into the project for its open-source nature and superior performance. This AI chatbot processes natural language queries and continuously learns from uploaded documents and conversations, providing informed responses reflecting the latest data. The system's memory, including episodic, declarative, and procedural components, provides relevant responses based on query context.

In a practical scenario depicted in Fig. 7, a user uploads a document detailing the discovery of human remains during an archaeological excavation in Tarquinia. Understanding the sources from which Cheshire Cat retrieves its information for a specific search query is insightful. As illustrated in last image of Fig. 7, a graph represents the query with a red dot, while other elements represent associated memories. The system's long-term memory (LTM) consists of episodic memory for recording past user interactions, declarative memory housing information from uploaded documents, and procedural memory containing Python instructions for system actions. During conversations, the system accesses these memories to provide relevant responses, updating them after each interaction. Memories closer to the query are considered more appropriate, aiding in identifying memory sources based on colour distinctions.

For instance, a researcher might upload an archaeological report describing the discovery of human remains and ask the system: "*What information is available on funerary rituals in Tarquinia during the Etruscan period?*" The system, utilizing its declarative memory to access the uploaded report and its episodic memory to account for previous interactions, could respond with specific details about the findings and link these data with other relevant sources stored in the system. The response might include information on burial methods, any artifacts found with the remains, and previous interpretations of such practices, thus offering a comprehensive and integrated view of the funerary customs of the time.

6 Impact on Archaeological Research and Knowledge Transmission

The new system has transformed traditional workflows by automating routine tasks, enabling archaeologists to focus on analysis and interpretation rather than data entry. The integration of tools like ArchMatrix has significantly reduced the time spent on data processing and improved the accuracy of data management, leading to more efficient excavation and research activities. This contribution

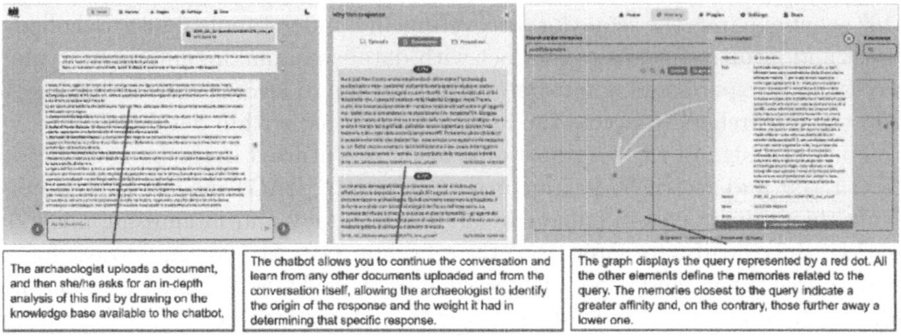

Fig. 7. In the first screenshot, the archaeologist uploads a document for analysis, and the CA provides detailed insights by utilising its knowledge base. Then, through ongoing conversation and learning from uploaded documents and dialogue, the archaeologist traces the origin and significance of each CA response. In the last screenshot, the graph displays the query represented by a red dot. All the other elements define the memories related to the query. The memories closest to the query indicate a greater affinity and, on the contrary, those further away a lower one. (Color figure online)

aligns with the goals of HWID, which emphasizes the design of environmentally friendly and human-centered workplaces. The paper argues that introducing advanced digital tools in archaeology, such as ArchMatrix, contributes to a more sustainable work environment by reducing the mental and physical burdens associated with traditional practices. By supporting bulk uploads via CSV files and utilizing visual query builders, the system minimizes manual input, which decreases errors and allows for rapid adjustments in data collection and analysis. These improvements not only streamline daily tasks but also make complex datasets more manageable for archaeologists, enhancing their ability to engage more meaningfully with data, generate insights, and focus on higher-level analysis and interpretation.

6.1 Broader Implications for Interdisciplinary Collaboration Between Computer Scientists and Archaeologists

The system fosters a more collaborative environment between archaeologists and computer scientists by utilizing an adaptable and customizable database model. This collaboration has been instrumental in the development of a flexible data modeling approach that accommodates the needs of both fields. By incorporating the CIDOC CRM conceptual model, the project facilitates interoperability, enabling seamless data exchange between archaeological and computational domains. Moreover, the adoption of AI-driven conversational agents further bridges the gap between these disciplines by allowing both archaeologists and data scientists to engage with the data without requiring specialized technical skills. This synergy enhances knowledge sharing and fosters a more cohesive research process, driving innovation in archaeological methodologies.

6.2 Democratising Access to Archaeological Data for Non-experts and the Public

The system has made significant strides toward democratizing access to archaeological data, extending its usability beyond experts to the broader public and non-technical users. The use of an AI-powered conversational agent enables intuitive natural language queries, simplifying data retrieval and exploration for users unfamiliar with database management. Visual and interactive query tools further support this goal, allowing non-experts to explore data relevant to their interests, fostering a deeper engagement with cultural heritage information. By making archaeological findings more accessible, the project promotes public understanding and appreciation of historical sites and practices, ultimately contributing to the preservation and dissemination of cultural heritage knowledge.

7 Conclusions and Future Works

In the ever-evolving landscape of archaeology, the proliferation of digital data presents unprecedented opportunities and challenges. This paper presents a new dashboard system within the archaeological framework, underscoring the critical need for innovative data management and analysis solutions. The paper also serves as a practical case study on the implementation and impact of digital tools in a real archaeological work environment, offering valuable insights into how human-centered design principles can be applied in this specific domain and contributing to the empirical knowledge base of HWID research.

Our research highlighted the transformative potential of advanced data modeling techniques, database query functionality, and graph-based visualization tools. These advancements enhance the efficiency of archaeological practices and enable more nuanced interpretations of complex datasets, such as those found at Tarquinia. Furthermore, by integrating the CIDOC CRM conceptual model, this work emphasizes the importance of data standards and data management practices in designing sustainable HWID systems, a relevant area of study for the HWID research community.

Moreover, incorporating AI, specifically conversational agents, represents a significant leap forward in democratizing access to research data. By facilitating natural language queries and providing intuitive interfaces, these agents bridge the gap between experts and non-experts, fostering broader engagement with archaeological knowledge. This study also underscores the potential benefits of interdisciplinary collaboration between computer scientists and archaeologists. The joint development of ArchMatrix and its related tools demonstrates the value of combining diverse perspectives and experiences to create innovative solutions that address the challenges of human work in the digital age.

Our interdisciplinary research demonstrates how technological innovation can serve as a catalyst for sustainable cultural preservation, enabling more efficient, accessible, and collaborative approaches to understanding human heritage that align with global sustainable development principles.

Our work addresses the immediate challenges archaeologists face in navigating vast datasets and lays the foundation for future innovation in the field. By embracing advanced technologies and fostering interdisciplinary collaborations, we envision a future where archaeological research is not only more accessible but also more insightful, leading to a deeper understanding of our shared human heritage. Building upon the groundwork laid out in this study, several avenues for future research and development emerge. Firstly, continued refinement and expansion of the dashboard system to accommodate diverse archaeological contexts and datasets are paramount. This solution may involve machine learning algorithms to automate data classification and enhance predictive analytics. Additionally, there is a need for ongoing evaluation and refinement of AI-driven conversational agents to ensure accuracy, usability, and inclusivity. Finally, fostering interdisciplinary collaborations between archaeologists, data scientists, and computer scientists will drive innovation in the field by leveraging diverse perspectives and expertise to develop holistic solutions that address the multifaceted challenges of archaeological research in the digital age.

References

1. Clemmensen, T., Campos, P., Orngreen, R., Pejtersen, A.M., Wong, W. (eds.) Human Work Interaction Design: Designing for Human Work: The First IFIP TC 13.6 WG Conference: Designing for Human Work, February 13–15, 2006, Madeira, Portugal, vol. 221. Springer (2006)
2. Barricelli, B.R., et al. (eds.): Human Work Interaction Design. Designing Engaging Automation: 5th IFIP WG 13.6 Working Conference, HWID 2018, Espoo, Finland, August 20–21, 2018, Revised Selected Papers, vol. 544. Springer (2018)
3. Bhutkar, G., et al. (eds.) Human Work Interaction Design. Artificial Intelligence and Designing for a Positive Work Experience in a Low Desire Society: 6th IFIP WG 13.6 Working Conference, HWID 2021, Beijing, China, May 15–16, 2021, Revised Selected Papers, vol. 609. Springer (2022)
4. Katre, D., ØrngreenR., Yammiyavar, P., Clemmensen, T. (eds.): Human Work Interaction Design: Usability in Social, Cultural and Organizational Contexts. Springer (2010)
5. Campos, P., Clemmensen, T., Nocera, J.A., Katre, D., Lopes, A., Ørngreen, R. (eds.) Human Work Interaction Design. Work Analysis and HCI: Third IFIP 13.6 Working Conference, HWID 2012, Copenhagen, Denmark, December 5-6, 2012, Revised Selected Papers, vol. 407. Springer (2013)
6. Abdelnour-Nocera, J., Baricelli, B.R., Lopes, A., Campos, P., Clemmensen, T. (eds.) Human Work Interaction Design: Analysis and Interaction Design Methods for Pervasive and Smart Workplaces: 4th IFIP 13.6 Working Conference, HWID 2015, London, UK, June 25–26, 2015, Revised Selected Papers, vol. 468. Springer (2015)
7. Jovino, M.B.: The tarquinia project: a summary of 25 years of excavation. Am. J. Archaeol. **114**, 161–180 (2010)
8. Gianni, G.B.: Tarquinia, tra spazio e tempo. appunti da una ricerca in corso. In: Chiaramonte Treré C. et al. (eds.), pp. 23–34 (2012)
9. Gianni, G.B.: Tarquinia. il deposito votivo reiterato: una preliminare analisi dei comparanda. Tarchna Suppl. **1**, 91–102 (2005)
10. Gianni, G.B., et al.: Past & present at tarchna & tarquinia: a flexible approach to make visible the invisible. In: Boriani, M., Gabaglio, R., Gulotta, D. (eds.), Built

Heritage 2013: Monitoring, Conservation and Management, Proceedings of the International Conference, Milan, 18–20 November 2013, pp. 163–175. Politecnico di Milano (2013)
11. Forte, M.: Realtà virtuale, beni culturali e cibernetica: un approccio eco sistemico. Archeol. Calcolatori **15**, 423–448 (2004)
12. Cataldi, M.: Il progetto t.arc.h.n.a.: conoscenza e divulgazione. In: Bagnasco Gianni G. (ed.), Tarquinia. Bridging Archaeological and Information Technology Cultures for Community Accessibility. Un ponte fra archeologia e informatica per un accesso condiviso, Roma, pp. 25–27 (2008)
13. Gianni, G.B.: The t.arc.h.n.a. project: aspects of the research. In: Bagnasco Gianni G. (ed.) Tarquinia. Bridging Archaeological and Information Technology Cultures for Community Accessibility. Un ponte fra archeologia e informatica per un accesso condiviso, Roma, pp. 29–36 (2008)
14. Tarchna, I.: Tarchna I, 1997 - IV, 2012. Publisher unknown (2012)
15. Marzullo, M.: Schede e materiali dalla "carta archeologica della civita di tarquinia". In: Bagnasco Gianni G. (ed.), Mura Tarquiniesi: riflessioni in margine alla città, vol. 14, pp. 311–341 (2018)
16. Tarchna. Tarchna IV, 2012. Publisher unknown (2012)
17. Gianni, G.B.: Introduzione, tarquinia project, aree di scavo e ricerca. In: Notootto: Progetti & Persone del Dipartimento di Beni Culturali e Ambientali Università degli Studi di Milano, vol. 6, pp. 1–6 (2023)
18. Doerr, M.: The CIDOC conceptual reference module: an ontological approach to semantic interoperability of metadata. AI Mag. **24**(3), 75 (2003)
19. Gianni, G.B., et al.: Past&present at tarchna&tarquinia: a flexible approach to make visible the invisible. In Proceedings of Built Heritage 2013: Monitoring, Conservation and Management, pp. 163–175 (2013)
20. Bødker, S., Grønbaek, K., Kyng, M.: Cooperative design: techniques and experiences from the Scandinavian scene, pp. 157–175. CRC Press (2017)
21. Barricelli, B.R.: An architecture for end-user development supporting global communities. Tesi di dottorato di ricerca, Università degli Studi di Milano (2011)
22. Herman, I., Melancon, G., Marshall, M.S.: Graph visualization and navigation in information visualization: a survey. IEEE Trans. Visual Comput. Graphics **6**(1), 24–43 (2000)
23. Harris, E.C.: Principles of Archaeological Stratigraphy. Elsevier (2014)
24. De Roo, B., Stal, C., Lonneville, B., De Wulf, A., Bourgeois, J., De Maeyer, P.: Spatiotemporal data as the foundation of an archaeological stratigraphy extraction and management system. J. Cult. Herit. **19**, 522–530 (2016)
25. Aho, A.V., Garey, M.R., Ullman, J.D.: The transitive reduction of a directed graph. SIAM J. Comput. **1**(2), 131–137 (1972)
26. Barricelli, B.R., Valtolina, S.: A visual language and interactive system for end-user development of internet of things ecosystems. J. Vis. Lang. Comput. **40**, 1–19 (2017). Semiotics, Human-Computer Interaction and End-User Development
27. Ceballos, A.G., Caruso, M.A., Klaus, K.: Criteria builder for query builder. US Patent 8,312,038 (2012)
28. Argyrou, A., Agapiou, A.: A review of artificial intelligence and remote sensing for archaeological research. Remote Sens. **14**(23), 6000 (2022)
29. Agapiou, A., Lysandrou, V.: Interacting with the artificial intelligence (AI) language model chatGPT: a synopsis of earth observation and remote sensing in archaeology. Heritage **6**(5), 4072–4085 (2023)
30. Gao, Y., et al.: Retrieval-augmented generation for large language models: a survey. *arXiv preprint*arXiv:2312.10997 (2023)

Author Index

Published by Springer Nature Switzerland AG 2026
B. R. Barricelli et al. (Eds.): HWID 2024, IFIP AICT 751, pp. 259–260, 2026.
https://doi.org/10.1007/978-3-031-95334-7

The manufacturer's authorised representative in the EU is Springer Nature Customer Service Centre GmbH, Europaplatz 3, 69115 Heidelberg, Germany. If you have any concerns regarding our products, please contact ProductSafety@springernature.com

Printed and bound by CPI Group (UK) Ltd, Croydon, CR0 4YY

30/09/2026

02225583-0019